The Two Powers

THE MIDDLE AGES SERIES

A complete list of books in the series
is available from the publisher.

The TWO POWERS

The Papacy, the Empire, and the Struggle for Sovereignty in the Thirteenth Century

Brett Edward Whalen

PENN

UNIVERSITY OF PENNSYLVANIA PRESS

PHILADELPHIA

Published by
University of Pennsylvania Press
Philadelphia, Pennsylvania 19104-4112
www.upenn.edu/pennpress

Printed in the United States of America on acid-free paper
1 3 5 7 9 10 8 6 4 2

Library of Congress Cataloging-in-Publication Data

Names: Whalen, Brett Edward, author.
Title: The two powers: the papacy, the empire, and the struggle for sovereignty in the thirteenth century / Brett Edward Whalen.
Other titles: Middle Ages series.
Description: 1st edition. | Philadelphia: University of Pennsylvania Press, [2019] | Series: The Middle Ages series | Includes bibliographical references and index.
Identifiers: LCCN 2018044569 | ISBN 9780812250862 (hardcover)
Subjects: LCSH: Gregory IX, Pope, approximately 1170–1241. | Innocent IV, Pope, approximately 1200–1254. | Frederick II, Holy Roman Emperor, 1194–1250. | Popes—Temporal power—History—To 1500. | Church and state—Holy Roman Empire—History—To 1500. | Papacy—History—To 1309. | Holy Roman Empire—History—Frederick II, 1215–1250. | Church history—Middle Ages, 600–1500. | Sovereignty—History—To 1500.
Classification: LCC BX1238.W47 2019 | DDC 943/.025—dc23
LC record available at https://lccn.loc.gov/2018044569

For Jack and Amelia

Contents

Map 1. Italy in the thirteenth century.

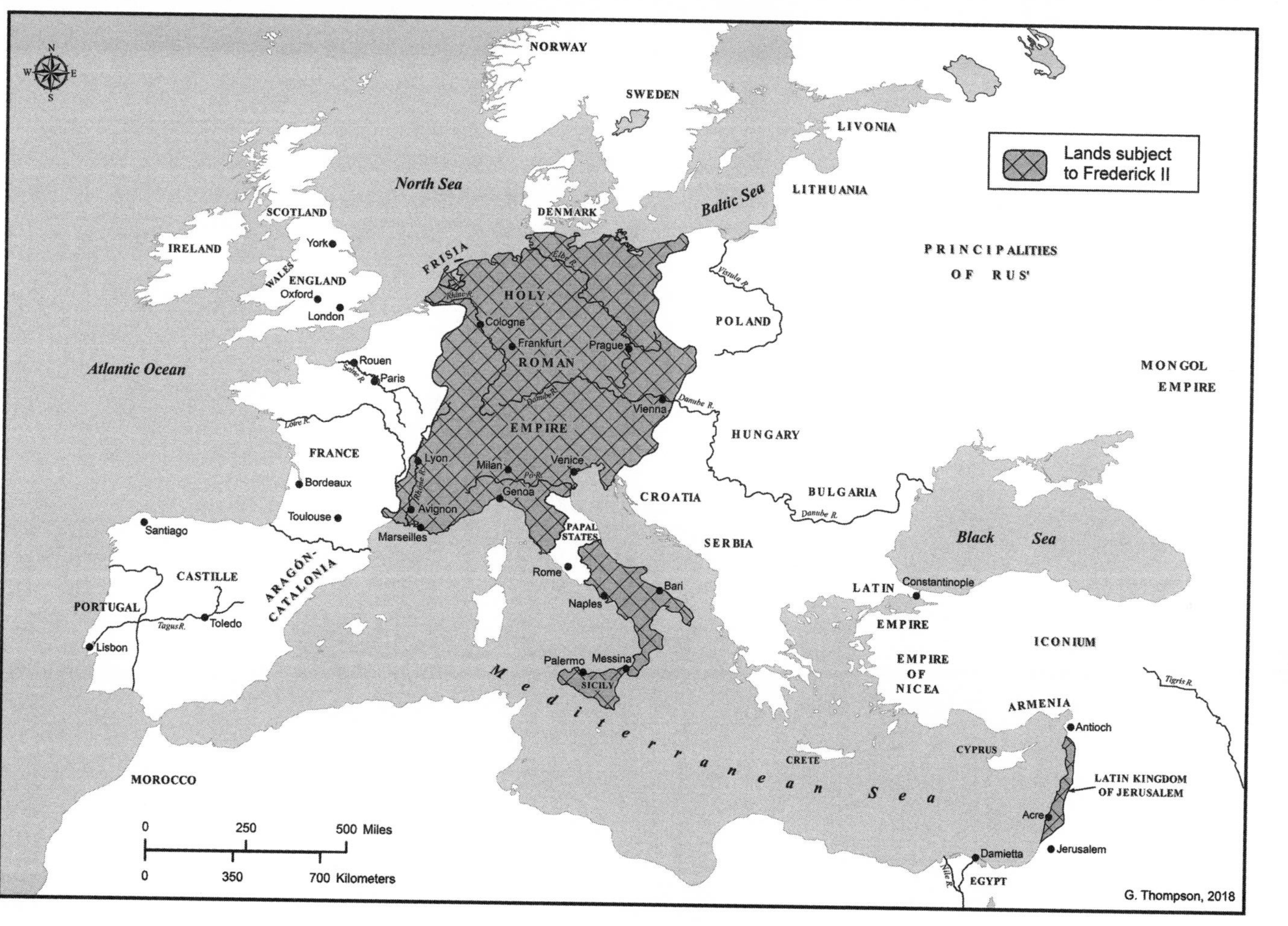

Map 2. Europe in the thirteenth century.

Introduction

Entering the chapel of Saint Sylvester in the basilica of Santi Quattro Coronati in Rome, one encounters a sequence of frescoes from the year 1246 that speaks to the dual nature of Christian sovereignty in the Middle Ages. The images present a meeting over nine hundred years earlier between Pope Sylvester, the bishop of Rome, and Constantine, the Roman emperor. Although this encounter never actually happened, medieval Europeans generally believed that that it did. The paintings commence with scenes of the pagan ruler's leprosy and refusal to bathe in the blood of slaughtered infants, a cure recommended to him by pagan priests, followed by his vision of the apostles Peter and Paul. The two saints instruct him to seek out Sylvester, who was hiding on the outskirts of Rome due to the imperial persecution of the Christian church at the time. The pope meets and baptizes the stricken ruler, healing him of his affliction. Out of gratitude, the emperor hands over his tiara to Sylvester, denoting his surrender of the Western empire to the Roman pontiff. A concluding scene shows Sylvester on horseback while Constantine humbly acts as his groom. By visualizing the past in this manner, the frescoes communicate a message about the proper relationship between the "two powers," that is, between the spiritual authority of priests and the temporal might of secular rulers, embodied above all by popes and emperors. As the example of Constantine and Sylvester revealed, emperors should ultimately defer to popes, recognizing their superior form of sacerdotal sovereignty.[1]

Outside the walls of the chapel, when its frescoes were new, Christians faced a far more turbulent relationship between the chief representatives of the two powers: a violent division between Pope Innocent IV and the Hohenstaufen emperor, Frederick II. Contention between the papacy and the imperial ruler had begun under Innocent's predecessor, Gregory IX, who excommunicated Frederick not once, but twice: for the first time in 1227, when the emperor failed to depart on crusade by an agreed-upon deadline, and again in 1239 (nine years after their previous reconciliation), when he was accused of various sins, crimes, and abuses of the church. The two had remained fiercely at odds when Gregory died in 1241. After his election one and a half years later, Innocent seemed poised to make peace with Frederick until negotiations between them collapsed and he fled to the city of Lyons. In July 1245, at the Council of Lyons, the pope deposed the Hohenstaufen ruler from his kingdoms and honors, a judgment rejected by the emperor as an illegal act of papal overreach into temporal affairs. Intensifying

Figure 1. The Donation of Constantine. Basilica of Santi Quattro Coronati, Rome. Getty Images.

conflict between the two sides followed for years to come. In 1250, unrepentant and excommunicate, Frederick died while still warring with the pope. Returning to Italy, Innocent spent the remainder of his life fighting with Frederick's heirs, until his own demise at Naples four years later.

Reading many of Frederick II's modern biographers, one gets the unmistakable impression that Gregory and Innocent in turn shared a deep-seated desire to destroy the emperor, viewing him as the principal danger to the papacy's territorial possessions on the Italian peninsula and their main competitor for universal sovereignty over Christendom.[2] Although such histories of the Hohenstaufen ruler are in many cases decades old, they continue to cast a long shadow over Gregory and Innocent, in part due to the lack of recent book-length studies on the two popes.[3] Perhaps not surprisingly, Frederick emerges as the clear protagonist in such works. While the emperor has enjoyed the reputation of being an iconoclast and a modern man born before his time, his papal opponents seem eminently "medieval" by comparison, that is to say, intolerant, narrow-minded, and determined to realize their theocratic aspirations at any cost. Desperate to eradicate Frederick, Gregory and Innocent squandered the church's wealth, discredited the crusades by turning them against their foe, and damaged their office's moral standing, setting the papacy on the slow road to decline and near ruin in the later Middle Ages.[4]

In this book, I retell and reevaluate the history of Gregory IX and Innocent IV's combative relationship with Frederick II from a different perspective: that of the medieval public. To influence, restrain, and combat the reigning emperor, the two popes had to convince the Christian community about the legitimacy of their cause, including not only kings, archbishops, and other highly placed elites but also members of the lesser clergy and lay nobility, crusaders and mendicants, merchants and burgers, and parish priests and their parishioners, among others. The papal confrontations with the Hohenstaufen ruler took place not just on the level of high politics and diplomacy but also in city streets, ports, plazas, and other open spaces. The battles between the popes and the prince could be heard in the proclamation of excommunications, the preaching of sermons, or the contrary silences imposed by interdict. Chroniclers with their own stakes in the outcome memorialized the clash between the papacy and empire in their historical writings, leaving traces of wider reactions to the turmoil disrupting their society: the circulation of wild rumors, the clamoring of the people, and the awe caused by apocalyptic signs of a world in crisis. Nothing less than the fate of Christendom seemed to hang in the balance between the discordant two powers.

The point of this study is not to turn the tables on Frederick, making Gregory and Innocent into heroes of the story, the emperor into the villain. Scholars with confessional sympathies have tried this before with equally skewed results.[5] In the pages below, however, I devote the majority of my attention to the means of communication, documentary culture, performances, and media that turned the papacy's spiritual and sacramental authority into consequential forms of social and political action.[6] While highlighting the papal side of the epoch-making struggles between the two powers, I also keep a close eye on Gregory and Innocent's other shared commitments, including their widely publicized mandates to create peace in Christendom, to promote crusading, and to eradicate heresy from the church. Those projects for the common good of Christendom, as the two popes presented them, shaped their response to Frederick's imperial reign, not the other way around. Ironically, perhaps, given the assumption of irreconcilable differences between him and the two popes, Frederick shared many of those same goals, albeit with his own ideas about how to realize them. In many ways, the popes and the prince disagreed so publicly and so violently because they agreed on so much.

By taking such an approach to the subject, this book seeks to restore a sense of contingency to the history of the thirteenth-century struggles between the papacy and empire, rather than viewing them as a more or less inexorable outcome of opposing political ideologies. Theoretically supreme in the theological and juridical realms, the bishops of Rome faced constant and unexpected challenges, constraints, and limitations to the enactment of their priestly sovereignty in the public realm. No one must have understood this better than Gregory and Innocent. Their contentious relationship with Frederick forced them to intervene in European politics and society in far-reaching and controversial ways, publicizing his excommunicate and eventually deposed status, attacking his reputation through propagandistic letters, deploying papal legates to act against his interests, declaring crusades against him, and transferring vast sums of ecclesiastical wealth to support the papacy's allies against Frederick's supporters. The results of those efforts remained imperfect and reliant upon forces that the popes could not easily or always control. Innocent, tellingly, was not on hand to see the frescoes of Sylvester and the deferential Constantine unveiled in Santi Quattro Coronati. He remained in exile at Lyons, unable to return to Italy for as long as Frederick lived and his allies dominated the road to Rome.

~

To a considerable extent, the history of Gregory IX and Innocent IV's battles with Frederick II remains inextricably bound to the larger question of the medieval "papal monarchy."[7] The term papal monarchy is a compelling and evocative one, but in some ways misleading—even in the Middle Ages, popes did not rule like kings over the faithful. In its technical, juridical sense, the concept of the papal monarchy denotes the pope's "fullness of power" (*plenitudo potestatis*) over the church and its offices, his position atop the ecclesiastical hierarchy and status as the final arbiter of canon law, able to grant dispensations, definitively settle disputes, and decide legal cases.[8] Used in a more capacious formulation, accurately or not, the papal monarchy suggests the awesome ambitions of the medieval papacy to stand as the supreme sovereign of Christendom, asserting the ultimate superiority of the priesthood (*sacerdotium*) over temporal rulership (*regnum*). Starting with papal reform movement of the eleventh century, building momentum in the twelfth century, and peaking in the thirteenth, the papal monarchy from this vantage point instantiated the ambitions of popes, theologians, and canon lawyers to realize the papacy's juridical authority over worldly princes of all kinds, thereby creating what has memorably been described as a hierocratic vision of the Christian political order.[9]

As will become evident through this book, theologically inflected legal concepts of sovereignty did indeed play a crucial role in the elaboration of papal claims to wield not just spiritual but also, in exceptional cases, temporal power over secular monarchs. But we need to look beyond the law in a narrow sense to discern the public contours of the thirteenth-century struggles between the papacy and empire. Needless to say, the vast majority of contemporary Christians were not canon lawyers and did not understand the technicalities of the canonistic tradition. They nevertheless possessed varying degrees of awareness about the papacy's jurisdiction over their lives, the pope's status as the Vicar of Christ, his fullness of power over the church, his "power of the keys" over sin, and his possession of the "spiritual sword."[10] These terms, at once sacramental and juridical, frequently feature in non-canonistic sources. In this regard, the dilemma of the two powers played out in what Daniel Lord Smail has called the "legal culture of publicity" in the Middle Ages. Powerful popes and rulers might seem far removed from the ordinary men and women that Smail describes in medieval Marseilles, who needed "to perform openly and in the public eye in order to inscribe facts in the memories and gossip networks that comprised the archive on which proof in subsequent legal quarrels might depend."[11] And yet, members of the papal curia and imperial court likewise argued about the law in the "public eye," sacrificing legalistic precision for sensationalism and seeking to create "public archives of knowledge" on a Christendom-wide scale.[12]

Certainly, one must be cautious when translating the medieval Latin word for "public" and its variants (*publicus, publice, publicare*), terms that commonly designated something as "lordly," "royal," or "official" or meant "to reserve as a royal prerogative" or "to confiscate for the fisc."[13] In our thirteenth-century sources, however, the word "public" suggested and designated many other things that come far closer to what we might now associate with public life. Canon law distinguished between the "internal forum" of the conscience and the "external forum" that encompassed "public or manifest transgressions of the Church's law or divine law."[14] Public acts included the presentation and reading of documents "in public" (*in publico*) before witnesses and crowds, deeds done "openly" (*palam*) as opposed to "secretly" (*clam*), and the bringing of news "to public notice" (*ad publicam notitiam*). The invocation of the public takes shape in descriptions of information spreading "among all the people" (*in universis populis*), "throughout the entire world" (*per totum orbem*) or "throughout all the lands of Christendom" (*per terras totius Christianitatis*), not only in written form but also as rumors and word-of-mouth news—much of it, what we might now call "fake news." Publicly embodying papal and imperial authority, apostolic legates and their imperial counterparts conveyed all sorts of communications to wider constituencies: "solemn," "public," and "open" letters or, by contrast, "closed" and "secret" ones, along with "letters of credence," "excusatory letters," and "exhortatory," "admonitory," and "testimonial" letters among them.[15] Rituals of anathema and the denunciation of sinners took place publicly, as did the convocation of citizens in communal spaces or the summons for Christians to assemble at church councils. One even finds a sense of "public scandal" (*scandalum publicum*), the outrage caused by shameful behavior and the reputations ruined by scurrilous gossip.[16]

Through routes that are sometimes but not always traceable, letters, documents, and orally transmitted information (or disinformation) made their way to monastic and civic chroniclers, who emplotted what they read and heard into narratives of their own design. The word "chronicler" conjures images of medieval scribes, removed from the events of the world they described, often with a confused sense of chronology or just a poor grasp on the facts. Yet the chroniclers that we will encounter in this book, and not just the ones that scholars label Guelf (more or less pro-papal) and Ghibelline (favoring the empire) possessed their own stakes in the battles between the popes and the Hohenstaufen prince: figures like the English monk Matthew Paris, outraged at the financial costs of the papacy's struggle with Frederick; or Salimbene of Adam, the well-traveled Franciscan friar, forced to traverse the war-torn landscapes of northern Italy during the years of conflict between papal and imperial allies.[17] Such history-writers did more than passively record events: they memorialized a certain version of the past from their presentist perspective. They preserved—to some extent, imagined—conversations, rumors and gossip, gestures, and rituals they judged worthy of remembrance.[18] In this regard, we can treat their mistakes, biases, and lack of factual accuracy as enriching their historical value rather than disqualifying them as unreliable primary sources, using them as a metric of sorts for contemporary reactions to the astonishing and sensational events of the thirteenth century.

At its most ambitious, this book suggests that we need to rethink the public nature of Christendom in the Middle Ages.[19] Among many other implications, this reconceptualizing of medieval Europe's Christian society has particular implications for the study of papal sovereignty. Historians have long emphasized the Roman papacy's contributions to the unity of Latin or Western Christian believers, who were bound together by their shared sacred language, rites, laws, and obedience to Rome as the "mother and head of all churches." Popes helped to shape that common identity through compelling ideas, stressing the unique role of their office as the unifier of the faithful on earth, and also through increasingly sophisticated forms of governance and communication, including the college of cardinals and consistory; the chancery and archives; a systematic tradition of canon law; and the staging of ecclesiastical councils, to name a few key examples. As an institution, the papacy acted as a leader in the broader information revolution that began to transform Europe starting in the eleventh century, with its well-known shift "from memory to written record."[20] By the thirteenth century, such changes in government, communication habits, and record keeping continued to accelerate. More effectively than before, the Roman curia functioned as the final court of appeals for ecclesiastical disputes; a source of privileges, immunities, and exemptions; a provider of benefices and dispensations; and a center for fundraising through taxes and subsidies, bringing petitioners and favor seekers to Rome (or wherever else the pope happened to be), while legates, envoys, and judge-delegates empowered by the Apostolic See conveyed papal letters, rescripts, and other documents into every corner of Europe and beyond.[21]

Some might nevertheless question the premise that Christendom formed a "public" or "open" realm. As a "feudal" society, it has been argued, medieval Europe did not possess a genuine public sphere, lacking as it did the requisite economic conditions, spaces of interaction, and forms of communication—namely, print—for an informed citizenry engaging in discourse about the public good.[22] Others have presented Christendom as a monolithic "religiously imagined community," its inhabitants lacking a self-consciousness of their own historicity.[23] In recent years, however, scholars have pushed back against dismissive views of medieval and early modern publics, demonstrating that premodern societies possessed their own performative cultures and communicative practices, their own open forums for debate over the social and political conditions of their lives.[24] Still others have stressed the public as a "powerful rhetorical and discursive concept" rather than an actual space or lived interaction of citizens, conceptualizing the public within a nexus of texts, forming part of a social imaginary, a "fiction, which, because it can appear real, exerts real political force."[25] This sort of discursive public need not be limited by putatively modern technologies, spaces, and social categories.

Viewed from this perspective, rather than as a hierarchical, feudal, or static society lacking public awareness, medieval Christendom formed a dynamic place of circulating people, texts, rumors, and shared performances. As the principal dilemma of Christian sovereignty in the Middle Ages, the relationship between the two powers took shape within that open realm and in turn helped to shape it.[26] Although far from the first conflict between popes and emperors, Gregory and Innocent's successive struggles with Frederick II marked an especially vital and intensive episode of public crisis over the proper ordering of Christendom, one with the potential for violence that spilled into the open on more than one occasion. Even so, rather than eagerly seeking combat to the death, the two popes and the emperor more often seemed to be searching for ways to defer, delay, or defuse their political confrontations, while other parties sought advantage in the turmoil caused by the division between the popes and the emperor. That history of reluctance, compromise, and occasional cooperation between the two sides forms an equally crucial, albeit largely forgotten, part of their relationship.

~

The chapters below are organized chronologically and divided into two parts. After a prelude describing Hugolino dei Conti's legation to Lombardy in 1221, before he became Gregory IX, Part I starts with the pope's election in 1227 and ends with his death in 1241. Chapter 1 examines Gregory's conflict with Frederick over the emperor's contested crusade vow, a conflict that lasted until their reconciliation in 1230; Chapter 2, the years from 1230 to 1235, an often overlooked period of dialog and cooperation between the two powers, including their alignment of interests over the crusades and the fight against heresy; Chapter 3, the pope and emperor's increasingly unrestrained arguments over Frederick's political actions in Lombardy and perceived abuse of ecclesiastical liberties; and Chapter 4, Gregory's second excommunication of Frederick and their ensuing battles until the pope's demise. An interlude between the two parts examines the intervening vacancy in the apostolic office.

Part II covers the period of Innocent IV's papacy. Chapter 5 explores the first year and half after his election, when the new pope pursued an unsuccessful peace with Frederick; Chapter 6, the Council of Lyons in 1245, where Innocent issued his formal judgment deposing the emperor; Chapter 7, the following years of unrestrained warfare between papal and imperial supporters until Frederick's death in 1250; and, Chapter 8, Innocent's fight with the deceased emperor's heirs until his own demise in 1254. A brief postlude follows, describing contemporary reactions to the pope's death and the immediate fallout from his battles with the Hohenstaufen dynasty.

The epilogue to this book speculates about the long-term significance attributed to the battles between *sacerdotium* and *regnum*. After all, medieval clashes between popes and monarchs feature in some of the most cherished narratives of modernity. Theorizing about the two powers, many argue, first suggested the possibility that human activity could be divided into autonomous spheres, one sacred, the other secular. Others assert that fighting between popes and worldly rulers formed an unintentional buttress against theocratic rule, assuring that neither party could realize their aspirations to complete dominion over Christian society and thereby creating space for the eventual retreat of religion from the public sphere. Between the "hammer and anvil" of such conflicts, as Francis Oakley recently put it, "political freedoms in the West were eventually to be forged."[27] There are sound reasons for locating such contributions to the western political tradition in the Middle Ages. Yet, in this present era of resurgent "public religions," I have come to wonder whether we should so confidently emplot the history of two powers into a narrative of progress from the medieval past, characterized by the imbrication of religion and politics, to the modern present that supposedly distinguishes between them.[28]

PRELUDE

The Legate

On 22 November 1220, before a crowd in the Church of Saint Peter at Rome, Pope Honorius III crowned Frederick II—already king of the Germans, of Lombardy, and of the Regno, the combined regions of Calabria, Apulia, and Sicily—emperor of the Romans. This event marked the beginning of Frederick's imperial reign as well as the culmination of years-long cooperation between the young Hohenstaufen ruler and the papacy, which had supported his rights in Sicily during his minority and backed his claim to the contested German throne. As part of the coronation ceremony, Frederick issued a number of constitutions, swearing among other things to recognize the territorial possessions, honors, and rights of the Roman church, to maintain a formal separation between the Regno and the empire, and to assure that his officials would take action against heretics of all kinds.[1] On that solemn occasion, he also renewed his crusading vow, first sworn during his royal coronation at Aachen in 1215. Richard of San Germano, a chronicler with ties to the imperial court, described how the emperor "publicly renewed his vow" at the hands of Hugolino dei Conti, the cardinal bishop of Ostia and Velletri and the future pope Gregory IX.[2]

A few months later, Honorius appointed Hugolino to the office of full legation in Lombardy and Tuscany to promote Frederick's promised crusade to the holy places. The elderly cleric, probably about seventy years old, had a long history of service at the papal curia and experience acting as a legate for Honorius and his predecessor, Innocent III, including a previous tour of duty in Lombardy.[3] When Frederick heard the news about Hugolino's assignment to the region, as he later wrote to the cardinal bishop, he was overjoyed to hear that the pope had assigned his "father in Christ and friend" to carry out the "business of the cross." Addressing the communities of northern Italy, the emperor signaled his support for Hugolino, authorizing him to absolve anyone subject to imperial banishment as long as they agreed to join the crusade and telling his subjects to honor the cardinal "like our own person."[4]

Papal legates like Hugolino dei Conti embodied the judicial and sacramental authority of the Apostolic See for those who might never lay eyes on the bishop of

Rome. They gave a public face and voice to the pope's fullness of power, conveying his sovereign rights over the faithful into the communities of Europe and beyond. The Roman pontiff, after all, could not be everywhere. But legally empowered legates sent "from the side" (*a latere*) of the pope came fairly close. Hugolino's legation represented only one such iteration of papal authority in this regard. Undertaking his duties, the cardinal participated in a wide-reaching network of envoys who represented the Roman curia, conveying and presenting documents from the papal chancery, passing along word-of-mouth instructions from the pope, and working to assure that local bishops, abbots, and other churchmen realized the directives of the Apostolic See. Without such means of communication and display, the impressive political and judicial prerogatives claimed by the Vicars of Christ would have meant little beyond their immediate orbit.[5]

Hugolino's particular legation to Lombardy in 1221 has a special significance for the subject of this book. Although the cardinal bishop did not know it at the time, his activities on Honorius's behalf anticipated the overriding concerns that would later shape his own papacy after he became Pope Gregory IX. These included the launching of a successful crusade to free the holy places from the "infidels," the effort to create conditions of peace that would enable such a crusade, and the commitment to eradicating heresy, which was perceived as a dire threat that endangered the faithful, threatened the peace, and undermined the crusades. In addition, Hugolino's legation made clear an inescapable fact of thirteenth-century politics: that the Apostolic See's ability to mobilize Christians for such goals remained linked, publicly and behind the scenes, to the reputation, fortunes, and decisions of the Hohenstaufen emperor.

An unusual amount of information about Hugolino's legation in 1221 survives thanks to the written register that remains of his activities: copies of various documents that the cardinal bishop or members of his traveling "household"—including his chaplains, treasurer, and notaries—judged important enough to archive. This invaluable collection of documents represents just a portion of the written artefacts that his legation must have produced, preserving one version of the letters, forms, receipts, and "public instruments" (*instrumenta publica*) that would have been copied, amended, and distributed to various recipients, signed and affixed with the legate's and other witnesses' seals.[6] Its texts often describe the scenes of their own inception, when they were drafted by notaries "before the legate" or "in the legate's presence" during or just after assemblies held in piazzas and other open spaces, communal halls, or the local bishop's palace, which doubled as a center for urban governance.[7] Hugolino staged or participated in many such gatherings that brought together notable citizens and officials, podestas and town councilors, bishops, abbots, and clerics of various rank, along with members of city militias and various urban societies. When the cardinal could not be present himself, he employed his own envoys, usually local prelates and abbots, "worthy" and "reliable" men sent with instructions to be delivered "aloud" (*viva voce*) and written documents to be read on his behalf. Such traffic went both ways, as "ambassadors" from various communes traveled to meet with Hugolino, sometimes ordered to appear before him by a fixed deadline, conveying their own oral instructions, letters, and documents.[8]

Hugolino's register makes plain his concern with launching the next crusade. The letter appointing him as legate highlighted this "burden," which was incumbent upon the pope and shared by his helpers, like the cardinal bishop.[9] That particular burden possessed an unmistakable urgency in 1221. Eight years earlier, Pope Innocent III had set plans in motion for what is now called the Fifth Crusade by issuing a number of bulls that called for a new expedition to liberate Jerusalem. As part of its deliberations in 1215, the Fourth Lateran Council had followed with the most elaborate formulation of papal crusading policy yet, laying down precise guidelines for the financing, moral comportment, and organization of the upcoming campaign. Among other measures, the council called for a universal one-twentieth tithe in support of the upcoming crusade, direct subsidies from clerical revenues, and personal donations as an act of penance for noncombatants, allowing women, the elderly, and the infirm to enjoy the same forgiveness of sins as those going to battle the unbelievers. After Innocent died in July 1216, Pope Honorius had immediately signaled his own commitment to the crusade, arranging for the systematic preaching of crusade sermons and assigning papal legates and other representatives to collect the crusade-related funds mandated at the recent general council.[10]

Two years later the crusade was launched, but it did not go as planned. During the late spring and summer of 1218, a substantial force of crusaders landed in Egypt, overseen in part by Honorius's legate Pelagius, cardinal bishop of Albano. In November 1219, after a long siege, the Christian army captured the port city of Damietta, apparently positioning them for further conquests. By the time of Frederick's imperial coronation one year later, however, the crusaders remained stuck in Damietta, undermanned and underfunded, their leaders divided. Rumors about the expedition's possible collapse spread around Europe, as letters circulated back and forth between the crusaders in Egypt and their friends at home, some telling of strange prophecies that foretold the coming of a mysterious figure known as Prester John, an Eastern Christian king who would rescue the stalled army.[11] Most of the crusader leadership pinned their hopes on Frederick's more likely arrival, which would bring fresh manpower, supplies, and funds. Honorius seemed to realize that the fate of the crusade hinged upon the Hohenstaufen ruler's timely intervention. In 1219, acknowledging Frederick's privileged legal status as a sworn crusader, the pope took him under the "special protection" of the Apostolic See, setting several deadlines for his departure, which was finally deferred until March 1221 after his imperial coronation. During the lead-up to Frederick's crowning in 1220, Honorius stressed the soon-to-be emperor's utmost responsibility to assist the crusade before it fell apart.[12]

Under these circumstances, securing the support of northern Italy's well-off urban communities for Frederick's upcoming crusade became a top priority for the pope and his legate. During his meetings with civic officials at places such as Siena, Florence, and Milan, acting by the "prayers of lord Pope Honorius, the highest pontiff, and lord Frederick, the emperor," Hugolino extracted sworn promises to collect and turn over monies still owed for the expedition, including in some cases the one-twentieth tithe still in arrears. His register includes a detailed list of such obligations, inventorying the troops and funds owed by communes, local lords, and bishops. As Hugolino cautioned in a letter to Berthold, patriarch of Aquileia, if people did not pay what they owed, their failure might embolden others to renege on their promises. Communities like Milan, Lodi, and Brescia agreed to make direct contributions of soldiers or offered to make fixed payments to other fighters taking up the cross. Hugolino also took a hand in directing the flow of funds to specific crusaders, figures such as the marquis of Montferrat, who were ready to depart soon for the holy places.[13]

The legate's public responsibilities for the crusade did not stop with securing financial contributions. They included a more ambitious, elusive goal: the establishment of peace. As evident at the Fourth Lateran Council, which called for a four-year universal truce throughout Christendom, the papacy insisted that crusading required peace among Christians. "Scandal," "rancor," and "discord" created the sort of conditions that endangered the church and drained the resources needed for a successful crusade.[14] After decades of far-reaching social transformation and changes in communal governance, the urban communities of Lombardy in particular had become sites of near endemic conflict, as powerful families and podestas, bishops, strongmen, and sworn associations vied for control of the region's cities and the surrounding countryside.[15] Responding to this volatility, Hugolino identified peace, public order, and protecting the church's "liberty" as the other priorities of his legation. He faced all sorts of disruptions that disturbed the tranquility of the region. In Piacenza, for example, he confronted an intractable struggle between two societies: the "popular party" and the "militia," that was dividing the city. Their fighting, he warned, represented precisely the kind of disruption that hampered a community's ability to fulfill its crusading commitments. In Milan, the commune had banned the city's archbishop, Henry, after he excommunicated—wrongly, the Milanese insisted—the neighboring town of Monza. By doing so, the legate declared, the podesta and counselors had violated church canons, as well as the recent constitutions passed by Frederick during his imperial coronation. The citizens of Lucca had likewise assaulted their bishop, expelling him and the cathedral canons. At Ferrara, Hugolino confronted another long-standing dispute over revenues from ecclesiastical estates at nearby Fiscaglia, money unjustly seized by the city. Dealing with a similar problem at Faenza, he accused the commune of assailing the church's liberty and infringing upon the rights of its neighbors.[16]

The cardinal bishop did not rely on goodwill and a shared sense of Christian devotion to end such conflicts and violations of the church. As a legate of the Apostolic See, he wielded forms of ecclesiastical censure, the "spiritual keys" of binding and loosening sinners through excommunication and interdict—cutting off individuals and groups from the body of the church and prohibiting divine services and select sacraments in a given community or the orbit of a certain person. Excommunication could also trigger the temporary suspension of all oaths and sworn obligations owed to the excommunicate party, bonds of fealty, and other associations.[17] In Lombardy, Tuscany, and the March of Verona, such forms of ecclesiastical censure worked in concert with the analogous imperial ban: after six weeks, persons subject to one sentence fell under the other, rendering them subject to exile, the loss of public offices, and the seizure of their property.[18] Hugolino did not only pass such judgments but also exercised the legal right to hear appeals from excommunicate parties, to confirm or nullify sentences passed by local bishops, and to set the conditions for absolution. Before relaxing a sentence, he sometimes required pledges in cash, money, or goods, including in one case some "scholarly books," to be deposited with a third party as a guarantee of good behavior while working out the terms for lifting the censure. In some instances, where such spiritual measures fell short, the legate authorized more direct forms of worldly punishment and coercion. At Ferrara, for instance, he revoked all of the city's ecclesiastical benefices and excommunicated anyone who traded with the commune after hearing about the ban, calling for other Christians to take up arms against its recalcitrant citizens, thereby giving license to "plunder the plunderers of the church."[19]

The issuing of such judgments and the negotiations surrounding them and their resolution created public scenes of give-and-take between the legate and his representatives and the envoys of the censured party. For excommunication and interdict to possess real political and social consequences, they required deliberate publicizing, such as the repeat performance of ritual anathema on Sundays and feast days, with the clergy gathered in church denouncing the sinner and casting down lit candles and extinguishing them. Letters were sent around the diocese, publicizing the ban.[20] To meet the conditions for absolution, the podestas of Piacenza, Treviso, and Faenza swore "public oaths" with hands on the Gospels during assemblies in the communal hall or bishop's palace. During such gatherings, the "lovers of peace and concord" swore to "obey the commands" of the

Roman church, to renounce further "rancor" or "quarrels" or "vengeance," and to release captives, pay fines, and drop any further appeals to the legate, the pope, or the emperor. Notaries on hand recorded these acts, producing and sealing the "public instruments" that memorialized the terms of the agreement.[21] But things did not always go as planned. Writing back to Hugolino about the unresolved dispute between the Milanese and their archbishop, the bishops of Bergamo and Lodi described a raucous meeting in which the assembled citizens refused to hear the charges leveled against them, protesting when the two prelates tried to read aloud the legate's letter detailing their misdeeds. Lasting peace always seemed to be elusive, although any peace remained preferable to scandal, discord, and war.[22]

During the course of his legation, Hugolino identified an especially subversive threat to the peace: heretics hiding among the faithful and undermining the church from within, waiting to burst into the open. Who were those supposed deviants? After decades of experimentation in religious life among the laity, especially among women and men living in urban areas, the line between orthodoxy and heresy could be sometimes hard to discern. Some new groups, like the recently formed mendicant orders, the Franciscans and Dominicans, secured legitimacy through formal recognition by the church. Hugolino knew this better than most, serving as the first cardinal protector of the Franciscan order starting in 1218.[23] Others, like the Waldensians, whose commitment to poverty and apostolic living did not look all that different from that of the mendicants on the face of things, fell on the wrong side of the church's determination between right and wrong behavior and belief. Scholars still debate over the identity—or, according to some, even the existence—of so-called Cathars, loosely defined as subscribers to a dualist cosmology with a pronounced streak of anticlericalism. In other instances, refusing to obey the commands of the Roman church could shade from a question of discipline into heresy, such as when excommunicate persons refused to acknowledge their status and thereby became "despisers of the keys," rejecting the clergy's power to loosen and bind sinners.[24]

By the time of Hugolino's legation to Lombardy in 1221, the fight against heresy had emerged as a prominent area of convergence between the interests of popes and emperors. The third canon of the Fourth Lateran Council, modeled after earlier legislation, had instructed bishops to investigate accusations of heresy in their dioceses with the help of secular authorities, calling up upon officials to brand heretics as infamous, to confiscate their goods, to bar them from public office, and when necessary to carry out capital punishment against them.[25] As seen above, at his coronation Frederick II affirmed his own commitment to battling "Cathars, Patarenes, Leonistas, Speronistas, Arnaldistas, Circumcisers, and all heretics of either sex, by whatever name they are called." As part of his legate's duties, Honorius expected him to ensure that the schoolmasters at Bologna add Frederick's constitutions to the law books, including his statutes against heresy of all kinds. Hugolino likewise insisted that communes in the region enter those same constitutions into their civil law codes along with the anti-heretical measures promulgated at the Fourth Lateran Council. At Piacenza, as part of the newly established peace, he specifically called upon both the popular party and militia to expel all heretics from the city and confiscate their property. During a public gathering at Mantua, summoned by ringing bells and trumpets at the legate's request, the civil authorities agreed to ban all heretics, giving them eight days to leave the city or face a penalty of one hundred imperial pounds. A herald proclaimed this policy on a bridge over the river Mincio in the middle of the city.[26]

Crusading, peace, and the fight against heresy: this trifecta that gave shape to Hugolino's legation in 1221 would continue to define the public commitments of his papacy years later. His time as a legate demonstrated the visible and audible ways that the authority of the Apostolic See reached communities beyond the orbit of the papal curia, through the travel and presence of the pope's representatives (or even the representatives of the pope's representatives), through the circulation of letters and other documents, through the convocation of crowds and assemblies, through face-to-face meetings, and through the ritual proclamation of excommunications, sentences of interdict, and scenes of absolution. As a papal legate, Hugolino enjoyed the open support of the newly crowned Roman emperor, who had been signed with the cross by the cardinal's own hand. As he began his return journey to Rome in October, the bishop of Ostia and Velletri had no way of knowing that the crusade to free the holy places, envisioned and publicized as a common enterprise for the papacy and the empire, would become a source of tension, distrust, and eventual antagonism between the emperor and himself after his own elevation to the highest office in the church.

PART I

Gregory IX

Chapter 1

A Contested Vow

Just one day after the death of Pope Honorius III on 18 March 1227, the cardinal clergy assembled at the Septizodium palace in Rome elected Hugolino dei Conti, cardinal bishop of Ostia and Velletri, as the next bishop of Rome. The new pontiff, then about seventy-five years old, took the name Gregory IX. As was customary, a few days later the pope dispatched a letter notifying "the entire world" about his elevation to the Apostolic See, sending that missive to prelates, nobles, and Christian rulers everywhere, including Frederick II, emperor of the Romans and king of Sicily. In addition to the news of Gregory's election, this announcement made one thing plainly clear: the pope's commitment to the upcoming crusade that was supposed to depart the upcoming summer. In the version of his letter sent directly to Frederick, which stressed his past affection for the prince while holding a "lesser office" as cardinal bishop, Gregory called upon the Hohenstaufen ruler to prepare himself "manfully and powerfully" for the upcoming passage to the Holy Land, reminding him about all of the pope's labors in the past to support crusaders.[1]

Over the following months, Frederick's unfulfilled crusading vow would become the source of a public crisis between the new pope and the emperor. By August, a force of crusaders gathered at Brindisi intending to accompany the emperor to Syria, but when pestilence struck the army, killing many and seriously sickening Frederick, he decided against sailing for the holy places. On 19 September, Gregory excommunicated him or, more accurately, formalized his excommunicate status, which had been automatically incurred by the violation of his previous oath to depart on crusade that summer. By doing so, the pope placed his priestly office at odds with the Christian emperor, a sworn crusader and vassal of the Roman church. Their confrontation continued even after the emperor left on crusade in 1228, still excommunicate, and persisted during Frederick's time in the Holy Land. In the meantime, Gregory widened his accusations against the Hohenstaufen ruler and his officials in the Regno, denouncing their abuses of the church's liberty, attacks on papal supporters, and what might now be called war crimes—allowing Muslim mercenaries to torture and kill priests. To oppose Frederick, Gregory eventually gathered a papal army and coordinated a military campaign against the emperor's supporters in southern Italy that was waged under the "banner of the keys," the sign of the pope's spiritual power as the head of the church and status as the temporal lord of the papal patrimony.

According to many scholars, Frederick's violation of his crusading oath gave Gregory the excuse he needed to humiliate and depose the imperial ruler. "Pope Gregory felt himself by stern necessity compelled to compass the destruction of the Hohenstaufen," Ernst Kantorowicz writes. "He seized the first opportunity of compelling the foe to fight." Others offer similar appraisals. For Gregory, who "knew little of conciliation or peace," Thomas Van Cleve claims, "the crusade *per se* was far less important than it had been to Honorius III. It was, indeed, secondary to a much more ambitious goal: the complete triumph of the papacy over the Empire in the struggle for predominance in Christendom." Or, as David Abulafia puts it, Gregory was "keen to indicate from the start the absolute primacy of his office over that of the emperor. . . . With his election, cooperation between the pope and emperor gave way to the idea of the subordination of emperor to pope."[2]

And yet, judging by Gregory's repeated declarations and actions, the crusade mattered immensely to his conceptualization of the papal office, forming a public red line between him and the emperor. After generations of summoning crusades, the Roman church had invested vast amounts of spiritual, political, and material capital in the unrealized goal of defeating the so-called Saracens and securing the holy places once and for all. As seen above, during his time as a cardinal legate, Hugolino dei Conti had devoted himself to the project of freeing Jerusalem. As pope, he became responsible for crusading at an especially critical juncture in its history, when disappointment and anxiety about crusading failures reached new levels due to the collapse of the Fifth Crusade. As his predecessor Honorius had warned Frederick and other notable figures on more than one occasion, the Christian people "murmured," "clamored," and made "public complaints" about the failure of their leaders to take up the business of the cross and work together to free Christ's patrimony. Now Gregory faced those same outcries. The need to find a solution to Jerusalem's captivity had never been greater, or at least, not so acute since the recapture of the city by Salah al-Din two generations earlier.[3]

In the ensuing struggle between the pope and the prince, communicating the causes and significance of their confrontation to the wider community created its own kind of battlefield, a means to isolate and pressure one's opponent by denying him moral and material support. Letters from the papal curia and imperial chancery circulated around Christendom, each side trying to generate sympathy for its cause.[4] Outside of official channels, rumors spread about the pope's decision to excommunicate the emperor and about the sensational events of Frederick's crusade. Once in motion, the confrontation between the two men escalated

Figure 2. A lead papal bull of Pope Gregory IX. Courtesy of the Portable Antiquities Scheme.

in ways that neither side could have anticipated, as a shockingly violent battle unfolded for control of the Regno. For contemporaries, these events provoked consternation and amazement, a sense of calamity in their world and uncertainty about how to restore the proper balance between the two powers.

The Delayed Crusade

By the time of Gregory's election as pope, Frederick's crusading plans had undergone many twists and turns since he had renewed his solemn vow in Hugolino's presence seven years earlier.[5] These developments set the stage for his subsequent confrontation with the pope. After Frederick's imperial coronation in 1220, Honorius III had set and reset deadlines for his passage, threating him with excommunication if he failed to leave but reluctantly granting him extensions when circumstances—such as a rebellion by his Muslim subjects on the island of Sicily—forced him to delay his departure.[6] The pope even helped to broker a marriage between Frederick and Isabella of Brienne, daughter of John of Brienne, the Latin king of Jerusalem.[7] Frederick's vow, Honorius reminded him, represented more than a private commitment: it was a public obligation that had been renewed on multiple occasions before lay and clerical witnesses. On 25 July 1225, in the presence of two papal legates—Jacob Guala, cardinal priest of San Silvestro e Martino, and Pelagius, cardinal bishop of Albano and former legate on the Fifth Crusade—Frederick had yet again "publicly" renewed his crusading vow at San Germano by swearing on the Gospels and setting a departure date for mid-August two years later. This time his solemn vow included the crucial stipulation that his failure to fulfill its terms would automatically trigger his excommunication and the interdict of his lands.[8]

Immediately after his election, Gregory also turned his attention to another major piece of unfinished business from Honorius's papacy: enforcing a peace agreement between the emperor and the Lombard League, an alliance of northern Italian cities, including Milan, Brescia, Mantua, Treviso, Padua, Piacenza, and Bologna, that opposed the Hohenstaufen ruler's rights in the region.[9] This political protest had turned violent in 1226, when the members of the league blocked Frederick's planned imperial assembly at Cremona, which had been called to reform the empire, eradicate heresy, and pursue the business of the Holy Land.[10] If, however, the rebellious Lombards expected papal intervention on their behalf, they must have been disappointed. Honorius's commitment to the crusade trumped an alignment of interests between Rome and the Lombard League. The pope and his representatives repeatedly signaled their support for Frederick, who invoked his protected status as a sworn crusader against the Lombards' "illicit conspiracy."[11] By January 1227, Honorius had formulated written oaths for the Lombards to swear, sign, seal, and forward to all of the concerned parties, including Frederick. Both sides had to commit to keep the peace and forego any further "rancor" toward the other, to restore all captives from their recent fighting, and to revoke all bans and other measures passed during their confrontation.[12] The Lombard cities also agreed to provide four hundred soldiers for a period of two years as a contribution to the upcoming crusade. The rectors of the league dragged their feet and did not return the signed agreements by the required February deadline. Honorius had to write to them weeks later, insisting that they send the required documents and expressing skepticism about their lame excuse that one of their envoys had dropped the pages into the water during their transport, rendering them illegible. The pope died shortly after sending this letter.[13]

His successor took immediate steps to secure the terms of this agreement, being committed to the idea that peace among Christians represented a necessary first step toward a successful crusade. On 27 March, Gregory resent Honorius's final letter to the Lombard rectors with minor changes, demanding that they send the promised "form of peace" (*forma pacis*) to him and the emperor as quickly as possible. Failing to do so might give Frederick a reason to delay his departure for the Holy Land, thereby provoking the anger of "God and men" against the Lombards. A few weeks after that, he wrote to the rectors again, observing that several signatures and seals were missing from the letters once they had arrived. For this reason, he had not forwarded the incomplete set of documents to the emperor. In writing and in verbal instructions given to the letter's bearer, he insisted that the rectors should send new versions of the documents with all of the appropriate seals. They also needed to ready the soldiers they were supposed to contribute in support of the upcoming crusade, as required by the terms of the recent peace agreement. If necessary, the archbishop of Milan would compel them to fulfill their obligations by ecclesiastical censure.[14]

In April, the pope announced the successful resolution of the conflict between Frederick and the Lombards to the archbishop of Cologne and prelates throughout Germany, calling upon them to instruct all of the sworn crusaders in their dioceses to ready themselves for the upcoming passage overseas. Crusade preachers, authorized by Honorius before he died, had been laying the groundwork for the campaign for months. Like every crusade before it, appeals for this latest expedition drew more enthusiasm from some corners of Europe than others, as the expedition faced shortages of manpower and financial means, stragglers, and reluctant crusaders. English monastic histories such as the *Waverley Annals* remember an outpouring of enthusiasm in England for this armed journey to the holy places, recording that people "inspired and strengthened by apostolic letters and advisements, signed and armed besides by the virtue and wood of the holy cross, desired to go forth to avenge the injuries done to God by the enemies of the Christian name." In his *Flowers of History*, the English chronicler Roger of Wendover pictures a "great motion throughout the world for the work of the cross," especially among "the poor." Authorized crusade preachers, bearing "written mandates" from the pope, did not have a monopoly on proclaiming the Lord's wishes for a new crusade. Roger also describes a fisherman who saw a vision of Christ's body with bloody wounds, pierced by the nails and lance from the crucifixion, who told everyone in the local marketplace about this miraculous sign.[15]

During the first few months of his papacy, therefore, Gregory's desire to destroy Frederick seems nowhere in sight. Writing to the emperor on 22 July 1227, just before Frederick's planned departure on crusade, Gregory struck a pastoral—if, perhaps, paternalistic—tone. The pope offered an exegesis of sorts on the five insignia of the Christian imperial office, including the relics of the cross and holy lance, the triple crown, the scepter for the right hand, and the orb for the left. All of these symbols served as reminders of Frederick's duty and devotion to Christ: the cross, of the Lord's suffering; the lance, of the blood that poured from his side; the triple crown, denoting grace, justice, and glory, of Frederick's crowns in Germany, Lombardy, and the imperial one bestowed upon him by the pope; the scepter, of earthly power to punish the wicked; and the orb, of dispensing mercy. In closing, Gregory stressed his past affection for the emperor and his present concern for his eternal salvation. On the eve of Frederick's planned departure for the Holy Land, the pope sought to valorize rather than undermine the imperial office, as long as its present occupant remembered the true nature of his calling in the service of the Lord.[16]

Various chronicles relate how a large crusading force gathered at Brindisi in July and August to await passage overseas. They also describe how the summer heat, spoiled food, and disease took a terrible toll on the soldiers camped outside the city. Some of the troops returned home, while others waited for transport as August turned into September. Frederick numbered among those who fell ill; Ludwig, landgrave of Thuringia, died of sickness. After an aborted attempt to set sail for Syria, the emperor decided to delay his own departure again until the following May, although a good portion of the crusaders left for Acre at his command, including Gerold of Lausanne, the patriarch of Jerusalem and the papal legate assigned to the army, and Hermann of Salza, the master general of the Teutonic Order. Opinions remained divided about the real reasons for the emperor's decision not to leave for the Holy Land. According to some, the emperor made the best of unfortunate circumstances, postponing his passage due to his illness. For others, he had only pretended that he planned to cross overseas and feigned being sick. The *Waverley Annals* claim that the "pagans" corrupted him with gifts, while the *Annals of Schäftlarn* say that other crusaders did not fall ill, but rather, Frederick had poisoned them. Roger of Wendover observes that the emperor's failure to depart brought "shame and harm to the entire business of the cross," adding that, "in opinion of many," his failure to depart was the reason why the Lord revealed himself on the cross in the vision described above, "placing his grievance against the emperor for the injuries caused by him before each and every one."[17]

Communicating Excommunication

On 19 September, Pope Gregory confirmed Frederick's self-inflicted sentence of excommunication at Anagni. As one of Frederick's modern biographers wryly observes, excommunication represented an "occupational hazard" for medieval emperors.[18] Gregory IX's anathematizing of Frederick II, however, hardly represented a run-of-the-mill excommunication, if there ever was such a thing. It placed the pope and the most powerful ruler in Europe publicly at odds during a moment when the fate of Jerusalem seemed to hang in the balance.[19]

Gregory's anonymous biographer, a member of the curia with close ties to the pope, describes the scene of the emperor's solemn excommunication in the *Life of Gregory IX*.[20] Gregory had come to his hometown in July. The bishops of Rome commonly left the city during the summer months to escape the heat. On 18 September, no doubt anticipating his plans for the following day, he elevated six presumably supportive clerics from the curia to the college of cardinals, promoting, among others, Sinibaldo Fieschi—the future pope, Innocent IV—as cardinal priest of San Lorenzo in Lucina.[21] On the Feast of the Archangel Michael, assisted by the cardinals and other archbishops and bishops and wearing his pontifical robes, Gregory delivered a sermon in the city's cathedral church on the Gospel of Matthew 18:7: "For it must be, that scandals come to pass, but woe to the man by whom that scandal comes." After delivering multiple warnings to Frederick about the need to fulfill his vow, the pope, like the "archangel triumphing over the dragon," had "publicly announced" Frederick's excommunication, affirming the sentence incurred when he had failed to depart on crusade as he had sworn to do at San Germano. Although the author of Gregory's vita does not say so, the solemn ceremony must have closely followed the guidelines for excommunication and anathema from canon law, including twelve priests holding lit candles, throwing them on the ground, and stamping them out.[22]

In canon law, the rules for excommunication give instructions for a letter to be sent throughout the appropriate parish announcing the sentence. In this case, the "parish" constituted nothing less than the entirety of Christendom.[23] The papal letter *In maris amplitudine* shows this messaging campaign at work. Issued on 10 October, the encyclical opens by describing the tempests that menaced the ship of Saint Peter on the storm-tossed seas: the "perfidy of the pagans" in the holy places; the "frenzy of tyrants" assailing the liberty of the church; the "madness of heretics" tearing Christ's "tunic" asunder; and the "perversity of false sons and brothers." For this reason, the Apostolic See had elevated and supported Frederick since his boyhood to act as a defender of the church. When he traveled to Germany to receive his crown, he had assumed the cross, a source of hope for the Holy Land. When crowned emperor "by our own hands, although in a lesser office," Frederick had "publicly" renewed his vow, planning to leave on crusade two years later. When the deadline drew near, however, with "many excuses," he had failed to depart. At San Germano, he had bound himself by another such oath, promising to make his passage by August two years later. The legates on hand, "publicly by the authority of the Apostolic See," had authorized a sentence of excommunication that would be triggered if he failed to meet these obligations. Now he had done so. Gregory's letter describes the gathering of the crusader army at Brindisi and its decimation by the summer heat, disease, and desertion, followed by the emperor's failure to depart for Syria, which left those crusaders who did set sail leaderless and endangered the Holy Land to the emperor's shame and the "shame of all Christendom." After lamenting the conditions overseas and emphasizing his commitment to the crusade, the pope had "unwillingly but publicly" pronounced the emperor as excommunicate, commanding him to be "shunned by all" and instructing prelates to announce his status publicly and gravely proceed against him if his stubbornness persisted.[24]

It is hardly surprising that this product of the papal chancery offers a one-sided picture of Frederick's actions. That was the point: to sway opinions and trigger indignation, leaving no room for doubt about the rightness of Gregory's decision. As intended, *In maris amplitudine* circulated widely, having been sent to prelates in Italy, Germany, England, and elsewhere. In his *Flowers of History*, Roger of Wendover includes a version of the text sent to Stephen, the archbishop of Canterbury. Roger did more than just "copy" or "transcribe" the letter. He narratively framed the letter, describing the pope's decision to anathematize the emperor by relating how Gregory "ordered the sentence of excommunication to be published in every place through apostolic letters." Other chroniclers offer similar observations about how the pope commanded Frederick "to be denounced throughout the empire," how he sent his "general letters throughout the entire west" regarding the emperor's public excommunication, or how he denounced the emperor "as excommunicate throughout the western church, through his letters sent to all the prelates, that is, archbishops, bishops, and archdeacons, so that they might denounce him in their dioceses."[25]

The emperor responded by sending out his own "excusatory" letters, including the encyclical *In admiratione vertimur.* This product of the imperial chancery lamented the unforeseen devastation of the crusading army at Brindisi, explaining the circumstances of Frederick's delayed passage overseas and complaining about the pope's "unjust" judgment. The emperor wanted the "entire world" to hear about his innocence and his grievances against Gregory, whose letters tried to "raise up hatred" against him in every land. *In admiratione vertimur* replays more or less the same version of events as *In maris amplitudine,* but in a different key, showing how Frederick tried to honor his crusading vow from the beginning, despite the Roman church's half-hearted attempts to protect and to assist him since his boyhood. Disregarding his doctors' orders, he had traveled to Brindisi and even set sail for Syria before his near-fatal illness forced him to debark. Fully intending to head overseas the following May, he had sent ahead numerous galleys and soldiers along with funds to support them, fulfilling his other obligations made at San Germano two years earlier. In the closing portions of this encyclical, Frederick gave instructions for the letter to be "read aloud and heard in public."[26] Richard of San Germano describes how the emperor sent one of his officials, Roffrid of Benevento, to do just that on the Capitoline Hill in Rome. In his *Flowers of History,* Roger of Wendover explains that "just as the pope had the issued sentence published in every Christian land, so the aforesaid emperor wrote to all of the Christian kings and princes complaining that the sentence had been injuriously passed against him." Roger relates that another such letter, sealed with Frederick's golden bull, arrived at the court of Henry III and warned the English king that Gregory wished to make all rulers into his "tributaries." Responding to both sets of letters, Henry tried to carve out a middle ground between the two sides for the good of the holy places, beseeching the pope to show compassion for the emperor and calling on Frederick to reconcile with the Roman church as soon as possible. This was not the last time he would find himself in this uncomfortable position.[27]

Chroniclers and annalists from every corner of Europe followed these astonishing events, implying or openly revealing their sympathies in the matter. The

Guelf *Annals of Piacenza*, so-called to designate their anti-imperial bias, describe how Frederick's failure to depart overseas provoked Gregory to "publicly anathematize and excommunicate the emperor before all of the people who had come to visit the threshold of the apostles Peter and Paul." The *Annals of Schäftlarn* state that Gregory "prudently" excommunicated him, while the *Chronicle of Burchard of Ursburg* says that he did so "for frivolous and false reasons, casting aside any judicial procedure." The *Waverley Annals* record that Frederick caused great harm to crusaders at Brindisi, prompting the pope to "solemnly" excommunicate him "at Rome and many other places," but the *Annals of Saint Emmeram of Regensburg* attribute the pope's decision to the "devil's instigation," nearly destroying the crusading expedition. The variety of attitudes in such historical works is striking and are indicative of the event's polarizing nature—and not just for chroniclers as the crafters and keepers of memory.[28]

The circulation of such misinformation and hard-edged accusations did not foreclose the possibility of reconciliation between the pope and emperor. To the contrary, by raising the public stakes in their confrontation, their propaganda seemed designed to build pressure for a negotiated settlement, each side seeking leverage to strike the best terms possible for their own set of interests. In September, after hearing about the pope's judgment against him, Frederick sent a group of envoys to meet with the pope during a provincial synod at Perugia to explain the reasons for his delayed departure. Frederick later complained about the pope's refusal to give his representatives a proper audience, despite the council's collective urging that he do so. According to the emperor, Gregory met individually with each bishop present, intimidating them into silence before allowing the envoys to speak and then dismissing them out of hand.[29] Such reluctance to deal with Frederick signaled to everyone that his reconciliation with the church would not come easily. On 18 November, after returning to Rome, Gregory seemed to reinforce this message, repeating his sentence of excommunication in the basilica of Saint Peter before a crowd of cardinals and other clergy. Yet the following month, the pope sent two cardinals, Otto, cardinal deacon of San Nichola in Carcere Tulliano, and Thomas of Capua, cardinal priest of Santa Sabina, to meet with the emperor at San Germano bearing a relatively conciliatory letter that expressed the pope's despair about the current "scandal" in the church and the lamentable state of the Holy Land, along with hopes for the emperor's speedy return to the church after he rendered sufficient satisfaction to God and justice to men.[30]

This posturing continued into the spring. On Maundy Thursday in 1228, a feast day traditionally linked with the excommunication and reconciliation of sinners, Gregory "publicly" reiterated the emperor's anathema before the large crowds gathered for Holy Week in the Church of Saint Peter.[31] Writing to the archbishops, bishops, and other clergy in Apulia that same month, instructing them to repeat and publicize this sentence on Sundays and feast days, the pope described how he had wielded the "medicinal sword of Peter" against Frederick in the "spirit of mildness," pronouncing the sentence of excommunication for the benefit of the ruler's soul, but also because the breaking of his crusader vow would cause a great "detriment to the faith and a grave scandal among the entire Christian people." Frederick, however, "showing contempt for the keys of the church," had ordered the divine mass to be celebrated—or rather profaned—in his presence. Gregory reiterated the terms of his excommunication and interdict: wherever the emperor went, there should be no celebration of the mass. Regardless of rank, anyone who celebrated the divine services in the ruler's presence before his reconciliation with the church would lose his benefice. If the emperor continued to attend mass, thereby refusing to acknowledge his excommunicate status, the pope would proceed against him as a "heretic and despiser of the keys," declaring all those who owed him fealty absolved from their oaths in accordance with canon law.[32]

By suspending the celebration of mass and certain sacraments in Frederick's presence, halting liturgical action and imposing silences, forbidding the ringing of bells, and instructing those with special permission to celebrate mass to do so behind closed doors with lowered voices, the interdict publicized the pope's judgment for those not exposed to his epistolary denunciations of the emperor. The papal interdict apparently had little impact in Germany, but its enforcement in the Regno clearly concerned Frederick. Writing to his officials in that kingdom, he declared his imperial duty to assure the proper performance of the "divine worship," thereby avoiding a "human scandal." He ordered them to inform all of the clergy under their authority that they must "publicly celebrate the divine offices in their churches," or else he would revoke all of the worldly goods, properties, and incomes attached to their positions.[33]

Rituals remained a flashpoint in other dangerous ways. The pope found this out for himself a few days after Maundy Thursday when a group of Roman citizens stormed into the Church of Saint Peter and assaulted Gregory along with the other clergy present. The pope's biographer, who probably witnessed the scene, insists that Frederick had turned the Romans against their bishop with his "bribes and lies." The mob, casting aside their fear of God, interrupted the pope while he said mass at the high altar over Saint Peter's remains, laying their "profane hands" on him and yelling "Crucify him!" much like those who crucified Christ. Other chroniclers agreed that the emperor lay behind this "sedition" in Rome. A few weeks later, the pope excommunicated the Romans and left for Perugia. He would not return to "the City," as contemporary sources called Rome, for two years.[34]

Jerusalem Delivered—or Not

In the summer of 1228, the public crisis between the pope and emperor entered a new stage when Frederick departed for Jerusalem. From start to finish, controversy surrounded this unprecedented situation in the history of crusading, wherein an excommunicate emperor and crusader, openly at odds with the pope, set out to free Jerusalem. During the months that followed, messengers and letters circulated back and forth between Europe and the Holy Land as the pope, emperor, and their supporters tried to shape public opinion about the expedition. In this "game played for high stakes," as one scholar has described Frederick's volatile crusade, controlling public perceptions of the expedition overseas became nearly as important as maintaining control of the crusade or even the holy city of Jerusalem itself.[35]

Throughout the entire period of his anathema, Frederick had continued to make and publicize his plans to embark on crusade, despite his excommunicate status. In a letter sent to Italian communes the preceding April, the emperor drew a clear contrast between his commitment to freeing Jerusalem and the pope's recent decision to speak against him on Maundy Thursday before the large crowds gathered for Holy Week. Rather than preaching about Frederick's crusade and encouraging his listeners toward the "service of the cross," the pope had raised the subject of Milan and other "traitors" to the empire, denouncing Frederick for not sufficiently compensating them after their recent rebellion. This revealed that Gregory did not have sufficient cause to judge him based on the "business of the Holy Land," given Frederick's past efforts toward that end and imminent departure overseas. Stressing his burning desire to fulfill his oath, as evident "before the entire world," and accusing the pope of damaging the crusade by favoring traitors to his imperial rule, the emperor called for his loyal followers to support the upcoming expedition. In a similar letter sent from the imperial court in June, he described how he had again sent solemn envoys to the curia bearing the written "form of satisfaction" that he would make so that he might cross overseas with the pope's blessing. Demonstrating his intransigence, Gregory rejected those terms but refused to explain what kind of satisfaction he would find acceptable to lift the ban. Frederick's message was clear. Although the pope had unjustly opposed him at every turn, the emperor refused to turn aside from fulfilling his duties in the Holy Land.[36]

The emperor set sail in August 1228. The course of his crusade is well known. After various stops en route, including a five-week stay on Cyprus, he landed at Acre on 7 September 1228. In November, Frederick marched with a mixed army of crusaders, local Christian nobles, and members of the military orders to Jaffa planning to fortify the city, which was within striking distance of Jerusalem. Ships reaching the port resupplied the army by year's end. Frederick, however, did not intend to free the holy city by military means, seeking instead to establish a truce with the Ayyubid sultan, al-Kamil. The Egyptian ruler had his own reasons for making such a deal, including political infighting with his brother and nephew, the sultans of Damascus. Negotiations had begun between the two even before the emperor left on his crusade. In February, they agreed to a ten-year peace: al-Kamil would restore Jerusalem to the emperor, along with Bethlehem, Nazareth, and various other villages, and allow the Christians living there access to the coast; both sides would release any prisoners they held; and the two rulers would pledge to support each other against their respective enemies. On 17 March, Frederick and the crusaders entered Jerusalem, completing their armed pilgrimage. On the following day, Easter Sunday, the Hohenstaufen ruler crowned himself king of Jerusalem in the Church of the Holy Sepulcher. The day after that, he began his return journey to Jaffa and Acre.[37]

Not surprisingly, the pope and his circle attacked the legitimacy of Frederick's expedition from the beginning. Gregory's anonymous biographer writes that when Frederick left Brindisi for Syria, he "set sail more like a pirate than an emperor, a transgressor of his vow and oath."[38] From the moment of his arrival in Acre, Frederick's excommunicate status reportedly caused disruptive scenes in the city. Roger of Wendover writes that the local clergy and people welcomed the emperor with great honor, but, "since they knew he was excommunicated," they refused to give him the kiss of peace or to eat with him, counseling him to "return to the holy church, making satisfaction to the pope." Canon law was clear on this point: those who kissed, prayed with, or ate with an excommunicate person were liable to excommunication themselves.[39] Not long after the emperor reached Acre, according to the *Estoire de Eracles*, an old French chronicle devoted to events in the Holy Land, a Franciscan messenger arrived bearing letters from Gregory to Gerold of Lausanne, patriarch of Jerusalem and papal legate, instructing him to "denounce the emperor Frederick, as excommunicate and foresworn." Frederick answered, laying his grievances with the pope "before the entire army" and denouncing the papal sentence against him as unjust.[40]

These sorts of demonstrations continued on the road to Jaffa and Jerusalem. Some chroniclers record that the Hospitallers and Templars greeted Frederick on bended knee, committed to serving him. Others, however, relate that the military orders, along with the friars, refused to march with the emperor's forces, declaring their obedience to the Roman church. They traveled instead to the east of the main army. Worried that the "Turks" might exploit this weakness, Frederick sent riders to cry out his commands "in the name of God and Christianity, without naming the emperor."[41] In a letter sent to the pope, which Gregory subsequently forwarded to other destinations, Gerold explained how the crusaders watched with fear and confusion as envoys passed back and forth between the Christian and Muslim camps, causing a "scandal" in the army. The patriarch, who remained at Acre but followed the crusaders' progress from afar, denounced Frederick's coziness with the sultan, who sent him "dancing girls and jugglers" and other unmentionable persons after he heard that Frederick preferred to dress, eat, and live "in a Saracen manner," behavior that the "army of Jesus Christ" found abhorrent.[42]

Gerold likewise portrayed Frederick's ten-year truce with al-Kamil as unrealistic, unsustainable, and a danger to the Christian presence in the Holy Land. He forwarded to the pope a French transcript of the pact that had been sent to him by Hermann of Salza, master general of the Teutonic Order, adding his own derisive commentary on its terms in Latin.[43] According to Gerold, the emperor gave away everything and got little in return. He even surrendered his breastplate, shield, and sword to the sultan, telling him that he never wished to take up arms against him again. Gerold stressed the "secretive" and "fraudulent" nature of the negotiations, as Frederick finally made his "hidden" plans "public," having agreed to the terms of the treaty without ever having them "read aloud or recited openly" before his fellow crusaders, thereby denying the bishops and members of the military orders accompanying the army a chance to consult with the Latin patriarch before they agreed to anything—hardly the behavior of a Christian prince and crusader.[44] Possession of the Temple Mount, including the Temple of the Lord, as the crusaders called the Dome of the Rock, was an especially sensitive point. Gerold highlighted the treaty's clause allowing the infidels continued access to the holy site. With "a greater multitude of Saracens coming to pray at the temple than the crowds of Christians coming to the sepulcher," he wondered, "how will the Christians be able to maintain their dominion for ten years, without discord and danger to their persons?"[45] The "clamor" of Saracens' call to prayer, proclaimed from that high place above the city, caused all sorts of confusion and uncertainty among the crusaders.[46]

With regard to the Temple Mount, Frederick seemed to realize that he possibly had a possible public relations disaster on his hands. In his letter *Letentur et exultent,* which celebrated his triumphs in the holy places, he carefully explained that the Saracens would enter the site "in the manner of pilgrims," unarmed and unable to spend the night, praying and departing. Apologizing for these upsetting sights and sounds, Hermann of Salza likewise stressed that Christians would also have free access to pray at the site, that the Saracens could keep only a few "unarmed, elderly priests" at the temple, and that the emperor's guards would monitor the gates into the site, deciding who could enter and exit. He even pointed out that the infidels allowed the Christians similar rights of worship in the cities under their control.[47]

Frederick's entry into Jerusalem and coronation in the Church of the Holy Sepulcher provoked more tense scenes. Roger of Wendover describes how the bishops accompanying the army ritually cleansed the city with processions, prayers, and holy water but did not allow any cleric to celebrate mass for as long as the emperor remained present. To the relief of some of the crusaders, a Dominican friar named Walter continued to perform divine services just outside the city walls.[48] In his letter to Gregory, Gerold reported that he "denied the pilgrims across the board license to enter Jerusalem or visit the sepulcher," telling them that the pope would not approve of such a visitation, which might endanger their souls.[49] Sent to Jerusalem by the Latin patriarch, the archbishop of Caesarea placed the Church of the Holy Sepulcher and all of the city's holy sites under interdict. The patriarch also instructed preachers to spread the word around the army that anyone violating this prohibition would have to seek absolution from the pope himself. These actions, Hermann of Salza wrote, caused a great deal of anger toward the church among the crusaders. Hermann also explained that Frederick "complained publicly before all of the bishops that the holy places, under the power of the Saracens for so long and now free by divine aid, placed under interdict, had been enslaved by the patriarch and restored to their earlier misery by the prohibition of the divine office." Addressing the pope directly, Frederick passed over these events in silence, except for the sardonic comment, "some other time and place, we will take care to explain fully just how much counsel and aid we received from the patriarch of Jerusalem, and the masters and brothers of the religious houses."[50]

Even Hermann of Salza advised Frederick to forego mass during his coronation ceremony in the Church of the Holy Sepulcher, despite the fact that others in the army advocated such a celebration. On Easter Sunday, speaking before a crowd of prelates and magnates, before the rich and poor, the master general of the Teutonic Order delivered an address in Latin and German. Speaking on Frederick's behalf, he declared that the emperor had fulfilled his crusade vow. He even made excuses for the pope, who had excommunicated Frederick and hounded him with letters sent across the sea after hearing that Frederick was gathering an army "against the church." If the pope had known the emperor's true intentions, he never would have written such things. Likewise, Hermann relayed, Frederick lamented the fact that complaints made against him by some of the crusaders had displeased the pope, causing "harm to the entire Christian people."[51]

The day after his coronation, Frederick began his return to Acre. A second letter attributed to the patriarch of Jerusalem, found only in the *Major Chronicle* of the English monk and historian Matthew Paris, describes more troubles after the emperor arrived there.[52] When Gerold and the leaders of the military orders objected to his "treacherous" and "fraudulent" treaty with the sultan, Frederick sent out a "public herald" to summon the crusaders for a gathering outside of the city. In a personal address to the crowd, he publicly denounced those opposing him, forbidding the soldiers on pain of death from staying in the Holy Land any longer. The letter also claims that he posted guards at the city gates, denying the Templars permission to enter; seized and fortified churches around the city; and sent his followers to harass the Dominican and Franciscan friars preaching on Palm Sunday. The streets of Acre erupted into chaos. Gathering the bishops and pilgrims on hand, the patriarch excommunicated anyone attacking church persons and property, passing a sentence of interdict over the city. Finally, after some half-hearted attempts to make peace with Gerold and the others, Frederick headed to the port by a hidden side street and on the third of May "secretly" set sail for Cyprus.[53]

Matthew observes that the patriarch's letter, which was written to defame the emperor and reached "audiences around the west," did considerable damage to Frederick's reputation. Commencing his chronicle seven or eight years later, the English monk—whose colorful and opinionated historical works will feature throughout the rest of this book—offers another provocative story about the hatred that developed between the military orders and the emperor.[54] According to Matthew, the Templars and Hospitallers sent a letter bearing their seals to al-Kamil, informing him that the emperor would soon be visiting the spot of Christ's baptism at the Jordan, the perfect place to ambush and kill him. Repelled by this treachery and hoping to create confusion among the Christians, the sultan forwarded the letter to Frederick, complete with the identifying seals, and foiled the plot.[55]

Other chroniclers, however, celebrated the emperor's remarkable achievement during this "year that will be long remembered by future generations." Burchard of Ursburg writes that the pope "cast aside and despised" Frederick's letters announcing the miraculous capture of Jerusalem to Christendom at large, while Richard of San Germano declares that things would have gone far better for the "business of the Holy Land" if the emperor had crossed over "with the grace and peace of the Roman church." He added that al-Kamil almost hesitated to negotiate with Frederick at all, knowing about the great "hatred" that the church held for him. The anonymous author of the *Brief Chronicle of Sicily*, proclaiming "I who write this, I was there personally, and do not diverge from the path of truth," layered his description of Jerusalem's liberation with references to the Book of Revelation, lending an apocalyptic resonance to Frederick's deeds. Even Roger of Wendover, who was not especially sympathetic toward the emperor in his chronicle, describes messages from God, marvelous signs, prophecies, and astrological predictions that foretold the holy city's restoration "to the Christian people generally, specifically to Frederick the Roman emperor."[56]

As for Pope Gregory, in still more letters sent to bishops, princes, kings, and communes around Europe during the summer of 1229, he made his perspective on Frederick's crusade unmistakably clear. Referring to the letters written by

Gerold of Lausanne and Hermann of Salza, the pope seemed especially concerned that false rumors and misinformation would reach Christian ears about the emperor's actions overseas. He accused Frederick of four particular crimes, among others.[57] First, Frederick had surrendered his armor and weapons to the sultan of Babylon, the "adversary of Christ," renouncing the "arms of the Christian soldiers, the power of the sword taken from the altar of Saint Peter, assigned to him by Christ through his vicar for taking vengeance against malefactors and honoring the good, for defending and preserving the peace of Christ and the faith of the church."[58] By doing so, Frederick had effectively abdicated the imperial office. Second, his pact allowed the followers of "Machomet" to "preach and proclaim" their nefarious law in the city while it simultaneously imposed "silence on the herald of evangelical truth." Third, he had left critical crusader castles and fortifications exposed to assault by the "pagans." Fourth, he had bound himself under oath to fight on the sultan's behalf against his enemies, including other Christians, meaning that he would have to take up arms against a future Christian army seeking to avenge Christ and cleanse the Holy Land of the nonbelievers. Frederick had committed nothing less than treason against the Lord, rendering him "infamous," subject to spiritual and temporal judgment, and unworthy of any honor or sacraments. Far from bolstering his reign by going on crusade, the emperor had publicly disqualified himself from ruling at all.[59]

Battle for the Regno

During the period leading up to Frederick's departure for Syria, Gregory's confrontation with him had expanded into a new theater of accusations and counter-accusations over conditions in the Regno, that is, the kingdom of Sicily, Calabria, and Apulia. The emperor nominally held these territories as a "vassal" of Saint Peter, making the pope his direct temporal lord with regard to their holding. This legal dimension enabled Gregory to bring a different kind of public pressure to bear on Frederick, accusing him of being a malfeasant vassal, not just an emperor who had abdicated his Christian duties. As time passed, this battle for the Regno would eclipse the emperor's unorthodox crusade as the primary site of contest between the two leaders.

Gregory's general complaints about the Regno echoed earlier ones made by Honorius III during the closing year of his papacy about disturbances in the region that had revealed Frederick's "ingratitude" toward the Roman church for the past and present benefits bestowed upon him. A "clamor" and "murmurs" had reached Gregory's ears about injustices in the kingdom, about how the emperor had denied bishops access to their sees, assaulted the clergy, despoiled widows and orphans, and violated papal vassals and other nobles in the region who enjoyed the protection of the Apostolic See. People now mocked those securities, seeing the rich and powerful reduced to beggary and exile. As seen above, the pope also denounced Frederick for forcing clergy to celebrate the divine office despite the interdict, making him a "despiser of the keys" and possible heretic. Under these circumstances, Gregory threatened in the spring of 1228 that Frederick should rightly fear the possibility that the pope would deprive him of his "feudal right" to the kingdom of Sicily, which he held as a vassal of the Roman church.[60]

The tense situation in the Regno continued to escalate after the emperor left for the holy places. In August, consulting with a provincial synod in Perugia, Gregory followed through on his threat to absolve Frederick's vassals in the Regno of their oaths of fealty to the Hohenstaufen ruler. As Gregory explained in letters addressed to "all the prelates of the church," Frederick, in addition to violating his crusade vow and "sneaking" off to Syria, was guilty of abusing the Roman church and its territorial patrimony, "usurping the spiritual and temporal rights" of the Apostolic See, and attempting to subvert the church's vassals through threats, lies, and bribes. The pope also accused him and his officials of allowing "Saracens"—in this case, meaning Muslim auxiliaries forcibly relocated to southern Italy and settled in Lucera after their rebellion in Sicily years earlier—to despoil churches and assault Christian clergy.[61] Aware of Frederick's efforts to counter papal messages, Gregory warned his audience not to believe any falsehoods they heard to the contrary, either sent in writing or told to them by the emperor's messengers. In addition, Gregory excommunicated and anathematized anyone who "shows him help and favor against the Roman church, either attacking its patrimony or illicitly usurping the spiritual and temporal rights of the Apostolic See." As always in such communications, instructions followed for the clerical recipients of these letters to publicize the contents in their cities and dioceses and enforce such papal judgments.[62]

Over the course of the fall, Gregory identified Raynald of Urslingen, Frederick's vicar in the Regno, as a particular culprit in the effort to subvert the papal patrimony in Ancona, where the church's enemies conspired "secretly" (*occulte*) and agitated "publicly" (*publice*) to corrupt papal vassals.[63] In a letter sent to Raynald on 7 November, Gregory denounced his destruction, burning, and occupation of various places that belonged by right to the Roman church. Even worse, according to what "people were saying," Raynald and his troops mutilated priests with unheard of sacrilege, allowing Saracens to crucify some clergy, blinding others. Now he had invaded Ancona, showing himself an "open enemy of the Apostolic See." Gregory gave him eight days from receiving this letter to withdraw; otherwise, the pope had given firm commands for his papal chaplain Cinthius to excommunicate him and all of his followers publicly, passing a sentence of ecclesiastical interdict over his lands.[64] In a letter written to the Genoese podesta and commune that same month, Gregory repeated his accusations about Raynald and the atrocities committed by his Saracen soldiers. When Raynald did not withdraw, Gregory excommunicated him, his brother Berthold, and his other supporters. Anyone supporting them would be excommunicated and deprived of their ecclesiastical fiefs or benefices. Only a year's service in the Holy Land would be considered a sufficient form penance for absolution.[65] Perhaps in response, Raynald ordered the expulsion of the Franciscans from the Regno, accusing them of bearing "apostolic letters" to the region's bishops. Just how much Gregory relied on the peripatetic friars to convey messages in the region is unclear, although no one could mistake his ongoing devotion to their order. A year earlier, at Assisi in July 1228, the pope had formally canonized Saint Francis.[66]

By this time, Gregory had begun to look beyond such epistolary denunciations, legal threats, and "spiritual" weapons, extending papal sanctions into the realm of armed conflict with Frederick's supporters on the Italian peninsula. Over the course of the winter, he started to coordinate the assembly of what chroniclers called a "papal army," or the "army of the lord pope." As the pope's biographer describes his decision, "since the punishment of the spiritual sword did not chasten the sinner, overcome by necessity, the successor of Peter took the step of wielding the temporal sword."[67] Acting in his capacity as the lord of the Papal States, Gregory fielded this force with the help of John of Brienne, Frederick's former father-in-law and a papal rector since 1227, along with John de Colonna, cardinal priest of Santa Prassede; Pelagius of Albano; and the papal chaplain Pandulf, who was "experienced" in military affairs. By the spring of 1229, this army, deployed as three smaller units, had pushed the emperor's vassals and allies from Ancona, Spoleto, and Campagna and began advancing into the Regno.[68]

When they talk about it at all, historians typically call this conflict the War of the Keys, named after the symbol featured on the papal army's banner. Discussions about this campaign typically revolve around the question of where it fits in the trajectory of so-called political crusades, in other words crusading campaigns called for the primary purpose of defending papal territories or subduing papal enemies within Europe.[69] The general consensus seems to be that the War of the Keys was a kind of "half" or "quasi" crusade authorized by the pope, promoted much like a genuine crusade but lacking important elements of "true" crusading, including the promised remission of sins for combatants—at least not until the closing stages of the conflict—and the actual use of the cross as a martial sign.

Clearly, the difference between symbols such as the cross and the keys made an impression on contemporaries like Richard of San Germano, who describes in his chronicle a pitched battle between a "crusader army" (*crucesignatorum exercitus*), a designation for supporters of the emperor who had recently returned from Syria while still bearing their crosses, and the pope's "keysader host" (*clavigeros hostes*).[70] For contemporaries, however, the controversy caused by the War of the Keys did not revolve around the question of whether the battle against the emperor constituted a crusade or not. It centered on a different issue—whether the pope possessed the legitimate right to wield the "material sword" (*gladius materialis*), as well as the "spiritual sword" (*gladius spiritualis*). Recent generations of theologians and canon lawyers had debated the exegesis of the "two swords" (Lk 22:38): Did God bestow each sword directly to its bearer, the emperor and the pope, the principal representatives of the two powers? Or did God grant both swords to the pope, who then delegated the material sword to the emperor to wield in defense of the church? Canon lawyers, in their glosses, offered a wide variety of opinions on the matter. Regardless, in either scenario the pope did not wield the material sword directly—the power of armed force, coercion, and punishment—but delegated its use to secular rulers, lay people who were not constrained by the clerical prohibition of bloodshed.[71]

When Gregory called for the raising of a papal army, the political theology of the two swords moved from canon law commentaries into the public eye as the pope sought to secure material support for his campaign. Deploying the material sword in defense of the church did not come cheaply. Facing an insufficient supply of local troops from the papal patrimony, Gregory appealed for aid from communities, clergy, and rulers around Europe, including the king of Sweden, the rectors of the Lombard League, and the Portuguese prince, Peter. In his *Flowers of History*, Roger of Wendover describes how Gregory's legate Master Stephen arrived in England to collect one-tenth of the kingdom's "moveable property," clerical and lay, "for his war undertaken against the Roman emperor." Gregory's "apostolic letters sent through various part of the world" enumerated the many reasons why he took this action, including all of Frederick's misdeeds while on crusade, his plunder of the military orders' properties in the Regno and overseas, his disregard for the church's interdict, and more. "For these causes," Roger writes, "the lord pope went to war against him, asserting it was just and necessary for the Christian faith for such a mighty persecutor of the church to be cast down from the imperial dignity." During an assembly called by King Henry III at Westminster, Stephen, bearing Gregory's "written authorization," read the pope's letters aloud, spelling out the papal demand for a special tax to sustain his war against the emperor.[72] Some of these written appeals survive in a register of letters, charters, and other documents from Salisbury, revealing how the pope pitched his war against Frederick as the response to a "common danger," insisting that a threat to the "head" of the church represented one to the "entire body." For these reasons, Gregory wrote, "we have begun to exercise the temporal power, gathering many armies with ample stipends for this purpose, for such possessions ought not to be spared, when the church is universally and bitterly assailed."[73]

These letters provide a striking example of the pope's unique public standing as the figure who could call for armed Christian action on behalf of the entire church as a "common" enterprise and a shared responsibility, summoning leaders to defend "the papacy and Saint Peter's regalia" and to fight "for the Lord under his commander Saint Peter" against the excommunicate emperor, who was a predator of churches, abuser of clergy, and friend to the infidels.[74] Gregory's unusual and to some extent unprecedented measures on behalf of the Apostolic See also remind us about the hard limits to the pope's actual reach. Assembling such armies always represented an ad hoc logistical affair that was constrained by financial limits, insufficient numbers, and uneven enthusiasm from the vassals, friends, and family members who comprised a typical medieval army. Gregory's papal army was no exception.[75] Judging by the pope's calls for the Lombards to fulfill their obligations to the church, the rectors of the league did not provide as much assistance as the pope would have liked. They did send troops, but not enough. Gregory also complained about their late arrival, about their lack of funds, arms, and horses, and about the fact that some of the levies were already planning to head home. He even forwarded them dispatches from the front lines, written by John of Brienne and John de Colonna and affixed with the papal bull, testifying to the desperate need for help.[76]

According to Roger of Wendover, the Apostolic See's demands for a direct tax to pay for the papal army—the first of its kind—met with reluctance and public protest. Realizing that Henry III would not prevent the pope's exactions, the English earls and barons emphatically refused to pay the tithe. After debating among themselves, the clergy decided to pay the demanded one-tenth, in part anxious about the legate Stephen's express power to excommunicate those who refused to render the funds or colluded to commit fraud in their collection. The pope's representative also had the right to demand that clerics swear an oath on the Gospels to make their payments, that they record the amounts on their "rolls" with seals affixed in testimony, and that they agree to censure anyone caught impeding the payments. Roger writes that the clerics in question had to pawn all sorts of sacred vessels and liturgical objects to meet the demands of such an unprecedented exaction. In this regard, the English clergy seemed less concerned with the pope's right to fight a Christian emperor in defense of the church than they were with how he planned to pay for it.[77]

Others challenged and denounced Gregory's decision to authorize armed force against the emperor. In a letter sent to Frederick during his stay in Syria, his bailiff Thomas of Acerra expressed astonishment that the pope, the emperor's "public enemy," had "decreed contrary to Christian law to vanquish you with the material sword, since, he says, he is unable to cast you down by the spiritual sword." Thomas asserts that Frederick's allies, especially among the clergy, could not believe that the "Roman pontiff could do such things, taking up arms against Christians, especially since the Lord said to Peter 'put your sword in its scabbard, for all those who strike with the sword, shall perish by it.' " They wondered by what right the pope acted, excommunicating thieves, arsonists, and murders on the one hand and then turning his authority to such ends on the other.[78] Chroniclers expressing sympathy for the emperor accused the pope's army, in turn, of committing atrocities, unlawfully invading the Regno, causing fearful locals to desert their homes, attacking crusaders or forcing those bound for the holy places via Italy to turn back, despoiling churches, and generally creating chaos in the region.[79]

Troubadours, some with close ties to the imperial court and others already critical of the Rome's aggressive attacks on supposed heretics in Provence, penned and presumably recited their own critiques of the papal war in the Regno. In a Provençal poem lamenting the general corruption of the church, Pierre Cardenal denounced the clergy for trying to expel Frederick from his "refuge" and emboldening the infidels, as "pastors" became "killers." Cardenal lamented a world turned upside down, because "kings and emperors used to rule the world, now the clergy possess such dominion." Guilhem Figueira lambasted the Roman church for shedding Christian blood, wrestling with Frederick over his crown, calling him a heretic, and offering false "pardons" for the sins of those who did the fighting. Yet others found the pope's actions justified. Responding to Figueira's poem, Gormonda di Montpellier celebrated Rome's battles against heretics, "worse than Saracens," defending the church's struggle against figures like the heretical Count of Toulouse and the emperor.[80] The Guelf *Annals of Piacenza* likewise valorized Gregory's decision to deploy the material sword. Seeing that Frederick intended the destruction of the Roman church and desolation of Italy, the pope first sent his envoys through the empire, announcing the emperor's excommunication, labeling him a heretic, and absolving his followers of their fidelity to him. When he saw that the "spiritual sword" lacked effectiveness, after taking counsel with others Gregory called upon the faithful of the Roman church to defend by force its rights and possessions.[81] Gregory's biographer, not surprisingly, struck a similar tone in his presentation of the pope's decision to gather an army, celebrating its victories at places like Monte Cassino, where "by God's judgment" papal forces expelled the imperial justiciar and a group of "Arabs" occupying the monastery.[82]

The pope himself recognized that his recourse to armed force in the Regno might raise particular problems for the church's reputation. As he wrote to his legate and military commander Pelagius on 19 May 1229, sometimes the church, rarely and unwillingly, had to "turn to the aid of the material sword" against tyrants and persecutors. It must do so, Gregory qualified, in the proper way, not thirsting for blood or to seize another's riches but to recall those in error to the path of the truth. The pope expressed dismay that some in the "army of Christ"—as he called the papal army in this instance—slaughtered the "lost sheep" that they were intended to find and restore to the flock, mutilating and killing prisoners who had freely surrendered. He denounced this behavior, including chopping off limbs and beheadings, and instructed Pelagius to protect those who fell into the "hands of the army of Christ." Such captives should enjoy more "liberty" as prisoners of the church than they previously enjoyed while ostensibly free, when they were really in bondage to the "pharaoh," Frederick. Thus, calling for mercy in the face of violence, the pope intended to protect his public reputation and that of the church from its detractors and the "deceitful stain of false opinion."[83]

Making Peace Public

By the summer of 1229, papal forces had made considerable advances, pushing back Frederick's vassals and allies on all fronts. Rumors of the emperor's demise circulated, demoralizing his allies. In June, however, Frederick returned from Syria, landing at Brindisi and quickly gathering his supporters to repulse the pope's forces. By the following summer, Gregory and the emperor had come to terms of peace, the Treaty of San Germano. Modern historians have puzzled over the apparently quick reversals that led to this agreement, wondering why Frederick—holding the upper hand in military terms—agreed to a negotiated peace rather than invade the Papal States. He generally receives high marks for restraining himself, or at least recognizing that he could not effectively rule while laboring under the "embarrassing" sentence of excommunication. For those who view the pope as utterly determined to destroy Frederick, the compromise reached at San Germano seems like a defeat for the "irascible" Gregory's hierocratic designs, a "deep humiliation" for the Roman pontiff who had wanted to "ruin the hated emperor." Exhausted from their struggle, then, both sides agreed to settle their differences, biding their time until they might resume their conflict.[84]

Such evaluations of the peace achieved in 1230 miss their mark. Peacemaking in the Middle Ages, as Jenny Benham observes, was about "public perception."[85] Gregory and Frederick, and their respective proxies and representatives, had fought their political battles in public for three years. Their peace took shape in a similar way: transcending individual attitudes and uncompromising ideologies, it was negotiated with a marked sensitivity to the difference between private and open discussions. When all of the relevant communications, letters, revised texts, and verbal exchanges are taken into consideration, Gregory, rather than humiliating Frederick or imposing unreasonable terms on him, emerges as a counter to centrifugal forces, trying to find a balance between sets of private interests involving members of the curia, papal vassals, the military orders, the citizens of Rome, and the Lombards, among others.

As Frederick no doubt intended, his military successes after his return from Syria clearly played a role in forcing Gregory to the bargaining table. Some returning German crusaders joined him, still bearing their crosses, although others apparently refused to fight on his behalf, given his excommunicate status. Richard of San Germano describes how the papal army began to dissolve almost immediately after Frederick landed, reporting that John de Colonna fled the battlefield, pretending he needed to return to the curia to secure pay for his troops. In August 1229, keeping up his own forms of public pressure on Frederick, Gregory again renewed his sentence of excommunication, circulating a written version of the sentence that revisited the now long list of sins and crimes committed by him and his agents, including Raynald of Spoleto. Suggesting the gravity of Frederick's crimes, the pope opened the sentence by excommunicating a stock list of supposed heretics, ironically the same list featured at the emperor's coronation. Frederick continued to send out "excusatory letters" to the "princes of the world" about his successes in the Holy Land, denouncing the patriarch of Jerusalem's defamatory letters and calling upon figures like the crusading bishop of Winchester and the master general of the Teutonic Order as his witnesses.[86]

While these dueling letters circulated and the fighting in the Regno continued, however, negotiations for an end to the discord between church and empire had already begun. Over the winter and spring, representatives including Frederick's envoys Hermann of Salza, Lando, archbishop of Reggio in Calabria, and Marinus, archbishop of Bari, joined by the pope's legates Thomas of Capua and John de Colonna, traveled back and forth between the papal curia and imperial court. In July 1230, a gathering of prelates, princes, and imperial officials met at San Germano and nearby Ceprano to negotiate the final terms of peace between the pope and emperor, leading to Frederick's absolution by the end of August. After three years of scandal and war, peace had returned to the Christian community.[87]

Scholars rarely seem to consider the full range of evidence available for the negotiations leading up to the Peace of San Germano, including a series of letters and documents exchanged between the pope, the curia, and Thomas of Capua during the months leading up to Frederick's absolution.[88] Written in a plainer style than papal encyclicals, the cardinal's letters reveal behind-the-scenes details, such as when Thomas commented on the heavy rains and flooding that impeded his travels in the Regno, or when he described how he found the cardinal bishop of Albano "more dead than alive" after spending months besieged by the emperor's forces in the monastery of Monte Cassino.[89] His on-the-road communications also suggest the limits of his willingness to commit things to writing during such challenging negotiations, since his letters contain frequent references to information that would be shared "verbally" (*viva voce*) by the bearer or writer of the letter at a later date. The written word possessed a permanence that could become a disadvantage, potentially exposing things that were meant only for certain ears—conversations that are now lost to the historian.[90]

What remains nevertheless reveals a great deal, exposing the conflicting interests, points of contention, and collective mediation that lay behind the Peace of

San Germano. The "form of peace" provided by the Roman church became an immediate source of debate. Initial versions called for the emperor to make amends for his occupation of ecclesiastical properties within one month. Later versions allowed for a window of three months if he was in the Regno, four months elsewhere in Italy, and five months beyond the peninsula. A dispute emerged about the possession of two towns, Gaeta and Sant'Agata, which the church would retain for one year while a solution could be found for their rightful disposition.[91] In February, the talks almost collapsed when a contingent of Lombards arrived at the papal curia with objections to the ongoing negotiations. A month later, Thomas informed Gregory that he might achieve his goals if he could offer absolution to Frederick immediately, but he knew that the representatives from Lombardy opposed such a move. The emperor desired peace, the cardinal legate insisted, but he also remained suspicious, in part due to disturbing "rumors" he had heard from the city of Rome about the church playing him false.[92]

Although negotiating the form of peace involved off-the-record conversations, guaranteeing its terms represented a public and collective commitment. Frederick was expected to swear various oaths, binding himself to obey the "mandates of the church," to make amends for his occupation of church lands, and to observe the truce that ended the fighting in central Italy, or he would suffer an automatic reinstatement of his excommunication. But he also had to secure the accompanying oaths of "worthy and sworn" princes, barons, counts, and others named by the church willing to pledge on his behalf (*fidejussores*), bound for eight months from the day of his absolution to assist the church against him if he failed to fulfill the agreed-upon conditions.[93] In the later stages of negotiations, papal and imperial envoys argued over the protections that would be extended to the church's faithful "adherents," guarantees that Frederick would "remit all rancor" and revenge toward them. The princes swearing on Frederick's behalf hesitated to give such assurances.[94] People who had suffered the "hardships of war," Thomas wrote, held high hopes for peace, but others were "throwing stones" without saying why, preferring to "fish in stormy waters" rather than seek concord. In response to his envoy's disillusionment, Gregory sent words of encouragement, calling upon him to persist in his labors for peace. One of the final documents sent from the curia to Thomas in early July contained instructions for the drawing down of forces in the region, the lifting of sieges, and the end of hostilities.[95]

By July 1230, only after months of performing such a balancing act, the stage was set for the ceremonial formalizing of this peace at San Germano at the foot of Monte Cassino. The siege of that monastery had ended; Frederick met in the town below with Gregory's envoy, Guala, the Dominican friar. Rather than the noises of war, the sound of ringing bells filled the town after Guala announced the emperor's agreement to the church's form of peace. On 23 July, before a "multitude" of German and Italian princes and prelates, cardinal legates, imperial officials, and local counts, Berthold of Aquileia, the archbishop of Salzburg, and the bishop of Regensburg recited the reasons for Frederick's excommunication, reading them aloud "in public." Thomas of Acerra, swearing on Frederick's behalf with his hand on the Gospels, rendered an oath to obey the "mandates of the church" before a number of witnesses, promising to observe the form of peace. The emperor agreed to restore lands seized from the Roman church and also from the Templars and Hospitallers; to allow displaced prelates in the Regno access to their sees; to exempt clergy from the jurisdiction of civil courts; to forego any tallages and taxes on clerical properties; and to keep the peace, taking no revenge on faithful papal vassals who had fought against him during the recent war.[96]

The princes committed to guaranteeing the peace on Frederick's behalf made their pledges, while the bishops present produced "testimonial letters" memorializing the oaths rendered aloud in Frederick's name and by others. Seal after seal was affixed to the written copies of these agreements, including those authenticated by Frederick's golden bull—documents that would be preserved in the papal archives and forwarded to interested parties. On 25 July, Guala returned from the Roman curia, lifting the interdict pronounced by Pelagius on San Germano, thereby allowing for the celebration of the divine offices there and elsewhere in the Regno. On 28 August, at nearby Ceprano, John de Colonna and Thomas of Capua performed the ritual of absolution for Frederick, "publicly and solemnly," before a crowd of cardinals, clergy, princes, and a "multitude of various people," to the "general joy of all Christendom." An encyclical sent from the imperial chancery in September describes this scene, telling its recipients that they deserved to know about the restoration of peace after receiving so many disturbing letters from the pope and emperor. Over the following months, Gregory circulated his own letters celebrating his agreement with Frederick, assuring the Lombards of his gratitude for their efforts on the church's behalf and asking the French King Louis IX to beseech God for their continued concord. Through such shared acts of ritual performance and remembrance, written assurances, and prayers, the scandalous discord between church and empire had come to an end.[97]

A few days after Frederick's absolution, on the first of September, Pope Gregory hosted the emperor at Anagni, welcoming him to one of his family's residences. They shared the kiss of peace and met together in the pope's private chambers and the next day shared a meal joined by Hermann of Salza. Later, Gregory's biographer reports, they spoke at length, "in secret discussions" and also "in public." According to Frederick's descriptions of this meeting in his letters, the pope received him kindly, explaining the reasons for his past judgment of the emperor and expressing his benevolence toward him, thereby wiping away any enmity Frederick might have harbored toward Gregory. "We hold him in all reverence," the emperor declared, "our only and universal father, showing ourselves to him as a devout son of the church in the bond of love that joins the priesthood and empire to one another." Two days later, with the pope's blessing, Frederick returned to Apulia, while Gregory and his entourage returned to Rome.[98] Even if the pope and emperor harbored personal resentments toward each other, this scene of public harmony struck the right chord after years of sensational conflict. What exact shape that reformed peace would take, however, still remained to be seen.

Chapter 2

Reforming the Peace

A year after Gregory IX and Frederick II agreed to settle their violent differences at San Germano, the emperor issued a sweeping new legislative code for the kingdom of Sicily, the Constitutions of Melfi. These laws presented the "crown" as the sole source of justice and peace, centralizing royal government over the centrifugal forces of the local nobility, clergy, and urban communities. The code also reinforced and clarified Frederick's rights over ecclesiastical offices and properties in the Regno. According to some modern commentators, the Constitutions of Melfi represented, among others things, a challenge to the universal jurisdiction of the Roman pope over the church at the expense of the king, a tacit rebuke to the "papal monarchy," a "gauntlet thrown down in the great struggle between the empire and papacy."[1] Certainly, when news reached Gregory about the planned legislation, he delivered a blunt rebuke to the emperor and to Jacob, archbishop of Capua, who had been tasked with helping to draft the law code. The pope warned Frederick that if he went through with his decision to issue the "new constitutions," acting by his own will or following the advice of "perverse men," he would rightly be called a "persecutor of the church and destroyer of public liberty."[2]

Other scholars, however, have cautioned against interpreting this episode as indicative of a deeply rooted conflict between the two powers, pointing out that Gregory made no objections to the final version of the Constitutions of Melfi, apparently a sign that his protest worked, and that Frederick modified the new laws accordingly.[3] Even as the pope called for the emperor to reconsider his forthcoming constitutions, he tried to avoid further escalation, stressing to the emperor in a subsequent communication that he had made his earlier complaints "in private not public, in secret letters, not cried aloud."[4] In yet another letter to Frederick that same month, which addressed persistent disruptions to the peace in the Regno, Gregory warned him about wicked men operating in the shadows who wished to destroy the state of concord between the two powers, the "two great lights" of the priesthood and empire.[5] As will become evident below, this was hardly the last time that the pope would show an explicit sensitivity to the vulnerable nature of his relationship with the emperor during the fragile period following their reconciliation.

After his meeting with Frederick in September 1230 and more or less for the first time since the beginning of his papacy, Gregory did not stand at odds with the imperial ruler of the Christian world. Once again, Frederick had become a beloved son who had chosen the way of peace, resuming his proper duties to serve and defend the Roman church. Over the following years Gregory would repeatedly emphasize the theme of harmonious unity between the two powers or the two swords, the spiritual and the material, making common cause for the defense of the faith, the protection of the papal patrimony, and the proper ordering of the church. As the Vicar of Christ, who was responsible for preserving and fostering the peace, he identified a number of challenges and projects that called for the emperor's assistance one way or another: settling the persistent strife on the Italian peninsula, above all in Lombardy; dealing with the imperiled conditions of the Holy Land; and combating the threat of heresy within the body of the faithful. When the Romans tried to cast off papal lordship and attacked neighboring communities that belonged to the Papal States, the pope even called for imperial assistance against the rebellious citizens of his own city.[6]

Rather than an elaborate ruse that masked the inevitable return of antagonism between Gregory and Frederick, these years of relative peace and cooperation in their relationship revealed the potentialities of public cooperation between the two powers in ways rarely seen before.[7] Frederick openly embraced his role as a "spiritual son" of the Roman church, its defender against infidels, heretics, and other enemies. Such obligations did not imply political subordination to the Vicar of Christ; they represented the fulfillment of his exalted position. In its preamble, the Constitutions of Melfi make this claim clear. As part of the "stewardship" granted to them by the Lord, rulers should not allow the "Holy Church, the mother of the Christian religion" to be "defiled by the secret perfidies of slanders of the faith." Rather, "they should protect her from attacks of public enemies" by the power of the "material sword" and "preserve peace," the sister of justice. The law code reaffirmed the prince's commitment to fight against heretics and his drawing the "sword of righteous vengeance against them," preventing their hostile attacks against the Roman church, "the head of all other churches, to the more evident injury of the Christian faith." Judged guilty of "public crimes," heretics would face the loss of their property and capital punishment, while their accomplices would suffer dispossession and exile.[8]

To be clear, peace did not always or necessarily mean the absence of contention and violence. Peace meant coercion and war deployed in the right directions, for the right purposes, by the right authorities for the common good. In Lombardy, the Holy Land, and even the city of Rome, the pope and emperor confronted signs of the devil's work, disturbers of the peace, warmongers, and sowers of scandal. As the head of the Roman church, Gregory possessed a compelling mandate for proclaiming peace, but he did not enjoy a monopoly over its creation. Papal and imperial networks of peacemaking ran on overlapping but sometimes divergent tracks. In different localities, the two Christian authorities confronted individuals and communities who refused their visions of peace or sought peace on different terms. Facing fluid political landscapes, Gregory and Frederick competed as much as cooperated, pursuing complementary but not identical ends, more often than not publicly rebuking each other for failing to live up to their divinely ordained duties. Rather than relieving the tensions embedded in the relationship between the two powers, reforming the peace transposed them into a different register.

Scars of War

Although the Treaty of San Germano had formally ended the fighting between the church and the prince, the process of turning that agreement into a meaningful political settlement on the Italian peninsula had just begun. By reconciling with Frederick, the pope shared public responsibility for the ruler's subsequent actions. As early as October, Gregory warned him about certain men around Foggia conspiring to destroy the new peace, "murmuring" and "clamoring" that the convergence of two great lights—that of the pope and emperor—was casting them into the shadows. Such accusations caused him "grief in private, shame out in the open." To prevent further blasphemy about "both our names," Gregory called upon the emperor to act with mercy and forbearance, rather than giving such critics further reason to reproach the pope for the faith that he placed in Frederick. Judging by a letter sent to Frederick on 3 December, Gregory remained watchful for any signs of noncompliance on the emperor's part. An envoy from the imperial court, a judge from Pavia identified only as G., had recently come to the papal curia with imperial "letters of security," the promises sworn by various magnates and prelates to ensure that Frederick observed the terms established at San Germano. When the pope inspected the letters, however, he discovered several things omitted, either out of negligence or oversight. As a consequence, he decided not to "publicize" them, since this might give their detractors cause to "murmur" against them both. Gregory informed Frederick that he was sending Jacob, archbishop of Capua, to the imperial court to collate a complete dossier of the necessary documents. He also asked the emperor to recall the judge in question, who had continued on the road to Germany with the imperfect versions of the fiduciary letters, despite the pope's instructions to suspend his journey.[9]

The War of the Keys had left the militarized Papal States and Regno in a disturbed condition. Not everyone was willing to lay down their arms and make the concessions demanded of them. The duchy of Spoleto remained a particular sore spot. The pope had appointed the bishop of Beauvais as its new duke, rewarding him for his service during the recent hostilities. When some of the locals rejected his lordship, he had to enter the duchy with an armed force.[10] Frederick faced his own troubles trying to pacify the war-torn region. Richard of San Germano records that the emperor revoked his followers' right to construct new fortifications, as permitted during the recent discord between church and empire. Gaeta remained another problem, since the fortified city refused to submit to the emperor's authority as stipulated in the Treaty of San Germano, despite Gregory's intervention on his behalf. This tense situation would last for years, until the commune finally acknowledged Frederick's lordship and swore fealty to his young son Conrad, born from his marriage to Isabella of Brienne. Frederick also demanded restitution for damages caused during the recent war at Città di Castellana, although the pope reminded him that the commune pertained by right to the Apostolic See, as made evident by "many public charters."[11]

More than anything else, however, the unresolved contention between the Lombard League and the emperor remained the true test of Gregory and Frederick's willingness, commitment, and ability to reform the peace. The underlying sources of tension between the two sides, such as the extent of the emperor's rights to appoint officials, dispense justice, collect tolls, and requisition supplies, remained unresolved. The fact that the "rebellious" Lombards had fought against him in the War of the Keys did not help matters. Gregory clearly viewed the stability of the region as critical to the new peace. In October 1230, when the pope informed the league's rectors about Frederick's reconciliation with the church, he had taken care to assure them about his ongoing support of their interests. He also forwarded to them some copies of the oaths sworn at San Germano by Thomas of Acerra on Frederick's behalf, which bound the emperor to forgive the Lombards and other supporters of the church and to revoke all judgments, edicts, and bans issued against them. The possibilities for renewed contention between Frederick and the league never seemed far away, compelling Gregory to warn the emperor about moving against the Lombards "by the power of strength rather than the rule of law."[12]

Positioning himself as the mediator for peace in the region, the pope did not unilaterally intervene on the Lombard League's behalf. In September 1231, Frederick announced his intention to hold an assembly at Ravenna the upcoming November intended "to reform the universal peace of the empire, put Italy into a prosperous and tranquil state, and settle the fervid disputes inside and outside of its cities, removing the foment of hatred and every disturbance among neighboring peoples." In the summons to the gathering, he stressed the fact that he proceeded by the counsel of the highest pontiff, a public sign of cooperation between church and empire for establishing peace in Lombardy.[13] According to one account of the Lombards' October meeting at Bologna, to assure a "good peace" the rectors of the league sent envoys to Pope Gregory, calling upon him to prevent Frederick from moving his forces into the region.[14] The pope, however, had already signaled his support for the imperial assembly. Writing to the bishops of Modena, Reggio, and Brescia and the bishop-elect of Mantua, the pope stressed his office's role in keeping the peace, assuring them that in formally sealed letters the emperor had committed himself to abide by papal arbitration in Lombardy. Gregory forwarded copies of those documents to them. He also called upon them not to impede Frederick's son Henry and the other German magnates coming to the assembly at Ravenna, adding instructions to assist the passage of Hermann of Salza, master general of the Teutonic Order, who was sent to Lombardy as the emperor's chief representative.[15]

The pope's concerns proved well founded. Much as they did in 1226, the cities of the Lombard League refused to send their envoys to the assembly and blocked the alpine passes leading from Germany into Italy, forcing Frederick to postpone the meeting until Christmas, and then again until March the following year. Responding to this worsening situation in January 1232, Gregory appointed James Pecorara, the newly minted cardinal bishop of Palestrina, and Otto Tonengo, cardinal deacon of San Nicola in Carcere Tulliano, as legates to mediate between the emperor and the recalcitrant Lombards.[16] The two cardinals, who had long and controversial careers ahead of them as papal-imperial mediators, headed to Bologna with letters of credence for a meeting with the envoys of the Lombard League. In early March, James and Otto presented them a list of "imperial petitions," including stipulations that the Lombards "swear an oath of fidelity to the lord emperor, as is customary," that they "renounce oaths made that infringe upon the honor and right of the lord emperor and empire," and that they bring their legal disputes "before the lord emperor or his vicars or legates in Lombardy." The representatives from Brescia, Milan, Lodi, Piacenza, and elsewhere provided the cardinals with a record of their objections to such demands, along with a list of their requirements for keeping the peace, insisting that Frederick "remit all rancor" against the league and placing a cap on the number of troops that could accompany his son Henry into the region.[17]

According to a description of these proceedings sent back to Brescia by the city's envoys, the cardinals insisted upon a "general" and "public" commission to negotiate with Frederick on the Lombards' behalf. The Lombard representatives agreed to their proposal, provided that Frederick likewise commit to their arbitration. In their letter to the podesta about the meeting, the Brescians present indicated that they placed great trust in the legates, since one, James, came from Piacenza and the other, Otto, from Vercelli.[18] In their own written proposition for this commission, the two legates said nothing of such personal affinities, highlighting the pope's concern that the turmoil in Lombardy "could inflict grave damage upon all of Christendom, especially by impeding aid to the Holy Land." If

James and Otto could not broker an agreement, they reserved the right to place the entire matter before the pope and the other cardinals, who would determine what needed to be done to "settle the discord" and "affirm the peace."[19] While the representatives of the league waited at Faenza under strict instructions to remain there, the two cardinals traveled to Ravenna to meet with the emperor. When they arrived, however, they discovered that Frederick had left the city by ship for Venice. Some chroniclers portrayed this decision as born from a pious desire to visit the basilica of Saint Mark, while others identified the emperor's dodge as a deliberate slight to the honor of the Roman church.[20]

Over the following months negotiations continued. On 13 May 1232, James and Otto oversaw a gathering in the bishop's palace at Padua, meeting first in the main hall of the cathedral chapter's canonry. They were joined by a number of prominent Lombard bishops, envoys from the cities of the Lombard League bearing "public instruments" of their commission to negotiate, and Hermann of Salza, who had been given full power by the emperor to make promises, agreements, and compromises on his behalf.[21] The following day, in the more formal setting of the bishop's hall, both sides committed themselves to the terms of arbitration provided by the two cardinals the preceding March, making solemn promises to observe their judgments and meet any deadlines imposed by them until the end of the negotiations.[22] Bringing the emperor back to the bargaining table proved difficult. Staying at Anagni, Pope Gregory made plans for a meeting between the concerned parties at the curia on Michaelmas, 29 September 1232. In July, after the emperor's envoy failed to turn up for preliminary negotiations at Lodi, the pope extended the deadline until the first of November to allow sufficient time for the cardinals to assemble for the deliberations. Although the Lombards and the emperor did send some representatives to the curia, sufficient numbers did not arrive for the formal November meeting to come off as planned.[23]

Peace in Lombardy and the March of Verona remained elusive. Heading into the spring of 1233, Gregory set a new date for the next meeting at Easter, assigning three cardinals—Otto, again, who was joined by John de Colonna and Stephen Conti, cardinal priest of Santa Maria in Trastevere—to oversee the next round of negotiations. Representatives from both sides met at the Lateran basilica on 24 May, submitting their written propositions for peace for review. Soon after, the pope and cardinals announced their decision. They undeniably gave the Lombards much of what they asked for: the pope called upon Frederick to "remit all rancor" against them, revoking all the judgments and bans issued against the members of the league, forgiving any of their past offenses, and receiving them in his grace. The Lombards likewise had to revoke any bans or edicts against the emperor or his loyal supporters and had to provide five hundred soldiers for assistance in the Holy Land over the course of two years. Both parties had to keep the peace and avoid further conflict. In closing, the pope instructed Frederick to send "patent letters" affixed with his golden seal confirming his commitment to these terms by Michaelmas the following September.[24]

Like most compromises, this agreement did not entirely satisfy anyone. On 7 June 1233, the Lombard representatives again met with the pope, taking issue with some of the specific wording in terms of peace and requesting clarifications. In a record of the meeting kept by a notary from Milan, the pope gave his responses, observing, for example, that the Lombard League could defend themselves against attacks without violating the terms of peace treaty.[25] When news of the decision reached Frederick, he delayed returning the patent letters that the pope had requested, telling Gregory in July that he would not send them until Hermann of Salza returned to the imperial court with a more detailed report of the proceedings at the papal curia.[26] He also wrote "in confidence" to the cardinal-bishop-elect of Ostia e Velletri, Raynald da Jenne, complaining about the pope's judgment that had let the Lombards off the hook, given the many injuries he had suffered from them. Frederick lodged a particular complaint about the Lombards' promise to provide five hundred soldiers for service in the holy places, when they still owed four hundred soldiers from their previous agreement with the emperor.[27] Intentionally or not, this "private" letter did not remain confined to Raynald's hands but was brought to the attention of the pope. On 12 August, Gregory sent a strongly worded response to the emperor, stressing all of his previous goodwill and efforts on Frederick's behalf and taking him to task for complaining to Raynald and the cardinals rather than writing to him directly. As for the four hundred soldiers previously promised by the league, that commitment had expired when Frederick embarked on his contentious crusade years earlier. In case he had forgotten the terms of that voided agreement, the pope sent him copies of the original documents taken from the papal archives.[28]

At this point, the logistical limitations of thirteenth-century epistolary communications made themselves felt. Soon after the pope sent this rebuke, Frederick's written ratification of the peace agreement arrived at the papal curia, before the pope's most recent complaints would have reached him. The reasons for the emperor's change of position are not entirely clear. Whatever misgivings he had, he apparently decided that an imperfect settlement remained better than no settlement at all, allowing him to turn his attention elsewhere, including to the Regno, where he faced an insurrection from rebellious barons. The representatives of the Lombard League likewise ratified the terms of the agreement.[29] Through papal intervention, the mediation of cardinal legates, the circulation of documents, oaths and sworn promises, the threat of fines and ecclesiastical censure, and solemn face-to-face meetings, peace between the emperor and the Lombards—messy, imperfect, incomplete—had been established, or at least, their open discord was settled until another day. In later years, the pope, emperor, and representatives of the league would accuse each other of acting in bad faith, of pretending to seek reconciliation while secretly conspiring to undermine their foes. At the moment, however, as one English monastic chronicler observed about the news, "thus peace was made between them."[30]

The Great Devotion of 1233

During those same summer months of 1233, the war-torn communes and communities of northern Italy experienced an unexpected movement of what we might now call religious revival: processions and sermons, miracles and other charismatic displays in the name of peace, all organized by itinerant preachers before crowds in churchyards, piazzas, markets, and fields on the edge of towns. Looking back at this Great Halleluiah, or Great Devotion, as he finished his *Chronicle* decades later, the well-traveled Franciscan writer Salimbene of Adam—who will reappear throughout the rest of this book—described it as a "time of tranquility and peace, when martial weapons were entirely laid aside, of happiness and joy, of gladness and celebration, of praise and jubilation."[31] Modern scholars have described the Great Devotion of 1233 as a "peace movement" that emerged from the particular mix of religious piety, social unrest, and endemic violence that characterized the urban landscape of northern Italy in the early decades of the thirteenth century. Opinions are mixed on whether the Great Devotion favored Gregory's or Frederick's interests in northern Italy. In his landmark work on Frederick II, Ernst Kantorowicz observed that for the emperor, "the Great Allelujah had the most inconvenient political consequences. The only person who profited was Pope Gregory." Others more recently see the pope as incidental to the Great Devotion, arriving "late and out of breath," showing "opportunistic" support for the charismatic preachers that led the revival.[32]

Neither of these appraisals captures the public complexities of the Great Devotion for the two powers. Its preachers did not uniformly favor the interests of either the pope or the emperor. Rather, their peacemaking initiatives presented opportunities and posed challenges for all sides in Lombardy, adding a new layer to an already complicated landscape of conflict and peacemaking. The Great Devotion cut across the supposed divides between the pro-imperial Ghibellines and the pro-papal Guelfs, convenient labels that mask a far more fluid set of shifting alliances and interested parties whose alignment with the party of the empire or that of the church formed a strategic choice, and not an irrevocable one. The charismatic peace movement of 1233 filled the public spaces left by the failure of established institutions to reconcile the warring factions of the strife-ridden Italian cities, rewiring the political and spiritual landscape of Lombardy and neighboring regions in the name of peace.[33]

Many of the Great Halleluiah's impresarios hailed from the mendicant orders, yet another demonstration of the rapidly expanding, highly visible role played by the relatively new friars in the public life of thirteenth-century Europe. They included Franciscans like Leo de Valvassori, who would later become archbishop of Milan. Leo arrived in Piacenza in the spring of 1233, after a year of street fighting between the city's militia and the popular party led by their captain, William de Andito. The two sides gave a commission for Leo to resolve their conflicts: he gathered them in the piazza before the city's cathedral church, where members from the various factions gave the ceremonial kiss of peace. The friar also arranged for the election of a new podesta, Lantelmo Mainerio.[34] Another Franciscan, named Gerard of Modena, along with a "simple and unlearned man" named Benedict de Cornetta, who was not a Franciscan but a "very good friend" of the friars, brought their version of peace to Parma. According to Salimbene, who saw both men with his own eyes, Gerard acted as podesta of the city, wielding "total lordship" over the Parmese so he might "bring peace to those warring against each other." Wherever Benedict went, dressed in his black sackcloth and blowing his small copper horn, large crowds would gather, waving palms, bearing candles, and singing hymns. Salimbene listened to him preach on the wall of the bishop's palace in Parma, then under construction.[35]

The Dominican friar John of Vicenza emerged as perhaps the most noteworthy of the Great Devotion's revivalist preachers, bringing his sermons of peace and miracles first to Bologna before touring around the Marches of Treviso and Verona in the summer of 1233. Verona represented a typical hot spot for armed conflict that involved all sorts of different individuals and groups but centered on Count Richard of San Bonifacio, a prominent magnate in the region, and his rivals, the Montecchi. Unrest in and around the city also demonstrated the limits of peacemaking through conventional means. In June 1230, Richard's enemies had seized him and his followers, imprisoning them in Verona. In response, Richard's allies from Mantua, joined by Azzo VII d'Este, jumped into the conflict. The powerful Romano brothers, Ezzelino and Alberic, backed the Veronese.[36] During a July 1231 meeting at Mantua, representatives from the communities caught up in the violence tried to broker a new confederation and end these hostilities.[37] Richard was released in September. During a subsequent meeting of the concerned parties at Bologna in October, an end to the violence seemed at hand until Ezzelino felt that he had been double-crossed by the Lombards' generous treatment of the count. Alienated from the Lombard League and its allies, he and his brother turned for support from Frederick, swearing fealty to the emperor, who took them under his special protection. In April 1232, Ezzelino and his supporters staged a coup of sorts in Verona, taking control of the city and moving it into the imperial orbit. Further armed conflict between the Veronese and Mantuans followed.[38]

Greeted by enthusiastic crowds at Verona and Vicenza, the Dominican friar John effectively became the "duke" and "rector" of those cities the following year.

Much like Leo de Valvassori and Gerard of Modena, he organized gatherings between warring factions in piazzas, fields, and other public spaces to exchange the kiss of peace and swear their commitment to his statues for resolving the endemic conflict in each commune. On 28 August at Paquara, a few miles south of Verona, he staged a particularly large and dramatic peace assembly, which was attended by representatives from Brescia, Mantua, Verona, Vicenza, and Treviso, the Romano brothers, the Montecchi, Azzo d'Este, Richard of San Bonifacio, Guala, the Dominican bishop of Brescia, and William, bishop of Modena, among others. Those gathered in the crowd listened to John's sermon that he delivered from a massive wooden stage, after which the antagonists rendered the kiss of peace and agreed to end their dissension.[39]

Viewed from the papal curia, these sorts of peacemaking scenes did not seamlessly align with the Roman church's priorities and interests in Lombardy. When news reached Pope Gregory about John of Vicenza's appeal and successes in Bologna, he instructed the Dominican friar to head next to Tuscany to negotiate peace between the warring cities of Siena and Florence. John apparently ignored these instructions. Years later, Thomas of Cantimpré described a telling episode about Gregory's first reaction to news of John. One of the Dominican preacher's detractors reported that the preacher was led into the city of Bologna on a white horse covered by a silk palanquin, acting as if he was the pope and publicly appropriating papal ceremonial. Consulting the cardinals, Gregory quickly planned to excommunicate the presumptuous friar until William of Modena swore before everyone on the gospels that he had witnessed an angel descend from heaven and affix a golden cross on John's forehead. Bursting into tears, the pope changed his mind and sent envoys to Bologna, who determined that the accusations against the miraculous preacher were untrue.[40]

At the same time, there are unmistakable signs that Pope Gregory recognized the public energies unleashed by the Great Devotion and worked, indirectly and directly, to channel them in favorable directions. Upon closer inspection, the religious revival that summer appears slightly less spontaneous and more strategic, linked to a wider set of papal designs for peace in northern Italy and not coincidently happening at the same time as Gregory's high-level mediation between the Lombards and the emperor. There is evidence of ties between John of Vicenza and ecclesiastical figures close to the pope who possessed previous hands-on experience as peacemakers in Lombardy, including Guala of Brescia and William of Modena. According to one account, when the citizens of Bologna tried to keep John in their city, William helped him slip away to begin his preaching tour around Vicenza and Verona.[41] More directly, Gregory issued a number of letters during the summer of 1233 enabling and bolstering John's public appeal, approving his safe passage throughout northern Italy, and granting indulgences for those who attended his sermons. In August 1233, no doubt anticipating the peace assembly at Paquara later that month, Gregory authorized John to reconcile Ezzelino da Romano, who had been excommunicated by the pope's own legates in Lombardy, if and when he rendered sufficient satisfaction for his sins. Chroniclers describing John's charismatic acts of reconciliation note that the warring parties swore to obey not only him but also the "mandates of the Roman church," thereby recognizing his authority to make peace given by the pope, the "lord Apostolic."[42]

The peace envisioned by the Great Devotion nevertheless proved to be particularly ephemeral. In Piacenza a few months after Leo de Valvassori's departure, many of the soldiers belonging to the militia abandoned the city with their families "privately" and "publicly," rejecting their reconciliation with the *popolo*. The confusion and disruption in Piacenza grew worse when a mob attacked the next itinerant preacher who arrived on the scene preaching against heresy, a Dominican from Cremona named Roland. The city's bishop imprisoned the perpetrators, but months of uncertainty and investigation followed while Pope Gregory tried to get to the bottom of things.[43] As for John of Vicenza, his meteoric rise was followed by an equally dramatic fall. Within days after the peace assembly at Paquara, a group of citizens from Padua who felt that the Dominican friar had shown too much lenience toward the Romano brothers took control of Vicenza with help from the inside. When John rushed back to deal with this surprising turn of events, his opponents in the city arrested and imprisoned him. Although he was released a few weeks later, John's charismatic effectiveness as a peacemaker was spent. During his captivity, he had to watch while the bishop of Vicenza and others sent a letter to the pope declaring the Dominican friar's statutes null and void. As the Vicenza notary and chronicler Gerard Maurisio observed about the months after the Great Devotion, "Now an even worse war sprang back up, in its accustomed manner."[44]

The peace movement that had so quickly seized the imagination of Italy's communes came to an abrupt end. Frederick II would eventually complain about wandering preachers like John of Vicenza, presenting them as subversive figures taking orders from the papacy. In 1233, there are no signs that the emperor identified the revivalists of the Great Devotion in this way, although someone at the imperial court composed a mocking poem that parodied the supposed miracles wrought by John and others.[45] By the spring of 1234, while endemic conflict continued to plague the communes of northern Italy and Frederick found new reasons to complain about his adversaries in the region, the Great Devotion was rapidly on its way to becoming a memory. The papacy's public efforts to broker peace, by contrast, remained vital and visible, while Gregory's legates at the imperial court secured Frederick's renewed commitment to placing the "Lombard business" in the pope's hands.[46] As charismatic preachers like John of Vicenza lost credibility, the papacy reminded everyone about its own role in supporting and celebrating the order's founder, adding Dominic to the catalog of saints on 3 July 1234.[47] In some sense, the failure of the Great Devotion to achieve a meaningful peace highlighted the enduring significance of papal intervention in Lombardy. Every time that the Lombards and the emperor agreed to Gregory's arbitration—before, during, and above all after the transitory Great Hallelujah—they publicly validated the Apostolic See's role as the true evangelizer of peace in the region.

Civil Strife in Holy Places

After the Treaty of San Germano, the reforming of the peace between the two powers remained linked to one goal more than any other: the freeing of Jerusalem. In his declarations about the search for peace in Lombardy, Gregory repeatedly invoked the need for concord among Christians as a means to liberating the holy places. In the early 1230s, the pope and Frederick faced another area being torn apart by civil strife between Christians, conflict that was eroding the support needed for the next crusade, namely, the crusader territories overseas. Certain factions in the region continued to rebel against Frederick's claims to the kingship of Jerusalem. During his earlier years of conflict with the emperor, Gregory, working through his legates and letters to the crusaders and Latin Christian inhabitants of the holy places, had tried to undermine Frederick's claims in crusader Syria and Palestine. After their broadly celebrated reconciliation, he reversed course, trying to stabilize the Hohenstaufen right to rule over the region. For both the pope and emperor, crusading represented one of the highest callings of their offices, a calling repeatedly invoked and widely publicized among contemporaries through rituals, oaths, letters, and sermons. They both possessed a stake in projecting harmonious cooperation between the two powers and peace in Christendom as a precondition to a successful crusade. In these terms, the crusades ideally formed the ultimate cooperative enterprise of the papacy and empire. It also created a means for either side to pressure the other openly, each accusing the other of neglecting one of their office's paramount duties. The "business of the cross" could publicly unite and yet still divide the two powers like almost nothing else.[48]

The pope's concern for Christians overseas did not abate after the end of hostilities between him and Frederick. In the early months of 1231, the Roman pontiff identified a new threat to the holy places: a coming assault by the "king of the Persians."[49] It remains unclear whom, exactly, the pope had in mind with this warning, but the danger struck him as quite real, having been relayed to him in letters sent to the curia from Syria by Gerold, patriarch of Jerusalem, and the leadership of the military orders.[50] In his blanket appeals for military and financial aid to the Holy Land, which were sent to Frederick, Henry III, Louis IX, and bishops throughout the church, Gregory drew upon well-developed themes from generations of crusade bulls, lamenting the Persian assault on the place where

Christ had shed his precious blood for humanity's salvation as a blow against all Christendom. Under these circumstances, he renewed his call for peace among Christians, including an end to ongoing hostilities between the French and English crowns. Writing to Frederick in August 1231, the pope stressed his obligation to defend Jerusalem against such "barbarous nations," insisting that the Hohenstaufen ruler send funds to rebuild Christian fortifications around the region. In a conciliatory gesture, Gregory addressed him in this letter for the first time as the "king of Jerusalem," a title that he and his predecessor, Honorius III, had withheld from their formal correspondence in light of the dispute between Frederick and the papal ally John of Brienne over the crown.[51]

By this time, however, Gregory faced another unprecedented situation in the history of crusading: a truce struck by the emperor of the Romans with the sultan of Egypt, one that had restored Jerusalem to Christian hands by peaceful means. Before reconciling with Frederick, the pope had done everything possible to spread disparaging news about this "traitorous" agreement. In a turnabout, he now recognized its temporary advantages in light of new threats. In February 1231, after receiving Frederick's complaints that the Templars had disregarded the commands of his bailiff and had begun marshaling troops in the region, thereby potentially violating the truce with al-Kamil, Gregory rebuked the master of Templar Order at Jerusalem. Although the pope commended the Templars' desire to fight the "enemies of God," he insisted that they show temporary restraint, since the disruptions of war might further expose Jerusalem to danger from the menacing Persian king and cause "confusion among the entire Christian people."[52] Taking advantage of these improved relations with al-Kamil, later that year Gregory wrote directly to the sultan, calling upon him to free a number of merchants from Ancona, who, according to rumor, were wrongfully imprisoned in Egypt. Over the coming years, seeing the possibilities of a temporary "détente" with the infidels, the pope dispatched a number of remarkable letters to the Egyptian sultan and other Islamic rulers around the Mediterranean, expressing his hopes for their conversion.[53]

During the years after the Treaty of San Germano, Pope Gregory also confronted something close to a civil war in crusader territories overseas that were still reeling from the disruptions caused by Frederick's recent visit to the Holy Land. In Cyprus and Syria, fighting had continued between the emperor's supporters and officials, including his new marshal in the area, Richard Filangerium, and factions that opposed his authority, including John of Ibelin, lord of Beirut, and a sworn association of nobles and citizens from Acre supported by the Genoese. The pope took steps to resolve this divisive conflict. Similar to his interventions in Lombardy, Gregory identified peace among Christians in the Holy Land as a necessary condition for concerted action against the infidels. In the region of Jerusalem, such discord among believers represented an existential threat. Latin

Christians, the pope recognized, represented an embattled minority in the crusader principalities.[54] To deal with this situation, Gregory pressed Frederick to fulfill one of his obligations stipulated by the peace of San Germano: restoring the goods and properties seized from the Templars and Hospitallers during his controversial crusade and the War of the Keys. Without the healthy military orders, the pope declared, there could be no successful defense of the holy places.[55]

For the most part, however, Gregory spoke out in support of Frederick's rights as ruler of Jerusalem. In this case, his change of policy put him at odds with his own legate in Syria, the patriarch Gerold, who had repeated the emperor's excommunication during his stay in the Holy Land and dogged his every step while on crusade, sending letters back to Europe that denounced Frederick's vile pact with the infidels. By the summer of 1232, the pope had decided to recall the patriarch to the papal curia, accompanied by the Templar and Hospitaller masters, to give a full accounting of their recent actions in the turbulent crusader principalities. The pope had instructed Gerold to cooperate with the emperor's representatives and help them to settle the political unrest in the region. News had reached Gregory's ears that Gerold instead had actively supported the rebels opposing Frederick's authority. Voices were crying out "openly and publicly" that Gerold worked to disturb the kingdom of Jerusalem, while some—mindful of Gerold's previous attacks on the emperor's reputation—blamed the pope for his actions. Proclaiming that the Devil was sowing "discord in place of peace, dissension in place of reform, hatred in place of love," the pope arranged for Frederick to provide Gerold with letters of safe conduct, enabling him to depart from Syria at the next available passage.[56] The pope commissioned Albert Rezzato, patriarch of Antioch, to replace Gerold, who would be stripped of his legatine status if he failed to return immediately to the curia. Albert set to work mediating between the warring factions in the holy places, trying to secure Frederick's rights along with those of his son Conrad, bringing the rebels back into line, and restoring peace to the area.[57]

In the summer of 1234, Gregory dispatched a special legate to Syria, Theodoric, archbishop of Ravenna, to enforce the terms of an agreement finally struck by Albert between the emperor and his opponents. Addressing the barons of Jerusalem, the citizens of Acre, the masters and brothers of the military orders, and all of the clergy in the kingdom of Jerusalem, the pope again emphasized the need for peace in the region as part of his developing plans for a campaign to the holy places, which were endangered by the endemic fighting there among Christians. At this point, he took extra steps to ensure cooperation with his legate, enjoining the recipients of his letters "by the remission of sins" to observe inviolably the established truce and informing them about his instructions for Theodoric to secure the full restoration of Frederick's possessions and rights as they existed before the recent uprising. As was often the case with such fully empowered legates, Gregory authorized the archbishop of Ravenna to compel obedience to his mandates through ecclesiastical censure, confirming in advance any judgment that Theodoric legitimately passed against the rebels.[58]

Intervening on Frederick's behalf and anticipating the end of Frederick's ten-year truce with al-Kamil in 1239, Gregory clearly hoped to advance his plans for a new crusading expedition. His summons for what became known as the "Baron's Crusade" served as a visual and vocal reminder of the pope's authority to mobilize Christians—men and women, clergy and laity, the powerful and the humble—for a common purpose. In the widely circulated bull *Rachel suum videns*, the pope tapped into the emotional and biblical language of past crusade appeals, reminding his audience about Christ's life and passion in the sacred places of Jerusalem. The loss of the Holy Land was a source of grief and scandal for the entire church. Among other measures, Gregory called for the observation of a "four-year general peace throughout the entire Christian world," threatening excommunication and interdict for those who violated its terms unless they had suffered injuries that justified violating the peace.[59] Through sermons and liturgies, prayers, pious bequests and tithes, the redeeming of vows, and more, Christians from all walks of life could contribute to the crusading cause. To enact these plans in public, the pope relied especially on the mendicant orders, who provided an unparalleled cadre of crusade preachers and fund-raisers. Matthew Paris, always ready to criticize the invasive mendicants, bore witness to the impact of such activities in England, even though he viewed the friars' preaching, commutation of vows, and other financial exactions as a fraud, since the monies collected for the Holy Land would never reach their goal.[60]

As will become clear below, Gregory's plans for the crusade would take some unexpected directions and eventually become a source of renewed tension between him and Frederick. In 1234, however, those problems lay in the future. During its earliest stages, the call for the Baron's Crusade illustrated the compelling public profile of the Roman pope as the spiritual leader of the universal church and evangelizer of peace working in concert with secular powers to achieve the common good of defending the Holy Land, where Christ had redeemed humanity. Mediating in October of that year between Frederick and the Lombards, who were still at odds over their past grievances and the extent of the emperor's rights, Gregory reminded them once again of the need for unity among Christians as a precursor to a successful crusade, especially at a time when the pope, moved to action by the "many clamors" reaching him from the Holy Land, sought to bring them expeditious aid. With Christendom at peace, Gregory envisioned, holy war would be exported beyond its borders.[61]

A Hidden Threat

As Pope Gregory publicized his plans for the upcoming crusade, he identified another threat to the peace in Christendom, a grave menace within the faithful: heresy. Heretics, the pope insisted, teaching their foul doctrines "secretly" and operating in the "shadows," tricked the simpleminded into questioning bedrock elements of their faith, such as the incarnation of Christ, the efficacy of the sacraments, and the resurrection of the body at the Final Judgment. They also tried to cast doubt on the pope's "fullness of power" over the church, his power of the keys over sin, and his right to excommunicate and interdict Christians. Eradicating heresy by wielding the spiritual sword against heretics represented one of Gregory's chief responsibilities as the bishop of Rome and leader of the universal church. Facing this duty, the pope needed a partner to wield the material sword, one who would coerce and, if necessary, execute those judged guilty of heresy: namely, the Christian emperor, among other representatives of the secular arm.

Much like the crusade to recover the holy places, during the years after the Treaty of San Germano the battle against heresy formed a point of convergence for the two powers, allowing the pope and emperor to stress their shared duty to root out and destroy that hidden threat. As observed earlier in this book, the papal effort to combat heresy did not start with Gregory, but his time as pope marked an important—for some, infamous—moment in the history of the medieval church: its "inquisitorial turn," the intensifying, centralizing, and institutionalizing of anti-heretical measures. In the popular imagination, *the* Inquisition summons images of dark dungeons, of clergy torturing more-often-than-not innocent victims far from prying eyes. To the contrary, the hunt for heretics in the thirteenth century involved the pope and his representatives in public displays of priestly authority, including acts such as preaching sermons, performing rites of excommunications, reading letters aloud and exhibiting their seals, receiving testimony in civic spaces, and publicizing anti-heretical statutes, among other "technologies" openly deployed against the hidden threat of heresy.[62]

For Gregory, acting as the bishop of Rome and lord of the Papal States, fighting heresy was in part a local duty that might have reminded him of his time as a cardinal legate in Lombardy years earlier. According to the pope's biographer, after returning to Rome in 1230 following his reconciliation with Frederick at San Germano, Gregory discovered that "Patarene" heretics had spread like a "contagion" throughout the city during his absence, seeking to cause "public harm" through "hidden means." After conducting an inquiry into the matter, in February 1231 the pope convoked a meeting of the Roman senate and people before the Church of Santa Maria Maggiore, where he condemned a great number of clergy and lay people, both men and women among the latter, based on the testimony of witnesses or their own confessions. The clergy suffered deposition, their sacred vestments removed before all the people. Richard of San Germano says that some of the Patarenes were converted back to the orthodox faith, while others were burned.[63] That same month, Gregory issued a new set of statutes regulating the investigation, prosecution, and punishment of heretics that was modeled on earlier examples of anti-heretical legislation. The edict called for the lifetime imprisonment of unrepentant heretics, barred them from holding public office, and anathematized their supporters. If they impeded proceedings against such "infamous" persons, judges and notaries should be deprived of their positions. The law banned the clergy from administering the sacraments to heretics or their supporters, taking alms from them, or giving them ecclesiastical burial. It also forbade clerics to dispute in "public or in private" with lay people about the catholic faith. Anyone who knew about the "hidden meetings" of heretics should tell their confessor or someone else who might notify their bishop.[64] In conjunction with the pope's efforts, the Roman senator Annibaldo, demonstrating the shared interest of clerical and secular authorities in wiping out dangerous heretics, issued a set of municipal statutes against heresy at the same time, committing himself under oath to prosecute heretics identified by the church's "inquisitors."[65]

Gregory's pursuit of heresy did not stop with the city of Rome. Later that year, while collecting still outstanding debts from the War of the Keys from communities in Campagna, he took action against the lords of the commune of Miranda, who were known by "public infamy" to be "supporters of heretics, violators of public roads, forgers of papal bulls, and counterfeiters of coins." After a siege of the town undertaken with allies from Rieti, Alatrin, a papal chaplain and rector of the duchy of Spoleto, met with Miranda's leaders and other witnesses called by a herald to the Church of Saint Mary in Terni. He received their surrender on the pope's behalf, taking the commune under the direct lordship of the Roman church.[66] In September 1231, Gregory issued the first of several warnings to Ezzelino da Romano, the father of the young warlord by that same name, calling him a "public protector" of heretics and causing an "enormous scandal in the general church." The pope recounted his personal meeting with the senior Ezzelino years before, during his legation in Lombardy in 1221, which led to a tearful scene when Ezzelino deceitfully declared his devotion to the church and hatred for the "heretical depravity." Gregory gave him two months to appear at the curia to answer for such charges and show his obedience to the church's commands. Otherwise, the pope would call upon the faithful to take actions against him, including occupying his lands and seizing his goods.[67] The Roman pontiff's support for the preachers of the Great Devotion—whose message of peacemaking included sermons against heresy and, on occasion, the burning of heretics—might have stemmed in part from his interest in opposing heresy through cities and communities of northern Italy.[68]

As the occupant of the Apostolic See, the pope's duty to oppose heresy extended beyond the Papal States and Italy. In principle, it reached throughout the universal church, wherever heretics might be lurking among orthodox Christians. In 1231, Gregory forwarded copies of both his and the Roman senator's antiheretical edicts to other communities outside of Italy, calling upon prelates to publicize solemnly their contents once a month in their dioceses and to make sure that local secular judges and officials implemented and enforced those regulations.[69] The pope's widely circulated calls for action against heretics, bulls like *Illi humanis generis* and *Vox in Rama*, painted a vivid portrait of heretical communities gathered in secret for foul rites, such as holding orgies, worshipping black cats, being visited by a diabolic "pallid man," and tossing the Eucharist in the privy after mass, among other foul deeds.[70] To prosecute the war on heresy, Gregory, rather than just relying upon poorly trained or lukewarm local bishops, authorized figures such as the Premonstratensian canon Conrad of Marburg to take the lead in searching for heretical communities. Above all, he turned again to the mendicant orders, the Franciscans and especially the Dominicans, whose commitment to fighting heretics had started with their founder.[71] Although the papal curia did not direct the daily activities of their investigations, such inquisitors publicly embodied papal authority, displaying letters and "written mandates" bearing the seal of the Apostolic See that empowered them to act in towns, cities, and parishes throughout Europe.[72]

As part of this campaign against heresy, Gregory publicly validated the antiheretical measures promoted by Frederick II, which were enshrined in the emperor's coronation oath and the Constitutions of Melfi. Richard of San Germano describes how the emperor sent his marshal and the archbishop of Reggio to seek out Patarenes in Naples in February 1231, at the same time that Pope Gregory had discovered them in Rome. In 1232, the emperor issued additional bans against heretics in Lombardy and the Regno along with legislation for the suppression of heresy in Germany, relying much like the pope on members of the Dominican order to abolish the "new and unheard-of infamy of heretical depravity" that had arisen there.[73] Proclaiming his own duty to destroy heretics, Frederick turned to the language of the two swords to elaborate how the empire and the church worked as separate but complementary entities for the defense of the faith. Writing directly to Pope Gregory, he celebrated how the "heights of heavenly counsel" had ordained the "priestly dignity" and "royal rank" for the rule of the world, disposing the spiritual sword to the one and the material sword to the other for the correction of errors in a time of growing malice and superstition among men. In each region of the Regno, he specified, a bishop would team up with an imperial justiciar to investigate possible heretics, keeping careful records of their findings. Just as the pope summoned the secular arm to assist the church, Frederick called upon the Roman pontiff, through his prayers and advice, to support his efforts against the "insanity of heretics," together turning the "judgment of both swords, whose power is given to you and us by divine foresight" against those who "arrogantly assume glory for themselves from their perverse dogma, in contempt of the divine power against the mother church."[74]

Gregory, in turn, celebrated the emperor's role in such "pious work," noting that both the material and spiritual swords had to work together to eradicate the heretical threat. This included groups like the Stedingers, rebellious peasants in the diocese of Bremen whose secret machinations had burst into the open when they attacked clergy, refused to pay tithes, and destroyed churches, causing a "scandal" in Germany. Channeling the language, symbols, and material and spiritual benefits of crusading, and following in the footsteps of his predecessor Innocent III, who had declared the Albigensian Crusade against supposed Cathars, Gregory authorized the preaching of armed campaigns against such enemies of the faith. In addition, the pope promised the same remission of sins to those who took up the cross to combat heretics as those going overseas and taking them under the special protection of the Apostolic See like other crusaders.[75] Sending a version of *Vox in Rama* to Frederick in 1233, the Roman pontiff called upon the emperor specifically to destroy such enemies through the power given to him and avenge the injuries done to Christ the Lord. "Stand forth for the eradication of that depraved and perverse people, who cast so many insults at the living God," Gregory exhorted the emperor, asking him to assure that the princes of Germany would take up the sword and wipe out the "ferment" of heretical depravity.[76]

Much like the crusades, the fight against heresy enabled a public conjuncture of the papal and imperial offices. During their period of reconciliation after the War of the Keys, Gregory and Frederick found themselves in a position to turn their energies toward the suppression of heretics, whose crimes threatened the Roman church and empire together and therefore constituted a form of treason. At the same time, again much like the crusades, the alignment of church and empire against heresy went only so far. Under certain circumstances, the pope and emperor could pivot and accuse each other of failing to defend the faith from heretics, a lapse in the duty of their office. In July 1233, praising Frederick's diligent opposition to heresy in the Regno, the pope felt it necessary to warn him about the scandal he might cause and the damage he might do to the imperial dignity if he burned rebels against his authority under the pretense of punishing heretics.[77] Years later, complaining about rampant heresy in Lombardy, the emperor would accuse the pope of favoring and protecting heretics rather than suppressing them. During the course of Frederick's first excommunication, Gregory had hinted of the possibility that the emperor might himself be guilty of heresy by despising the Roman church's "power of the keys," a charge difficult to prove and one that the pope did not openly pursue. When he excommunicated Frederick for the second time, this accusation would return with less reticence. For the time being, however, the two powers, wielding the spiritual and material swords, stood united against the common threat of heretical depravity in their midst.

War with the Romans

In May 1234, Frederick made a personal appearance before Pope Gregory, who was then staying at Rieti. During this meeting, they discussed the unsettled conditions overseas in the holy places, but they also spoke about more pressing business. According to the pope's biographer, Fredrick came as a supplicant, bringing his son Conrad with him and seeking assistance against his other son, Henry, the king of Germany, who had rebelled against his father. Gregory likewise had reasons for welcoming Frederick. Much like the emperor, he faced his own problems with inside agitators who questioned his authority as the lord of the Papal States and bishop of Rome, in this case facing an uprising by the inhabitants of his own city. This meeting at Rieti set the stage for perhaps the most unexpected and understudied episode of public cooperation between Gregory and Frederick during the years after the peace of San Germano, as the two former opponents agreed to assist each other against their present enemies.[78]

Historians generally view this alliance as one of undisguised convenience: the pope aiding the emperor against his traitorous son, the emperor assisting the pope to wage war against his own city. This convergence of Gregory's and Frederick's interests, however, should not be dismissed as merely opportunistic. Much like the papal promotion of other common causes with the emperor, such as freeing Jerusalem and wiping out heresy, Gregory's turn toward the "material sword" represented an advantage of the peace between the two powers. While the pope mobilized Christians to fight for the common cause of defending the Roman church's liberty, Frederick could fulfill his imperial duty as that church's primary defender. To some extent, the war with the Romans validated the harmony between two powers, even if the results of their cooperation fell short of papal expectations. At the same time, Gregory's war against the Romans with imperial aid raised complaints about the pope's use of ecclesiastical resources to field a "papal army" on the Italian peninsula. Much like the War of the Keys, the pope's fight against the Christians of his own city did not sit well with everyone.

Gregory hardly represented the first pope to experience troubles with Roman aristocratic factions and communal government, a problem shared by generations of his papal predecessors. But as Peter Partner observes, his relations with the city were "notoriously bad."[79] As seen in the previous chapter, after the pope repeated Frederick's sentence of excommunication in the basilica of Saint Peter in 1228, a mob had driven him and several cardinals out of the church and eventually out of the city. By the time that the Gregory and Frederick agreed to the Treaty of San Germano, the pope had more or less made peace with the citizens of Rome, who had been "assailing the churches of the City and harassing the Patrimony's vassals with various burdens," as the author of the pope's vita describes the situation. He also claims that the flooding of the Tiber in winter 1230, clearly a punishment from God, convinced the Romans to change their wicked ways. However, problems persisted between the Roman pontiff and the Romans due primarily to the city government's territorial ambitions in central Italy. In the spring of 1231, Roman forces attacked Viterbo, part of the papal patrimony, and seized the town of Monteforte, near Naples, the following summer, using it as a base to "subjugate the remainder of Campania to their dominion." In June 1232, Gregory left Rome for Rieti, not only to escape the summer heat but also because of his growing tensions with the Romans.[80]

During this episode of conflict with the civil government of Rome, the pope turned to Frederick for help, seeking his assistance against the "pride of the Romans." At Gregory's request, the emperor took Viterbo under imperial protection in 1231 and tried to ensure that the Viterbans would cooperate with papal legates assigned to broker a peace agreement, Thomas of Capua and Raynald da Jenne. Throughout his correspondence with Frederick relating to this situation, Gregory emphasized the emperor's role as the defender and advocate of the Roman church, who was responsible for protecting its rights, which were indelibly linked to those of the empire. At an especially evocative moment, he described his joy that the "imperial right hand" brandished the "triumphal sword taken up from the body of blessed Peter, received from the hand of Christ's vicar," wielding it vengefully against such malefactors. On more than one occasion, Gregory enjoined Frederick by the "remission of sins" to aid the Roman church.[81] In one of his replies to the pope, Frederick expressed similar sentiments, remarkably describing the ultimate unity of the "two swords," the spiritual power of priests and the temporal power of emperors, formed from one substance and joined in the "sheath" of the church.[82]

Despite these promises, actual military aid from the emperor was not forthcoming. Facing an uprising in Sicily, Frederick returned to the Regno with his forces in the late fall of 1232, leaving the pope to make peace with the Romans as best as he could. In letters sent to Frederick the following February, the pope described his earlier satisfaction when the emperor's envoys had informed him that Frederick was "manfully preparing to fight in defense of the faith, for the preservation of ecclesiastical liberty, and for the preservation of Saint Peter's Patrimony." Subsequently, Gregory heard rumors that Frederick planned to return to the Regno, abandoning his obligations as the defender of the church. In closing, the pope called upon him to fulfill his duties with "deeds, not just words."[83] Gregory's biographer, looking back at these events after 1239, when the pope excommunicated Frederick for the second time, claims that the emperor never really intended to help the church but instead secretly conspired with the Romans against the pope.[84] Through a series of negotiations led by the cardinals Thomas and Raynald, who smoothed things over by cash payments to the Romans, the pope nevertheless helped to forestall the assault on Campania. In March 1233, representatives from Rome approached the pontiff while he was staying at Anagni and begged him to return to the city. A few months after that, the pope helped to broker a truce between Rome and Viterbo in which the Romans forgave any damages caused by the Viterbans during the recent fighting and the Viterbans swore fealty to the Romans, both sides releasing their captives.[85]

By the spring of 1234, however, this peace between the pope and the Romans began to deteriorate again. According to Gregory's biographer, a new senator named Luke Savelli renewed the city's military push into the surrounding regions and issued statutes "damaging the liberty of the church and causing enormous harm to the Apostolic See," trying to enslave the papal patrimony and overturn its privileges that dated back to the days of Emperor Constantine.[86] By this time, news of the discord between the pope and the Romans had begun to make an impression on wider audiences around Christian Europe. Roger of Wendover, for example, describes how the Romans tried to "usurp" ancient rights in Rome, seeking among other things immunity from excommunication and interdict, a demand that the pope refused. While lesser than God, as Saint Peter's heir and their spiritual father he possessed the right to stand in judgment over them. By May, the pope again left Rome for Rieti, where he passed a sentence of excommunication against Luke Savelli and several other leading Roman citizens due to their seizure and fortification of Monte Alto, a town belonging to the Patrimony of Saint Peter; their taking hostages from that same community; and their extraction of oaths from papal vassals, all actions contrary to the interests of the Roman church.[87]

At Rieti, Gregory also began to make plans for a coordinated assault on the "rebellious Romans," assisted by the emperor, who placed himself "at the service of the church" against the citizens of the city.[88] Neither the pope nor the emperor dissembled the fact that Frederick expected help against his rebellious son, who was allied with some of the Lombard cities in resisting Frederick's rights. In July, Gregory wrote to the archbishop of Trier and other German prelates, denouncing Henry for violating his promises of fealty to his father and instructing the bishops to publicize Henry's excommunication throughout the kingdom. He specified that the prince's actions triggered the suspension of any oaths rendered to him by ecclesiastical and secular magnates.[89] The anonymous author of the *Life of Gregory IX*, writing after 1239 with retrospective disapproval of the emperor's every action, claims that Frederick arrived uninvited at Rieti, offering his son Conrad as a hostage and pledge of his commitment to the understandably suspicious pope—a commitment he never intended to keep after getting what he wanted. Fortified with such "papal letters," Gregory's biographer claims, the emperor acted like "new legate of the Roman church," taking advantage of the pope's written support to turn the German magnates supporting his son against him.[90]

Although Frederick indeed left for Germany to confront his rebellious son, other sources claim that he left a sizable force of troops behind at Viterbo to support the pope. Over the summer, Gregory began to widen his appeals for armed help against the Romans well beyond those he made to the emperor. In July, he wrote to the cities of the Lombard League, stressing this need to employ the "ministry of the imperial arm" in defense of the church and calling upon them not to impede the transit of Frederick's forces. At the same time, still in the middle of peace negotiations between the Lombards and the emperor, he assured them that he would not abandon their interests.[91] The following month, the pope informed the cities and leaders of Tuscany about the appointment of Rainier of Viterbo, cardinal deacon of Santa Maria in Cosmedin, as the leader of the assembling papal army, which was intended for the defense of the papal patrimony and the liberty of the church. A few months after that, Gregory directed a letter to Siegfried, archbishop of Mainz, reminding him about an oath he took to protect the Patrimony of Saint Peter, instructing him to come with or send troops by the following March.[92]

Around this time, the "pope's army" and the "emperor's army," as Roger of Wendover describes the two forces, coordinated their assaults on the outskirts of Rome, destroying a number of surrounding villages. Roger tells us that Gregory also gave Peter, bishop of Winchester, a leadership role in the papal army, valuing him for his military skills and riches, not to mention the contingent of English foot soldiers and bowmen he brought with him. Later in October, when a large body of Roman troops made an undisciplined sally against Viterbo, the pope's combined troops delivered a crushing blow against them, killing thousands and taking many more captive. As Matthew Paris adds in his *History of the English*, elaborating on Roger's account, the slaughter was so great that "the hearts of Pagans rejoiced, far and wide."[93] The Romans never recovered from these defeats, although they sent a defiant message by passing a series of edicts that condemned Rainier of Viterbo and banned the pope from returning to Rome until he paid a large indemnity for damages caused during the war.[94]

During the following months, Gregory continued to solicit armed support from every corner of the Christian world, calling upon Eberhard, archbishop of Salzburg, and thirty-two other German bishops to provide troops with stipends for three months of service. He made a similar request to the archbishop of Rouen and nineteen other prelates in France and Spain, denouncing the Romans, who "ought to be special sons of the church, but, degenerating from sons into stepsons, are showing themselves to be disloyal and ungrateful, so that scarcely a spark of loyalty or gratitude remains among them." In this letter, the pope identified the rebellious Romans' desire to "enslave the Roman church," not only by seizing its temporal goods but also by abusing its spiritual persons and offices, as a "public not private" problem.[95] Closer to home, Gregory summoned the citizens of Velletri to the service of the Roman church, promising "the full remission of sins for those who made confession with a contrite heart."[96] The pope also took specific measures to raise funds for his campaign against the Romans while depriving the city of its own financial resources. In December 1234, citing the "malice of the Romans," he instructed bishops in the kingdom of France to retain all revenues from benefices belonging to absentee Roman clergy, excepting papal chaplains, and to send the proceeds to Master Simon, an official from the papal chancery. In a similar letter to the archbishops of Canterbury and York, Gregory instructed them to forward such funds to the Templar master at Paris. The *Tewksbury Annals* record that some Romans were in fact deprived of their benefices, the revenues of which were forwarded to Canterbury.[97]

Whether the money in question ever reached the pope is unclear. There is little evidence that bishops besides the opportunistic Peter of Winchester provided serious logistical support, in terms of either troops, funds, or supplies. Nevertheless, by the spring of 1235, Gregory's overall efforts had worked, bringing his opponents to the bargaining table. In April and May, the pope's legates in Rome—Romano, the cardinal bishop of Porto, John de Colonna, and Stephen Conti—negotiated peace terms with a new senator, Angelo Malebranca, and other leaders of the city, receiving their solemn oaths to render satisfaction to the Roman church and the emperor during a public ceremony staged on the Capitoline. Frederick had already given his approval to the plans for peace, assuring the pope of his support, even if he could not be on hand in person. Captives were released on both sides. Gregory soon returned to Rome.[98]

Compared to the pope's ambitious plans for the next crusade to the holy places, or even his past calls for assistance against Frederick's forces in the Regno, Gregory's efforts to pitch an armed campaign against the citizens of his own city as a shared responsibility of all Christians seems to have had limited publicity and minimal impact. The pope never called for a direct subsidy or special tax to fund his campaign against the Romans, perhaps due to lingering complaints about his levies on clerical incomes in 1228, which had been raised to pay for his campaign against Frederick in the Regno after the emperor's excommunication. Nor did he authorize any sort of preaching campaign to drum up support for this struggle against the "pride of the Romans." There are no signs that the papal army directed against the Romans marched under the sign of the cross or even under the banner of the keys, an indicator of the limits on how far the papacy could push such spiritually and politically charged symbols in public. Beyond Matthew Paris's sardonic comment about the joy brought to pagans by Christians killing each other, it remains difficult to determine what this war with the Romans meant for contemporaries increasingly habituated to hearing papal calls for military action in defense of the church. Judging by their silence, many chroniclers ignored the fighting between the Roman pope and the Romans, or perhaps never heard much about it.

In this regard, Gregory's struggles with the Romans remained to a large extent a local affair rather than a concern for the entirety of Christendom. But the episode nevertheless remains an important and telling one. The papal campaign against the citizenry of Rome once again reveals the capabilities of the thirteenth-century papacy to publicly authorize violence in defense of the church, even against orthodox Christians: promising the remission of sins for those serving the papal cause and taking them under the "special protection" of the Apostolic See, styling the fight as a common challenge for the entire church, and attempting to draw upon ecclesiastical resources from around western Europe. Every time the pope became involved in any sort of military action, it mattered for the wider Christian community, possibly reaching into their pockets and disrupting their lives. Gregory's fight with the Romans also demonstrates how Italian problems, so to speak, could become everyone's problems. In this instance, the pope and emperor stood on the same side of the fight. Moving forward, that would not be the case.

~

Writing to Gregory from Worms in late July, Conrad, bishop of Hildesheim, expressed the joy felt by the "universal Christian people" that peace had returned to the Roman church after an end to the pope's hostilities with the city of Rome.[99] Through that settlement, there lay "hope for future tranquility and peace for all churches." Conrad also shared news about Frederick's marriage to Isabella of England, King Henry III's sister, earlier in July. During the matrimonial negotiations, Gregory had supported Frederick and Isabella's union. He may have even first suggested it as a means to ally the English crown and Roman empire—one more way of promoting the peace and furthering the cause of the new crusade. Frederick's son Henry had attended the ceremony, having been received back into his father's good graces, his rebellion at an end. (In fact, Frederick soon banished Henry to the Regno, where he died in 1242 after years of captivity.) Conrad concluded that the emperor and other magnates gathered for the wedding would be heading next to Mainz to hold an assembly on 15 August, a convocation intended for "the general good of the peace and the benefit of the entire church."[100]

For years, despite the undeniable stresses and strains placed upon the relationship between their two offices, the pope and emperor had maintained a public state of concord between the two powers, preserving their agreement struck at San Germano. Gregory's apparent concessions and reversals during this period—seeking to broker a settlement in Lombardy, embracing Frederick's truce with al-Kamil, praising the emperor's efforts against heresy, supporting him during his son's rebellion, and even calling for imperial aid against the Romans—revealed something more than political expediency. These changes of direction signaled the vital appeal of harmony between the spiritual and temporal powers as the working balance for the good of Christendom. In his capacity as the Vicar of Christ, Gregory placed unparalleled demands upon Frederick, ones that the Hohenstaufen ruler openly embraced as a duty of his office. Or at least he did, as the pope had once complained, in "words" if not "deeds." In this sense, Conrad of Hildesheim's confidence, his sense that a time of crisis had passed for both the Roman church and empire, was understandable, if misplaced.

Chapter 3

The Widening Gyre

Writing to Frederick in September 1235, after years of celebrating the harmony that lay between the two powers, Pope Gregory acknowledged the tension and mistrust that had recently begun to change the tone of their relationship. Much went unsaid in this letter. During an imperial assembly at Mainz a month earlier, the emperor had openly declared his intention to subdue the rebellious cities of Lombardy, despite his previous commitment to place the "Lombard business" into the "hands of the church." He now seemed to suspect that the pope and papal legates were working against his interests in the region. Overseas, the emperor faced a continued challenge to his rights in the Holy Land, another sign that papal mediation had failed him, perhaps by design. Responding to these unspoken disturbances, Gregory assured Frederick that he was still on his side, blaming recent troubles on those who preferred to "fish in muddy waters" and to work "in the shadows," sowing "quarrels and complaints" and seeking to "dissolve the bonds of love in the hearts of princes with their poisons." Such men, the pope reminded Frederick, had harmed the interests of the papal curia and the imperial court in the past. Specifically, Gregory told him not to believe "secret letters and documents" falsely attributed to the pope and meant to cast doubt on his commitment to the emperor's rights. His past actions on Frederick's behalf in the kingdom of Jerusalem and Lombardy served to demonstrate his sincerity. Frederick should "block out" the words of such liars and write back to the pope when the truth became known from Gregory's actual letters.[1]

Nothing remains of such forgeries, and the pope remained vague about the identities of the "liars" trying to destroy the peace. But the sentiment behind his letter, the sense of erosion in his relationship with Frederick, was quite real. Over the following three years, the Hohenstaufen ruler followed through on his military plans to subdue the seditious cities of northern Italy, campaigning with his own troops, his local allies, and even Muslim mercenaries imported into the region from the Regno. The emperor's decision to settle the Lombard business by force placed Pope Gregory in a difficult position: the "evangelizer of peace" confronted a high-profile war on the Italian peninsula that he had spent years trying to prevent. During this same period, other problems surfaced, swept up in the widening gyre of discord between the pope and the prince as they began to dispute over conditions in the Regno, the emperor's supposed abuse of the clergy, and the pope's interference in Frederick's kingdoms. They argued about dilapidated churches, vacant clerical offices, feudal rights and talliages, and the free movement of envoys. They even disagreed over the whereabouts of a missing Tunisian prince, who was supposedly on his way to Rome to be baptized when he disappeared, somewhere in Apulia.[2]

As these disputes and grievances accumulated, Gregory and Frederick faced a growing public crisis between their offices that neither party seemed entirely to want but did not necessarily know how to avoid. The relentless political problems in northern Italy became a particular source of tension between them. Responding to the centrifugal forces spinning them apart, the pope and emperor slowly hardened and publicized their positions, leaving them less and less room to maneuver. Undeniably, the tone of their direct communications took on an increasingly confrontational posture. At the same time, these years of worsening relations were also ones of persistent if fraying restraint, each side repeatedly stepping back from an outright confrontation. Both parties had good reasons to avoid another costly and disruptive confrontation. Neither of them had particularly benefited from their last open confrontation, while their years of relative cooperation had brought undeniable benefits. Above all, the two Christian leaders remained committed, in the capacity of their respective offices, to the greater goals of peace, crusading, and wiping out heresy. Another battle between the papacy and empire would endanger those projects, as Gregory and Frederick repeatedly reminded each other, each trying to pressure the other into backing down for the common good.

Almost four years would pass before Gregory deployed the "nuclear option," excommunicating Frederick for the second time. If the pope was eager to annihilate the emperor, he certainly took his time going about it. At the very least, he knew that he had to proceed cautiously. After years of celebrating the concord that ought to exist between their offices, he began to erase the record of their cooperation, reminding everyone about his previous struggles with Frederick and accusing him of ingratitude, double-dealing, and sedition. The emperor broadcast a similar revision of the past. The peace, it turned out, had been a false one that concealed true enmity. As the rumor mill churned and new sources of scandal arose, as the sights and sounds of war began to drown out calls for harmony, the two powers once again stood on the verge of open conflict, provoking a renewed sense of anxiety in Christendom.

Angels of Peace and Sowers of Dissension

By the summer of 1235, even as Frederick married Isabella of England with the pope's blessing, if not encouragement, Gregory knew that trouble lay on the horizon with regard to the volatile situation in Lombardy. As it had since the beginning of his papacy, the immediate circumstances of the "Lombard business" continued to shape the pope's interactions with the emperor across the board. Gregory continued his efforts to thread the needle between supporting the Lombard League while stopping short of an open break with the emperor, sending his legates to the region to act as "angels of peace" and to counter the shadowy figures who tried to sow dissension with their lies and deceptions. Meanwhile, Christians around Europe followed news of the growing escalation between Frederick and the Lombard League, recognizing that the growing chances of war in northern Italy affected the Roman church directly and indirectly concerned the entirety of Christendom.

In July, anticipating the emperor's upcoming assembly at Mainz, Gregory sent a batch of letters to the clergy and lay nobles at the imperial court. Declaring that the time approached for the planned crusade to redeem the holy places, the pope called upon the recipients of his communications to lay aside any "rancor" toward the Lombards, working instead with the emperor for peace. Further discord, he insisted, would serve only to undermine the upcoming crusade's prospects for success. Gregory also reminded the recipients of his letters that Frederick had previously placed the Lombard business in the mediatory hands of the Roman church. If they needed evidence of that fact, he forwarded copies, bearing the papal seal, of the agreement struck a year earlier between the emperor and the Lombard rectors in which both sides promised to abide by the pope's arbitration in Lombardy, the March of Treviso, and Romaniola.[3]

The pope had good reasons for communicating his concern. On 24 August, Frederick wrote to Gregory, informing him about the proceedings at Mainz. Coming on the heels of Henry VII's unsuccessful rebellion, the imperial assembly proclaimed peace in Germany.[4] But it also formed a council of war against the cities of Lombardy that continued to reject Frederick's authority. As the emperor described the scene for the pope, not wishing to "conceal" anything from him, the nobles present swore to avenge all of the wrongs perpetrated by the Lombards against their ruler, taking an oath to that effect "with their hands raised in the air, as is customary among them." Divided into two forces, the emperor's armies would march into Italy the following April. As for the agreement made with the pope in Tuscany the previous spring, Frederick, submitting his dispute with the Lombard rebels for papal judgment, insisted that he still desired to follow the pope's "paternal counsel" and honor that commitment. As evidence of his restraint, he would delay his final decision about the campaign until the upcoming Christmas, allowing for the rectors of the league and the Roman pontiff to reach a favorable accommodation. Otherwise, there would be no more delays, no more chances for the Lombards to put him off with "sweet-sounding words" and "false promises."[5]

Frederick indicated that a papal notary, Master Peter, who was retained at the imperial court until the end of the deliberations at Mainz, would give the pope this letter and inform him more fully in person about the emperor's intentions. There is no way of knowing what Peter might have said off the record. Regardless, despite his publicly stated intentions to wage war against the Lombard League, the emperor had still not closed the door to papal mediation. To the contrary, he likely intended his open threats against the Lombards to place pressure on both the league's rectors and the pope to reach a political solution before a costly, disruptive, and hazardous military campaign became necessary. At the same time, by marshaling his forces and allies north of the Alps and setting a firm Christmas deadline for further negotiations, the emperor sent a clear message to everyone involved that he would no longer tolerate the status quo in Lombardy.[6]

In response, Gregory turned to his highest-ranking legate in northern Italy, Albert Rezzato, patriarch of Antioch. As discussed previously, Albert had already represented papal and imperial interests in Syria, helping to broker peace in the crusader kingdoms during the Ibelin uprising. Gregory had first sent Albert—bishop of Brescia before his promotion to the patriarchate of Antioch—to Lombardy in March 1235, instructing him to act as a mediator between the warring communes of Bertinorio and Faeza, whose conflict violated the crusade-related truce declared in 1234. In May, Gregory tasked Albert with a "full legation" to Lombardy, the March of Treviso, and Romaniola, deputizing him to "reform the peace" in the conflict-ridden region after years of devastating losses in lives, goods, and properties, which damaged the crusade to free the Holy Land and impeded the church's effort to wipe out heretics, the "little foxes" in the Lord's vineyard. After hearing about Frederick's threats to invade Lombardy, the pope relied upon Albert to ensure that the rectors of the Lombard League would send their fully empowered ambassadors to the papal curia by the first of December, well in advance of the Christmas deadline imposed by the emperor.[7] Recognizing the dangerous escalation in the conflict between the league and Frederick, the pope projected a measured but firm tone with both sides. In September, writing to the emperor and Hermann of Salza, who was once again acting as a go-between for the imperial court and the papal curia, Gregory assured them that he was doing everything he could to bring the Lombards to the negotiating table. Around this time, he addressed the letter to Frederick described at the beginning of this chapter, warning him about the liars and sowers of dissension that wanted to drive them apart. Corresponding with Hermann and calling upon him to convince the emperor to extend the deadline for this "arduous business" past Christmas, Gregory stressed the preparations underway for the new crusade that would be imperiled if Frederick broke his word to abide by the pope's mediation and invaded Lombardy, a move that the church would not bear. Just what actions the pope might take remained unsaid. Communicating with the Lombards, the pope was far more explicit about possible consequences for noncompliance, threatening them with excommunication if their envoys failed to appear on time and assessing a penalty of thirty thousand marks if they failed to show up.[8]

The fall and winter months, however, proved just how intractable the situation in Lombardy had become. In November, during an assembly in the bishop's palace at Brescia, the cities of the Lombard League renewed their alliance against the emperor, adding Ferrara to their ranks and securing a promise from the city's podesta to block the Germans and their allies from using any roads and rivers under Ferrara's control.[9] The following month, disregarding the pope's threats, the rectors of the league failed to send their envoys to the papal curia installed at Viterbo by the December deadline, prompting Hermann of Salza, who was on hand for the planned negotiations, to leave the city. As Gregory later explained to Frederick and several high-ranking German bishops, the Lombard delegation, having been delayed for legitimate reasons, had arrived just a few days after Hermann left. When the pope tried to recall the master of the Teutonic Order to the curia, he declined to return, citing letters from the emperor demanding his immediate return to the imperial court. Moving forward, the pope tried to pick up the pieces, calling upon all the parties involved to remain committed to future peace talks, stressing the need to observe the general truce declared in advance of the upcoming crusade, and warning everyone about the negative consequences if they violated the church's mandates.[10]

Heading into the spring of 1236, Frederick made no secret of his imminent march into Lombardy, rallying his friends and allies and intimidating his enemies. In March, Peter de Vinea and Thaddeus of Suessa, two prominent members of Frederick's court with a long future ahead of them as imperial representatives, staged a public gathering at Piacenza's communal palace for just such a purpose, joined by the emperor's supporters from Verona, Pavia, Cremona, and elsewhere.[11] The choice of Piacenza for this open-air convocation was not a coincidence. Months earlier, the popular party and its captain, William de Andito, had sent the city's "golden keys" to Frederick as a sign of their submission to the emperor.[12] Gregory made his own plans in advance of Frederick's arrival, seeking as much leverage and advantage as possible. In March, he appointed a new legate to Lombardy—Marcellino, bishop of Ascoli, sent as an "angel of peace" to the war-torn region. Writing to Marcellino to impose limits on his ability to pass sentences of excommunication and interdict against communities without a "special mandate" from the Apostolic See, Gregory specifically placed Verona,

Piacenza, and other "disturbers of the peace" outside of that constraint. With those communes, Marcellino was free to employ ecclesiastical censure as he saw fit. In his legatine commission to the bishop of Ascoli, the pope specifically asked him to intervene in Piacenza, informing the soldiers and citizens of the city about his special concern for their community.[13] The following month, Frederick declared his intention to hold an imperial council at Piacenza in July, which would deliberate over the eradication of heresy, the reform of the empire, and the effort to free Jerusalem. Once peace was restored to the region, the riches of Lombardy would be at the crusade's disposal. In his summons for this gathering, the emperor menacingly declared his intention to pay back what he owed to his friends and enemies alike, subduing the rebels against his rule in Italy.[14]

In June, Gregory sent yet another "angel of peace" to Lombardy: James, cardinal bishop of Palestrina, who was endowed with full legatine powers to work for the abolishment of heresy and the business of the Holy Land for the honor of church and empire. Gregory knew that some parties might object to this choice, telling Frederick not to listen to those who disparaged James or questioned his motives. The emperor had wanted Albert of Antioch sent back as a legate to the region, a request that the pope denied for unclear reasons.[15] A native of Piacenza, James quickly intervened in the civil strife disrupting his hometown. The Genoese chronicler Bartholomew records that the Piacenzans "wisely" expelled their podesta at James's urging. The Ghibelline *Annals of Piacenza*—always suspicious of the church's motives—describe how James "under the guise of peace" effectively staged a coup, bringing troops into the city after some of the citizens exiled William de Andito and his sons before electing a new podesta, a Venetian named Rainier Zenum. From that point forward, this chronicler observes, Piacenza stood in a state of rebellion against the emperor.[16]

Scholars sometimes view Gregory's appointment of James as his legate to Lombardy as a provocative move, a sign that he was not truly committed to peace with Frederick and perhaps even worked behind the scenes to oppose him. Or, James's actions might reveal that he and some of the other cardinals decided to act against the emperor for their own reasons, regardless of what the pope wanted.[17] Regardless, by this time Frederick had begun to express increased skepticism about the pope's willingness or ability to broker peace in Lombardy. In a widely circulated letter addressed to the French king Louis IX in June 1236, the emperor revisited all of his past grievances against the Lombards, from their blockading of the Alpine passes before his planned assembly at Cremona in 1226 to their involvement in his son Henry's conspiracy and their recent failure to appear on time at the papal curia for peace talks. Every time he had placed the matter into the pope's hands, the results had been more lies and treachery by the Lombards. Frederick emphasized his undiminished commitment to the upcoming crusade, rejecting Gregory's insistence that the cause of freeing Jerusalem outweighed the emperor's obligation to quash the rebellion against his rule in northern Italy. "Surely," Frederick queried, "we are not to believe that the pope intends the business across the seas to blunt the sword of justice?"[18]

Rumors of the approaching war in Lombardy spread far and wide, contributing to confusion about the current state of affairs between the emperor and pope. Taking note of the emperor's growing "rage" and "inexorable hatred" for the Italians, Matthew Paris writes in his *Major Chronicle* that Frederick turned to the pope for help against them, creating a great deal of "anxiety and worries" for the Roman church when the pope gathered the entire curia for deliberations about how to "reform an honorable peace" between the two sides. He did this not for altruistic reasons, Matthew observes, but rather because he knew that he might need Frederick's help in the future against his own enemies. In his narrative of these events, the English chronicler includes a letter that he attributes to Frederick, proclaiming the emperor's hereditary authority over Italy, denouncing the heretical Lombards for impeding his new crusade, and calling upon the pope to support him. According to Matthew, not wishing to seem indifferent to the emperor's demands, Gregory acquiesced to his plans—for the time being.[19]

Trouble Overseas

During this period of rising tensions on the Italian peninsula, Gregory and Frederick continued to wrestle with the equally unsettled conditions of the crusader kingdoms "across the sea," another unraveling area of cooperation between the two powers. Preparations for the so-called Baron's Crusade had continued to move forward since 1234, anticipating the expiration of Frederick's ten-year truce with the Egyptian sultan, al-Kamil. Bearing letters and "written warrants" from the pope, mendicant friars and other papal envoys had fanned out around Europe to raise support for the upcoming campaign by preaching the cross, offering indulgences, and collecting funds through donations and pious bequests. They also raised money through the redemption of crusader vows, which were sworn and immediately redeemed by a cash payment. This intensive effort in England raised further complaints from Matthew Paris, who was always ready to excoriate the greed of the friars and papal curia.[20] In 1235, Gregory made the decision to split the crusading campaign into two forces, directing one toward Syria and the other toward the embattled Latin Empire of Constantinople, which was being assailed by the "schismatic" Byzantine emperor-in-exile, John III Doukas Vatatzes. According to Matthew, much of the blame for the schism between Latins and Greeks again lay with the greed and corruption of the papal curia, which had alienated the Greeks and caused their rejection of Rome's authority. No longer willing to stand such disobedience, Matthew writes, the pope decided to send a "universal army signed with the cross" against them.[21]

As shown above, Gregory's determination to mobilize a major crusading expedition had played a significant role in conditioning his public relationship with Frederick. The pope's efforts to achieve a peaceful settlement between the Lombard League and the Hohenstaufen ruler repeatedly invoked the needs of the crusades as requiring an end to strife between the two sides. Peace between the Christians living overseas, and even forms of strategic peace between Christians and certain Muslims, was equally critical for the success of any future effort to free Jerusalem. In March 1235, in a remarkable sign of how Frederick's truce with al-Kamil had changed the diplomatic playing field between Christian and Muslim powers, Gregory exchanged a number of letters with the sultan of Konya, 'Ala ad-Din Kaiqubad, exploring the possibility of "friendship and peace" between them, the same "friendship" that the Muslim leader enjoyed with the "lord of the Germans, Frederick." This unusual exchange illustrated the opportunities posed for Christian diplomacy when the pope and emperor did not stand at odds. Gregory met face-to-face with the sultan's envoy, a Christian named John de Gabra, who had been sent to the papal curia via Frederick's imperial court. John, carrying 'Ala ad-Din's letters and bearing other information that he would only relay in person, shared the sultan's proposal to form an alliance to destroy their mutual enemies and help the Christians "recover Jerusalem and all of the lands that they held in the days of Saladin." After his meeting with Gabra, the pope sent him back to Frederick's court to continue with these negotiations. This is the last thing ever heard of the sultan's emissary and the proposed peace between the Muslim ruler and the bishop of Rome.[22]

Peace among Christians living in the crusader kingdoms remained just as elusive, despite the truce established in 1234 by Albert of Antioch and the archbishop of Ravenna between John of Ibelin and Frederick's officials. When news reached the pope in the summer of 1235 that John and his supporters at Acre were planning an assault on Tyre, which was held by Frederick's imperial marshal, Richard Filangerium, Gregory again tried to intervene on the emperor's behalf. Writing to the Hospitaller, Templar, and Teutonic orders in Syria, calling for "peace and tranquility" rather than "dissension and scandal," he instructed them to work for the "preservation of imperial rights" and stop the attack on Tyre. An injury against the emperor, Gregory stated, is like "an injury to us." He sent a similar message to John of Ibelin and the citizens of Acre, threatening them with ecclesiastical censure if they did not reverse their confrontational course.[23]

In his letters to the various parties concerned, the pope did not disguise or dissemble his reasons for supporting Frederick. Damage to the emperor's power would equally harm the church and impede the upcoming crusade. After the emperor's recent service, meaning his support against the rebellious citizens of Rome, Gregory felt especially beholden to back the Hohenstaufen position overseas. Writing directly to Frederick in September 1235 and celebrating the empire as the "strong-arm and defender of the Apostolic See," Gregory reviewed his past efforts to defend Frederick's rights in Syria. With this address, he included a separate "form of peace," laying out the new terms for a settlement in the kingdom of Jerusalem that would restore the status quo before the recent rebellion against the imperial marshal. In that same letter, however, Gregory also tried to explain his controversial decision to lift the sentence of interdict passed against Acre by his own legate, Theodoric of Ravenna, after proctors from the city at the papal curia provided sworn assurances of their good behavior moving forward. The pope did so because of the particular situation in that city. With so many different kinds of Christians and kinds of worship in the city, he worried that leaving the ban in place might encourage some citizens to abandon the Roman rite altogether, allowing for the spread of heresy. Gregory must have realized that Frederick would question his decision to lift the interdict before finalizing the terms of peace, so he asked Peter de Vinea, who was present at the curia for negotiations over the problems in Lombardy, to approve of the papal agreement with the citizens of Acre. To Gregory's disappointment, Peter refused, since his mandate from the emperor did not authorize him to do so.[24]

The pope's efforts to settle the civil strife in Syria continued along these lines. As the Vicar of Christ, Gregory reminded Frederick, he bore the responsibility to "weed out the scandals" from the Holy Land and "sow the things of peace."[25] After a subsequent meeting involving Hermann of Salza and some ambassadors from Acre in February 1236, the pope sent an updated version of his plan for peace to Frederick, an agreement that called for the full restoration of the Hohenstaufen ruler's rights and the dissolution of the illicit commune in the city, including the surrender of its communal bell and the removal of its civic officers. The citizens would swear public oaths of fidelity to the emperor that would supersede any oaths previously sworn against him or his son. Due to the bad blood between the rebels and Richard Filangerium, he would be replaced by a temporary bailiff for Acre until Bohemond V, prince of Antioch, could take up that position and rule the kingdom of Jerusalem and the city of Tyre in the emperor's name. The treaty called upon the emperor to receive the citizens of Acre back into the "fullness of his grace," guaranteeing security for John of Ibelin and his family within the bounds of the crusader kingdom. In separate letters sent to the archbishop of Nazareth and the bishop of Acre, the pope, in recognition of the new peace, authorized them to relax any sentences of excommunication and interdict passed on account of the recent conflict.[26]

Much like the pope's other attempts to broker a settlement between Frederick and those resisting his rule, Gregory's plans for the kingdom of Jerusalem satisfied no one. According to the *Estoire de Eracles*, when the envoys from Acre returned to the city with papal letters laying out the new terms for peace, the citizens protested angrily, viewing the agreement as slanderous and shameful, since it presented them as the treacherous party. The pope's instructions to dissolve the commune at Acre, along with the limits he placed on the guarantees for John of Ibelin's security, did not sit well either. The leaders of the commune dispatched another envoy to the pope, a knight from Cyprus named Joffrey le Tor, who came to Viterbo bearing not only letters of protest about the peace agreement but also lavish gifts for Gregory and the cardinals. The pope, the *Estoire de Eracles* continues, carefully listened to Joffrey and agreed with his objections, sending him back to Syria with letters promising the people of Acre the full support of the church. Whether this story was true or not, Frederick refused to ratify the pope's settlement. Whatever his intentions, Gregory's designs for peace in the crusader kingdoms had done little to end the dissension overseas and nothing to improve his relations with Frederick.[27]

Lines in the Sand

As the year 1236 passed, Frederick remained in Germany for a few months longer than planned. In May, he attended the ritual translation of Elizabeth of Hungary's holy remains into a new shrine at Marburg. The archbishops of Mainz and Trier joined him, as did Conrad of Hildesheim. In retrospect, the ceremony has a calm-before-the-storm feel about it.[28] In August, the emperor marched into Italy with several thousand soldiers, going first to Verona, where he joined up with Ezzelino da Romano and his supporters from Parma, Cremona, and elsewhere. Anticipated and feared for months if not years, war had come to Lombardy. More than anything else, Frederick's commitment to campaigning against the Lombard rebels greatly intensified the building public pressure on him and the pope, who reacted by delivering a series of sharply worded ultimatums to the emperor. As the relationship between the two powers began to deteriorate, each side also began to argue over the circumstances of their past falling out, calling attention to perceived double-dealing during their attempts to settle the strife in Lombardy. Christians everywhere needed to know where the fault lay for the escalating violence.

Frederick's choice of Verona as a staging ground was not made lightly. Political control of the city, which sits at the foot of the Brenner Pass across the Alps, had changed hands a number of times over the past year or more. The region had remained caught up in local feuding between Azzo d'Este and Richard of San Bonifacio on the one hand and the Romano brothers and the Monticoli family on the other. In April 1235, two papal legates, Nicholas, bishop of Reggio, and Tyso, bishop of Treviso, had arrived on the scene for the purposes of "making peace by the advisement of the lord pope." Recalling the days of John of Vicenza and the Great Devotion, the two clerics staged an assembly in a nearby field, bringing Richard and some of his enemies together to share the ceremonial kiss of peace.

Acting on behalf of the pope, as one chronicler described the situation, Nicholas and Tyso also secured the election of a new podesta, Rainier Borgarello, who took an oath in Verona's communal palace to "preserve the liberty of the Roman church and obey its mandates."[29] In June 1236, the city experienced another regime change when an imperial official named Gaboard arrived with a force of five hundred foot soldiers and one hundred archers and took control of Verona in the emperor's name.[30]

Over the course of the fall, Frederick and his allies marched against armies fielded by the cities of the Lombard League, including Milan, Mantua, Brescia, Bologna, Ferrara, Lodi, Vercelli, Novara, and Alexandrina. Azzo d'Este and Richard of San Bonifacio fought alongside the cities of the league. Although his brief siege of Mantua ended inconclusively, Frederick dominated the fighting. On the first of November, he sent an unmistakable message that he meant business in Lombardy when his soldiers captured Vicenza, burning large portions of the city.[31] In his *Major Chronicle,* attributing his source of information to Baldwin de Vere, an envoy of Henry III sent to Frederick's court for "secret negotiations," Matthew writes that Gregory did not oppose Frederick's campaign at the time. Instead he pretended to go along, emboldening the emperor. When the panicked Milanese appealed for help from the pope, Gregory immediately expressed his support for them in disregard of Frederick's rights, hoping to extort money from the city. This two-faced attitude astonished everyone.[32]

Contrary to Matthew's report, Gregory had tried to restrain the emperor from the beginning. Before Frederick even crossed the Alps, in February 1236 the pope had written the first of several confrontational warnings to the emperor, *Dum preteritorum consideratione.* He sent this address as a response to complaints made by the emperor in a letter that no longer survives. Based on the pope's replies, it is possible to discern the gist of Frederick's objections. Gregory opened his address with sentiments of optimism about Frederick's future support for the catholic faith, based on the consideration of the past cooperation between them. The spreaders of lies, however, had once again been busy, trying to "wound the unity between church and empire," seeking to turn the emperor against the Apostolic See, which had defended his rights since his childhood. The pope again reminded Frederick about his promises to submit to papal arbitration in Lombardy. In particular, he defended the actions a year earlier of his legates in Verona, who had created a "good peace" in the city by installing his "faithful" man, Rainier Borgarello. Gregory assured Frederick that he had not acted out of prejudice toward his rights and did not instruct the new podesta to block the "king's highway." He also denied that the Lombard League had renewed its society at the church's prompting.[33]

Going on the offensive for the first time in years, Gregory also raised the subject of disturbing rumors that had reached him from the Regno about imperial officials infringing upon the rights of bishops, despoiling church properties, jailing priests and dragging them before civil courts, imposing tallages on clerics, and other disturbing news. Oppressing the clergy in this way, above all limiting their ability to preach, allowed heresy to flourish. In a sign of things to come, the pope called attention to the "Saracen mercenaries" settled by the emperor at the town of Lucera—Muslims forcibly relocated to the Italian peninsula from Sicily after their failed rebellion years earlier. The pope's awareness of their presence in the region was hardly new. Years earlier, after complaining about the destruction of church buildings by the Saracens with Frederick's consent, he had appealed to the emperor to assist proselytizing Dominican missionaries among the Muslim population there. Now, he again highlighted rumors that the "Hagarenes" were using stones from ruined churches to construct their own "gymnasia," places of worship where they praised the "damnable Machomet." Finally, Gregory denounced the imperial abuse of certain nobles who had sided with the church during the War of the Keys, clearly violating the peace agreement made at San Germano six years earlier. Calling upon the emperor to fulfill his past promises to the church and forbid future such abuses and proclaiming that the "clamor" reaching his ears and even to heaven compelled him to act, Gregory told Frederick that he could not keep silent any longer without causing harm to his own reputation and conscience.[34]

Responding to the pope's letter in April, Frederick likewise attributed the accusations about his abuses of the church in the Regno—beyond his rightful exercise of feudal rights and traditional prerogatives over clerical elections—to those "spreading lies," calling upon the pope to close his ears to such malicious fabrications. The emperor was not embittered toward the pope because of such falsehoods but rather toward the people responsible for inventing them. Replying in general terms to Gregory's vague complaints, Frederick denied any knowledge of the misdeeds attributed to his officials in the Regno, including the plunder of churches, the despoiling of ecclesiastical properties and goods, and the assaults on the clergy. The cities and individuals who had sided with the church during the past split between the emperor and pope continued to enjoy the peaceful tranquility of his reign. As for the Saracens in Apulia, he knew nothing about their destruction of churches. To the contrary, he had gone through a great deal of trouble and expense to subdue those unbelievers in Sicily before moving them to the mainland, where many had embraced the Christian faith. Addressing the situation in Verona, Frederick denounced the pope's decision to excommunicate those citizens who, "publically crying out our name and that of the empire," had ejected the newly installed podesta and his cronies, who had been corrupted by bribes from the Lombards. There were some who suspected that Gregory desired to bring Verona over the side of the league. Although Frederick did not think it true, he called upon the pope to prove them wrong through his actions. In closing, stressing his affection for the pope and the church, Frederick asked Gregory to reconsider the bitter tone expressed at the end of his letter, signaling his intention to write to the pope further when he entered Italy.[35]

After Frederick's arrival in northern Italy, the pope again designated James of Palestrina, with his "erudite tongue," to defend the church's interests at the imperial court. Gregory knew that James might be an incendiary choice for his primary legate to the imperial court. Addressing the archbishop of Milan, he specifically asked him and his fellow bishops to assure Frederick that the cardinal bishop's recent actions at Piacenza, forging a "good peace" in the city at the request of its citizens, did nothing to compromise the emperor's rights. If James could not be present, or perhaps if the emperor refused outright to meet with him, the pope expected others—including Guala, bishop of Brescia; William, archbishop of Milan; the deacon Gregory da Romano; or all of them—to defend the Roman church against the emperor or any others seeking to "sow tares" of dissent by disparaging the church "publicly or secretly."[36] The pope armed his representatives with a list of grievances about Frederick's abuses of ecclesiastical persons and properties in the Regno, picking up where his letter to Frederick written the preceding February had left off. According to the terms struck at San Germano in 1230, the emperor had three months to correct such violations if he were in the Regno, four months if elsewhere in Italy, or five months if he were outside of Italy, or else he would suffer a "certain penalty," which seemed to imply that he might trigger his own excommunication.[37]

Publicly, Gregory did not signal any overt intention to excommunicate the emperor. Writing to Hermann of Salza earlier that summer, the pope had assured him that he had no such plans to censure Frederick, wondering where Hermann got the idea that he might do so.[38] In August, however, Gregory da Romano presented the emperor with another list of grievances that restated some of the pope's earlier complaints about conditions in the Regno, while adding new ones.[39] The document charged that imperial officials in the Regno were robbing the church's liberty, despoiling churches, jailing prelates, forcing clerics to appear before secular judges, and imposing tallages on them. Those officials also prohibited preaching for the defense of the faith and the business of the Holy Land, thereby allowing heresy to flourish, while permitting Saracens to exercise lordship over Christians by the use of stones from ruined churches to build their own houses of worship. Frederick's agents also allowed Jews to sell hocked ecclesiastical goods. The document followed those charges with a specific list of monasteries and churches that Frederick had destroyed, kept vacant, or allowed to fall into ruin, while preventing the construction of any new ones. The charges closed with a complaint that the emperor's officials had seized and detained a Tunisian prince en route to Rome to receive baptism.[40]

From his camp at the siege of Mantua, Frederick responded to these latest accusations with his point-by-point replies to the record of events that Gregory remembered or preserved in his archives. He pleaded ignorance of some matters that the pope raised, dismissed others, and explained the perfectly good reasons for his actions in still other cases, but he denied violating the church's liberty, unless by chance Gregory referred to his lawful exercise of feudal privileges. "For we, in our ancient temporalities and dignities, exert ourselves to preserve our right inviolably," he informed the pope about the balance of powers between them, "just as, with regard to your spiritualities, we in no way intend any infringement upon the duty of the papal office or your fullness of power." The emperor rejected any claims that his officials had prevented preaching in the Regno, above all for the upcoming crusade, a duty that rested on his shoulders more than most. But he also insisted that, under the pretext of such sermons, some chose to speak openly against his rule, trying to assume control over the goods, towns, and castles of his faithful followers in the name of the church, such as when the Dominican preacher John "in his letters named himself the duke and rector of Verona," or in Apulia, when a certain friar gathered a host of simple young boys to his banner. Frederick would continue to restrain such men even as he granted complete freedom to those who confined their preaching to the word of God.[41]

When the emperor's envoys brought this response to the curia, they handed over another list of complaints made in turn by Frederick to the pope. Gregory's register records his replies to this set of charges, which he may or may not have sent to the emperor. As before, many of their disagreements revolved around particular places and the public actions of certain individuals rather than around abstract principles. The pope defended his own actions and those of his representatives; for example, he had disciplined the abbot of Saint Vincent because his monks accused him of wastefulness, not because he sided with the emperor. As for John of Vicenza, who made "peace among the people of Verona," he had done so without Gregory's awareness. If he had called himself duke and rector of that city, the pope knew nothing about it. Gregory likewise denied appointing Rainier Borgarello podesta of Verona, a choice made by the citizens. Last but not least, the pope rejected Frederick's claim that he sent James of Palestrina to work against his rights in Piacenza, defending his legate as a "just and God-fearing man, desiring peace and working for tranquility of the province, who has done or arranged for nothing, saving for the right of the empire, without causing any harm."[42]

In October 1236, Gregory sent yet another letter to Frederick addressing these sources of controversy, *Si memoriam beneficiorum*.[43] Modern historians have sometimes pointed to this address as revealing the pope's true designs to assert the ultimate superiority of the papal office over that of the emperor.[44] Such appraisals are mainly based on Gregory's decision to stress the ultimate responsibility of emperors to submit to the judgments of the Apostolic See, as the examples of past rulers showed. In this letter, Gregory reminded Frederick specifically about the so-called Donation of Constantine, the (spurious but believed authentic) record of that emperor's surrender of the imperial regalia to Pope Sylvester and his successors along with lordship over the Rome, its surroundings, and the entire western empire.[45] Constantine's famous deed, the pope stated, was "publicly known throughout the entire world." Subsequent popes later transferred that power of empire to Charlemagne and the Germans, Frederick's own ancestors. The emperor, Gregory wrote, borrowing a line from his predecessor Gregory VII enshrined in canon law, had clearly forgotten that "the priests of Christ are held to be masters and fathers of kings and princes, of all the faithful."[46]

Si memoriam beneficiorum undeniably struck a remarkably different tone than anything produced by the papal chancery since the pope had reconciled with the emperor at San Germano, invoking the historical examples of the past to assert the ultimate dominance of the priesthood over secular rulers. Clearly, Frederick's invasion of Lombardy had raised the stakes in the relationship between him and the pope, provoking Gregory's less-than-compromising tone. And yet the fact that such ideological elements constitute a small part of the letter should not be overlooked. Gregory spent far more time defending the actions of his legate, James of Palestrina, who, the pope insisted, had taken no actions contrary to Frederick's rights in Lombardy. Rather, the cardinal bishop had worked to "reform the peace" in the region, following up on Frederick's earlier promises to consign the "Lombard business" into the hands of the church. The pope also had sent James there for the purposes of wiping out heresy, fostering aid for the holy places, and recovering the rights of both church and empire, goals that Frederick declared as his own. Rather than hampering James's efforts in this regard, the emperor should be helping him. Gregory also recalled how Hermann of Salza had publicly praised James at the papal curia years earlier, when he and Otto of San Nichola had intervened on Frederick's behalf Lombardy. If James had wronged Frederick, the pope was prepared to render justice on this account, but the emperor had failed to prove any such crimes.

Much of this letter also turned upon conditions in the Regno. Gregory rejected Frederick's protestations of ignorance concerning abuses in the kingdom, expressing his skepticism that any one of the emperor's agents acted there without his permission or commands. No one "lifted a finger or moved a foot" there without his consent. Rather than firing a shot in an ideological battle between the two powers, Gregory's invocation of the Donation of Constantine and stress on the subordination of emperors to priests seemed designed mainly as a rebuke of the emperor's interference with ecclesiastical persons and properties, thereby trying to usurp the pope's "fullness of power" over the church. Worse than all of these other accusations, Gregory denounced Frederick's attempts to limit public preaching in the Regno, which impeded the business of the cross. In closing, the pope called for the emperor to proceed with humility and make amends for these injuries, so that God might not avert the eyes of his majesty from the emperor's steps and the pope might celebrate Frederick's successes in the Lord.[47]

If *Si memoriam beneficiorum* signaled Gregory's intentions to censure Frederick, he was clearly nowhere taking such drastic action in public. To the contrary, despite the violence in Lombardy and the less restrained tone of the letters exchanged between the emperor and the pope, negotiations for some sort of settlement in Lombardy continued as winter approached. In November, after conferring with Peter de Vinea and Herman of Salza, Gregory authorized two new legates to Lombardy: Raynald of Jenne, cardinal bishop of Ostia, and Thomas of Capua, cardinal priest of Santa Sabina. Given their past success as mediators between the papal curia and imperial court, the choice of these two ambassadors might have represented an attempt to de-escalate his worsening relations with Frederick. Their mandate included the now familiar goals of securing the church's liberty, reforming the state of the empire, abolishing heresy, and enabling the business of the Holy Land, none of which could happen with Lombardy in flames.[48]

As they often did, unexpected events intervened when the emperor left northern Italy for Germany to deal with an armed uprising by Duke Frederick of Austria. The emperor accused the duke of undermining his authority, conspiring with the Milanese against him, and even trying to hire a Saracen Assassin from the Old Man of the Mountain to kill him. Despite Matthew Paris's suggestive comments that the Roman church or some other "enemies of the empire" conspired to draw Frederick away from his planned siege of Milan, there is no evidence that Gregory had any hand in his rebellion. Frederick did make the claim that the duke of Austria tried to draw "the most holy father in Christ, the highest pontiff" over to his cause, but he had failed to do so. Regardless, the rebellion north of the Alps came at an opportune time for the hard-pressed Lombards and the pope, giving them some breathing room.[49]

The Turning of the Tide

After subduing the rebellious duke of Austria and wintering in Germany, in the spring of 1237 Frederick began to prepare for the next year's campaign against the cities of the Lombard League. The war in the region had begun to achieve a momentum that would prove difficult to arrest, one that seemed to favor the emperor as news spread around Europe about his victories over the Lombard rebels. His incentive to cooperate with Gregory and his representatives had never been lower. The pope clearly recognized this fact, as the sources of tension with Frederick expanded to regions outside of Lombardy, including the territories of Arles and Provence. The relationship between the two powers began to reach a public tipping point, from showing persistent restraint over their differences to undisguised confrontation.

As in previous years, negotiations to end the fighting continued heading into the summer months, before Frederick actually committed his forces. While acknowledging that Raynald and Thomas represented a major improvement over James of Palestrina, the emperor evinced skepticism that anything constructive would happen on their watch. They basically offered the same unacceptable terms for peace as their predecessor. Frederick nevertheless recommitted his own envoys to the peace process, including the now familiar faces of Peter de Vinea, Thaddeus of Suessa, and Hermann of Salza. In May, Pope Gregory gave instructions for Milan and ten other Lombard cities to send envoys for an assembly at Mantua under the direction of the two cardinal legates. Complications for such peace talks emerged from all sides. In February, Ezzelino da Romano unexpectedly staged a coup in Padua, seizing control of the city and bringing it over to the emperor's side.[50] During the general chapter meeting of the Teutonic Order, the German princes present, crying out for blood in Lombardy, tried to prevent Hermann of Salza from returning to the bargaining table. They relented only when he displayed the pope's letters instructing him to do so.[51] When the cardinal legates, the representatives of the Lombard League, and the imperial envoys finally gathered in July at the castle of Florentiola, not far from Piacenza, things did not go well either. While the emperor's men tried to convince the Lombards to relax the bonds of their illicit society and swear fealty to Frederick, they insisted among other points that the rebels restore to his position the exiled podesta of Piacenza, William de Andito. Suddenly, Rainier Zenum, who had taken over the city when the citizens expelled William, burst in on the deliberations, rejecting any peace that did not include his native Venice and throwing the whole meeting into chaos. When he returned to Piacenza, he arranged for the citizens to swear that they would never allow William or his sons back into the city. At this point, Raynald and Thomas gave up on the current round of talks and returned to the papal curia.[52]

Meanwhile, the fortunes of war continued to swing Frederick's way, giving him more and more latitude to press his political advantage. In September, he returned to Italy from Germany. Assembling forces at Verona, he arranged for several thousand Saracen archers to join him at the city. He stationed other Muslim troops in Ravenna and Faenza. The visible presence of these non-Christian mercenaries made a strong impression on chroniclers such as Salimbene of Adam, who described the large number of Saracens present at Frederick's siege of Montichiari, near Brescia. The emperor also marched with an elephant, which had a large wooden tower, adorned with banners, strapped to its back. Then, on 27 November, Frederick delivered a dramatic military victory over the increasingly isolated Milanese and their allies at Cortenuova, slaughtering thousands, capturing the city's podesta, and seizing its carroccio, the ceremonial war wagon carrying a portable altar and Milan's battle standard.[53]

Numerous chroniclers memorialized this disastrous defeat for the Lombards. Frederick made sure that news of his heaven-sent victory spread close to hand and far afield. He paraded the captured carroccio around Cremona with the Milanese podesta strapped to it and later sent the war wagon to Rome. Frederick also circulated letters celebrating the battle to various individuals, courts, and communities around Europe, where they were to be read and read aloud with the intention of eliciting joy over the empire's exaltation. In his *Major Chronicle,* Matthew includes a copy of one such address that was sent by the emperor to his brother-in-law Richard of Cornwall—an imperial letter affixed with the emperor's golden bull. What goes unmentioned by Matthew is the fact that Frederick sent a similar letter directly to the pope and the cardinals, openly savoring his victory.[54] According to some reports, the arrival of the carroccio in Rome grieved Pope Gregory almost to death, as evidenced by his unsuccessful attempt to prevent the emperor's supporters from bringing the war wagon into the city. This public display of Milan's defeat divided the city: the Ghibelline *Annals of Piacenza* record that the emperor's sympathizers arranged for the carroccio to be displayed on the Capitoline hill, although Salimbene of Adam claims that some of the Romans later burned the war wagon in a show of contempt for Frederick.[55]

Seeing this string of victories and the collapse of Frederick's opponents, the city of Treviso submitted to him, followed by Azzo d'Este, the citizens of Mantua, and Richard of San Bonifacio. After their loss, even the Milanese showed signs of capitulating to the emperor. The Ghibelline *Annals of Piacenza* describe how the Franciscan friar Leo, one of the charismatic preachers of the Great Devotion in 1233, arranged for a meeting with Frederick at Cremona, where he made proposals for peace between the emperor and Milan. Even Rainier Zenum, the recalcitrant podesta of Piacenza, seemed ready to submit to Frederick when he heard the news about Milan's possible surrender, making a "public pact" with the bishop of Piacenza and the city's Dominican prior to make peace with Frederick. This whole plan fell through when some envoys from Milan told Rainier not to believe the rumors about their capitulation. Rainier recalled his representatives from their meeting with the emperor's envoys at Lodi, causing them to storm off in the middle of dinner. The war in Lombardy would not be coming to an end anytime soon.[56]

After wintering in Italy, Frederick began to lay the groundwork for the next season of campaigning against the rebellious Lombards, announcing plans for an assembly to meet at Verona in May with the declared intention of "pacifying the state of our faithful followers and subduing the pride of the traitors with an iron rod." During this same period, the political strife and violence in northern Italy showed signs of spilling over into the neighboring territories of Arles, Provence, and Toulouse. Due to Frederick's tenuous but still meaningful claims to rule over the kingdom of Arles as part of the empire, the area represented another sphere of imperial influence and possible contention between the emperor and the pope. Raymond, count of Toulouse, was one of Frederick's vassals, although not always as responsive as his lord would have liked. In late April, Frederick dispatched a strongly worded address to the count that rejected his excuses for his planned absence from the upcoming assembly at Verona.[57] Conditions in the supposedly heretic-infested region of Toulouse weighed on Gregory's mind as well. Raymond had his own long and controversial relationship with the Roman church. Excommunicated as heretic and Cathar sympathizer under Honorius III, Raymond had reconciled with Rome in 1229 but faced a renewed ban by Gregory in 1236 after his officials—or so the pope understood—had expelled the Dominicans from Toulouse and banned them from preaching against the "heretical depravity." A number of friars and cathedral canons were beaten during the ensuing violence. Ratcheting up the pressure on the count, Gregory insisted that he depart on crusade, as he had sworn to do as an act of penance. Otherwise, he would face ecclesiastical censure.[58]

In May 1238, Gregory assigned James of Palestrina as his new legate to Provence, thrusting the controversial cardinal bishop back into the spotlight. The pope dispatched James with the declared purpose of "confounding" the persistent "heretical depravity" that plagued Toulouse and its surroundings. He also instructed James to absolve Raymond of Toulouse, now styled a "noble man" in papal letters, after confirming the terms of his reconciliation with the Roman church.[59] The choice of James for this high-profile legation again raises difficult questions about Gregory's motives: Was he trying to get the combative cardinal bishop out of Italy and out of the way? Was his overriding concern with the problem of heresy, as stated? Or was the pope sending his chief provocateur to undermine the emperor's rights in the region? Frederick certainly did not object to the goal of wiping out heretics. In May and June, addressing all the princes and officials of the empire, he reissued legislation designed to eradicate heresy, which was an insidious threat to his kingdoms and empire.[60] But he left no doubt about how he viewed Gregory's decision to assign James of Palestrina as his legate to Provence, rejecting the pope's written request for a letter of safe conduct that would allow the cardinal bishop to cross through imperial territories. The emperor did not dissemble his reasons for blocking James and circulated letters that denounced him as a "sower of scandal," "preaching scandal among the people," who came to Lombardy "not to evangelize peace, but to raise up the sword of disruption." Whether James did this with or without the pope's knowledge, the emperor stated, remained unclear.[61]

The days of celebrating the joint effort of the two powers to eradicate heresy seemed over. Indeed, new sources of contention were emerging between the pope and the prince everywhere one looked. That same spring, apparently seeking to counterbalance Frederick's growing influence over the Tyrhennian Sea, Gregory had signed an agreement with the Genoese, who had recently been denounced by Frederick as rebels against the empire.[62] The local chronicler Bartholomew the Scribe describes how the citizens of the commune angrily rejected Frederick's demands for fealty during a public assembly after the emperor's envoys read a letter stating his demands aloud. The Genoese sent two ambassadors to Rome in a well-armed galley to meet with Gregory, who took Genoa under the "special protection" of the Apostolic See. In the presence of the pope and joined by envoys from the formerly imperial city of Venice, the Genoese and Venetians confirmed a new peace between the two naval superpowers. Although not stated explicitly, this alliance set them squarely against Frederick and close to the orbit of the papal curia.[63] By this time, Gregory may have heard the rumors that Frederick's illegitimate son, Enzio, was planning to marry Adelasia of Torres, the widowed wife of the lord of Sardinia. From the papacy's perspective, the island pertained to the "special right" of Saint Peter's patrimony and was part of the Papal States. The pope called upon Adelasia to marry someone faithful to the Apostolic See. In October, however, she married Enzio, who assumed the provocative title of king of Sardinia.[64]

Gregory's widely publicized plans for a new crusade likewise began to expose divisions rather than concord between church and empire. As the end of Frederick's truce with al-Kamil drew near, Gregory and the emperor remained committed to the crusade, but they increasingly diverged about how to realize that goal. For the pope, the crusade provided the impetus for peace in Lombardy, as well as the rest of Christendom, binding the emperor to the promises he had made to the Roman church. For Frederick, pacifying Lombardy by force represented the first step toward a successful crusade, which would enable him to bring the riches of northern Italy to bear on the next campaign overseas, one he might even lead himself if he could secure his rule at home. Under these circumstances, the rapidly approaching deadline for the expedition became something of a moving target. In the fall of 1237, the pope had announced his plans for the crusaders to depart by the Feast of John the Baptist in June 1238. Frederick, however, sent letters to Richard of Cornwall and another group of crusaders gathering near Lyons asking them to delay the expedition for one more year, until the end of his ten-year truce with al-Kamil.[65] He also encouraged such crusaders to pass through the Regno en route to Syria, so he might better assist them and provide them with supplies. Gregory, who found himself in the difficult position of ordering crusaders *not* to leave until the authorized time of departure, agreed to the extension of the deadline but wanted to make sure that the emperor would honor his commitments to the crusaders the following year. The pope's plan to redirect some of the crusaders to Greece cast further uncertainty over the upcoming expedition. In a series of letters sent to Frederick in March 1238, Gregory called upon him to support sending an army against the "disobedient" and "heretical" Greeks. The fact that Frederick maintained relatively close diplomatic ties to the Byzantine emperor-in-exile John Vatatzes, the target of that crusading force, went unmentioned, although the pope did mention the emperor's unspecified "objections" to the planned diversion.[66]

Meanwhile, the war in northern Italy continued. In July 1238, Frederick committed his forces to an all-out assault on Brescia. Chroniclers close to the action and at a distance described the emperor's "international coalition" of forces: soldiers from around the empire, including troops from Germany, Lombardy, Apulia, and Provence, and also English, Greek, and Saracen fighters. Even by the standards of war-torn Lombardy, the siege displayed moments of exceptional violence, such as when Frederick ordered the construction of a large scaffold in sight of the city walls and hanged his Brescian prisoners where their friends could see them. The besieged citizens tied their own imperial captives to the walls, where the stones thrown by siege-engines would strike them. Franciscan friars played a notable role inside the city during the siege, carrying water to its defenders and aiding the wounded.[67]

By this time, Christians around Europe could not ignore the worsening violence in Italy and its impact on relations between the pope and emperor. Albert of Stade describes how the "pope and emperor began to fall out somewhat, for the pope favored the Lombards, and the emperor planned to assault them."[68] Gregory's biographer remembered this period as a time when Frederick's animosity against the Roman church, which had been hidden for a long while, finally burst into the open again, as revealed his many crimes against the pope and cardinals.[69] In his *Major Chronicle*, Matthew Paris transcribes a letter supposedly sent by John de Colonna, cardinal priest of Santa Prassede, to Otto of San Nichola in Carcere Tulliano, currently acting as Gregory's legate in England. John lamented the conditions of the Roman church that had leapt into the "wolf's jaws": losing her liberty; falling into servitude, imprisonment, and confusion; losing her tranquility; and falling into a "state of desolation" that John could not amend despite his best efforts. Otto was lucky to be in a faraway land, so that he did not have to see his friends' suffering. The cardinal bishop of Sabina had recently died, while the cardinals sent by the pope as envoys to Lombardy, that "land in dissension from its prince," had returned after accomplishing nothing, leaving behind no "footprints of peace" and having been defeated by the "followers of discord." Faced with these "rising tides of scandals and many storms," John told Otto that he should make himself ready to return to the papal curia to aid their "mother" in her time of need.[70]

In October, Frederick ended the siege of Brescia, unable to break through its defenses, the first meaningful military failure he faced in Lombardy since his declaration of war two years earlier. Later that month, perhaps sensing an opening after the emperor's setback, Gregory arranged for a delegation of German and Italian prelates to appear before Frederick at Cremona bearing papal letters that included a detailed list of "certain articles" against the emperor.[71] As the *Royal Chronicle of Cologne* described the scene, "The pope sent numerous bishops as admonishers to the emperor, so that he might desist from injuring churches, especially the Roman church."[72] The prelates, writing back to the pope, told him how they obediently followed his instructions, presenting the charges before a gathering at imperial court that included themselves, the abbot of San Vincenzo, and a number Dominicans and Franciscans. The list echoed specific grievances and the overall tone found in Gregory's accusations against the emperor two years earlier. Frederick had despoiled monasteries, had destroyed churches and prevented their repair, had failed to restore properties unjustly taken from the military orders (as stipulated by the Treaty of San Germano), had imposed talliages upon clergy (allowing some to be imprisoned or slain), had kept church offices vacant, and had seized goods and lands from papal allies during the War of the Keys, likewise contravening the peace struck at San Germano. Other accusations focused on specific people, including a missing Tunisian prince, who had been detained somewhere in Apulia en route to Rome seeking baptism; Peter Saracen, an envoy of King Henry III, likewise imprisoned while coming to the curia; and James of Palestrina, whom the emperor ordered to be arrested.[73] Gregory also charged Frederick with arousing sedition against the pope in Rome and impeding aid to the Holy Land by refusing to make peace in Lombardy, despite the best efforts of the church and the Lombards to reach some sort of reconciliation with him.[74]

The bishops read the church's complaints aloud to the emperor and provided him with copies of the pope's letters. He replied point by point to the accusations, recording the responses, which the prelates present forwarded to Gregory.[75] Frederick's defense involved a mixture of pleading ignorance (for example, he denied knowing anything about the despoiling of certain monasteries and churches, although he had appointed a special envoy to look into the matter), careful qualifications (he imposed tallages upon clergy not for ecclesiastical properties or things but for feudal and patrimonial holdings), and outright denial (he wanted vacant churches to be filled, keeping in mind the traditional rights and dignities owed to him over appointments). He likewise denied abusing former papal supporters in the Regno. He countered that the pope had violated the peace of San Germano by retaining the town of Castellana and taking payments from its citizens, even as Frederick helped Gregory in his conflict with the Romans at great expense to himself. He had not incited the Romans against the pope, although he did stand by some of his loyal subjects in the city when they faced troubles at the hands of their enemies. Nor had he ordered James of Palestrina seized, although he rightly could have, since James preached rebellion against him in Lombardy. He had no idea about the location of the missing Tunisian prince, who had fled northern Africa out of fear for his life, not because he wanted to be baptized. Sometimes the emperor admitted to doing what the pope said, such as imprisoning Peter Saracen, his enemy and not a genuine envoy. As for the situation in Lombardy and the ongoing effort to aid the Holy Land, Frederick turned the tables on Gregory, accusing him of bad faith in their previous dealings over the matter, and of contradicting himself, as revealed by a comparison of his promises and his previous letters. Frederick, to the contrary, had made his commitment to the crusade under the church's direction quite clear in letters sent to "all the kings of the world" and the assembling crusaders themselves.

As this exchange makes clear, the pope and emperor were not just feuding between themselves, but were also performing for wider audiences, anticipating what now seemed to be an imminent and public break between them. As the *Royal Chronicle of Cologne* observes, copies of Frederick's response to the pope's list of charges were "sent and heard throughout Germany." Frederick later sent versions of the charges and his replies to England.[76] After years of exchanging letters and legates, negotiating for peace in the war-torn region of northern Italy, and accusing each other of bad faith in their dealings while holding out hope for renewed harmony between the two powers, the prince and the pope had begun to talk past each other, more interested in broadcasting the legitimacy of their respective grievances than solving them and inscribing them into the public record before the imperial court and papal curia, their immediate supporters, and ultimately the entirety of Christendom.

In February 1239, Frederick recommitted to his war against the Lombard League, issuing an edict against the "traitors" to the empire that forbade his faithful subjects from making any agreements with such parties, from receiving their letters or envoys or pledges, and from selling them weapons and horses. Anyone who might violate this ban was threatened with infamy.[77] A month later, even as yet another round of envoys and legates moved back and forth between them, the emperor recognized the likelihood that the pope planned to censure him formally, most likely on Maundy Thursday. In early March, Frederick sent the letter *Cum Christus sit* to the college of cardinals, stressing his rightful authority and expressing his amazement that the pope had acted so openly against him. He called upon the cardinals to "avoid a scandal" in the church and to restrain the Roman pontiff so as to prevent the emperor's private vengeance against the pope from spilling over and damaging the Apostolic See. Frederick carefully emphasized his piety and devotion toward the Roman church, insisting that he rejected Gregory as an unworthy occupant of the papal office, who was wielding the "spiritual sword" for all the wrong reasons, while making it clear that he did not question the spiritual authority of the papal office. This letter would later provide Gregory with considerable ammunition against the emperor and would be spun by him as revealing Frederick's true bloodthirsty nature.[78]

~

While news of the worsening relations between church and empire spread around Europe, Christians faced an unexpected source of terror as they began to hear wild rumors about strange barbarians destroying the lands of believers and nonbelievers alike in the east. The threat posed by those invaders, the Mongols, was quite real. At the time, medieval Europeans knew little for certain about them, except what they learned from confused reports, prophecies, and stories, some dating back to the time of the Fifth Crusade if not earlier. In his *Major Chronicle*, Matthew Paris shares such materials, first mentioning the Tartars in 1238. According to him, Saracen envoys who came to the French and English courts described how a "monstrous and inhuman race of men," impious, inexorable, and speaking an unknown language, had burst forth from the eastern borders, led by their ruler named "Caan." The Saracens sought aid against them from the Christians. Matthew and other chroniclers speculated about the barbarians' origins and intentions, theorizing that they might be Jews from the ten lost tribes of Israel, who had abandoned the Mosaic law and Hebrew language. *The Deeds of the Bishops of Trier* introduces the Tartars in apocalyptic terms, indicating that they would dominate the world for "eight weeks of the world, that is, fifty-six years, and do many wicked things." The author of this historical work also relates that a number of Jews believed the Tartars' arrival to be a sign of their messiah's coming and their freedom from bondage under the Gentiles, leading to the suspicion that they were somehow assisting the pagans.[79]

As Matthew's *Major Chronicle* and his *History of the English* brought their coverage of the year 1238 to a close, all sorts of sensational news and disturbing rumors seemed to be circulating around Christendom. Matthew writes that the Milanese again made proposals for their submission to the emperor, offering him copious amounts of money and troops for the imminent crusade and proposing to burn the city's military banners as a symbol of their submission. But Frederick refused, unwilling to accept anything less than their unconditional surrender, thereby making him look like a tyrant compared to the reasonable Milanese. Frederick's reputation suffered as stories spread about his penchant for Saracen dancing girls along with graver accusations that he refused the sacrament of the altar and blasphemed Christ, lumping him together with Moses and Muhammad as a charlatan. His enemies said such things to darken his name. It remained unclear, Matthew observed, whether they sinned or not by doing so.[80] The "spreaders of lies" had been busy. If there were people hoping for a rupture between the two powers, they were about to get their wish.

Chapter 4

Christendom in Crisis

On Palm Sunday in 1239, before a gathering of cardinals and other clergy in the Lateran basilica, Gregory IX anathematized Frederick II for the second time. The pope's anonymous biographer describes the pronouncement of the emperor's ban like the severing of a "putrid limb" from the body of the faithful. The emperor, Gregory explained in the sentence of excommunication, had aroused sedition in Rome, trying to expel the pope and cardinals from the city. He had prevented the papal legate and cardinal bishop James of Palestrina from fulfilling his mission to combat heresy in Provence. He had trampled the liberty of the church, refusing to repair cathedrals and churches, imprisoning and killing clergy in his realms, imposing tallages and taxes upon clerical persons and properties, keeping ecclesiastical offices vacant, and physically destroying sacred buildings. In addition, violating the terms of the peace he made with the pope after his first excommunication, Frederick had occupied lands that rightfully belonged to the Roman church and its vassals, despoiling the Templars and Hospitallers while impeding the effort to free the Holy Land and defend the Latin Empire of Constantinople. For these reasons and more, the pope bound the unrepentant ruler with the chain of excommunication and anathema. As for the "clamor" made "throughout the entire world" that Frederick had deviated from the catholic faith, Gregory would look into such accusations in due course, following proper procedures.[1]

Scholars commonly view the pope's second excommunication of Frederick as a natural, inevitable extension of the first after their grudging and temporary truce.[2] To some extent, this second round of conflict did replay the circumstances of the first. As with the emperor's excommunication a dozen years earlier, news of the papal sentence circulated around Europe through papal letters, legates, and repeat performances of the ban in cathedrals and parish churches. Propaganda came out of the papal chancery attacking Frederick as nothing less than Antichrist, denouncing his past sins and crimes and ties to the infidels. The emperor again performatively rejected the papal anathema, while letters written in his name emerged from the imperial chancery denouncing Gregory's judgment and accusing him of violating his spiritual office. Guelf and Ghibelline forces battled on the Italian peninsula, as Pope Gregory tried to channel the wealth of local churches from places like England and France into the papacy's war effort and to support papal allies against the emperor and his loyalists.

By other measures, however, the public stakes in this new round of conflict between the two powers stood much higher than they had the first time that Gregory excommunicated Frederick: the tone of their polemics more apocalyptic, the mutual slander more intense, the fighting more widespread, and the financial consequences for the church even greater. At San Germano, the pope and emperor had committed themselves to peace after their initial confrontation over Frederick's crusading vow. Over the following years, the two powers had publicly realigned for the common good of Christendom. To explain their renewed discord, the pope and emperor began erasing that history of cooperation. Their peace, it turned out, had been a false one, filled with treachery and secret dealings. Years of worsening conflict over the situation in Lombardy and conditions in the Regno, among other points of contention, had exposed the truth that one of the two powers had acted in bad faith and violated the sacred trust of their office. Which one, of course, depended upon whom you asked. During the War of the Keys, Gregory and his representatives refrained from deploying the sign of the cross against Frederick or preaching a crusade against him. Starting in 1239, they showed no such restraint, as the papal war machine moved quickly into action. Unlike his first excommunication of the emperor, the pope immediately absolved Frederick's subjects from their oaths of fealty and passed a sentence of interdict wherever he went. More than anything else, Gregory's decision to summon a general council to meet at Rome and address this new crisis, something never planned or attempted during his first confrontation with Frederick, illustrated the pope's acknowledgment of the need for collective action on behalf of the Christian community in defense of the church.

Christendom stood divided, even as a new and terrible threat—the invading armies of the Mongols—created a sense of panic about nothing less than the possible destruction of the Christian religion. For those who knew where to look, that disorder became manifest in marvelous signs and prophecies, divine forms of communication: an eclipse around the time of Frederick's excommunication, signifying the emperor's darkening of the church that "illuminates humankind like the sun"; some dead whales washed ashore in England after tearing each other apart, an apparent sign of the "discord between the priesthood and the empire"; a prophecy mysteriously scrawled on the walls of the pope's bedchamber; a dragon-shaped apparition that flew across the skies near Cologne. Dangerous and dark times had befallen both church and empire, whose disunion seemed to place the entire Christian world in jeopardy.[3]

Anathema and Its Discontents

As with Frederick's first excommunication, publicizing the ban represented a major priority for the pope. Christendom had to be made aware of the papal judgment, and it could not be allowed to forget it. Regardless of its spiritual implications, the sentence would otherwise mean little in political and social terms. After the ceremony in the Lateran Church on Palm Sunday, Gregory immediately began signaling to wider audiences his reasons for anathematizing the emperor and his expectations for how the Christian community would observe that sentence. Based on the "evidence of the facts," his encyclicals *Apostolica sedes* and *Cum nuper in Fredericum* explained, nearly the "entire world" knew about the Apostolic See's past support for Frederick as a child, favors that he repaid with ingratitude, thus forcing the pope—unwillingly, on account of the emperor's sins—to pass judgment against him. *Apostolica sedes* reviewed the principal charges laid against the emperor by Gregory, who had no choice but to pass judgment against him and all those who rendered the emperor "counsel, aid, or favor," while absolving his vassals from the bonds of fidelity owed to their ruler "for as long as he remained bound by the chain of excommunication." *Cum nuper in Fredericum* additionally specified that crusaders, who typically enjoyed immunity from excommunication, would nevertheless incur excommunicate status if they rendered aid, military assistance above all, to Frederick. Any cities, fortresses, towns, or other places that the emperor visited should be placed under interdict, suspending the celebration of mass and sacraments "publicly or in secret" (*publice vel secreto*) for the duration of his stay. Following the formula from canon law, the pope called for the clerical recipients of his missives to "solemnly publicize and announce" (*solempniter publicare ac nuntiare*) the sentence on Sundays and feast days with ringing bells and lit candles. Prelates should make sure that this performance took place throughout their diocese.[4]

Contemporary history writers of all kinds memorialized this disturbing rupture between the two powers. Copies of the pope's announcements about Frederick's excommunication reached chroniclers such as Matthew Paris, Albert of Stade, and the author of the Ghibelline *Annals of Piacenza*, who added them to their histories, giving their readers some sense of how the news traveled. In his *Major Chronicle*, Matthew Paris describes how Gregory excommunicated the emperor in a "spirit of burning anger," inspiring terror in all those listening. Other English histories record that Frederick became "gravely infamous" throughout the world because of his excommunication, with many "clamoring" about his misdeeds. In his *Annals*, Albert of Stade likewise transcribes the pope's sentence of excommunication, observing that Gregory called upon archbishops and bishops everywhere to denounce Frederick. The Cistercian chronicler Albert of Trois-Fontaines describes the "seventeen clauses" issued against the emperor, including his blasphemy against the Christian law, while the *Annals of Saint Justina* state that Gregory "publicly" excommunicated Frederick, seeing that "his spirit was turned toward the oppression of the church and that he would subjugate Lombardy if he could." Others made observations about the pope's decision to "publicly" bind the emperor with the "chain of excommunication," about the letters he "sent into every province" announcing the anathema, and about the "pernicious discord" between the pope and emperor that struck "a not inconsiderable fear into all of the faithful."[5]

To spread the word of Frederick's excommunication, Gregory turned specifically to his legates already present in other parts of Europe or those newly dispatched from the curia for that purpose.[6] They received, carried, and passed along copies of the pope's letters and read the sentence aloud in churches, monasteries, royal courts, and other locations, trying to ensure conformity with papal instructions. Gregory could rely on such direct agents more consistently than clergy and monks in local communities. Publicly proclaiming the sentence of excommunication meant openly taking sides, and not everyone was eager to do so, for understandable reasons. Based on his past experiences, one imagines, Gregory did not disguise the fact that he anticipated possible breakdowns in his messaging or instructions, warning the recipients of his letters to "fulfill our mandate in such a way that you cannot be accused of any negligence whatsoever, so we shall not be forced to proceed against you otherwise."[7]

In England, the pope assigned Otto, cardinal deacon of San Nicola in Carcere Tulliano, the job of publicizing the ban against Frederick throughout the lands covered by his legation, including Scotland and Ireland. Matthew Paris tells us that Otto personally read the sentence of excommunication aloud at St. Paul's Cathedral following the pope's commands, a process repeated by others "throughout the diocese of London, and the entire kingdom." On another occasion, Otto announced the ban at Matthew's own monastery of Saint Albans during his return journey south from a visit to Scotland. He did so because the monks possessed a special privilege exempting them from pronouncing any such sentence. Not everyone was so fortunate. Matthew also relates the desperate appearance of some monks from Monte Cassino before the Roman curia, where they informed the pope that Frederick had expelled them from their house because they had repeated the sentence against him, as required. Replying only that "your obedience will be your salvation," Gregory sent them away empty-handed.[8]

Albert of Stade observes that the pope tried to stir up opposition against Frederick throughout Germany by calling upon archbishops and bishops in his letters to denounce the emperor.[9] Gregory charged his legate Albert Beiham, a canon from Passau, with announcing the ban and making sure that local prelates followed his commands to solemnly publicize the excommunication and observe the terms of the interdict.[10] Some prelates did follow papal commands, including the bishop of Bremen, who proceeded against Frederick "like a lion." Initially, Albert enjoyed support from a number of highly placed magnates in the region, including Frederick, duke of Austria; Otto II, duke of Bavaria; and Wenceslas, king of Bohemia. But the pope's envoy and others like him faced considerable resistance from other nobles and clergy. Albert of Stade writes that some German prelates begged Gregory to reconsider his decision, thereby avoiding a "scandal" for the church. Other bishops, like Siegfried of Regensburg, challenged Albert Beiham's right to enforce the sentence, demanding to see his written authorization from the pope. Others pleaded for more time to make such public announcements, stressing their imperiled positions in the middle of imperial territories, such as the bishop of Strasburg, who told Albert "day by day" that he would announce the emperor's ban as soon as he had enough support from other bishops. Some prelates threatened anyone bearing papal letters with excommunication, and one went so far as to trample "publicly" the pope's letters underfoot. Still others declared Albert's sentences of interdict and excommunication null and void.[11]

Pope Gregory sent James of Palestrina to seek support from Louis IX and his mother, Blanche. In his letters, reviewing all of the glorious service rendered in the past by the French crown to the Roman church, the pope asked for "counsel and aid" in defense of the catholic faith, denouncing Frederick's mendacious claims that Christ's vicar, the church, and its ministers—including the cardinal legate James—represented "capital enemies" of the empire. Gregory suggested that the struggle against Frederick, who schemed to overturn the church entirely, formed a more important Christian duty than the crusades to recover the Holy Land.[12] James of Palestrina apparently had another goal in France: that of pursuing the possibility that the imperial office might be transferred to the French ruler or his brother, Robert of Artois. If Gregory considered this possibility, he did not seem willing to make it widely known: not a single letter entered into his official register raises the subject. Behind the scenes, however, the pope apparently pursued the possibility. Matthew Paris, for example, includes a letter in his *Major Chronicle* that he attributes to Gregory and that had been read "solemnly and memorably" to Louis and his barons proposing this plan. Although reluctant to disregard the pope completely, the barons, evincing skepticism about papal attacks on the emperor's catholic faith and fearing his wrath if they opposed him, sent envoys to meet with Frederick at the imperial court. After the emperor assured them of his orthodox faith in Jesus Christ, the satisfied barons rejected any such scheme to transfer the imperial dignity to Gaul.[13] Apparently, Albert Beiham also broached the possibility of holding a new election with Otto II. If the magnates did not act, he suggested, the pope might transfer the imperial dignity to another king or nation. Supposedly Otto replied, "Would that he had already done that." Albert of Stade makes a similar observation about Gregory's plans to elevate a new ruler, claiming that the electors rejected such a plan, saying to the pope that "it is not your right to substitute an emperor, but only to crown the one elected by the princes." Whatever public support the pope expected from the German nobility, in the short term they more or less closed ranks around Frederick after his son Conrad marshalled their support during an assembly at Eger in June 1239.[14]

As the months passed after Gregory anathematized Frederick, the sentences of excommunication and interdict did not stop with the emperor. In Germany, Albert Beiham excommunicated scores of bishops and other clergy who refused to enforce and publicize the ban. In November 1239 the pope anathematized Frederick's son, Enzio, who had invaded the March of Ancona on his father's orders.[15] Gregory also excommunicated the former Franciscan minister general, Elias of Cortona, due to his ties with the excommunicate emperor. As recently as 1238, the pope had employed Elias as a go-between with the imperial court. Salimbene of Adam, whose own entry into the Franciscan order depended on Elias's intervention, describes him as "a special friend of both men, who thus made sense as a mediator between them."[16] On Pentecost 1239, however, after hearing complaints at the Franciscan general chapter meeting about the minister general's decadent behavior and poor management of the order, Gregory had removed him from his position. Elias soon joined Frederick's camp and began to make all sorts of accusations against the pope. Salimbene, who did not hide his disapproval of the disgraced friar, says that Elias accompanied Frederick everywhere, while still wearing his Franciscan habit, "causing a great scandal for the pope, the church, and his own order." Matthew Paris writes that Elias became a vocal critic of Gregory and accused him of assaulting the empire for his own greedy reasons, despising "prayers, masses, processions, and fasts," a source of comfort for those suffering oppression, while fraudulently appropriating money intended for the Holy Land. He also claimed that Gregory filled out dispensations as he pleased in his private chambers without consulting the cardinals and gave out blank documents with the papal seal already affixed to them so that his legates could fill them in as they pleased. Elias even took it upon himself to absolve people excommunicated by the pope, creating further "scandal in the church." Frederick later complained that, when the Franciscan friar approached Rome for a meeting with the pope on his behalf, Gregory treacherously planned to arrest him despite his letter of safe conduct from the emperor. Elias only escaped because he had sent some envoys ahead of him, who got wind of the pope's plan.[17]

The conditions created by interdict had their own indirect ripple effect, causing others to incur ecclesiastical censure due to their deliberate or unintentional transgression of the ban. All kinds of uncertainties resulted. In December the pope wrote to Berthold, patriarch of Aquileia, who had triggered his own excommunication by celebrating mass on Pentecost with the emperor, giving him the ceremonial "kiss of peace," and eating with him. Salimbene of Adam, who says that he knew Berthold well, describes the patriarch's attempt to avoid this conflict of interests when Frederick's messengers summoned him to celebrate mass: he had a barber come and bleed him and then protested to the emperor that he was too weak to attend the divine services. Frederick insisted, however, and Berthold finally obeyed his summons, fearful of arousing his anger. Gregory informed Berthold that he had authorized Peter, bishop of Castellano, to absolve the excommunicate patriarch, as soon as Berthold set out for Rome for a personal meeting with the pope. In a separate address to Peter, Gregory asked him to forward Berthold's letters, which bore the patriarch's seal, including a word-for-word version of the oath that the patriarch would take to make satisfaction for his sin. In July 1240, faced with a similar situation, the pope absolved the bishop of Saint-Vincent, who had incurred excommunication when he failed to stop mass as Frederick and others, including Berthold, his own bishop, entered his church.[18]

Much as he did during his first experience facing excommunication and interdict, Frederick immediately began damage control, trying to counter the papal sentence both close to hand and farther afield. The emperor was in Padua on Palm Sunday in 1239 and heard Easter mass there a week later. The notary and chronicler Roland of Padua describes the scene in his native city on that feast day, when the people began to "murmur" about news of the pope's judgment. The emperor called for an assembly in the city's main piazza. While he sat "serenely," the imperial judge and counselor Peter de Vinea, known for his education, erudition, and poetic skills, stood forth to "instruct and educate the people" about the benevolence and justice of Frederick's imperial reign, the greatest since Charlemagne ruled the world. He also shared with them the emperor's grief over the unjust sentence and his amazement that the other ministers of the church had consented to such an "incautious" judgment.[19]

Beyond his immediate orbit, Frederick sent out "excusatory" letters to the "princes of the world," explaining how the pope had falsely proceeded against him. As seen in Chapter 3, the emperor, anticipating the pope's ban, had begun this process even before Gregory actually excommunicated him, sending his letter *Cum sit Christus* to the cardinals. By design, the letter reached far wider audiences, as evident in the works of chroniclers like Albert of Stade and Matthew Paris, who added it to their histories alongside news of the emperor's excommunication.[20] Indeed, in his encyclical *Apostolica sedes,* Gregory warned others about the contents of *Cum sit Christus,* quoting the emperor's threat to take vengeance on the pope and his family. Frederick, he stated, thereby revealed "just how much devotion he shows for his mother, the Roman church, for the Roman pontiff and his brothers." Both the pope and emperor tried to convince the wider Christian community that the cardinals supported their position. Whenever he described his decision to excommunicate Frederick, the pope typically stressed that he did so with the "counsel of his brothers." Frederick protested that the majority of the cardinals—the "saner" part—opposed the pope's passing of the sentence against him. Only the cardinals from Lombardy had approved.[21]

Judging by the emperor's reaction to the publicizing of the ban in other parts of Europe, he took its harmful impact seriously. Writing to Henry III in October 1239, Frederick expressed his disappointment that the English king allowed Otto to publish the pope's "injurious" sentence throughout his kingdom. He made similar complaints in a letter sent to the English barons and other nobles in the realm. Matthew Paris writes that the king, showing his typical weakness where the papacy was concerned, responded to Frederick that he had little choice but to follow Gregory's wishes, due to his status as a papal vassal.[22] At Frederick's urging, the canons at the cathedral church of Passau eventually expelled Albert Beiham from their ranks, condemning him for his agitations against the emperor. The bishop of Salzburg even declared a crusade of sorts against the papal envoy. In other instances, the emperor took blunter measures to counter papal communications. Chroniclers took note of his efforts to seal off Rome: shutting up the pope and cardinals, so that they could "scarcely breathe," by closing off roads and seaways. According to the *Annals of St. Pantaleon*, these blockades forced James of Palestrina to put aside his habit and travel in disguise while journeying to France. Richard of San Germano writes that the cardinal bishop dressed like a pilgrim to escape detection.[23]

No doubt based on experience from his first excommunication, Frederick recognized that members of the mendicant orders represented important agents for conveying papal messages. Soon after his excommunication, he ordered any mendicants hailing from Lombardy to be expelled from the Regno, putting all others on notice not to "offend" the emperor. Eventually, Frederick simply ordered all the friars to leave. Over the following months, broader restrictions followed, including a ban on clerical travel to the Roman curia without express permission from the imperial justiciar. Frederick instructed his naval commander in Sicily to appoint trustworthy men to inspect boats entering the kingdom, interview their occupants, and compel them to swear that they did not bear missives against the empire or emperor. Any such communications discovered should be impounded; those concealing them should be hanged. Individuals bearing "letters of credence" should explain their provenance and purpose. If their confession indicated intentions to harm the prince, they should suffer capital punishment.[24] Crisscrossing the fraught lines between Guelf and Ghibelline territories in Italy, Salimbene describes how he began to write his own letters in code, fearful of their interception because he knew that imperial agents were executing people bearing missives against Frederick. Possessing the wrong letter in the wrong place and time had become a matter of life and death.[25]

The Battle for Public Memory

During the months after Gregory excommunicated Frederick, their circles turned again to the production of elaborate encyclicals written to attack and defame their opponents. Europe had never experienced a propaganda war of this intensity, not even during previous periods of public contention between popes and emperors dating back centuries. These epistles, more like what would now be called political pamphlets, had several purposes as shapers of public opinion. One was simply to defame. But the letters also relied upon a contemporary familiarity with the duties and prerogatives of the two powers to raise more sophisticated questions about the proper ordering of Christian governance and its violation. Beyond that, these polemics tried to rewrite the history of Gregory and Frederick's relations, especially the memory of their apparent, but in fact deceptive, cooperation during the period between the emperor's two excommunications.

This new round of polemical epistles started with Frederick's *Levate in circuitu* on 20 April 1239, followed by the apocalyptically charged *Ascendit de mari* on 1 July 1239, and the emperor's response, *In exordio nascentis*, which was issued later that July. Another round of letters circulated during the spring and summer of 1240, starting with the emperor's missive *Triplex doloris* on 16 March 1240 and *Collegerunt pontifices* in June 1240, quickly followed by the papal response, *Convenerunt in unum*.[26] Although Gregory and Frederick undoubtedly played a role in shaping and authorizing their contents, professionals at the papal curia and imperial chancery—such as Rainier of Viterbo, cardinal deacon of Santa Maria in Cosmedin, and the imperial judge, Peter de Vinea—had a hand in crafting these uncompromising communications.[27] Contemporaries certainly did not miss the dialogic, dueling nature of these widely publicized exchanges. Copied down in "letter books" memorializing these rhetorical battles, they later served as models for the art of letter writing.[28]

These encyclicals took a no-holds-barred approach to slandering the opposition, trading in emotive language and uncompromising imagery. *Ascendit de mari* stands out particularly, as it injects an apocalyptic intensity into the accusations against Frederick, blasting the emperor as the beast that "rises from the sea, full with the names of blasphemy, with the feet of a bear and the mouth of a lion" (Rev. 13:1–2). This letter symbolically defamed the emperor, associating him with the dragon "pouring forth the waters of persecution for the destruction of the church from his mouth, like a river," calling him the "staff of the impious" and the "hammer of every land, who is seeking to overturn the earth, to strike down kingdoms, and to turn the world into a desert." Frederick embraced his role as a "forerunner of Antichrist."[29] Responding to these apocalyptic charges, *In exordio nascentis* linked Gregory to the "red horse" of the Apocalypse (Rev. 6:4), which was given the power to "take peace from the earth," and called him the "father of discord, not mercy, of desolation, not consolation." The letter accuses him of creating a "scandal throughout the world" through his "deceitful and venomous writings" against Frederick, which were sent everywhere.[30] Striking a similar tone, *Collegerunt pontifices* denounced Gregory for misusing ecclesiastical wealth for his own gain, declaring, "The mother church weeps that the shepherd of the Lord's flock has become a rapacious wolf," while *Convenerunt in unum* attacked the emperor for his use of Muslim mercenaries. "What other Antichrist should we expect," the letter asks, "when he, Frederick, has already come, as revealed through his deeds, the author of every evil, stained by the vice of his every cruelty, invading Christ's patrimony and seeking to destroy it with the Saracen people"?[31]

While these epistolary attacks on the present occupants of the papal and imperial offices possess an ad hominem feel, they also targeted informed audiences who understood the rightful jurisdictions of the priesthood (*sacerdotium*) and secular rule (*regnum*). *In exordio nascentis* opens by declaring that God created the "sun and moon" in the beginning of all things, two lights, one greater and lesser but each with its respective "zone" in the sky. In a similar fashion, the Lord wished there to be "two kinds of rulership in the firmament of the earth, namely the priesthood and the empire," one for the care and the other for the defense of the church. In this way, both served to restrain sinful men, assuring "peace throughout the entire earth, beyond all limitations."[32] The emperor's polemics took aim at the pope's status as the Vicar of Christ, turning that pastoral title against the current pontiff by calling Gregory a "false vicar" (*falsus vicarius*) and calling out to him, "If you were a true vicar of Christ and successor to Peter, as you claim, you would not stray so utterly from the path of Christ and Peter." The pope had abused the "power of the keys" and misdirected his spiritual authority against a just and legitimate ruler. Remembering the harmonious relationship between Pope Sylvester and Constantine, who gave the church "whatever it possesses of liberty and honor today," *Collegerunt pontifices* casts Gregory as an unfit successor to Sylvester because he was treating Frederick poorly and unjustly.[33] Turning the tables on Frederick, papal letters denounced his failure to act as a proper emperor, which was evident in his dealings with Muslim rulers and use of Muslim mercenaries against Christians, his lack of commitment to the crusades, his past attacks on papal territories, and his abuse of church liberties. Responding to *Collegerunt pontifices*, *Convenerunt in unum* compares Frederick unfavorably to Constantine: while the latter honored the clergy, the former preyed upon them, abandoning his duties and leaving the empire bereft like a widow. The letter asks, "Surely you promised to act as the sword and shield of Christendom? But your sword is bloodied by shedding the blood of the catholic faith with a barbarous people."[34]

As Daniel Lord Smail observes about the "legal culture of publicity" in medieval Europe, "All facts worth knowing, especially legal facts, were public facts: known everywhere, at all times, and by all."[35] Exchanging accusations that each side had violated their respective offices, the pope and emperor invoked competing versions of recent events to support their position, publicizing their version of the facts about their relationship dating back to Frederick's boyhood, his rise to power, and Gregory's first excommunication of the emperor in 1227, through his expedition to Syria and ten-year truce with the Egyptian sultan, al-Kamil, followed by the troublesome situation in Lombardy, the rebellion by the Romans against Gregory, and the pope's efforts to support Frederick's rule in the crusader kingdom overseas. *Ascendit de mari* repeatedly accuses the emperor of lying about these events in his letters sent out to the wider public: of lying about his reasons for delaying his crusade; of lying that Gregory tried to oppose him while he campaigned overseas; and of lying that the pope's dealings with the Lombards were intended to undermine Frederick's imperial rights. The letters issued from imperial circles made similar charges against the pope, accusing him of operating deceitfully against Frederick, opposing his effort to liberate Jerusalem, invading the Regno while he went on crusade, undermining the emperor's officials in Acre and elsewhere overseas, and conspiring with the Lombard cities that opposed him.

Of course, the pope and emperor did not have to rely exclusively on living memory and verbal exchanges or on rumors and gossip to substantiate their public claims. Both the papal curia and the imperial chancery had archives at their disposal, which were some of the more sophisticated means of preserving official documents known in thirteenth-century Europe. After circulating widely, papal and imperial letters were retained in royal archives and monastic cartularies, and were inscribed into chronicles and other histories. The accessibility, publicity, and archiving of such texts opened up another arena of dispute between the pope and emperor over their communications in the past. Repeatedly, the letters written on Frederick's behalf referenced other letters: letters written by the pope that had been intercepted and retained by the emperor as "public testimony" of Gregory's double-dealing, whether sent to the sultan of Egypt (conspiring with him against Frederick), to his own legates (revealing promises he later failed to keep), or to the citizens of Castellano (whom the pope had encouraged to withdraw from their obedience to the emperor). When these "secretly sent letters," "hidden obstacles," and "furtive envoys" failed to accomplish their purpose, the pope moved against Frederick openly, eventually excommunicating him without consulting the majority of the cardinals. The epistles written on Gregory's behalf likewise highlighted Frederick's letters as evidence of his crimes and double-dealing, such as those that authorized Raynald of Urslingen to invade the papal patrimony in 1228, or the letters that recorded his promises to the pope at Rieti in 1234, which were preserved as evidence of his later treachery. In this regard, papal and imperial seals became especially important markers of authenticity, testifying to the genuine nature of damning letters.[36]

Throughout these exchanges, the pope's and emperor's letters self-referentially invoke their own importance as sources of information and shapers of public opinion. In its opening section, *Levate in circuitu* calls upon its readers to look around them and see the "general scandal of the world," as news of the emperor's justice and the pope's depravity came to the "public notice of the world." *Ascendit de mari* expressly responds to "lies" spread about the pope that had been made in "detestable letters" that the emperor had sent "into every corner of the world." By publicizing his views in this way, Frederick revealed that he no longer planned to operate in the shadows but rather was bringing his "works of darkness into the light." These included things that he said but did not dare to write down, such as his claim that Moses, Jesus, and Muhammad had deceived the entire world, or his heretical doubts about the virgin birth of Christ. In closing, *Ascendit de mari* called upon its recipients to prevent the emperor from spreading his "vicious lies" and "to explain faithfully all of the things written above to the people and clergy subject to you." *In exordio nascentis* responded in kind on the emperor's behalf, denouncing Gregory, who sent "papal letters filled with lies throughout every part of the world," making baseless accusations against Frederick's faith. Both sets of papal and imperial missives repeatedly accused the other party of creating a "public scandal" or "public disturbance," of being a "public enemy" or causing a "scandal throughout the world" by their actions, including the sending of mendacious letters everywhere.[37]

Reputations were on the line during these epistolary battles. Gregory's biographer, no doubt familiar with all of these exchanges, described how Frederick poured forth his "venomous cunning in public" through his letters to the cardinals and the citizens of Rome, calling attention to the "false batch of letters" he sent to the "ends of the earth," which showed his contempt for the "keys of the church." Matthew Paris likewise took note of how these letters circulated and the impression they made. "A murmur began among the people," he writes about Frederick's reputation, "that God might turn aside from such a prince, who made a pact with the Saracens a long while ago and proved more a friend to them than to Christians." Frederick's enemies tried to stoke such rumors, including the belief that he considered "Muhammad, as well as Jesus and Moses, to be imposters," deliberately trying to "darken his reputation." Whether they sinned or not by doing so, Matthew wondered, only God knew.[38] After transcribing a copy of *Levate in circuitu* into his chronicle, he describes how the emperor sent that letter "with different titles and a few words changed" to the king of England and many other rulers "throughout the world." Frederick's letter enraged the pope, who crafted a "longer letter"—*Ascendit de mari*—that he sent "to princes and prelates in every land" to render the emperor "damnable and infamous throughout the entire world."[39] After the pope sent this address "throughout the world, to many kings and princes and magnates, with the title changed, a great fear and horror and wonder struck the hearts of the faithful." Many started to doubt the contents of Frederick's previous letter. And yet, Matthew continues, the Roman curia's own reputation for avarice blunted the effectiveness of its messaging, otherwise the "entire world" might have turned against the emperor as a "foe of the church and enemy of Christ." People everywhere did not know what to think. After inscribing *Triplex doloris* into his chronicle, the Benedictine monk followed with the observation: "When these things were heard and known throughout the world, the pope's reputation and authority experienced a serious blow and turn for the worse. A scandal was born, as wise and holy men began greatly to fear for the honor of the church, the lord pope, and the clergy in general, afraid that the Lord might inflict an incurable wound upon his people in his extreme anger."[40]

The Papal War Machine

The rapidly escalating confrontation between the two powers did not remain one of just spiritual weapons and propaganda. Their confrontation quickly turned to one of armed force, once again requiring Gregory to leverage his priestly authority for the purpose of realizing military goals by communicating to Christians around Europe the legitimacy of taking up weapons against Frederick and calling upon them to provide material support for the endangered Roman church. Given his experience with previous campaigns in Italy, not to mention his nearly constant planning for crusades overseas, the pope knew well the necessary steps to plan for such military action: the letters summoning Christians to aid the Apostolic See in remission of their sins, the exhortatory sermons, and the calls for financial assistance, voluntary or otherwise. As before, these calls for Christians to fight on the papacy's behalf created public controversy over the lawfulness of such fighting and how to pay for it.[41]

After excommunicating the emperor in 1239, Gregory immediately put the papacy on a war footing. In his *Annals*, Albert of Stade tells us that Gregory raised up as many adversaries against the emperor as he could after he excommunicated him, calling for the "cross to be preached" against all of the Apostolic See's enemies in Germany. On the Italian peninsula, Gregory promised and renewed various papal privileges for cities and individuals that remained faithful to the Roman church, encouraging his secular allies, like Alberic da Romano and Azzo d'Este, to oppose the emperor and taking their persons and lands under the "special protection" of the Apostolic See. In Genoa, according to the civic chronicler Bartholomew the Scribe, the pope's envoys arrived in 1240 to "preach about taking up the cross against the rebels and enemies of the most holy church, approving by his authority the same remission of all sins for those assuming the cross as for those going beyond the sea for the recovery of the holy land."[42]

At Milan, the papal effort to invigorate Frederick's military enemies involved a particularly controversial figure, Gregory of Monte Longo.[43] First sent to Milan in April 1238, Gregory occupied a place on the front lines of the Lombard League's military conflict with the emperor. The *Annals of Piacenza* report that upon returning to Milan after Frederick's excommunication, Gregory signed citizens "with the cross" and raised up two banners bearing the papal symbols of "the cross and keys" that were similar to the standard carried by the papacy's allies in 1228 to 1230. The *Annals of Saint Justina* describe how the papal notary and legate strengthened the flagging resolve of the Milanese and inflamed them toward war against Frederick, throwing himself into the fight against the church's enemies personally. Starting in February 1240, Gregory of Monte Longo and Milanese troops joined the siege of Ferrara, working with a number of Guelf nobles and papal allies, including Azzo d'Este, Count Richard of St. Bonifacio, and Alberic da Romano, alongside Mantuan and Venetian forces. When Frederick's vassal Salinguerra finally surrendered, the legate joined the other leaders of the army during their victorious entry into the city.[44]

Salimbene of Adam, who met Gregory of Montelongo, presents him as a colorful figure, admiring him for his martial experience and courage, even if he had gout and problems remaining chaste. Quoting Ecclesiastes 3:8, "a time of war, a time of peace," he observes that the legate always knew "the proper time for battle and the proper time to cease battle." Gregory owned a book on the "subtle art of war," not to mention a talking crow. Matthew Paris, on the other hand, offers a far less flattering picture of the legate, informing his readers that Gregory's presence made the people of Milan that much more belligerent, leading them to attack and devastate imperial towns and cities—showing no mercy for the besieged, sparing only their lives and none of their property. Such atrocities made many "holy and religious men in Christian lands" wonder about the church's unprecedented use of the "material sword" to cause such misery. They feared God's wrath in particular since the "papal party" no longer seemed to value fasting, masses, and processions as a source of triumph over its oppressors, "placing all of its hope" instead upon the "treasure of coin and rapine."[45] Matthew's negative view of Gregory of Monte Longo no doubt owed a lot to the Benedictine monk's familiarity with Frederick's letters. In them, the emperor more than once expressed particular outrage toward the papal legate, first sent by the pope to Milan as a "simple notary" but who wielded extraordinary powers in opposition to the emperor. Pope Gregory appointed the legate at the head of a "veritable papal army" in Milan, where he dressed in armor, wore a sword like a soldier, and absolved people of their sins if they fought against Frederick. Through his warmongering, his slaughtering of men, his sieges of cities and more, this so-called priest created a "universal scandal" in the church. Regardless, the pope continued to defend his legate, insisting that he was sent to Lombardy to prevent the "slaughter of war" rather than cause it.[46]

In this battle for control of northern Italy, the pope also turned to Sinibaldo Fieschi, cardinal priest of San Lorenzo in Lucina, who had been appointed as rector in the March of Ancona years earlier. In the late spring of 1239, under the leadership of the local noble Paul Traversario, a group of citizens in Ravenna had revolted against Frederick's authority, expelling his supporters from the city and aligning themselves with Venice and Bologna. Although the details remain hazy, Sinibaldo was clearly involved. From the beginning of his communications with Ravenna's civic leaders, praising their opposition to Frederick in defense of the church, Gregory made sure to send copies of those letters to his rector in Ancona. The *Annals of St. Pantaleon* record that the pope actually sent "Swenebaldo" to Ravenna to work against the emperor.[47] Frederick later complained about the role of a "cardinal legate," identified in one copy of *Triplex doloris* as "S," who had encouraged Paul Traversario to revolt against him.[48] In July 1240, leveraging another kind of ecclesiastical power, Gregory wrote to Sinibaldo about his transferal of the cathedral see from Osimo, a town supporting the emperor, to the loyal commune of Recanti. Since Recanti had never enjoyed the episcopal dignity before, the pope gave Sinibaldo instructions to endow the town with sufficient properties to support the new bishop and cathedral chapter—some of them taken from Osimo as a further punishment.[49]

Gregory also relied on the Roman church's maritime allies, negotiating an agreement with the communal governments of Venice and Genoa in support of a planned naval campaign against Frederick's holdings in the Regno. In September 1239, acting through Robert Somercotes, cardinal deacon of Sant'Eustachio, the pope promised payments to arm twenty-five galleys and pay for their upkeep for up to six months, with three hundred soldiers and additional funds provided by the Venetians. The two communes also promised not make peace with Frederick without the church's approval, otherwise they would face excommunication and a fine of six thousand silver marks. This planned invasion fleet never materialized, perhaps due to lack of funds. In June 1240, Pope Gregory pressed his legate in Lombardy, Gregory of Monte Longo, to guarantee that the Milanese would make payments they owed to Venice for the galleys. Regardless, by bringing the potential for sea power into the mix, the papal alliance with Venice and Genoa further raised the military pressures aligned against Frederick on the Italian peninsula.[50]

As the war between church and empire heated up, it spilled over into other regions of Europe, fueling local conflicts and dynastic struggles in places like Flanders and Provence. In his *Major Chronicle*, Matthew Paris describes how Thomas, count of Flanders, enriched and emboldened after a visit to Henry III—

his nephew by marriage to Thomas's niece, Eleanor of Provence—attacked the bishop of Liege, one of Frederick's supporters. Eventually, facing Frederick's wrath, he called off his assaults.[51] In southern France, fighting broke out between Count Raymond Berengar of Provence, an "adherent" of the Roman church, and Raymond of Toulouse, who sided with Frederick. In November 1239, James of Palestrina, working through his deputy in Provence, the Bolognese archpriest Zöen, secured a public oath from Raymond Berengar to provide soldiers for the defense of the faithful against their adversaries. Wielding the "sword of ecclesiastical power," James also sought to pressure those who fought against Raymond Berengar along with John, archbishop of Arles, and other supporters of the church. According to Matthew Paris, the violence in the region started to cause problems between Frederick and Louis IX, Raymond Berengar's son-in-law, until the emperor convinced Louis that he was not responsible for any attacks on the king's subjects in the region. In July, Zöen excommunicated Raymond of Toulouse just two years after his apparent reconciliation with the Roman church. During a mass in Viviers called especially for that purpose and before a crowd of prelates, clergy, and lay people, Zöen charged him with assaulting Raymond Berengar and others after they had "received their crosses for the aid of the church against Frederick and his supporters."[52]

This multifront war on Frederick required far more money than the resources of the papal patrimony and other regular streams of revenue could possibly provide. In Provence, Pope Gregory authorized James of Palestrina—who was described by Frederick as a "rapacious wolf"—to share the revenues from a special subsidy with Raymond Berengar for the purposes of defending the church. James also allowed the count of Provence to retain any funds raised in the region by the commutation of crusade vows for cash.[53] Following the precedent set by the War of the Keys, the pope tried to raise funds for the fight against the emperor in England by passing a one-fifth tax on ecclesiastical and monastic properties and by the monetary commutation of crusader vows. Matthew Paris describes how Pope Gregory's legate Otto, joined by another papal envoy, Peter Rosso, and helped by members of the mendicant orders, took the lead in collecting these funds. During a gathering of bishops and abbots at Reading, Otto, explaining the necessity of the pope's mandate to all of those listening, delivered a sermon about the hardships and insults caused by Frederick against the Roman church. His reputation for raising money spread far afield, even coming to the notice of the *Annals of St. Pantaleon*.[54] Informed by his "spies," Frederick was well aware of Otto's fundraising efforts. In his letters to Henry III and the English barons, the emperor expressed indignation that the king had allowed Otto and other papal representatives to gather such funds from the "treasure of the king, the goods of clerics, the tallages of churches," which the pope funneled into the hands of the Milanese and other rebels against the emperor's rightful rule. Frederick asked

Henry to expel Otto from his kingdom, something the English king declined to do, replying to Frederick's envoy Hugh Chalbaot that, being a vassal of the pope, he had little choice but to obey Gregory's commands.[55]

Although Matthew tells us that the archbishop of Canterbury consented to the one-fifth tax, in a replay of 1228 some of the English clergy strongly objected to Gregory's latest fiscal demands. During assemblies at Northampton and in Berkshire, they raised a number of complaints about the proposed use of the subsidies to spill Christian blood and make war on the emperor, an ally of their king, including the fact that Frederick—while admittedly excommunicate—had not been convicted of heresy by ecclesiastical judgment. They also pointed out that the Roman church possessed its own patrimony and resources, which should suffice for its defense. Churches elsewhere belonged to the lord pope in terms of their "care and solicitude," not their "dominion and proprietorship," meaning that Gregory did not have the right to make such demands. Above all, money intended for the relief of the poor should not be turned to such improper ends. Such exactions, the bishops and abbots declared, created a "scandal spread about throughout the entire world," and must be rejected. Even simple-minded people, Matthew observes elsewhere in his *Major Chronicle,* found all of the Roman curia's moneymaking schemes absurd; they were merely fleecing the faithful for silver and gold. Eventually, by getting the king on his side and undermining the protesters by offering some of them promotions and greater dignities, Otto broke their resistance.[56]

During their meeting at Berkshire, the prelates and abbots highlighted, among their other complaints, another dilemma caused by the pope's financial demands, pointing out that crusaders heading for the Holy Land could not afford to fulfill their financial obligations for that "arduous business" and contribute to the pope's subsidy at the same time.[57] This tension between two papal projects, the crusade overseas and the war on Frederick, became particularly pronounced, and not just in England. After years of preparing for the Baron's Crusade, whether bound for Syria or Constantinople, Gregory suddenly confronted the possibility that crusader forces in places like England or the army assembled at Lyons under Theobald of Navarre and Henry of Champagne might be diverted into the fight with Frederick—but on the wrong side. Rumors and confusion swirled around the crusader forces and the plans for their departure. Matthew Paris explains that Gregory sent instructions to his legate Otto asking him to make sure the crusaders stayed put in England, reversing his earlier calls for them to depart that spring. If they insisted upon leaving, they would not enjoy the "indulgence of their sins" promised to them. Later that year, a group of crusaders gathered at Northampton to accompany Richard of Cornwall to Syria swore to leave on schedule despite the pope's change of plans, stressing their stated intention to fight only in the holy places, not to "shed Christian blood" in Greece fighting in defense of the Latin empire of Constantinople, nor in Italy battling the emperor.[58]

Matthew further relates that Gregory likewise commanded the crusaders gathered at Lyons to remain there or even to return to their own homes. The papal envoy sent to the army produced written authorization from the pope confirming these instructions. Given the pope's complaints elsewhere about crusaders "taking off their crosses" and refusing to fulfill sworn vows, it seems unlikely that Gregory tried to disband the army at Lyons, although its disposition plainly concerned him.[59] Regardless, the way that Matthew Paris tells things, the crusaders at Lyons reacted with great indignation to the proposed delay, railing against the pope for encouraging them to take up the cross, setting a date for their departure, and now trying stop the expedition when it had gathered its supplies and was ready to set out.[60] Frederick sent his own communications to the crusaders at Lyons. Writing to them in July 1239, he proclaimed his desire to lead them personally in support of their "noble vow," while complaining about the fact that the pope's support for the Lombard rebels left him unable to do so. Gregory, who should foster peace and facilitate the business of the cross, instead fed "the flames of a public disturbance and scandal," raising up "public hatred" against Frederick. Corresponding with the crusaders, the emperor did not ask them to delay their departure, but he did ask them to pass through his territories en route to their destination—precisely the sort of scenario that Gregory seemed to fear. Trying to stay out of the entire mess, most of the crusaders departed from ports in Provence by late summer. In a letter sent to Theobald in January 1240, soon after the count landed at Acre, the emperor continued his complaints about the pope, who "preaches scandal instead of peace" and who created a "public scandal" that prevented Frederick from joining Theobald on the crusade.[61]

Later that same month, the emperor brought the war right to Gregory's doorstep, moving his forces to the vicinity of Rome. Some of the Romans apparently welcomed his arrival, crying out, "Let the emperor come! Let him receive the City!" In response, on 22 February, the feast day celebrating Saint Peter's position as the bishop of Rome, Gregory led a procession bearing relics of Peter and Paul along with a piece of the True Cross to the basilica of Saint Peter, accompanied by the cardinals and other prelates, and a crowd of citizens. In his letter *Attendite ad petram*, which describes the procession, Gregory insisted that he could have relied upon his military allies to oppose Frederick, who tried to turn the Romans against their mother church, seeking to subject the see of Peter to "gentile rites" and desiring to "seat himself in the Temple of the Lord" and "usurp the office of the priesthood." Rather than calling upon the "temporal sword," however, the pope relied upon divine justice, bearing the relics of the saints with honor before the gathered Romans. He described the remarkable effects: promised a "general indulgence," the people received the "sign of the cross" from the pontiff's own hands and took up arms to defend their city, men and women alike, young and old. Thus fortified by the "armor of the catholic faith," they opposed the "true

Antichrist." The pope's biographer reports that the emperor ordered anyone caught bearing such a cross to be mutilated. One priest, who refused to remove the sign, was burned alive. In his subsequent letters, Frederick tried to dismiss the pope's actions, declaring that Gregory had only prevailed upon some boys, old women, and a few mercenaries to "take up the cross" against him. Regardless, he soon withdrew from the vicinity, realizing that the siege would not be successful. If the crusading spirit did come to Rome, it had arrived just in the nick of time for the beleaguered pope.[62]

The Call for a Council

As the sensational conflict between the pope and the emperor continued to shock Christians on all sides, certain groups and individuals continued to hope for some form of reconciliation between the two powers. Historians fixated on the notion of relentless antagonism between the church and empire often seem to forget or overlook such contemporary voices of moderation, which recognized the devastating impact of that conflict on their community. One solution to the division in Christendom started to emerge before all others: the calling of a general council to deliberate over the best course of action for the Christian community. Plans for such an assembly, however, quickly became a new source of tension between the pope and the emperor, as questions emerged about the legitimacy of such a council and whom it might favor.

Impulses for peace came from all sides. In September 1239, a group of German prelates wrote to the pope, opening their appeal for peace with a reference to the "two swords"—the foundation of the "church militant"—noting that one could not be weakened or destroyed without causing harm to the other. Stressing their devotion to the Roman church and acknowledging the legitimacy of at least some of Frederick's grievances, they called upon the pope to "take heed of general good and public cause by reforming the peace," offering to help in any way that they could. Writing to the pope a few months later, Ferdinand, king of Castile, asked Gregory's permission to send his envoy, the abbot of Saint Facundus, to the imperial court as a negotiator for peace. In late spring 1240, another group of German clergy and magnates wrote to Gregory complaining about the present discord, stressing their fidelity to the Roman church but calling upon the pope to grant an audience to Conrad, the new master general of the Hospitallers, who had been sent to the curia with their proposals for peace. The fight between the pope and Frederick, they declared, represented the devil's work, causing treacherous plots, wars, murder, and other ills, not to mention impeding the Christian effort to recover Jerusalem.[63]

Those dangers to Christendom seemed to be escalating. By that time, news had reached Europe about a disastrous crusader defeat at Gaza in Palestine, when

Egyptian forces routed an ill-advised raiding party led by members of the Baron's Crusade. In letters sent back to friends and family at home, witnesses and survivors described the slaughter, including the loss of lives, horses, and supplies and the capture of numerous Christian nobles.[64] Frederick sensed an advantage. In his letter *Communem causum*, written in April 1240, he stressed how, through his "frequent letters and solemn envoys," he had advised the crusaders to delay their departure until he or his son Conrad could take command of the forces after Frederick had settled the "difficult business of the empire" in Italy. The pope, however, heedless of the consequences, had instructed them to set out immediately, ignoring the emperor's concerns. "This Roman priest," Frederick stated, "out of hatred for us, holding all these things in contempt and driving everything toward ruin, more insistently compelled the crusaders to make their passage." When he realized Gregory's intention, the emperor had encouraged the crusaders at least to pass through his lands so that he might better assist them. Now, after their horrible losses, he grieved for the "ignominy of Christendom and the mediator of mankind, Jesus Christ." The emperor declared in closing that he had written to the Muslim leaders holding the crusaders captured at Gaza, threatening swift vengeance if they mistreated the prisoners. Here it becomes evident how Frederick tried to turn his diplomatic ties with Saracens from a liability to a benefit: if the deceased Egyptian ruler al-Kamil had still lived, the emperor wrote, he would have freed the captives out of his affection for Frederick's person. The emperor still planned to pursue their release with the sultan's son. According to Matthew Paris, this letter restored the flagging confidence of Frederick's allies, as did the menacing letters that he sent to the sultans of Damascus and Egypt promising retribution if they mistreated their Christian captives.[65]

Meanwhile, wild stories about the "Tartars" continued to spread about Europe, as did the sense of an existential threat they posed to the Christian kingdoms of the West. The latest news of the invaders reached the papal curia in letters sent from the Christian queen of Georgia that begged for help against the barbarians despite her recent victory over their forces. Responding in January 1240 and expressing his regrets, the pope informed her that help—an "army of the Roman church"—was not on the way. Too many infidels lay between their lands, he observed, while the Roman church struggled to defend itself in Italy, Spain, and Syria.[66] In his *Major Chronicle*, Matthew Paris relates a particularly disturbing rumor shared by some people, who said that Frederick was actually conspiring with the Tartars, like Antichrist or Lucifer, in a desire to possess "monarchy over the entire world." But God forbid, Matthew editorialized, that "so much wickedness to reside in any one mortal body."[67]

For those seeking peace between the two powers, the challenge that remained was how to break the apparent impasse between the pope and emperor. From the moment of his ban, Frederick had offered one solution to the problem: to bring his grievances against Gregory before the cardinals, the "hinges of the church," and some "future Roman pontiff, a general council, the princes of Germany and more generally the kings of the entire earth and other Christians."[68] Matthew Paris makes the claim that the cardinals as a whole were no longer willing to tolerate the pope's attacks on Frederick, which placed "all of Christendom in danger," and agreed to a general council with the emperor's consent. This scenario seems unlikely, given the long-standing canonistic acknowledgment that only the pope could summon such an ecumenical assembly.[69] By the summer of 1240, rumors had indeed begun to circulate about a truce between the pope and emperor, a cessation of hostilities until a general council might meet at Easter the following year. Following these developments, Matthew also tells us that James of Palestrina denounced Gregory's truce with the emperor, begging the pope to continue the war. Changing his mind, Gregory told John de Colonna—who had helped to broker the agreement in the first place—to inform Frederick that he would no longer observe any such truce. John objected stridently, complaining to the point that Gregory declared, "I won't have you as a cardinal anymore." John replied, "I won't have you as pope," before storming off, the two friends becoming enemies. Richard of San Germano likewise records that the cardinal priest began to side with the emperor and seized control of several castles in the vicinity of Rome "out of hatred for the pope."[70] Based on a letter from the pope to Raymond Berengar, James of Palestrina had nothing to worry about: Gregory told the count of Provence not to believe any stories that he might hear about "secret peace talks" between him and Frederick.[71]

Plans for a general council to meet at Rome on the following Easter, however, turned out to be quite real. Matters of this magnitude for the Christian community made the calling of such an assembly by the pope, who sought consent, counsel, and consensus, a logical next step. As the legal aphorism from the canonistic tradition put it, "That which concerns everyone, ought to be discussed and approved by everyone."[72] In his first call for the council, which was dispatched to hundreds of recipients on 9 August, Gregory emphasized the dire necessity for such a gathering, which would be a source of solace and support for the Roman pontiff. "Eternal providence," he declared, desiring to safeguard the church, had ordained that its one head and pastor possessing the "fullness of power" (*plenitudo potestatis*) remain in communion with the other pastors who possessed a "part of the care" (*pars sollicitudinis*) for the governance of the faithful.[73] In the pope's presence, bishops or their proctors might provide counsel for the "ship of Saint Peter," which was threatened by stormy waters. Although he referred in some versions of this encyclical to the "disturbances of the world," the pope made no explicit mention of Frederick. He did not have to. Everyone involved would have realized the main reason for the gathering, even though Gregory did not spell out his precise intentions—

whether he planned to pressure Frederick into some sort of settlement or depose him from office.[74]

As the summer passed, the announcement of this general council created more, not less, controversy. Frederick soon reversed course and declared his opposition to such an assembly. Complaining about the pope's persistent violence and support for the Lombard rebels when writing to Henry III in September 1240, the emperor insisted that Gregory's planned assembly was nothing more than a trap. He wrote a similar letter to King Louis IX of France and to the Dominican minister general at Paris, warning the friars against circulating the pope's letters. The emperor insisted that Gregory had selectively invited sympathetic prelates and nobles to the gathering, including his enemies Alberic da Romano, the Venetian doge, and the marquis d'Este, among others. While preparations for the council went forward, the pope continued to amass funds for his war chest, revealing his true intentions. Gregory also insisted that the Lombards be included in their truce until next Easter, secretly giving them time to act against the emperor. "So, you can see plainly before your eyes," the emperor wrote, that the pope "calls this council more for discord than peace." That same fall, an unknown author penned an open letter addressed to the English and French clergy, warning them against the dangers of sea travel. Frederick controlled the ports near to Rome, and even if the clerics did reach the city, they would find a scorpion pit of corruption and treachery. The upcoming council really had only one purpose: destroying Frederick. Why should they bear that burden for the pope?[75]

Heading into the new year, Frederick repeated instructions for his followers to close the roads and sea-lanes to Rome, telling them to seize any clergy heading to the council and confiscate their possessions, especially monies intended for the Lombard rebels.[76] Aware of these threats, Gregory nevertheless moved forward with his plans, repeating his general summons for prelates and lay envoys to attend the assembly even though he knew about the emperor's orders to close off access to Rome.[77] Successfully organizing such an assembly under wartime conditions presented particular challenges with regard to communication, logistics, and finances. First, the pope expected his cardinal legates and other representatives around Europe to return to Rome, bringing with them recently accrued revenues from exactions, fees, and specific subsidies intended to fund the military opposition to Frederick. Matthew Paris describes the legate Otto's departure from England bearing immense wealth plundered from the English church, wealth that—as the Benedictine monks observed with some foreshadowing—he would later lose to Frederick. Other prelates from England set out for the council, Matthew observes with another bit of anticipation, although some decided to hole up in France before proceeding any further. Over the following months, Gregory also recalled Gregory of Monte Longo from Lombardy and Sinibaldo

Fieschi from Ancona.[78] Realizing that overland transit through Lombardy had become next to impossible, the pope began to coordinate with the Genoese his plans for transporting the prelates, abbots, other clergy, proctors, and lay envoys. Writing to Gregory da Romano, a papal chaplain and Gregory's legate to Genoa, the pope instructed him to commission a fleet of ships and galleys to bring the council's attendees to Rome. The passage money for the ships, the pope cautioned, should be raised "cautiously" and "secretly" to prevent Frederick's agents or allies from hearing about the preparations. In a series of follow-up letters, he gave further instructions for his envoys to receive a "secret oath" from the podesta to keep these preparations hidden. Raising money for this fleet represented an immense financial burden that required the pope to borrow large sums of money from various Italian mercantile creditors for the "defense of the church and ecclesiastical liberty." Gregory also relied on James of Palestrina to transfer funds raised in France to Genoa as down payment for the fleet.[79]

The Genoese chronicler known as Bartholomew the Scribe provides an insider's view of these negotiations and the tensions that they provoked in a city whose communal government backed the pope, while some of its citizens continued to favor the emperor. While Gregory de Romano negotiated for the construction of the fleet, the podesta William Surdus and other representatives of the commune faced constant challenges to their agreement with Gregory's legate. First, a number of Pisan envoys came to the city, threatening the Genoese with disaster if they followed through on the plan to transport the prelates and others to the council, but the Genoese refused to back down, declaring their fidelity to the Roman church. Next, a group of Ghibelline citizens "publicly" challenged the commune's arrangement. Someone also found secret letters, which had been smuggled into Genoa sealed in a loaf of bread, sent from Frederick to his supporters inside the city. To avoid a scandal and possibly disrupting the transportation of the clergy, the leading men of the civic government convinced the podesta to keep these missives secret until after the fleet took the prelates to Rome. William Surdus agreed, Bartholomew writes, although ongoing trouble with the city's dissident factions later forced his hand, leading him to read the one of the letters aloud and indicate its intended recipients. During the ensuing months, fighting broke out around the city and its surroundings while the preparation of the fleet continued apace.[80]

By March 1241, a number of highly placed prelates en route to Genoa had gathered at Lyons, including the cardinals James and Otto, joined by Robert, patriarch of Jerusalem, and a number of prominent bishops and abbots. From there, they made their way to Nice, where Genoese ships picked them up and brought them to Genoa. A considerable crowd headed for the council had gathered in the city by that time. On 15 March, Pope Gregory wrote to Gregory de Romano, telling him that sixteen galleys were not enough for the job and ordering him to work with the patriarch of Jerusalem to arrange for further ships. The pope also warned him that the "persecutors of the church," meaning Frederick's son Enzio and his Pisan allies, had prepared their own fleet of twenty-five ships to stop the Genoese convoy.[81] His worries proved well founded. On 3 May, a few days after the vessels bearing the churchmen and others left Genoa for Rome, a Pisan flotilla intercepted them near Isola di Giglio. A number of bishops from Provence and Spain who had not arrived in time to embark from Genoa with the main fleet wrote to the pope a week later, describing how Pisan naval forces operating under Enzio's command had assaulted the Genoese ships, sinking some, drowning and killing numerous clergy, tossing their corpses into the sea, and plundering the vessels thoroughly, generally despising the "fear of God," the norms of "natural law," and the honor of the cross. Enzio and the Pisans also captured many prominent members of the clergy, including the two cardinals, Otto and James.[82]

News of this sea battle made its way around Europe, which was described by historians such as Matthew Paris and Albert of Stade and in chronicles like the *Deeds of the Bishops of Trier* and the *Annals of St. Pantaleon*, among many others.[83] Writing to Henry III, Frederick celebrated his victory as a sign of God's favor, particularly relishing the capture of his longtime opponent, James of Palestrina. Tapping into the language of the two powers, Frederick presented the destruction of the fleet as a sign that God had decreed "that the machine of the world is to be governed, not alone by the priesthood but by the royal power and the priesthood." The emperor sent out a number of such letters that also praised the fact that his forces had successfully captured the city of Faenza after a long siege. Around this time, Pisan forces on land counterattacked a raiding party from Milan led by Gregory of Monte Longo, capturing their "banner of the keys" and the commune's standard along with a number of Gregory's companions. Frederick did not know, at that point, whether the papal legate had survived the battle.[84]

Not everyone, however, greeted the sinking of the Genoese fleet with such enthusiasm. Matthew Paris reports that many of those who heard about the attack and the emperor's celebratory letter believed that he had taken things a step too far.[85] Pope Gregory condemned the attack in the strongest terms. Writing to the captured prelates in June and seeking, perhaps, to exculpate himself after his many previous guarantees of their safety, he not-so-subtly blamed Gregory da Romano for failing to secure enough ships to protect the fleet bound for Rome.[86] The Genoese podesta, William Surdus, reacted just as strongly against Frederick's assault. In his letter to the pope, he stressed his relentless desire to take vengeance on the emperor for the glory of Christ, the Roman pontiff's honor, and all the faithful. Genoa planned to construct an even larger fleet to take action against Frederick, the "son of Perdition," after his assault on the prelates coming in public to the council. He also noted the "clamor among many" that the Hohenstaufen

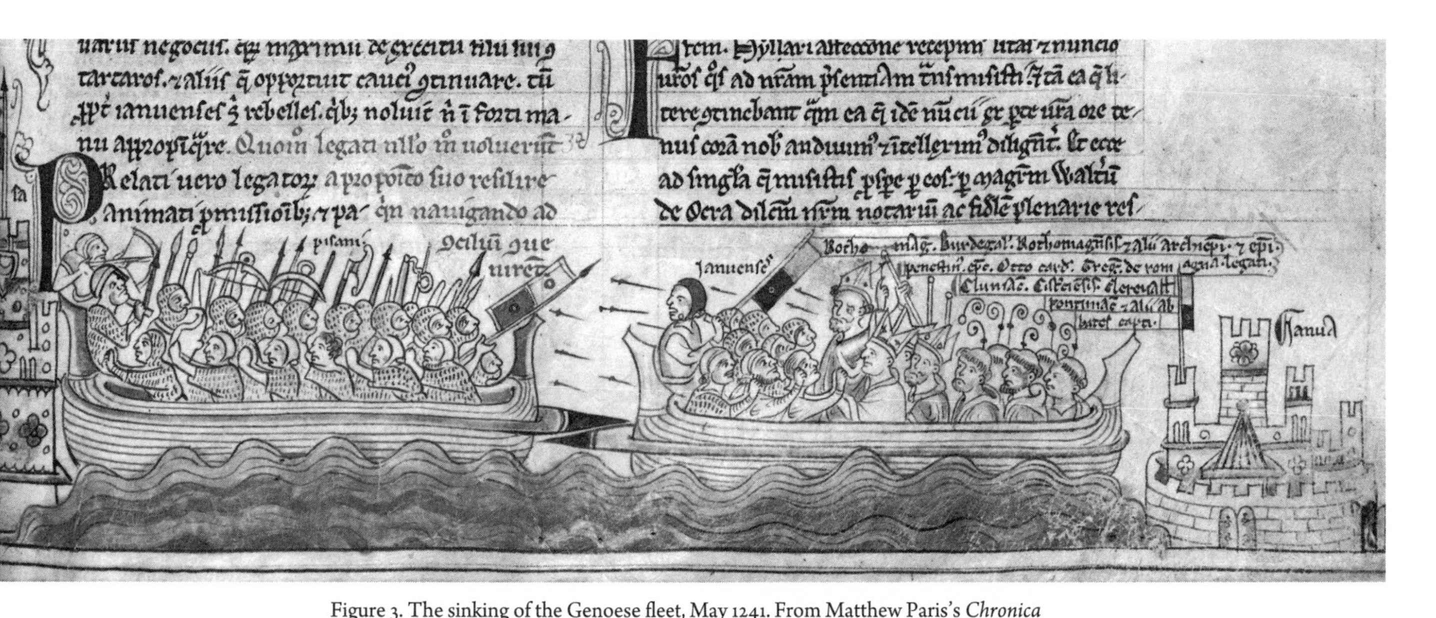

Figure 3. The sinking of the Genoese fleet, May 1241. From Matthew Paris's *Chronica maiora*. Courtesy of the Parker Library, Corpus Christi College, Cambridge, MS 16, f. 147r.

ruler be deposed so that the church would not have to remain under the fearful threat of his imperial power. William ended the letter to Gregory stressing Genoa's fidelity to the pope and promising the city's obedience to apostolic commands. Those opposed to Frederick would not let others forget his act of "sacrilege," which turned the sea red with the blood of holy men.[87]

Weeks after the sinking of the Genoese fleet, Frederick began to move his forces back into the vicinity of Rome, bottling up the pope and some of the cardinals in the city. In June, Frederick wrote to the Roman senate about the terrible devastation caused by the Tartars, who had attacked Poland and Hungary two months earlier, scattering Christian kings and planning to destroy the Christian religion. A month earlier, his son Conrad had taken the cross at Esslingen with a number of other German magnates, while Christians in the empire prayed, fasted, and staged processions, beseeching God for his mercy. Calling for the faithful to unite against the invaders, the emperor informed the senators that he was coming to Rome to settle his discord with the pope, hoping for paternal counsel about repelling the invaders. Yet he did not have high expectations in that regard, given how the pope had invaded the Regno, had incited the Milanese against him, and had forbidden Christians from helping the emperor when he went on his crusade to fight the Saracens years earlier. News of the dissension between him and the pope, he believed, served to embolden such barbarians. Writing to Henry III and other princes, Frederick denounced Gregory for preaching the cross through his legates and envoys "against us, the strong arm and defender of the church," rather than against the "tyranny of the Tartars and Saracens invading and occupying the holy land."[88]

In fact, Gregory had authorized the call for a crusade against the Tartars in Hungary, telling King Bela IV and a number of Dominican priors in the region that he was offering the same remission of sins for those fighting the barbarians as crusaders going overseas. But he also commissioned crusade preaching against Frederick in the same region, despite the clear and present danger posed by the Tartars.[89] In any case, after the devastating attack on the Genoese fleet bearing funds for his war effort to Rome, which stopped his planned council dead in its tracks, the pope's options for taking meaningful action against the emperor had undeniably narrowed. In June, someone at the curia penned another apocalyptically toned letter in Gregory's name, this time denouncing Frederick for his vicious attack on the bishops and other clergy bound for the pope's council at Rome. This address ended with the call for a "virtual" council of sorts, asking the prelates who received the letter to assemble their suffragan bishops, cathedral chapters, abbots, priors, and other prelates to deliberate among themselves about what they might do to aid the Roman church and its imperiled leader. There are no signs that this final polemic circulated widely at all, an apparent sign of the besieged pope's growing isolation.[90]

~

Even at this dire stage, overtures for peace between the two powers did not stop entirely. Perhaps because of the Mongol threat or the hope of taking advantage of the pope's compromised position, Frederick continued to reach out to Gregory. So did others, like the duke of Carinthia, who was close to the front lines of the fight with the Mongols and who sent letters to the pope offering to intercede for peace on the emperor's behalf. Gregory replied that he would welcome Frederick back to the mother church as soon as he showed himself ready to rejoin the faithful. Reading between the lines of this terse letter, the pope seemed to be saying that it would never come to pass. That summer, Frederick asked Richard of Cornwall, who had stopped in Italy while returning from his crusade to the holy places, to visit the Roman curia, giving him a written commission to negotiate on the emperor's behalf for the "reformation of the peace." According to Matthew Paris, Richard found Gregory in an "uncompromising and rebellious" mood: he refused any rapprochement with Frederick and demanded that he swear an oath submitting entirely to the pope's judgment. The English crusader returned to the emperor with nothing accomplished. In one of the last letters of his papacy sent to the Genoese on 16 August, in which he adopted a belligerent rather than conciliatory tone, Gregory praised them for their commitment to avenging the losses of the Roman church.[91]

On 22 August, the elderly pope, who must have been in his nineties, if not nearly one hundred years old, passed away. The most detailed account of Gregory's demise comes from the distant but always curious Matthew Paris, who says that the summer heat contributed to the pope's death, since he could not leave Rome for the healing baths at Viterbo as usual. But he also died of grief, after hearing that Frederick had captured one of his family's castles in Campagna and hanged a number of the pope's relatives. When the "public rumor" of Gregory's demise reached the emperor in his camp at Crypta Ferrata, he expressed his gratitude that God had seen fit to settle "the general scandal that has very much burdened the faithful of Christ in modern times," as he informed his brother-in-law Henry III. Mindful of the threat posed by the Tartars, who were trying to "demolish the worshippers of the Christian faith," Frederick also shared his hopes for a new occupant of the Apostolic See who might correct the wrongs of his predecessor, provide "peace for the entire world," and direct the "maternal love of the church" toward the emperor. Frederick and the rest of Christendom, however, would have a long wait before discovering who that person might be and what steps he would take toward reconciliation with the prince.[92]

INTERLUDE

The Vacancy

In the fall of 1241, about four months after Gregory IX's death, several cardinals who had fled from Rome to take refuge at Anagni wrote to their brothers still back in the city. The other cardinals had sent them letters, begging them to return for the business of electing a new pope after the demise of Gregory's short-lived successor, Celestine IV, who had held the office for just seventeen days. The cardinals at Anagni could barely believe this request, given their traumatic experiences during the lead-up to Celestine's election. In their response, they reminded their brothers how the Roman senator Matteo Rosso had ordered the cardinal bishops dragged through the streets like thieves and locked them in the Septizonium until they chose a new pope. During their confinement, they suffered heat, hunger, and other horrid conditions, such as when the guards urinated through cracks in the roof, wetting those sleeping below, or when rain water ruined their parchment spread out for writing. One of their number had died. Under these circumstances, they would not be leaving Anagni for Rome anytime soon.[1]

Whether or not the cardinals writing this letter exaggerated the deplorable conditions of the first-ever conclave, they meant it when they said they would not return to Rome. The papal office would remain vacant for another eighteen months until a sufficient number of cardinal clergy gathered at Anagni to elect a new pope. From November 1241 to June 1243, the lack of a Roman pontiff became a new source of concern and public scandal for Christians around Europe. The prolonged vacancy raised a profound question about the sovereignty of the Apostolic See. Where did authority in the church reside when Saint Peter's chair sat empty? By the thirteenth century, canons lawyers had elaborated an answer: in-between popes, authority was vested in the "corporate" body of the church, above all in the college of cardinals. But this abstract legal solution did little to settle the sense of uncertainty surrounding the vacant papal office during these years of perceived danger for Christendom. With one of the two powers missing its chief representative, the unresolved struggle between the papacy and the excommunicate emperor remained in a sort of limbo, even as partisans on both sides continued to fight in the name of the "church" and the "empire." Meanwhile, foreign enemies—the Mongols—still threatened to destroy the Christian religion entirely.[2]

Matthew Paris' *Major Chronicle* offers some of the most sensational details about the conclave and vacancy following Gregory IX's death. By the traditional standards of historical evidence, his presentation of events is filled with errors.[3] In some ways, this makes his disjointed account ideal for measuring the confusion that surrounded these events. The English chronicler places ten cardinals at Rome when Gregory died. Five of them—Rainier of Viterbo, John de Colonna, Stephen Conti, Giles de Torres, and Robert Somercotes—supported Geoffrey Castiglioni, cardinal bishop of Santa Sabina and the candidate favored by Frederick. Three others—Sinibaldo Fieschi, Raynald da Jenne, and Richard Annibaldi—backed Romano Bonaventura, cardinal bishop of Porto e Santa Ruffina and Matteo Orsini's preferred choice.[4] Romano Bonaventura had an unsavory reputation, Matthew insists, and was known for harassing scholars at the university of Paris and sleeping with Louis IX's mother, Blanche. Since the election of a pope required a two-thirds majority among the cardinals, the group remained deadlocked in a "great schism."[5] As the deliberations dragged on, Robert Somercotes died, poisoned by his enemies who feared that the foreign Englishman might become the next pontiff. Meanwhile, resentful of John de Colonna's past support for Frederick, the Romans seized and imprisoned him[6]

Around this time, the emperor paroled Otto of San Nicola in Carcere Tulliano, who had been captured during the sinking of the Genoese fleet the previous May. Matthew writes that Richard of Cornwall convinced Frederick to free Otto with the provision that, if Otto himself was not elected pope, he would return to captivity after the election. The emperor still blamed Otto for repeating the papal sentence of excommunication against him throughout England during the previous years. As the deliberations dragged on, the cardinal deacon had to return to captivity.[7] The remaining cardinals finally settled upon Geoffrey Castiglioni—Geoffrey of Milan, Matthew calls him—as the next pope. Geoffrey took the name Celestine IV but died just seventeen days later, before he could be consecrated. Rather than face another conclave, the cardinals scattered, some hiding with their families and others remaining in Rome. "So it was," Matthew observed, "that the house of God, which requires union to ensure its strength, could not be properly supported by them."[8]

Concern about the turbulent conditions of the Apostolic See extended far and wide. In late in 1241, Matthew's *Major Chronicle* continues, a group of English prelates including the archbishop of York, the bishops of Lincoln and Norwich, and many other high-ranking clergy gathered to discuss the "many desolations of the church." In a public display, these prelates arranged "special prayers with fasts to happen in the church and generally throughout England, so that the Lord might judge it worthy to relieve and restore the Roman church, destitute of its pastor, taking as their example the church's constant prayers when Paul was imprisoned in the Acts of the Apostles." They agreed to send envoys to Frederick, calling upon him to "remit all of his rancor and indignation" toward the church, above all since those who offended him were now dead, making him seem like a tyrant for persecuting the innocent. When it came time to choose those ambassadors, however, everyone made excuses why they could not go. Finally the bishops settled upon some mendicants as their envoys, those used to "wandering through every province." The emperor, however, remained far from accommodating. He asked the friars why he should not impede the next papal election, since the church had tried to cast him down from his office, excommunicating him, defaming him, and spending its money to oppose him. The English bishops' intervention thereby came to nothing.[9]

Others chroniclers besides Matthew Paris speculated about the conclave and wondered about Frederick's role in preventing the election of a new pope, expressing their astonishment about the circumstances of the prolonged vacancy. *The Deeds of the Bishop of Trier* claimed that someone poisoned Celestine IV, while Albert Stade reported that the cardinals picked yet another pope immediately after Geoffrey of Milan died but refused to tell the Romans who it was. Describing an eclipse in late 1241, the Premonstratensian monk and chronicler Menko offered a natural explanation for the event—the moon, he observes, passes between the earth and the sun—but also suggested a prophetic meaning for the celestial sign. First, Pope Gregory, the "most strenuous defender of the church" who had excommunicated the disobedient Frederick, had died. The newly elected Celestine quickly died too, leaving the Apostolic See vacant for over a year. "For the emperor, Frederick," Menko continued, "was both secretly and openly impeding the election, since he held captive two cardinals without whom the election could not take place. Thus it came to pass in accordance with the prophecy, 'I see Israel, scattered like a sheep with their shepherd.'"[10] Salimbene of Adam likewise reported that Frederick kept watch on the highways, trying to seize as many of the cardinals as he could, worried that one of them would manage to become the next pope. "I was captured several times myself around this time," the Franciscan friar recalls. "It was then that I devised and developed a method of writing my letters in various kinds of code."[11]

Rulers as well as chroniclers closely followed the twists and turns of the failed papal election and prolonged vacancy, not hiding their sense of alarm. Late in the year 1242, King Louis IX wrote to the cardinals, encouraging them to proceed with the choice of a new pope. He clearly had the impression that they were worried about reprisals from the emperor if they picked someone not to his liking. The French king assured them that he remained committed to their physical and financial protection. His letter also accused Frederick of "wanting to be called king and priest." The law, however, did not allow the royal power to be combined with the priesthood in one person. Thus, Louis wondered, "it remains to be seen by what right he claims the priestly dignity."[12] Matthew Paris reports that the French king sent "solemn envoys" to the cardinals, beseeching them to elect a new pope for the "solace of the universal church." Otherwise, Christians on the other side of the Alps would have to choose their own highest pontiff, obeying him instead.[13]

In his correspondence about the vacancy, Frederick made no such claims to be called priest as well as king. To the contrary, the emperor had good reason to desire the election of the next pope. Without a Roman pontiff, no one could restore him to the graces of the Roman church and lift the sentence of excommunication against him. Judging by his own letters, rather than the rumors surrounding him, Frederick demanded that the cardinals end their disagreements and proceed to the election. When the news of Gregory's death had first reached his camp outside of Rome, the emperor informed King Henry III that he had grieved to hear the news, even though he had good cause to hate the deceased pope. But he also took heart in the chance to elect a new pontiff, following the demise of the one who created such a "general scandal, a great burden among the faithful of Christ in modern times."[14] In similar letters sent to the cardinals, to Baldwin of Constantinople, to the French king, and to other unspecified supporters, Frederick stressed the need for a true shepherd to guide the church, a "friend of peace and striver for justice, through whom the church and empire might be reformed." Addressing the cardinals as the "hinge and column" of the church, which was left in the state of a bereft widow without a pope, Frederick blamed them for failing in their duties to their mother.[15]

Such correspondence with the cardinals left unsaid what must have seemed obvious—that new bishop of Rome, the "friend of peace," should be inclined to work with the emperor and reconcile him with the church on favorable terms. Apparently, Frederick pressured the cardinal clergy to act beyond writing them letters. In July 1242 and May 1243, his troops pillaged the outskirts of Rome. In his letters, the emperor declared that he deployed such force against the rebellious citizens of the city to protect the cardinals from mistreatment by the latter. The Romans' imprisonment of John de Colonna, one of Frederick's allies, probably had something to do with this claim.[16] According to Matthew Paris, however, Frederick also intended his attacks to send a message to the cardinals, blaming them for the schism in the college and the failure to elect a pope. By not acting, they darkened the emperor's reputation. Fed up with the delay, Frederick issued an edict that targeted the cardinals' churches and estates for plunder by his troops. Those forces included Saracens, who devastated Albano its surroundings until the cardinals begged Frederick to stop, promising to choose a new pontiff who would be "worthy of the church and the empire."[17]

Meanwhile, the "war between church and empire," as the Genoese chronicler Bartholomew the Scribe describes the situation, continued unabated on the Italian peninsula despite the lack of a pope to lead the effort against Frederick. Fighting largely for local reasons, papal and imperial allies invoked the grander conflict between the two powers as the ultimate cause of their struggles. Bartholomew describes a battle in 1242 between the Genoese and the Pisans. The Genoese bore a relic of the True Cross before them, wearing crosses on their right shoulder guards, fight like penitents for the "honor of the church." He also records a "public assembly" staged outside Genoa, where Boniface of Montferrat, along with other nobles, switched sides, abandoning the emperor and swearing to defend Genoa, Milan, and Piacenza. On hand for the convocation and still in the field after years of fighting, Gregory of Monte Longo took the marquis and others under the special protection of the Apostolic See. That same month, Vercelli revolted against Frederick, allowing Gregory and six thousand Milanese troops to enter the city, turning that commune to the "service of the Roman church."[18]

Fighting persisted in Germany as well. The *Annals of St. Pantaleon* describe how the archbishops of Cologne and Mainz battled against Frederick's son Conrad and his allies, invading and pillaging the area around Wetterau. The two prelates publicly repeated the emperor's excommunication and attacked his reputation. Because of the vacancy in the Apostolic See caused by Frederick, they claimed, they had to act like "godparents" for the faithful sons of the desolate Roman church. In this way, the disapproving writer of the chronicle observes, rather than rightly submitting their grievances against the emperor for judgment to the church, they did it great harm.[19]

The dangers to Christendom during the vacancy came from the outside as well. Addressing the need for the election of a new pope and for peace among Christians, Fredrick called attention to the continued threat posed by the Tartars.[20] Unaware the Mongols had in fact pulled back from their assaults on Eastern Europe and would not return, everyone ranging from rulers to refugees remained obsessed with the strange barbarians that had come out of nowhere. Numerous letters circulated about the Tartars, copies of which made their way into Matthew of Paris's hands. He added some of them to his collection of documents, the *Book of Additions,* a kind of appendix to his *Major Chronicle.* In these letters, which express fear and astonishment about the warriors who desired to "conquer the world" and whose arrival perhaps signaled the coming of Antichrist, the panic looming over Europe due to the "devil's horsemen" seems palpable. Those writing such missives struck a common note, assigning blame for the devastation to the discord among Christians and failure to work together for a common peace. The situation seemed dire. As one Franciscan from Cologne put it, the Tartars grew stronger every day, joining together in a confederation with "pagans, heretics, and false Christians who form a great multitude. It ought to be greatly feared, lest all of Christendom fall into ruin."[21]

During the late spring and summer of 1243, Frederick and cardinals negotiated over the release of the two cardinals held captive by the emperor, Otto and James.[22] The college lacked the numbers for a proper election: Romano Bonaventura and Richard Annibaldi had died the preceding year, while John de Colonna remained imprisoned by the Romans. The remaining cardinals pressed Frederick to free their brothers, insisting that the papal election could not be held without them. One of them wrote to Peter de Vinea, lamenting James of Palestrina's horrible treatment: his being moved from prison to prison, confined in small spaces, and not allowed visitors. Frederick made his willingness to release Otto clear, but he continued to resist freeing James, an "open enemy" of the empire. In June 1243, after further appeals from the cardinals, the emperor finally agreed to let James go, declaring that the "public good" of the Christian republic trumped his own private desires. Writing to King Louis IX that same month, Frederick described how he had withdrawn his troops from the vicinity of Rome, doing everything he could to enable the cardinals gathered at Anagni to reach a decision.[23]

On 24 June, the Feast of John the Baptist, the cardinals at Anagni renewed their deliberations over the election of a new pope. On 25 June, they announced their unanimous decision: they had chosen Sinibaldo Fieschi, cardinal priest of San Lorenzo in Lucina, as the next bishop of Rome. He took the name Innocent IV, because, according to Menko, he wanted to live "peacefully and innocently."[24] Numerous other chroniclers recorded the election of the pope, which finally ended the disturbing vacancy in the papal office.[25] With a new bishop seated on the Apostolic See, the curia could resume important business that had been delayed or deferred for more than a year and a half. One question, however, must have weighed on everyone's mind above all others: Would peace be restored between the two powers or would the crisis of Christendom continue?

PART II

Innocent IV

Chapter 5

A New Hope

Pope Innocent IV's biographer, the Franciscan Nicholas of Carbio, does not start his account of the pope's life with Sinibaldo dei Fieschi's youth or with his earlier station as the cardinal priest of San Lorenzo in Lucina, or even with his election to the Apostolic See. He begins instead with the conflict between Gregory IX and Frederick II, who turned "from an emperor into a tyrant, a protector into an attacker, a defender into a persecutor of the church." Before ever mentioning Sinibaldo, Nicholas describes Gregory's decision to summon a council to sit in judgment of the errant ruler, although the pope was prevented from doing so by Frederick's closure of the roads and sea routes into Rome, followed by the destruction of the Genoese fleet carrying the cardinals and other clergy to the city. He continues by narrating Frederick's siege of Rome, Gregory's death, the forced conclave and election of Celestine IV, Celestine's quick demise, and the long vacancy. Finally, the cardinals at Anagni elected a new pope, Sinibaldo dei Fieschi, who took the name Innocent IV: "Genoese by birth, of a noble family, but more noble in his life, exceptional in his learning and endowed with the honesty of his moral bearings."[1]

For more than a year and a half, Christians around Europe had reacted to, speculated about, and debated the scandalous vacancy in the papal office. The election of a new pope raised more questions, possibilities, and uncertainties about the conditions facing Christendom, above all that concerning the fight between the Roman church and emperor. Writing the pope's vita shortly after Innocent's death and knowing about all the twists and turns of his relationship with Frederick, Nicholas makes it clear to his readers that the emperor never intended to make peace with the Roman pontiff, even if he pretended otherwise. Most of the Hohenstaufen ruler's modern biographers seem to agree that there was never any chance for reconciliation between the two, but they blame the pope's intransigence for that state of affairs.[2] A sense of inevitability thereby hangs over Innocent and his contentious relationship with Frederick, pointing inexorably toward the pope's controversial decision to depose the emperor at Lyons in July 1245.

And yet, no one—including Innocent himself—knew that his pontificate would lead to that controversial outcome when the cardinals elevated him to the Apostolic See two years earlier. Whatever they felt about each other, publicly, Innocent and Frederick embraced the opportunity to de-escalate the battle between the papacy and empire. When scholars assume that the pope desired to annihilate his imperial opponent from the beginning, they miss the chance to explore the strategies, negotiations, and performances that characterized his interactions with the emperor. Taking a close look at the first year and a half of Innocent's papacy provides an opportunity to track the centrifugal forces, problems, and contingencies that made a meaningful settlement difficult to reach. During this period, particular people and places rather than ideological principles emerged as stumbling blocks to the new hope for peace, as did events that neither the pope nor emperor could control entirely. The struggle between their offices had taken on a difficult-to-arrest momentum involving individuals and communities whose interests did not seamlessly align with the either side of the conflict between the "church" and the "prince."

Despite these challenges, for a brief moment, during a ceremony at Saint Peter's Basilica on the Feast of the Last Supper in 1244, when Frederick's envoys swore on his behalf to render satisfaction to the church before the pope, cardinals, and a large crowd gathered for Holy Week, the restoration of peace seemed achievable, if not actually achieved. Within a few months, however, Innocent had fled from central Italy for Genoa and eventually to Lyons. Both sides resumed their public effort to discredit the other, exposing the bad faith that had lain hidden behind their previous gestures of reconciliation. By the time that Innocent IV reached his new refuge at Lyons in December, anxieties and uncertainties over the conditions of Christendom seemed just as acute and palpable as ever, worsened by continued uncertainty over the whereabouts of the Tartars and the spreading news of Jerusalem's recent sacking by the Khwarezmian Turks. The window of cautious optimism that the crisis between the two powers might be resolved had closed, creating the illusion that it never existed in the first place.

The Search for Peace

In the customary letter announcing his election, Innocent opened with a long and formal preamble about the divine ordering of the celestial and earthy hierarchies, including the church, the body of the faithful headed by Christ's vicar.[3] Disrupted by the death of Celestine IV soon after Gregory IX's passing, "on account of our sins and the malice of the times," the papal office had experienced a long vacancy until the cardinals unanimously elected Sinibaldo dei Fieschi. Presenting himself with customary humility, the new pope declared that although he was unworthy of the office, he was nevertheless willing to undertake that burden. Innocent called upon the clerical recipients of his missive to care for their own flocks and to pray for him, beseeching God each day to bring peace to the Christian church and people, and to repel the "ravishments of the barbarians"—meaning the Tartars—from their borders. In this inaugural epistolary address, Innocent made no direct mention of the papacy's problems with the emperor, although in one version of the letter sent to Milan and its citizens, he called upon them as his "special sons" to remain steadfast and obedient to the Apostolic See—a formulaic appeal but perhaps an oblique reference to the ongoing military conflict in Lombardy.[4]

Nevertheless, the new pope's intentions regarding Frederick II represented the biggest question mark surrounding his new papacy and the possibilities for peace. Remarking on Innocent's failure to mention the church's conflict with the emperor in the announcement of his election, with his typical suspicion of papal motives, Thomas Van Cleve has called that letter "a masterpiece of evasion."[5] But the pope's circumspection might also be considered an attempt to avoid an inflammatory start to his newly configured relationship with the emperor. A number of histories, including Matthew Paris's *Major Chronicle*, Menko's *Chronicle*, and the *Annals of Saint Justina* observe that Innocent immediately renewed Frederick's sentence of excommunication after his election. If he did so, and it seems likely that he did, he repeated the ban with little fanfare. The opening weeks of his papacy include no announcements about the anathema, no instructions to publicize the ban, and no revisiting of the numerous charges leveled against the emperor. Over the following months, papal circles produced none of the apocalyptically charged polemics against the Hohenstaufen ruler so common during the final years of Gregory IX's time as pope. In this regard, public restraint rather than evasion seems to characterize the start of Innocent's papacy.[6]

The challenge posed by Frederick did not occupy Innocent to the exclusion of his other self-arrogated responsibilities for the common good of Christendom. The ongoing threat from the Mongols clearly concerned him from the moment he became pope. At that point, no one knew where they were or when they might return. Innocent tried to learn what he could to prepare for the next attack. In July, less than a month after his election, he wrote to Berthold, patriarch of Aquileia, instructing him to organize the "preaching of the cross" against the "impious people of the Tartars," the "envoys of Satan," promising the same indulgence of sins for crusaders who went to Hungary as those going to the Holy Land. The pope also enlisted the Dominican provincial prior in Serbia to absolve sinners who would normally have to visit the papal curia, such as arsonists and those who assaulted clerics, if they swore to fight the barbarians.[7] Flexibility ruled the day. Writing to the archbishop of Trondheim, he approved the Norwegian king's request to commute his crusade vow for Jerusalem into one against the Tartars if they attacked again within the year.[8] Innocent also looked to endangered frontiers overseas, assigning legatine status to a number of highly placed prelates in crusader territories, including Robert of Nantes, patriarch of Jerusalem; Albert of Antioch; and Nicholas da Castro Arquato, patriarch of Constantinople. The pope paid particular attention to the condition of Jerusalem's defensive walls, which had been razed by Muslim forces during the course of the Baron's Crusade, instructing Robert of Nantes to raise tithes for rebuilding the fortifications and calling upon Christians "in remission of sins" to contribute manpower and funds for that project. The current infighting between the sultans of Damascus and Cairo provided the faithful with a window of opportunity to consolidate their hold on the city. Innocent also authorized special subsidies for the defense of Constantinople, which was endangered by resurgent Byzantine power in the region.[9]

Frederick's reaction to the new pope's election seemed equally nonconfrontational. Admittedly, Matthew Paris writes that the emperor, reacting angrily to his renewed excommunication and disappointed in the new pope, closed the roadways, ports, and bridges to prevent Innocent from dispatching any letters or receiving any money at the curia. He also hanged two Franciscans bearing letters with instructions from their superiors to foment rebellion against his rule. In a manner similar to that of Matthew Paris, the *Annals of Saint Justina* declare that Innocent spent two years trying to make peace with Frederick but was deceived by him "in words and deeds." Elated with pride, the emperor never stopped planning to humble the clergy, not even bothering to conceal his "sacrilegious intention" and thereby exciting the hatred of prelates from around the empire. Salimbene of Adam and Menko likewise describe how Innocent kept trying to establish peace with Frederick but eventually had to flee from Rome because of the emperor's disobedience to the church. For Menko, this called to mind Matthew 10:23: "When they persecute in one town, flee to the next."[10]

These history writers, however, clearly collapse the circumstances of the pope's election and later events, anticipating the failed negotiations between the two sides, Innocent's flight to Lyons, and his eventual deposition of the emperor. Richard of San Germano, to the contrary, who ends his chronicle in October 1243, reports that Frederick ordered hymns sung throughout the churches of the Regno when he heard the news of Innocent's election. In his own correspondence, the emperor expressed his hope that Innocent's election would enable his reconciliation with the Roman church. Although he had denied Gregory's legitimacy as pope and fought to protect his imperial rights from the abusive pontiff, he insisted that he did not question the spiritual preeminence of the papal office. With a different pope occupying the Apostolic See, negotiations for peace could begin again. Writing to the Duke of Brabant just days after Innocent's election, Frederick described the new pope as numbering "among the noble sons of the empire," explaining that Innocent had "always been friendly toward us in words and deeds." Frederick also wrote that the newly elected bishop of Rome would "with paternal affection procure the unity of our friendship, a general peace, and the good state of the empire, and therefore, we embrace him as a father and he embraces us as a son."[11] Addressing Innocent directly just over a month after his election, Frederick congratulated him on his change in status, whereby an "old friend" had become "a new father," indicating his confidence that the pope would keep "peace and justice inviolate." The emperor dispatched this letter with envoys sent in the "spirit of devotion" to the pope, led by his longtime officials and confidantes Peter de Vinea and Thaddeus of Suessa, along with Girard Malperg, master general of the Teutonic Knights; Ansaldus de Mari, admiral of the imperial naval forces; and Frederick's chaplain from Messina, Roger Porcastrella. These legates, the emperor declared, possessed intimate knowledge of his own will and were fully empowered to negotiate with the pope for the "honor of the church and the favor of ecclesiastical liberty in every way," offering as many concessions as possible while "preserving the right and honor of the empire."[12]

Nicholas of Carbio describes a similar mood at Anagni: a receptivity to the possibilities for a new peace that would end the discord between church and empire. Immediately after Innocent's election, the friar writes, the pope began to speak with the cardinals about reestablishing "the peace and concord of the church," organizing his own party of negotiators led by Peter da Collemezzo, archbishop of Rouen; William, abbot of Saint Facundus; and Nicholas, bishop of Reggio.[13] In August, he drew up articles for a proposed peace given to this legation—minus Nicholas, replaced by the pope's penitentiary, William of Modena—before they journeyed to the imperial court at Melfi. In this document, the pope called upon Frederick to release the clergy he still held captive since the destruction of the Genoese fleet bound for the council at Rome two years earlier. He empowered the legates to hear the emperor's satisfaction for the wrongs he had committed that led to his excommunication. The church likewise stood ready to make amends for any harm done to Frederick, although the pope did not believe that the church had actually harmed the emperor. If Frederick felt unjustly accused or believed that the church had injured him unjustly, Innocent stood ready to bring their disagreements before a council of "kings, prelates, and princes, both secular and ecclesiastical, held some place safe, so that he or his envoys might come there." The pope promised to abide by the assembly's adjudication to the extent of lifting the sentence of excommunication, as long as its judgment demanded nothing contrary to the honor of the church. Last but not least, he insisted that the Roman church's "friends and supporters" must enjoy "peace and full security," suffering no harm in the meanwhile.[14]

In instructions given separately to the papal legates, the combination of old and new sticking points faced by the pope and emperor can be seen. Innocent informed his envoys that Frederick expected him to recall the controversial Gregory of Monte Longo from Lombardy, claiming that the cardinals had promised to do so during the vacancy in the papal office in exchange for the release of Otto of San Nicola and James of Palestrina. Innocent refused to withdraw Gregory before the emperor made peace with the Lombards. Frederick also insisted that the pope secure the release of his follower Salinguerra, who had been captured by the Venetians after the surrender of Ferrara. The pope had no direct say over Salinguerra's captivity, and even if he did, he saw no reason to push for the release of a former vassal who had betrayed his oaths to the Roman church. Nevertheless, he promised to look into the matter. The emperor complained that the pope had warmly received Archbishop Siegfried of Mainz, an open rebel against Frederick's rule for years, endowing him with legatine powers and refusing to hear any accusations against him. The archbishop remained a "great prelate," Innocent observed, and the pope planned to honor him further. If Frederick made peace with the church, however, Innocent would certainly try to restore the allegiance of the church's friends to him. Frederick expressed further displeasure about the bishop-elect of Avignon, Zoën, appointed—the emperor claimed—by the pope to work against his interests in the region. Innocent denied such a motive for installing Zoën, who had been sent at the request of local Dominicans who sought aid against the rampant heretics in Provence.[15]

The ideological question of the two powers, of whether emperors ultimately answered to popes or the other way around, makes no explicit appearance in these exchanges. Rather, the two parties mainly disputed over various individuals and groups of persons—demanding the release of captives and protesting the public actions of certain office holders—thereby signaling a limited commitment to compromise in the future. Only in regard to combating heresy did the profile of the discussion change. Toward the close of the letter to his envoys, the pope observed that Frederick had complained that the church was failing to suppress the heretical depravity in Lombardy and Tuscany. Innocent denied this accusation, pointing out that, in fact, the emperor ignored heretics in own backyard and farther afield. Before the recent conflict erupted with Frederick, as everyone knew, the papacy had fought heresy everywhere. By blockading the roads and preventing the free travel of papal legates, Frederick had disrupted the Roman church's efforts against heretics, close at hand and elsewhere. In closing, the pope emphasized his desire for peace and his hope that the prince would show proper devotion to the Apostolic See and turn the arms he bore "against the church" against "heretics, schismatics, and other enemies of the faith," for the salvation of his soul. If Frederick balked at Innocent's response to his complaints, the pope instructed his legates to end the negotiations and return immediately to the curia.[16]

These high-profile negotiations proceeded in a highly scripted, performative manner. In September, Innocent wrote again to his envoys at the imperial court, giving them specific instructions for how they would receive the emperors' excommunicate envoys, including Peter de Vinea, Thaddeus of Suessa, and

Bernard, archbishop of Palermo, when they returned for a second time to the papal curia. The pope had refused to meet personally with Frederick's delegation during their first appearance at Anagni in August. The emperor had complained about this treatment, although Innocent wondered at his surprise, given the fact that the pope would never formally receive an excommunicate person before absolution. Innocent, anticipating the arrival of the second delegation, outlined his plan for receiving the emperor's representatives. Peter da Collemezzo, William of Modena, and the abbot of Saint Facundus would absolve the imperial delegation in the presence of the pope when he gave them verbal go-ahead to do so—with the exception of Bernard, who would be absolved at a later date. As a highly placed member of the church, his opposition to the pope and support for the emperor was less easy to forgive. Innocent specified that absolving him for the purposes of this meeting did not mean that he would be free to enjoy the revenues or other benefits from his position. Letting him off the hook too readily might send the wrong message and encourage others in their bad behavior.[17]

A few months after Innocent's election, things seemed on track for a settlement between the Roman papacy and Hohenstaufen prince, negotiations reminiscent of those that preceded the peace of San Germano in 1230. The exchange of envoys, letters, and documents; the trading of complaints about each side's past actions with an eye toward their remediation; the staged moment of reconciliation for the imperial delegation: such displays signaled the possibilities for concord between the pope and emperor. Innocent's professed willingness to submit their dispute to a general council in particular seemed designed to pressure Frederick into making some sort of accommodation with the Roman church before such a move became necessary. The emperor had done everything in his power to prevent Pope Gregory's planned council from meeting at Rome. Presumably, he still wanted to avoid such a public airing of his disputes with Innocent, proceedings that the pope might play to his advantage. In late September, Nicholas of Carbio reports, Peter de Vinea and Thaddeus of Suessa came to the papal curia bearing letters sealed with the Frederick's golden bull and making all sorts of promises on his behalf. These commitments were fraudulent ones, the Franciscan friar observes with hindsight. But at the time, both Innocent and Frederick had a great deal to gain from pursuing a new peace or, at the very least, broadcasting their willingness to end the scandalous division plaguing Christendom.[18]

Casualties of War

After becoming pope, Innocent also turned his attention toward more immediate problems facing him as the sovereign lord of the Papal States. Determining the future political landscape of the Italian peninsula represented one of the greatest challenges to restoring a state of concord between the Roman church and empire.

This fact would not have been lost on the pope. As the former rector of the March of Ancona, he possessed ground-floor knowledge of the ties of vassalage, networks of clerical administration, and financial resources that would enable papal governance despite the unsettled conditions created by years of fighting in the region. While he claimed awesome spiritual powers as the successor to Peter, his ability to manage the saint's "special patrimony" would play an important role in determining the capabilities of his new papacy to sustain the war against Frederick or bring it to an end.

Over the first several months of his pontificate, Innocent tried to undo some of the damage and uncertainty caused in the Papal States by the long vacancy in the papal office by appointing new rectors in Spoleto and Tuscany and confirming his administrative successor in the march, Marcellino, bishop of Arezzo.[19] The pope reached out to communities and individuals that had suffered the hardships of war on the church's behalf, dispatching clerical messengers bearing "consolatory" letters to them. In these addresses, Innocent praised their service of the church and called upon them to remain steadfast in their loyalty and obedience, promising such allies the special protection of the Apostolic See; renewing and confirming various ecclesiastical rights, privileges, and statutes made in the past for their benefit; and declaring the emperor's bans and judgments null and void. He assured them, too, that he would not agree to any peace with Frederick that did not include the church's friends and supporters in its terms.[20]

These letters expose the possibilities and limitations of what the new pope and his agents could do, try to do, or simply not consider under present conditions. Innocent leveraged the power of penance and absolution where he could, authorizing prelates in places like the March of Ancona and Sardinia to reconcile excommunicate but sufficiently repentant imperial supporters, including Adelasia of Torres, who—misled by the bad counsel of others—had agreed to marry Frederick's son Enzio years earlier.[21] Writing to the civic leadership in Radicofani, he praised their willingness to surrender hostages to Gregory IX's notary, Bartholomew, as a guarantee of their loyalty. Out of gratitude for their good faith, Innocent promised to pay for the upkeep of the hostages, to compensate the commune for its losses due to the "war between the church and prince," and to help fund construction of the town's fortifications. In his communications with the podesta and commune of Assisi, Innocent recognized all of the persecution they had suffered as "fighters of Christ" (*pugiles Christi*) and grieved that he could not offer them more substantive aid at this time. The Roman church, he stressed, had a long memory and would reward the people of Assisi in the future. Meanwhile, the pope recognized the commune's right to seek compensation for damages caused by the neighboring towns of Foglino and Spello and to confiscate the property of some nobles from Assisi who had conspired to hand the town over to the "enemies of the church."[22]

Looking beyond the papal patrimony, Innocent continued to monitor conditions on the ground in Lombardy. In September, he updated Gregory of Monte Longo on the proposed "reformation of the peace" between the Roman church and the emperor. Much like he did elsewhere, the pope reassured him and the rectors of the Lombard League that he would not make an agreement with Frederick that excluded them. Later that fall, apparently concerned about the negotiations taking place between the curia and the imperial court, Gregory contacted the pope through his own "envoys and special letters," asking to be recalled from his legation. Innocent refused the request, however, insisting that he remain in Lombardy and continuing his effort to preserve the unity of the faithful and to defend the church's liberty.[23] The political situation on the Italian peninsula remained volatile. If people needed a reminder about that fact, they received one during the first week of September, when a faction of citizens in Viterbo revolted against the imperial party that had been in control of the city for the previous three years. Various accounts of this event, including letters from the different parties involved, describe how Rainier of Viterbo, cardinal deacon of Santa Maria in Cosmedin, acted "suddenly and secretly" (*subito et clam*) to turn the Viterbans against the emperor. One especially detailed narrative of this putsch survives in the cardinal deacon's "letter book" and narrates how the reverend cardinal deacon, with a group of sworn friends, relatives, and other nobles, sneaked though one of the city gates during the dead of night on the Feast of the Nativity of Blessed Virgin. This band quickly seized control of twenty-eight towers and the palace belonging to the cardinal's family, surrounding the garrison in the citadel, which consisted of three hundred soldiers commanded by Simon of Teatino. "On that day," the account proclaims, "nearly the entire city went over to the side of the church with joy."[24]

Viterbo's unexpected uprising created an immediate spectacle, becoming a source of rumors and public news, sensational scenes, and hard-to-believe stories even for the war-torn Italian peninsula. In a series of letters sent to Frederick and the count of Caserta, the imperial vicar for the region, Simon and his besieged companions in the citadel begged for relief against the "thieves, perjurers, and condemned men" that Rainier had assembled against them. Simon lamented that the "cowardice of priests" had weakened the count of Caserta's strength "without even a battle." He claimed to have written so many letters asking for aid that he was running out of ink and parchment.[25] By mid-September, Frederick arrived and personally laid siege to Viterbo, the "Philistines gathered in battle against Israel's phalanx," as the letter in Rainier's collection describes the situation. Panic struck when those inside the city heard a rumor that Rainier had secretly fled by night. When they found him still at the cardinal's palace, he rebuked them for their cowardice. Inspiring them with strong words and sending them back to fight "like lions," the cardinal deacon ordered lamps to be kindled to illuminate the city.

The citizens, half-dead with fear, rushed forth as if reborn, foiling a plot by some traitors to open one of the gates to the enemy.[26]

What role did Innocent play in these events? Was he pretending to "reform the peace" with Frederick and conspiring with Viterbo behind the scenes? The reality of the situation seems more complex as the pope tried to balance competing interests and reacted to events after the fact. The description of the revolt found in Rainier's letter collection says that he acted by the "counsel" of the highest pontiff and cardinals. Writing to Rainier in early October, the pope made it clear that he had met with the cardinal deacon sometime late in the summer and listened to his proposal to recover Viterbo for the church. Speaking personally with Rainier, the pope had refused to incur any expenses for this plan, although he did not forbid him from making the attempt. This decision forced Rainier to borrow money against his own goods and properties along with those of his friends and family. After the fact, recognizing the danger to Viterbo and the bad example it would set if the church's allies fell to their enemies, Innocent agreed to transfer twenty-five hundred ounces of gold and five hundred silver marks to a Florentine merchant to provide a month's stipend for soldiers to defend the city.[27] Innocent, who had heard that the troops coming to fight for the church at Viterbo "desired to attain the remission of their sins," also granted Rainier the right to make indulgences as he saw fit, based on the quality and amount of the military service rendered. From Innocent's perspective, with minimal commitment from the papacy, the "flipping" of Viterbo might strengthen his hand in his ongoing negotiations with Frederick rather than derail them.[28]

By all accounts, the city saw savage fighting during Frederick's siege: the emperor summoned soldiers from around Lombardy and Tuscany to join the siege, while others arrived to help the Viterbans, attracted by the promise of indulgences. The celebratory narrative in Rainier's letter book endows the ensuing struggles with a biblical sense of sanctified war, relating how the defenders' initial slaughter of the "excommunicate ones" inspired fear in Frederick's later levies, who worried that they might lose their lives and their souls for the price of their stipends. The imperial armies attacked furtively by night and built siege engines to assail the city by day, blasting the walls with Greek fire. At one point, when the fighting turned against Frederick's troops in the defensive ditches dug around Viterbo, they used as shields "crucifixes and icons of the blessed Virgin, stolen from nearby leprosaria and churches." The emperor spent money without restraint, seeking to bribe some of the Viterbans over to his side. He even sought help from a local pair of Cathar heresiarchs, Peter and John d'Orta, giving their followers security and free license "to preach publicly," as if "faith and salvation lay with them, not with the Roman church, its pontiffs, prelates." This claim was difficult to believe, even the pro-Viterban narrative admitted, but it was corroborated by several heretics who later wanted to return to the catholic faith. Increasingly vindictive, Frederick hanged a dozen young men from Orvieto who had been captured on the road as they came to aid the Viterbans.[29]

Whatever role he played in green-lighting the coup or not, afterward Innocent tried to play the role of mediator in this escalating confrontation, sending Otto, cardinal deacon of San Nicola in Carcere Tulliano, to act as a broker between the emperor and the Viterbans. According to Frederick in his own letters about the siege, the cardinal deacon—my "dear friend," he sardonically calls him, a "good and pure man"—only made matters worse.[30] Cardinal Rainier, also described by Frederick as a "good friend," marshaled the anti-imperial forces in the city, while mendicant friars tended to the wounded and promised the "remission of sins" to those fighting against the emperor's troops, whereby they could "more safely and freely kill our men."[31] Finally, Frederick relates, he reached an agreement that would allow Simon of Teatino and his forces to withdraw from the garrison along with other loyal citizens, who could leave the city unharmed and unspoiled. When they did so, however, Rainier and his men attacked, slaughtering some, imprisoning others, and looting and destroying property belonging to the emperor's supporters. When confronted in the imperial camp by the bloodstained Rainier, Otto did nothing. The Romans, fighting with the Viterbans, the emperor continues, fought "like those sailing for the liberation of the Lord's sepulcher," emboldened by the remission of sins. As the emperor withdrew his forces, the Viterbans and their allies continued to attack unarmed and defenseless men, acting "as if guaranteed paradise." Writing to Otto, Frederick emphasized that he would "complain to everyone" about his promises made and broken.[32]

Judging by the emperor's letters and the reports by distant chroniclers like Matthew Paris, news of the fierce fighting around Viterbo, presented by Frederick as a perverse mockery of a "holy war," spread far and wide. After this final sally from the Viterbans in late November, when even the city's "fragile" women fought like the biblical heroines Judith and Esther, the emperor ended his siege, his forces dissolving at the end of their stipendiary service despite appeals for them to remain.[33] Frederick withdrew to Pisa. Matthew Paris tells us that the emperor's reputation suffered considerably from this turn of events, throwing fuel on the fire of other rumors that Frederick never attended mass, slept with Saracen concubines, and allowed the infidels to build "fortified cities" in his lands. A number of prominent nobles, including Boniface of Montferrat, abandoned his cause. For the Benedictine chronicler, this humiliation called to mind Psalm 82:16: "Fill their faces with shame, and they will seek your name, O Lord."[34]

Peace Achieved

During the months-long battle for Viterbo, plans for some sort of reconciliation between the pope and the emperor continued to move forward. The public openness of both leaders to some sort of accommodation was especially striking, given the sensational scenes of violence surrounding the city. The loss of Viterbo to Cardinal Rainier and his "church party," far from turning Frederick against Innocent, might have given him further incentive to reach a negotiated settlement that would have allowed him to focus attention on pacifying Lombardy without his enemies receiving indulgences and wearing crosses while fighting him. Much like Gregory and Frederick at San Germano thirteen years earlier, for Innocent and the emperor to make peace they did not have to settle all of their differences, just enough of them to end their open discord.

In October, with the coming of cooler weather, Innocent had felt secure enough to begin the return journey to Rome, where he had not set foot since the conclave and death of Celestine IV. It seems unlikely that he would have done so unless he believed that the peace talks with Frederick were more or less on track. Coming back to Rome made a statement. According to Nicholas of Carbio, the pope left Anagni on 16 October but did not enter the city until 20 November. The Franciscan friar did not provide a detailed description of the itinerary in between, but the pope's travels and visits to local communities in between Anagni and Rome would have offered a ceremonial display of the pope's presence and reassertion of his authority after the long vacancy in the papal office. When he finally reached Rome, Nicholas reports, a joyous crowd of clergy and Roman citizens greeted him.[35]

Soon after his arrival, however, Innocent confronted a problem that would continually complicate the dynamics of his papacy—overwhelming debt related to war against Frederick. Much like the Jews who received Christ in Jerusalem with honor on Palm Sunday but later turned their backs on him, Nicholas continues, a group of merchants in the city soon confronted Innocent, demanding the repayment of sixty thousand marks borrowed by Gregory IX. They hounded the pope so much that he lost his appetite and began hiding out in his private chambers. Eventually, outlasting them with his patience, he managed to settle the debt, giving the merchants less than they wanted.[36] This was the first and last time the Franciscan friar mentions the Roman church's financial problems in his vita of the pope, but the costs of war would remain a central concern for the remainder of Innocent's papacy. This cash crunch represented more than just a financial dilemma. It encouraged increasingly intensive measures to raise money through the commutation of crusader vows, the call for direct subsidies by the Apostolic See, and the authorization of bishops to raise revenues for the defense of the church's liberty by levying taxes on clerical properties and incomes, among other measures. Such fiscal activities, in turn, contributed to increasingly hostile forms of criticism and complaints about the papal curia's greed and pastoral failings. Innocent's personal headaches at Rome represented just one small sign of a looming public relations problem.[37]

Regardless of his troubles with creditors, with the pope back in Rome, his negotiations with Frederick continued to gather momentum. At this stage, a new mediator joined the discussions between the two powers, Raymond of Toulouse. The count's on-again, off-again relationship with the Apostolic See had changed yet again when he came to Rome for the first time as Frederick's representative in December. At this point, Innocent authorized the archbishop of Bari to relax the sentence of excommunication leveled against Raymond due to the charges of heresy made against him by Dominican inquisitors in Toulouse, after receiving sufficient oaths and testimonial letters guaranteeing his obedience to the church.[38] In January, when Frederick announced his plans to hold an imperial assembly at Verona, he shared his hopes for the successful outcome of Raymond's negotiations after years of abuse by the Milanese and their accomplices, including the "scandal of public dissension" caused by Gregory IX's sentence of excommunication.[39] The following March, the emperor issued and reissued a written authentication for his other longtime negotiators, Peter de Vinea and Thaddeus of Suessa, to act with special and full power in the case of his excommunication, authorizing them to swear on his behalf to "obey the mandates of the lord pope and church."[40]

On the Feast of the Last Supper, 31 March, this carefully scripted exchange of letters, envoys, and formulas for peace seemed to pay off. As Nicholas of Carbio describes the scene, Peter de Vinea, Thaddeus of Suessa, and Raymond of Toulouse gathered in the Lateran church before the pope, cardinals, and Roman senators and citizens, along with a "very large crowd of others from various parts of the world who had come on that day to visit the apostles' threshold for the Feast of Easter." Baldwin, Latin ruler of Constantinople, was also on hand after traveling to western Europe to seek military and financial aid for his beleaguered empire, as were envoys from the Lombard League and the French and English crowns. During this ceremonial gathering, the imperial representatives swore on the emperor's behalf to obey the mandates of the church and pope, submitting to the specific articles of peace negotiated beforehand. According to Frederick, writing to his son Conrad about this turn of events and asking him to bring this news to the "public notice," Innocent preached a sermon before the crowd, calling Frederick a "devout son of the church" and a "catholic prince," provisionally readmitting him to the unity of the faithful.[41]

Those terms for peace mainly revolved around specific violations of church properties and clerical persons and were intended to more or less restore the status quo ante, that is, before Frederick's second excommunication and the subsequent violence it unleashed between the two powers. The agreement called for the emperor to restore seized lands belonging to the church and its supporters at the time of his excommunication; to free any remaining prisoners from the attack on the Genoese fleet, releasing them from any coerced oaths taken during their captivity and providing them with letters testifying to this fact; to forgive all offenses predating the current conflict between him and the church, revoking his bans, judgments, and sentences; to allow all exiles, clerical and lay, safe passage back to their homes; and to compensate the church for damages caused by imperial officials, although not armies. The articles made specific provisions regarding Gregory of Monte Longo, guaranteeing peace and security for him and his family and restoring lands that belonged to the church's ally, William, count of Tuscany. As for the accusation that Frederick had shown "contempt for the keys of the church," the most troubling of the charges, the agreement recognized his excuse that he had not intended to disregard the sentence of excommunication. The emperor had acted instead on the advice of unnamed German and Italian bishops who had told him that, since he never received formal written notification of the judgment passed against him, he did not have to observe its terms. A failure of communication, not willful heresy, explained his apparent rejection of papal authority. He subsequently realized that he had acted wrongly in this regard, acknowledging that the pope possessed "the fullness of power over all Christians in spiritual matters."[42]

In this manner, the sworn peace of March 1244 seems intended to act as a placeholder, a means of deescalating the current conflict between the papacy and the Hohenstaufen ruler and of setting the stage for further negotiations. The agreement left many issues unresolved, pending forms of "satisfaction" rendered by the emperor, including his provision of funds and soldiers for the "good of Christendom," meaning his contributions toward future crusades, along with other displays of penance, fasting, and the giving of alms according to the pope's instructions. As for causes of Frederick's conflict with the Lombards before his breach with the church, the emperor swore to abide by further mediation from Raynald, cardinal bishop of Ostia; Stephen, cardinal priest of Santa Maria in Trastevere; and Giles, cardinal deacon of Santi Cosma and Damiano, promising to obey the commands of the pope and church, albeit preserving—again, the important caveat—the "honors and rights" that pertained to his empire and kingdoms. Much like the peace struck at San Germano, the agreement made in 1244 called for kings, princes, magnates, and others to provide fiduciary promises on Fredrick's behalf. Presumably, the envoys on hand from these various courts received copies of the articles. Judging by their appearance in Matthew Paris's *Major Chronicle*, where they were partially transcribed by the English monk, the terms for peace did indeed circulate beyond papal and imperial circles.[43]

Looking back at this moment, Matthew Paris and Nicholas of Carbio declared that Frederick had made these compromises fraudulently, deceiving the pope and never intending to honor his commitments.[44] After the ceremony in the Lateran church, however, relations between Innocent and Frederick seemed primed for reconciliation. Sometime in April, an anonymous supporter of the emperor penned an address to all those remaining in captivity from the past years of conflict, celebrating the imminent opening of prisons everywhere. Writing to his son

Conrad, Frederick indicated his expectation that a personal meeting would take place with Innocent sometime soon, when the pope would formally lift the ban against him: a replay, in effect, of the emperor's convivial gathering with Pope Gregory at Anagni after the lifting of his first excommunication. The emperor would then proceed to Lombardy with a "strong arm" to settle matters there. In a letter to the commune of Bergamo, Frederick offered similar predictions, adding that, with the establishment of peace, he would be in a position to join them at last and finally settle the rebellion against his rule.[45]

Frederick's plans to subdue Lombardy from his newfound position of strength served as a reminder that the brokering of peace between him and the Roman church would not come easily. Indeed, no sooner had Innocent, the cardinals, and many others witnessed the solemn oath sworn on Frederick's behalf in the Lateran church than new complaints, uncertainties, and accusations began to arise. An unnamed cardinal wrote to the emperor of Constantinople expressing concerns that the pope did not truly believe in the emperor's promises, due to his support for seditious factions in Rome trying to undermine the peace.[46] A similar letter, likewise attributed to a cardinal and addressed to Frederick, informed him about people in Rome spreading money around in his name—some "in public" (*in publico*), others "in secret" (*in occulto*)—and scheming to create a renewed "scandal" that would draw the emperor away from the church.[47] Writing to Innocent in late April, after hearing news of such happenings, Frederick assured him that he had nothing to do with those who were "sowing the tares of scandal" in Rome by fabricating and circulating letters in his name.[48]

By this point, Innocent seemed to recognize that his planned peace with the emperor was falling apart. On 30 April, the pope wrote to Henry Raspe, landgrave of Thuringia and a possible rival to the Hohenstaufen ruler for the German crown, describing the recent scene in the Lateran church, where Raymond, Peter, and Thaddeus had sworn on the emperor's behalf to obey Innocent's commands insofar as they related to his excommunication by Pope Gregory. Frederick, however, had already begun to reject rather than observe the terms of their agreement. Innocent assured Henry of his support and encouraged him to persist with the business he had begun—an unspoken reference to Henry's possible election as the new "king of the Romans," an idea that had been gaining currency over the previous winter, despite the landgrave's past support for Frederick.[49] Things remained tense in Germany, which was the scene of bitter fighting between local magnates and prelates allied with either the church or imperial party. That same month, Innocent instructed the archbishop of Mainz to renew and announce solemnly on Sundays and feast days with bells and candles all sentences of excommunication and interdict issued against the enemies of the church to assure that their "immense temerity" did not provide a "pernicious example" for others.[50] Invoking the "fullness of power," he also issued a dispensation for Henry to marry

Beatrice, daughter of Henry II, duke of Brabant, despite their relation within the forbidden four degrees of marriage. He issued similar dispensations to other German nobles allied with the landgrave, magnates who opposed to the Hohenstaufen dynasty, along with another privilege for the landgrave of Thuringia: a three-year exemption from being excommunicated without direct papal approval of the sentence. As will become clear below, this was not the last time that the pope would leverage his power to grant dispensations for the purposes of bolstering Frederick's potential enemies.[51]

Judging by a letter he sent to Louis IX in early June, Frederick also realized that the situation was deteriorating quickly. Raymond of Toulouse had recently returned from the papal curia to the imperial court, updating him not just on the pope's intentions regarding the peace, but also on those of the French king. Presumably, Louis and Raymond had been in direct contact with one another or had exchanged news through the envoys of the French crown present in Rome. In this letter, Frederick stressed his commitment to reconciling with the church despite his belief that Innocent, "whom we profess as our most eminent father above all of the princes of the world, cruelly and nefariously chooses to wage war rather than keep the peace." People on all sides complained about the recently arranged agreement between him and the pope, which had achieved through the efforts of a few "strivers for peace." Forces at the curia conspired to impede his preparations to enter Lombardy and to reject the overtures of his envoys. Nevertheless, the emperor intended to ask Innocent to send one of the cardinals back to the imperial court to continue the negotiations for his reconciliation with the church, to whom "we might reveal the innermost intentions of our heart." In closing, Frederick informed Louis of his plans to send Raymond of Toulouse back to the pope one more time, where he would make the emperor's will known to Innocent and the French king. Peace was not off the table entirely, but the hope for a settlement seemed to be vanishing fast.[52]

The Pope on the Run

In June 1244, Innocent made a consequential decision that would shape the remainder of his papacy and its reputation in the wider Christian community. He not only abandoned his negotiations with Frederick, but he also fled from Rome, first traveling to his native Genoa and eventually to Lyon, nominally an imperial possession but effectively an independent principality ruled by the city's bishop. By doing so, he set the stage for his future course of confrontation with the emperor, sending an unmistakable signal that he had no intention of reconciling with Frederick on the terms previously considered—perhaps on no terms, ever. His dramatic flight to Lyons opened a new phase in the public perception of his papacy and the struggle between the two powers, changing the trajectory of his relationship with Frederick and his heirs.

On 28 May, in the Basilica of Saint Peter, Innocent had ordained a new group of cardinals, elevating his former negotiators, Peter Collemezzo and William of Modena, to be the cardinal bishop of Albano and cardinal bishop of Santa Sabina, respectively. He also promoted three cardinal priests and three cardinal deacons, including his cousin, William Fieschi, who became the cardinal deacon of San'Eustachio. More than a week later, responding to Frederick's request, the pope sent Otto da Tenengo, recently raised from cardinal deacon of San Nicola in Carcere Tulliano to his new position as cardinal bishop of Porto, to the imperial court as his envoy for continued peace talks with the emperor.[53] At this point in their negotiations, things became especially murky, as Nicholas of Carbio informs his readers that the pope left Rome for Civita Castellana, wary of the emperor's presence at nearby Interampnum. Frederick, the Franciscan friar insists, was planning "a secret ambush," scheming to seize the pope and cardinals while his envoys maintained the pretense of searching for peace.[54]

Recognizing this imminent treachery, Innocent turned to his native Genoa for help, an early sign of how his family connections would shape the nature of his papacy. He sent a Franciscan named Boiolus to Genoa to meet with a number of his relatives and the current podesta, Philip. Bartholomew the Scribe describes in elaborate terms how the pope sent Boiolus bearing the "most secret letters," with instructions for Philip, along with Innocent's nephews Albert and Jacob Fieschi, to pick up the endangered pontiff at Civitavecchia. Philip revealed the letters to the leading citizens of the city, and they formulated their plan to divert twenty-two galleys, a force prepared for battle against Ansaldus de Mari and his allies from Saône, for the rescue of the pope. They faced the problem, however, of how they might include Innocent's nephews in this subterfuge without tipping their hand to the emperor's friends and allies in the city. The Genoese nobles devised an ingenious performance to enable their plan. Albert and Jacob would ask the podesta for permission to attend one of their relatives' wedding in Parma, a city allied with Frederick, something he would loudly and angrily refuse. They would ask their friends to beg him to reconsider so that the news of their request would "reach the ears" of everyone in Genoa. The charade proceeded along these lines. After the fleet sailed to nearby Voltri, the pope's nephews confronted Philip on his ship. He forbade them to raise the matter again until he returned from the expedition to the coast of Provence, leading them to declare before the gathered crowd that they planned to go to Parma whether he liked it or not. The podesta did not back down and pressured them into swearing an oath that they would accompany him to Provence. Those watching this angry exchange could not believe it. "Behold, we're making war against the lord emperor and with other peoples, and now, we're starting a war with the lord pope," Bartholomew described the Genoese as saying. "We're going to need to seek help from Saracens and Jews, because we're at war with all the other Christians!" At this point, with the podesta in one boat and the pope's nephews in another, the fleet changed course and headed instead for Civitavecchia.[55]

Meanwhile, again according to Nicholas of Carbio, Innocent had traveled to Sutri, where he planned to celebrate the Feast of Saints Peter and Paul on 29 June. Maintaining a "prudent fiction," the pope and his entourage pretended to prepare for celebrating mass. The night before, however, accompanied by a small group of relatives, including his cousin William, along with a number of chaplains and his future biographer, Innocent slipped away and made an exhausting journey to Civitavecchia, where the Genoese ships awaited him. The next day, five more of the cardinals joined him there. Wearing his tiara and apostolic robes, Innocent "blessed the galleys and all those who had come in them, offering the indulgence of sins to everyone." After that, the pope and his entourage boarded the ships and set sail for Genoa. On 7 July, after several harrowing days dealing with storms and uncertain seas, the pope reached his native city. The podesta and other leaders of the commune, the archbishop, and overjoyed citizens turned out to greet him at the port. Bartholomew the Scribe and Nicholas of Carbio describe a similar scene upon Innocent's arrival before a large crowd, the ships and city streets festooned with silks and golden clothes and young boys singing psalms while others played horns, cymbals, and drums.[56]

Whether Innocent acted out of bad faith or genuinely feared for his safety, the sensational news of his secret flight spread far and wide. Despite Matthew Paris's general willingness to give Frederick the benefit of the doubt, in his *Major Chronicle* he writes that the emperor had laid traps for the pope, sending three hundred soldiers to seize him en route to their meeting, although he adds that some believed the pope fled less from fear of the emperor and more out of eagerness for the many gifts he might receive from people elsewhere. Abandoning his papal garments, Innocent "once again became Sinibaldo" and secretly fled to the Genoese galleys accompanied by a small band of cardinals.[57] The *Annals of Saint Justina* record that the pope "secretly and cautiously" fled to Genoa after realizing that the emperor had deceived him with false promises, while the Ghibelline *Annals of Piacenza* accuse Innocent of fleeing in the middle of negotiations, provoking Frederick's outrage at his betrayal. In response, the emperor gathered together as many bishops and clerics as he could, those leaving Rome for their homes in "various parts of the world," and asked them to spread the word that he still desired "concord with the Roman church."[58]

According to Matthew Paris, Frederick denounced the pope's flight, observing with a reference to the Book of Proverbs that only a guilty person flees when no one chases him.[59] In an encyclical sent to all the faithful later that summer, Frederick reviewed the past negotiations between him and Innocent, exposing

Figure 4. Pope Innocent takes flight. From Matthew Paris's *Chronica maiora*. Courtesy of the Parker Library, Corpus Christi College, Cambridge, MS 16, f. 178r.

the contention, scheming, and double-dealing behind their apparent reconciliation.[60] He provided numerous examples of bad behavior by the pope and his representatives, including saying one thing and then doing the opposite, such as when the cardinal legate Otto had promised "in public sight" to allow the withdrawal of imperial forces from Viterbo but then allowed the Viterbans to slaughter Frederick's troops. Such double-dealing was "manifestly proven by many public witnesses and legitimate documents."[61] The emperor revealed Innocent's "cunning" manipulation of the peace talks at Rome, demanding that the emperor place the Lombard business into his hands. Frederick, now "experienced in the dangers of compromising with the church in this way," had refused, reviewing the instances when the church had made promises but did not keep them. The pope also acted deceptively regarding the prisoners still held by the emperor, retroactively claiming that the draft articles of their agreement, which called for the release of captives seized during the sinking of the Genoese fleet and afterward, included those captured at the battle of Courtenuova years earlier.[62]

Frederick insisted that the restoration of church property and the unsettled situation in Lombardy remained the real stumbling blocks to peace. During the negotiations, Innocent had said—not openly, but privately (*non palam sed clam*)—that he would not give an inch where the Lombards were concerned, not even when Raymond of Toulouse and Baldwin of Constantinople begged him to reconsider. After the emperor's envoys had rendered their vows on Frederick's behalf the pope, thinking the emperor trapped by his oath, appeared before the Lombards' legates, weeping and acting upset, trying to reopen the topic of the emperor's rights in Lombardy. Seeing his open display of affection toward the Lombards, Frederick's representatives vainly protested. In many other ways, the pope had shown that he had no real interest in peace, such as when he agreed that the details of their settlement would not be made public until finished and affixed with the appropriate seals. And yet, after adding conditions that were never discussed or agreed upon, Innocent exposed the terms "before everybody, to the point that anyone who wanted a copy could purchase one for six denars in the Lateran Church." As evidence of this shocking behavior, Frederick called upon the "public testimony of the cardinals, who were greatly upset by this." In addition, he claimed, the pope told ambassadors from the French king that he would continue to help the Lombards fight against the emperor, even if he absolved Frederick.[63] Disregarding these betrayals, Frederick had still hoped for a personal meeting with Innocent in Campagna. The pope had agreed to speak with him. In early June, the emperor met with the cardinal bishop Otto to parse two different versions of an earlier peace agreement with the Milanese that was never concluded. Frederick indicated his willingness to follow either of them. The pope could choose which one. Then a rumor reached Frederick that the pope, armed and dressed like a soldier, had secretly fled from Sutri to the coast and been carried away by a fleet of Genoese galleys to Liguria or somewhere north of the Alps, where he might proceed to "our detriment, and that of the empire."[64]

A number of chroniclers tell us that as word spread "throughout the entire world" of Innocent's presence in Genoa, friendly observers stood amazed by his great wisdom in seeking refuge there. Envoys came from cities in Lombardy, including Milan, Brescia, Piacenza, and others, along with Boniface, marquis de Montferrat, whom the pope greeted with honor and the "kiss of peace." Around this time, Matthew Paris writes, the pope again reached out to Henry, landgrave of Thuringia, calling upon him to take up the "imperial dignity" until the princes might properly elect him and asking him to make war on Frederick as a "general and public persecutor of the church." The emperor's reputation continued to suffer due to the stories about his refusal to "walk on the path of the Lord's law" and his preference for the company of infidels. Making a sudden and secret trip to Germany, Frederick met with Henry and diverted his "womanly spirit" from this plan. The two parted as the best of friends for the time being.[65]

By the early fall, Innocent had begun to make plans for his departure from Genoa. In his *Major Chronicle*, Matthew Paris describes how the pope sent an "elegant letter" to the Cistercian monks gathered for their general chapter meeting at Cîteaux in September, beseeching them to beg the French ruler and his mother Blanche for help against the "the emperor's insults." When Louis and Blanche arrived at the chapter meeting, the brothers made this request on bended knees with clasped hands, inspiring the king to declare his support for the pope against the emperor, even to the extent of welcoming him to the French kingdom in exile. Louis made this promise despite the presence of Frederick's own envoys at Cîteaux, trying to counteract Innocent's appeals. Later in his chronicle, Matthew suggests another possibility for the pope's fleeing: that he eventually planned to reach England, having secretly asked an unnamed cardinal to send a letter to Henry III proposing such a move. Innocent, the cardinal intimated, would love to see the "wonders of Westminster and the riches of London." The English king, showing his typical lack of judgment, would have joyfully gone along with this "treacherous plan," although his counselors managed to convince him otherwise, spelling out the financial damage this would cause to the kingdom, which was already overrun by usurers like the "Cahorsins," Italians, and Romans. France and Aragon likewise denied entry to the pope, Matthew observes, because they were repelled by the "evil name" and "stench" of the curia.[66]

Bartholomew the Scribe, describing Innocent's nearly fatal illness after he reached Genoa, tells us that the pope had a clear destination in mind from the beginning of his flight: "I wish to go to Lyons before I die," he told the Genoese, "to show Christians, prelates and princes of the church, the hardship and injury that the church of God has suffered. If I cannot ride, I will have to be carried." In light of his recent traumatic experiences aboard ship, Innocent refused to travel by sea. Carried in a bier, Innocent left Genoa on October 5 with several cardinals, notaries, chaplains, and other officials, bearing some version of a mobile archive containing papal records. Mindful of the dangers he faced, he left accompanied by Genoese soldiers.[67]

Innocent's hazardous journey from Genoa to Lyons took just under two months. Nicholas of Carbio, who made the trip with him, describes his passage with great detail and pathos: the sick pope, nearly dying, was greeted joyfully at various towns along the way, although he still feared treachery from the emperor's allies. His transit created some tense scenes. At Asti, a town controlled by imperial officials, the citizens denied Innocent entry, shutting their gates against him. The pope and his party stayed instead at a nearby monastery, humbly received by the brothers. The next day, however, after a fierce debate among the townspeople, the podesta and leaders of the commune emerged at dawn, welcoming Innocent and humbly begging his forgiveness for their injurious behavior. Floods of men and women came out to greet the pope. A few days later, at Susa, six more cardinals, who came from Sutri and France, joined Innocent's entourage, including Hugh of Saint-Cher, cardinal priest of Santa Sabina, and Eudes de Châteauroux, cardinal bishop of Tusculanum. Finally, after experiencing "the dangers of the sea, rivers, roads, enemies and other kinds of sickness with equanimity," Innocent traveled up the Rhone and reached Lyons with "great joy and exaltation" on 2 December 1244, received by the people of the city, clergy, and laity with great honor. Although the pope could not have known it at the time, he would remain in residence there for over seven years.[68]

~

During the summer and fall of 1244, as Christians around Europe followed the ins and outs of Innocent's deteriorating relationship with Frederick, they also began to hear dire news about disturbing events abroad. The "most cruel and inhumane" Khwarezmian Turks, expelled from their homeland in Persia by the advancing Mongols, had invaded Palestine and sacked the holy city of Jerusalem in August. Thousand were slaughtered, even those taking refuge in the Church of the Holy Sepulcher, which, many chroniclers lamented, the Turks thoroughly sacked.[69] By October, the leaders of the remaining Christian forces in the region, including the patriarch of Jerusalem and the master generals of the military orders, assembled an army at Acre to repel the Khwarezmian army. Muslim allies from Damascus and Homs joined the crusaders as they marched south to engage the Khwarezmians, who were reinforced by their own ally, the sultan of Egypt. When the two sides met in battle near Gaza on 17 October, the Turks and Egyptians routed the Muslim forces from Homs and Damascus, who abandoned the crusaders to their fate: thousands died, including a great number of bishops, nobles, and the leaders of the military orders.[70] Desperate to tell their coreligionists back in Europe about these horrible events, Robert, patriarch of Jerusalem, sent a widely circulated letter to the Western church signed by numerous prelates from the Latin church in the east, describing the recent sack of Jerusalem, the desecration of the Holy Sepulcher, and the destruction of the crusader forces at Gaza and calling desperately for military aid.[71]

Jerusalem lost again, the Church of the Holy Sepulcher defiled, Christian armies wiped out. The signs of such ill news for Christendom could be found in marvelous places, Matthew Paris wanted his readers to know. After describing the Khwarezmian Turks' invasion of the holy places, he pointed to some prophetic happenings that had preceded these shocking developments and that truly fulfilled the Lord's predictions that "not a stone will remain on another" in the city of Jerusalem. A few years earlier in Mecca, when a statue of Muhammad had fallen over, Christians had mocked his followers. Now, the Saracens said, by the grace of God and Muhammad, the "Chrosomins" had laid waste to the Christians' lands and holy places. Referencing the preaching of the Dominicans and Franciscans, spreading the word of God in foreign lands, Matthew cited Romans 18:18, "Their voice has gone out to the ends of the earth." Portents were everywhere: the sterility of the land and sea, two eclipses of the sun in three years, stars falling from the heavens. As for the "church and empire," he observed, "there is a greater discord between them than ever known before." If Pope Innocent could have read these words after his harrowing journey to Lyons, he no doubt would have agreed with this assessment. For Matthew and others like him, the question must have remained, what would the pope, installed at Lyons, do about these calamities facing Christendom?[72]

Chapter 6

The Council

Two days after celebrating Christmas in 1244, Pope Innocent delivered a sermon on the Feast of John the Evangelist announcing his intention to hold a general church council at Lyons on 24 June, the next Feast of John the Baptist. In that act of "public preaching," as Nicholas of Carbio describes the scene, he summoned Frederick II to appear at that council to present his case before the assembly and face judgment for his sins and crimes.[1] On 3 January 1245, Innocent broadcast his decision to hold a universal synod at Lyons with a widely circulated letter, *Dei virtus et*, calling for the "kings of the earth, the prelates of the church, and other princes of the world" to attend the planned assembly or send worthy envoys to join its deliberations. In this address, the pope laid out a clear agenda for the synod: to alleviate the deplorable suffering of the Holy Land; to aid the endangered Latin empire in Romania; to find relief against the Tartars and other persecutors of the Christian people; and, finally, to "settle the business that lies between the church and the prince." Innocent informed the recipients of this letter that he had issued a summons for Frederick to appear in person or through his envoys to answer the charges against him.[2]

The Council of Lyons met as planned during the following summer for three sessions, on 28 June, 5 July, and after a deliberate delay, 17 July. Frederick stood accused of four principal crimes: perjury, violating the peace, sacrilege, and suspicion of heresy. Thaddeus of Suessa, his principal representative present for the deliberations, denounced the proceedings as illegitimate and appealed to a future pope or a general council for judgment. During the third session, after hearing written and oral evidence against the emperor, Innocent issued a formal judgment deposing Frederick of his honors, his empire, and his other kingdom.[3] Perhaps not surprisingly, controversy and debate have surrounded this decision down through twentieth-century scholarship on the subject. For some, Innocent's pronouncement stands as a landmark in the history of the papal monarchy. As Walter Ullmann once evocatively declared about the trial, "The hierocratic idea had indeed achieved a resounding victory at Lyons: the pope, the master of the world, had become the embodiment of an idea."[4] That idea found expression in the Old

Testament figure of Melchizedek, both a priest and a king, who foreshadowed the true King of Kings, Jesus Christ. Passing his sentence against the emperor, Innocent acted as just such a priestly and royal figure, combining the two powers in his apostolic office.[5] For others, the council's deliberations were mere window dressing for a decision already made by the pope and his inner circle, nothing less than a judicial "farce." Still others have insisted that the trial properly followed canonical procedures, legitimating the pope's action against the emperor.[6]

Beyond its ideological or judicial implications, the Council of Lyons provided a high-stakes forum for the building of a public case against the Hohenstaufen ruler. Hundreds of clergy and lay representatives gathered at the assembly, where they watched liturgical performances, listened to sermons, and heard letters read aloud and verbal testimony delivered against Frederick. Some attendees protested or cautioned against the emperor's deposition. Those on hand would have conversed and gossiped about the pope's decision and other dire happenings in Christendom before returning home to share the news about what they had seen, said, and heard. From this perspective, rather than the arbitrary act of an aspirational priest-king or legal farce, Innocent's deposition of Frederick at Lyons seems like the sensational trial of the century, fascinating and dividing contemporaries.[7] Convincing Christians that this particular pope had made the right call by deposing this specific emperor required more than just legal certitude. It involved an equally important effort to communicate the reasons for the papal decision to depose Frederick, spelling out the consequences of that judgment for the emperor, his subjects, and the Christian community as a whole. Not surprisingly, Frederick openly contested Innocent's interpretation of events and tried to cast aspersions on the pope's judgment. Those caught in the middle faced the hard decision of how to respond to such pressures. As a result, rather than resolving the discord between the chief representatives of the two powers, the Council of Lyons intensified the public breach between the pope and emperor like never before.

Rome on the Rhone

By making his dramatic flight to Lyons in the fall of 1244, Innocent had created an unusual situation in the history of the medieval church, more or less permanently installing the papal curia somewhere else than Rome. As seen earlier in this book, popes commonly spent time outside of the City, leaving willingly or unwillingly for nearby communities. During times of previous trouble in Rome, some of them had even sought refuge north of the Alps.[8] Innocent's decision to settle at Lyons for the foreseeable future, while planning for a general council to meet there, signaled a far more consequential move, rerouting the lines of communication that led to the administrative, financial, and to some extent symbolic nexus of the Roman church. As the canonistic formulation put it, *Ubi est papa, ibi est Roma*: "Where the pope is, Rome is there."[9] Accordingly, Christians around Europe had to reorient themselves toward a new working center for Christendom.

After reaching Lyons, Nicholas of Carbio tells us, Innocent, the cardinals, and other clergy at the curia installed themselves in the church of Saint Just and the cathedral church of Saint John the Baptist, reorganizing the city "like the battle-line of a military encampment." The pope also established a school for studying theology and canon law. Innumerable people began to arrive "from every part of the world," making the city into "another Rome," while Innocent exercised his apostolic duties to relieve the oppressed and condemn their oppressors, dealing with everyone according to their merits. The everyday management of the papal monarchy—confirming elections, hearing appeals, granting dispensations, and more—brought a flood of clerics, petitioners, proctors, and envoys to Lyons. The long vacancy in the papal office before Innocent's election, Nicholas observes, had left a backlog of unsettled business.[10] Numerous bishops from Gaul and Spain came to the pope at Lyons, as did the archbishop of Cologne, "whom the pope received and honored among the greatest dignitaries."[11] In his *Major Chronicle*, Matthew Paris describes how a number of English clergy—including Robert Grosseteste, bishop of Lincoln, in the middle of a fight with Lincoln's cathedral canons over his rights of visitation, along with Boniface, the newly elected archbishop of Canterbury, who had been consecrated by the pope in January 1245—immediately departed for Lyons for various reasons.[12]

As noted above, when Innocent fled from central Italy, he and his household staff brought with them his papal registers and other records. Innocent had good reasons to bring those detailed records with him. Escaping to Lyons did not mean escaping from the Roman church's overwhelming debt, much of it linked to previous years of warfare with Frederick and his allies. Soon after reaching the city, the pope renewed his efforts to collect overdue payments from Gregory IX's 1228 tithe in England, monies still owed for the "defense of the catholic faith, ecclesiastical liberty, and the patrimony."[13] Matthew Paris did not conceal his disapproval about the ecclesiastical goods—gold, silver, precious vestments, liturgical vessels, and other riches—that flooded into Lyons, brought by visiting prelates, favor seekers, and papal agents who managed to evade "imperial snares" and reach the city. Abbot Hugh of Cluny sent thirty, or perhaps as many as eighty, palfreys with saddles and accouterments to the pope, including one for each cardinal. So many people arrived at Lyons bringing gifts, Matthew observes, that some began to suspect Innocent came to the city to rake in such wealth, not because he had been forced to flee from anyone.[14] Matthew also relates that in May a fire broke out in Innocent's chambers, where those materials were housed. In his *Major Chronicle*, the English chronicler suggests that the pope started the fire deliberately, hoping to use the losses as an excuse to extort money from visitors to Lyons, but the blaze got out of hand. But in his *History of the English,* he changed his story, claiming that one of the pope's ministers in the chancery caused the fire by neglect and then blamed it on "secret arsonists" sent by the emperor to kill the pope.[15]

Given all of this traffic and the accompanying demands of the curia, Matthew continues, the papacy's installation at Lyon caused tensions with the locals. The canons of the cathedral chapter, for instance, protested when Innocent, true to form, tried to assign several prebends to his relatives. The canons threatened to toss any such office seekers into the Rhone. On another occasion, the pope's doorkeeper refused entry to a citizen from the city. An altercation broke out and the irate burger cut off the cleric's hand. When the injured doorkeeper showed his mutilated limb to Innocent, the pope demanded vengeance according to the "laws of the city," although Philip of Savoy, bishop-elect of Valencia and "guardian of peace" in Lyons, managed to smooth things over.[16] Security was tight, given the pope's antagonistic relationship with Frederick. Philip acted as the leader of what Matthew Paris calls a "papal militia" in the city. The anonymous *Account of the Council of Lyons,* an important eyewitness source for the ecclesiastical gathering, states that members of the military orders acted as guards for the curia, incurring considerable expenses.[17]

As the time for the council drew near, travelers continued to arrive at Lyons, some coming from far afield, bringing with them letters, news, and rumors. One of the exotic visitors was a Russian archbishop named Peter, who came seeking aid for his people against the Tartars. He did not know Hebrew, Greek, or Latin and had to speak before the curia through a translator. Questioned by the clergy present, Peter gave a long and detailed account of the barbarians' religious beliefs and rites, their habits and ways of fighting, and their desire to rule over the entire world.[18] Such long-distance traffic went both ways, since Innocent dispatched representatives to points beyond Europe's borders, relying especially upon members of the mendicant orders as missionaries endowed with special rights and privileges. In his vita of the pope, Nicholas of Carbio celebrates how Innocent, "burning with the desire to enrich heaven with the souls of lost Gentiles," sent from Lyons "solemn legates and envoys bearing solemn letters to the barbarian nations of diverse provinces, apostate peoples, so that they might recoil from their errors and worship of idols, and the 'fullness of the Gentiles' might enter into the holy catholic faith."[19] Those missionary-diplomats included the Dominican friar Andrew of Longjumeau and the Franciscan John of Plano Carpini, both of whom left Lyons in March 1245. Andrew journeyed to the Eastern Mediterranean and Persia, while John conveyed papal letters to the "great khan" Güyük, explaining the pope's status as the Vicar of Christ and calling for the pagan ruler's conversion.[20]

Through such messengers, news of the contest between the two powers in Europe reached distant places. When he returned to Lyons two years later, Andrew brought back letters from several Eastern Christian prelates outlining the articles of the "Nestorian" and "Jacobite" faiths. According to one such letter, which had been sent by the Catholicus of the Eastern church Simon Raban-ata to Pope Innocent, traveling merchants had told him about the struggle between the Roman pontiff and the emperor. Stressing the great damage done to the holy places in recent years, Simon called upon Innocent to forgive Frederick's sins and reconcile him with the church for the common good. He also sent a letter to Frederick. Quoting Matthew 12:25, "A kingdom divided against itself will be ruined," the Syrian churchman beseeched the emperor to submit to the pope's judgment, to do penance for his sins, and to seek the pontiff's advice about the "business of the Holy Land and Christendom."[21] It remains unclear whether Frederick ever received this letter or responded to this distant expression of concern over his fight with the Roman pope. After John of Plano Carpini returned to Lyons in 1247, he wrote a book about his travels in central Asia. Salimbene of Adam, who listened to him read aloud from its pages, describes how the khan questioned the Franciscan friar during his stay at the Tartar court, asking about the number of rulers in the "Western lands." There were two, John replied, the pope and the emperor and all others derived their leadership from them. Which one was greater, the khan queried? The pope, John answered, and then read him one of Innocent's letters to prove it. Güyük remained unimpressed, sending John back with his own letter and demanding that the pope submit along with the other princes of the West—or else, face destruction.[22]

Setting the Stage

In the spring of 1245, Güyük Khan's menacing reply to Innocent's overtures still lay two years away, but the threat posed by the Tartars continued to weigh heavily on the minds of Christian communities and leaders around Europe. The clergy gathering at Lyons had only to listen to the Russian archbishop Peter, speaking through his translator, to be reminded about the Tartars' bizarre habits, strange ways, and ruthlessness.[23] The situation in Jerusalem likewise consumed people's attention, as letters from the holy places describing the Khwarezmian Turks' horrific sack of Jerusalem circulated around western monasteries, churches, and courts. The *Annals of St. Pantaleon* report that one such letter, "written, it was said, in human blood," had reached Pope Innocent in December 1244, soon after his arrival in Lyons.[24]

The internal struggle between the two powers, however, dominated the lead-up to the council more than anything else. The wider Christian community knew that the pope planned to pass judgment, one way or another, against Frederick.

Dei virtus et informed its recipients that Innocent had summoned the emperor to attend the synod, either personally or through his envoys, to defend himself. A version of that encyclical sent directly to Frederick might have served as his written citation. In his *Annals*, Bartholomew the Scribe writes that Innocent called the council wishing to show everyone how Frederick, "under the guise of peace, sought to devour the church, and so that he might consult them about what to do." Bartholomew goes on to say that the pope summoned the emperor to appear "through solemn envoys and apostolic letters." The Ghibelline *Annals of Piacenza* also mention a "form of citation" sent by the pope to the emperor.[25] Nicholas of Carbio, however, says that Innocent's Christmas-day sermon provided the only citation Frederick ever received, implying that the excommunicate ruler's blockade of roads and seaways prevented papal messengers from reaching him with a written summons, as required by canon law.[26]

During the months preceding the gathering, the pope and his representatives kept up the pressure on the emperor. Whoever wrote in the *Chronicle of Worms* for the year 1245, friendly toward Frederick and his son Conrad, describes how Innocent "solemnly" and "publicly" denounced the emperor on Easter at the urging of Frederick's enemies, the archbishops of Mainz and Cologne.[27] The pope also instructed bishops in the region not to accept any letters or envoys from the prince, calling upon them to remain steadfast in their loyalty to the church and to inviolably observe any sentences rightly passed by the archbishop against "rebels."[28] As always, publicizing the emperor's anathema caused tensions and problems in various localities. The *Chronicle of Worms* describes how Landulf, bishop of Worms, feared denouncing Frederick as instructed by the archbishop of Mainz, since the majority of the city's inhabitants stood by the emperor and his son. To avoid doing so, he paid off the archbishop with gold and jewels, incurring significant debts. Around the time of Lent, according to Matthew Paris, clergy in France and England likewise renewed and repeated the ruler's ban in churches and other visible locations, spreading the "infamy of his name throughout Christendom." In the city of Paris, one priest balked, delivering a sermon to his entire parish about his instructions to issue the solemn sentence of excommunication against the emperor and performing the full ceremony of anathema with candles burning and bells ringing. The priest did not understand the reasons why he should do this, other than the fact that an "unquenchable hatred" had arisen between Frederick and the pope. With a levity typical of the French, Matthew observes, he said he would excommunicate whichever party was truly causing such injuries to "all of Christendom" and absolve the other. Word of this jest spread far and wide. When Frederick heard about it, he sent the priest a gift; the pope, failing to appreciate the joke, punished him.[29]

During those same months, negotiations between the curia and Frederick did not stop entirely, even if they assumed a less solemn profile than previously. The lines of communication remained open in March and April, thanks in large part to Albert, patriarch of Antioch, who was still active after years of representing papal interests in the Holy Land and Lombardy. During a previous meeting with the pope and cardinals, Albert had informed them about his time spent at the imperial court, where he found Frederick willing and inclined toward making a "good peace." As Innocent made clear, Albert did not have a special commission to treat with Frederick, but the pope indicated that would not stand in Albert's way if he wished to return to the imperial court. In March, Albert still remained in the dark about the pope's plans and narrowly missed meeting with Frederick on at least one occasion. Given Frederick's excommunicate status, Albert must have expected to engage with him through intermediaries when he finally managed to track him down.[30] In his ongoing correspondence with Innocent and Cardinal Rainier, the patriarch continued to insist that Frederick remained genuinely committed to some sort of reconciliation with the church, blaming his officials for committing many of the wrongs attributed to the emperor. In April, Frederick wrote directly to Innocent, expressing his confidence in the patriarch, a "longtime friend," and his continued willingness to go on crusade in accordance with the pope's instructions.[31] Albert, meanwhile, expressed his reticence to make any firm commitments without approval from the pope and awaited "apostolic orders." Writing to Rainier, the patriarch of Antioch adopted a far more assertive tone, calling on him and his supporters not to take harmful actions that might impede the possibilities for peace. According to Albert, Frederick had said that a state of concord between him and the church might already have been achieved if not for the revolt at Viterbo a year and a half earlier. Responding to the patriarch that he remained "favorable toward peace," Innocent said that he would still be willing to reconcile with Frederick if the emperor honored the commitments he had made just over a year ago at the Lateran church. The time for such an agreement, however, was running out, since the start of the pope's planned general council lay just two months away.[32]

That spring, while Albert played the role of cautious mediator between the papal curia and the imperial court, Viterbo again became a flash point when the emperor laid siege to the city for a second time. Writing in May to the podesta and civic leaders of his birthplace, Rainier informed them about his ongoing correspondence with Albert, forwarding some of the patriarch's letters to them, but he cautioned them against placing faith in the emperor, even after he withdrew his forces from the siege. Frederick did not end his attack out of any love for them or their city. Quite the opposite: the emperor told Albert, who passed the news on to Rainier, that he would spare the papal patrimony further attacks, except for the Viterbans, who had willfully violated the peace agreement struck during his first siege of the city two years earlier. "If he was dead," Rainier quoted the emperor as saying, "he would want his bones to rise up, if able, and to surge forth for the destruction of Viterbo." If he had one foot in paradise, the emperor reportedly continued, he would drag it out and move personally to wipe out the city. The cardinal deacon also warned the citizens that Frederick had spoken publicly about his hopes for treachery within the city to enable its conquest from without. Rainier had it on good authority that the emperor never would have besieged Viterbo a second time without the expectation of aid from his loyalists inside. Writing back to Rainier and stressing their fidelity to the church, the citizens of Viterbo called for further aid, now that the "winter of war" had been renewed and the "summer of reconciliation" drawn to an abrupt close. The cardinal deacon's support did not extend to additional financial contributions. Corresponding with podesta and city government after Frederick lifted his siege, Rainier told them not to ask for more money, reminding them about his heavy debts and informing them that pope had not given him a single denarius for such expenses.[33]

Meanwhile, clergy and laity of various ranks and origins had begun to arrive at Lyons in serious numbers. When not generalizing about the "multitudes" present, contemporary history writers offer figures anywhere from one hundred and fifty to three hundred bishops and abbots joining the majority of the cardinals and other members of the curia. The patriarchs of Antioch, Constantinople, and Aquileia were present as well. Along with such churchmen and their proctors, the crowd included prominent nobles such as Raymond of Toulouse, Raymond of Provence, and the Baldwin of Constantinople and lay envoys from England, Spain, France, and the cities of Lombardy. The details of the delegation from England—Earl Roger Bigod, John Fitz-Geoffrey, William de Cantilupe, Philip Basset, Ralph Fitz-Nicholas, and William de Powick—are especially well known.[34] Attendees from Germany and the Regno were fewer in number due to the difficulties of traveling territories held by Frederick or his allies. The devastation caused by the Tartars and Khwarezmian Turks prevented still others from attending. Last but not least, Frederick's representatives—Thaddeus of Suessa, Peter de Vinea, Walter d'Orca, and Bernard, archbishop of Palermo—and other clergy still favoring the imperial party arrived at Lyons before the council began.[35]

In his *Major Chronicle,* Matthew Paris describes a meeting of the council's attendees on 26 June held in the refectory at the Church of Saint-Just, two days before the first session. At this gathering, Baldwin of Constantinople spoke first about the deplorable conditions in Greece and the near loss of the entire Latin empire to the resurgent Byzantines. Innocent, according to Matthew, said nothing in response. The English delegation raised another part of their business at Lyons: seeking the canonization of Saint Edmund, something that the pope wished to put off until more serious matters were addressed. Thaddeus of Suessa also spoke to those present, stressing that his lord Frederick continued to desire peace and concord with the pope and promising on his behalf to return the schismatic Greeks to the unity of the Roman church, to battle the Saracens and other enemies of the church, and to restore the church's properties. Insisting that Frederick had made such promises before and failed to fulfill them, Innocent rejected Thaddeus's proposal for the French and English crowns to stand as guarantors of the peace, which would leave the pope at war with all three powers when the emperor inevitably broke his word. Finally, the attendees heard further news about the Khwarezmian Turks. Waleran, bishop of Beirut, asked his companion, the Dominican preacher Arnulf, to read aloud letters that described their horrible attack on the holy places. Waleran and Arnulf had come personally bearing such correspondence, reaching Venice from the Holy Land in May before coming to Lyons.[36]

On the eve of the council, other letters apparently circulated at Lyons behind the scenes rather than being read aloud or presented openly. During the lead-up to the first session, someone from the ranks of the Roman church, a person mostly likely linked to Cardinal Rainier's circle, composed two scripturally charged, apocalyptically themed letters against Frederick: *Iuxta vatacinium Ysiae* and *Aspidis ova reperant*. Scholars have sometimes suggested that Innocent IV, with his logical legal mind, had little use for such visceral works of propaganda. Their production, however, did not diminish under his papacy and seemed to indicate that the pope encouraged or did not discourage such attacks on the soon-to-be-judged emperor.[37] There is no way of knowing how many people read or heard these letters at Lyons, but the contents of both addresses closely mirrored the charges subsequently laid against Frederick in the sentence deposing him. Copies of both epistles are found in the letter book associated with Cardinal Rainier, who was in Rome during the synod, but they are also included in the letter collection that belonged to the papal legate, Albert Beiham, who was present for the deliberations.[38]

Iuxta vatacinium Ysiae resumed the apocalyptically charged themes of earlier polemics against the emperor that were produced just after his excommunication in 1239. This new political broadside assailed Frederick's reputation, referring to him as a "tyrant, a destroyer of the church's teaching, an inverter of the faith, master of cruelty, changer of the age, waster of the globe, and hammer of the world." Channeling imagery from the Book of Daniel and Revelation, the letter narrated Frederick's past abuses of the faithful, including his siege of Pope Gregory in Rome, his attempts to bribe the cardinals during the vacancy in the papal office, his attack on Viterbo when the city abandoned his rule, and his false promises of peace that eventually drove the Roman pontiff to seek refuge north of the Alps.[39] *Iuxta vatacinium Ysiae* rolled out every rumor, charge, and accusation leveled against the emperor to date, denouncing his unlawful dominion. "Like a type and forerunner of Antichrist," the letter declares, "he does not permit anyone under his authority to pass through lands subject to his rule, or to buy or sell, unless that person bears the mark and number of his name on his right hand." This polemical text also highlighted Frederick's links to the Saracens at home and abroad, along with his plundering of church property, blocking of roads, and abuse of captives. The need for judgment stood above doubt: "Cast him from the sanctuary of the Lord, so that he does not reign over the Christian people any longer!"[40]

In similar terms, *Aspidis ova reperant* denounced the "seed" of Frederick I and Henry VI, the boy favored by the church as a youth who had turned on his mother.[41] This letter placed a particular emphasis on all of the vows that the emperor had broken, those taken as a vassal of the Roman church and his oath to go on crusade. When the emperor made peace with the church at San Germano, he set the stage for another act of perjury, creating the conditions for his renewed excommunication in 1239. The letter compares Frederick with Ozias, the biblical king struck by leprosy when he usurped the powers of the priesthood, just as the emperor was struck by the "leprosy of excommunication" when did not desist from his wicked deeds.[42] In addition to other crimes, Frederick had threatened the pope and cardinals with his "imperial letters," defaming Pope Gregory throughout the world, and had forced clergy to celebrate the mass for him, despising the pope's "power to bind." By doing so, he manifestly revealed himself to be a heretic.[43]

By making these accusations, the emperor's opponents did their best to blanket the synod with a review of his supposed crimes and an unforgiving attack on his character. Some people might have needed convincing. Even at this late date, Frederick's allies saw room for some sort of maneuvering or at least believed that not all of the cardinals stood entirely against him. In a letter addressed to the cardinals, which was brought to Lyons by Thaddeus of Suessa, the emperor opened with a particular emphasis on his unswerving commitment to Christian doctrine and practice, stressing his fidelity as a "devout son and special defender of those with zeal for the Christian law and orthodox faith," whose "sacred mysteries we catholically observe and venerate with the reverence of our entire heart and body." He still desired to settle the "cause of dissension" between him and the "highest pontiff, our most holy father." Aware that the pope had turned against him, Frederick expressed his fear that Christ's vicar—"would that he was a just judge!"—would raise up "the spiritual sword against us in a temporal way, and proceed, if it might be said so, less than justly." For this reason, facing the pope's "oppression and iniquitous trial," the emperor had sent his envoys before the cardinals to lodge their appeal for judgment by a future pope, along with the princes of Germany, and generally all of the kings and princes of the world and other Christians. Frederick clearly wanted to cast doubt on the legitimacy of the council before it even started.[44]

The First Session

On 28 June, the vigil of Saint Peter, Pope Innocent formally convened the general council of Lyons in the Cathedral of St. John the Baptist. The anonymous *Account of the Council of Lyons* describes in detail the highly formalized staging of the opening ceremonies. Innocent sat in an elevated space near the high altar with Baldwin of Constantinople seated to his right and other lay princes to his left, joined by the cardinal deacons, the vice chancellor of the curia, the auditor of contradictory letters, the corrector of papal letters, additional subdeacons, chaplains, and notaries. Below, arranged in the nave according to their rank, sat the patriarchs of Constantinople, Antioch, and Aquileia, the cardinal bishops, and well over a hundred other bishops, abbots, and procurators from various cathedral chapters. Envoys from other lay powers also sat in the nave, including the emperor's envoys. A series of standard hymns and litanies followed, chanted by the pope accompanied by Giles, cardinal deacon of Sainti Cosma and Damiano; Ottoviano, cardinal deacon of Santa Maria in Via Lata; and a papal chaplain named Galitianus.[45]

After completing this liturgical sequence, Innocent approached the high altar to deliver a sermon, taking as his theme Psalm 93:19, "According to the multitude of my sorrows in my heart, your comforts have given joy to my soul." Echoing the language of his earlier call for the general council to meet at Lyons, he explained to those listening the five sorrows in his heart: first, corruption among the clergy; second, the "insolence of the Saracens," including the recent sack of Jerusalem by Khwarezmians; third, the "schism of the Greeks," who threatened the Latin empire of Constantinople; fourth, the "savagery of the Tartars," who had invaded "the land of the Christians"; and fifth, "the persecution of the Emperor Frederick."[46] Innocent described how the emperor had assailed the church and his predecessor, Pope Gregory, as made clear "publicly" in letters that the emperor had sent "throughout the entire world" claiming that he opposed that pontiff personally but not the entire church. This was patently untrue, since he had continued to afflict the church during the vacancy in the papal office.[47]

With this sermon completed, the pope made his case against the emperor. The *Account of the Council of Lyons* describes what happened next:

> And after he said many things about afflictions of this sort, he had read a certain charter fixed with the emperor's golden bull when he was still king and granted to the pope's predecessor Honorius. Among other things, it chiefly contained how he had sworn an oath of fidelity to him, like a vassal to his lord. And a certain other charter, in which he acknowledged that the Regno of Sicily and Apulia was a special patrimony of Saint Peter and that he held it as a fief from the church, conceding and guaranteeing that, if he

> held any right of election in the churches of the aforesaid Regno, he would make them free and clear, immune from any exactions. Likewise, the pope had read many other charters fixed with the golden bull granted to the church, when he was king and afterward emperor, in which it was held that he had waived his rights over, bestowed, recognized, and confirmed the boundaries of papal lands from the town of Radicophani to the town of Ceperani, the March of Anconi, the Duchy of Spoleto, the Exarchate of Ravenna and Pentapolis, the County of Bertinoro, the lands of Countess Mathilda, and many others that were there.[48]

Thaddeus of Suessa then took the floor: "After all of this was said, Thaddeus, one of the emperor's envoys, rose and replied to near every point that the pope had raised, and marvelously seemed to excuse the emperor. He asserted the many ills that, he said, the church had committed and arranged against the emperor, and he demonstrated this with many parts of letters. His response was welcome to many. But the pope replied well to each in turn, as if he had foreseen them, and excused the church. And thus the first day's session came to an end."[49]

Matthew Paris describes a similar scene, although his presentation does not separate the events of the first and second sessions so clearly. According to him, after Innocent's opening sermon, the pope described the emperor's enormous crimes, including sacrilege and heresy, along with his construction of a city "populated by Saracens" in Christendom and his foreign ties with the sultan of Babylon. Innocent also accused him of perjury and not keeping his promises. In order to "certify these things among those listening," Matthew relates, the pope produced "many and more letters, fixed with golden, imperial seals." Thaddeus of Suessa, "unbowed in public," produced his own letters with "papal bulls" that seemed to say the opposite. Upon close inspection it was determined that the letters did not contradict each other: the pope's letters expressed things in "conditional" terms while those of the emperor put them in "absolute" ones, suggesting that Frederick had failed to fulfill what he had promised. Thaddeus produced still more papal letters, revealing that the pope failed to keep the promises made in them, thus freeing his lord from his related obligations.[50]

Instead of dueling ideas about the two powers, dueling documents, produced and read aloud before the assembly, took center stage. In those performances, the charters and letters' seals feature prominently as visual forms of testimony to their authenticity, embodying papal and imperial authority for those involved in the process of evaluating competing claims. Perjury stood as the main issue of contention, relating to Frederick's feudal responsibilities as a vassal of the Roman church. This orientation on the record of oaths, promises, and obligations represented a high-stakes contest, a dispute between the two preeminent political figures of the Christian world with the integrity of the papal patrimony and the liberties of the Roman church in the balance. The anonymous observer's comment that Thaddeus's defense of the emperor was "welcome to many" suggests that the public case made against Frederick needed to have real teeth, that is, a compelling and persuasive argument that relied upon documented wrongdoings rather than sweeping accusations, polemical charges, or theologically inflected statements of papal primacy in both the spiritual and temporal realms. As the self-proclaimed aggrieved party at Lyons, the pope stood first and foremost as a lord betrayed by his vassal rather than as the Vicar of Christ asserting himself over the ruling emperor of the Christian world.

The Second Session

On 5 July, Pope Innocent convened the council's second session. After those responsible performed the same liturgical offices as on the opening day, the *Account of the Council of Lyons* relates what followed:

> The bishop-in-exile of Carinola in the kingdom of Apulia, from the Cistercian order, arose and marvelously described the progress of the emperor's wicked and ignominious life since his boyhood, and his desire—since he intended this thing above all else—that prelates and clergy revert to the same state of poverty as the primitive church. He made this most plain through letters, which he sent throughout the world against the clergy and church. Afterward, the archbishop from Spain arose, he greatly encouraged the lord pope to proceed against the emperor, referring to his many actions against the church and how it was his utter intention to suppress the church as much as he could. He and the other prelates from Spain, who attended the council in greater numbers and with greater pomp than any other nation, promised to assist the pope personally and with their resources, according to the pleasure of his will. Many other prelates at the synod made the same promise.[51]

Again, Thaddeus rose to Frederick's defense, attacking Peter of Carinola as an untrustworthy source of testimony for personal reasons rather than for any commitment to justice. Matthew Paris describes a subsequent argument that occurred when relatives of those captured with the Genoese fleet four years earlier complained to Thaddeus about their seizure and treatment, leading him to protest that Frederick never intended for the prelates and clergy to be caught up in the sea battle. The pope pressed on this point: if Frederick knew they were innocent, why not release them immediately? Because, Thaddeus replied, the "exasperated" emperor knew that Gregory had invited his open enemies to the planned council at Rome. He had explicitly warned the bishops and others not to attempt the journey by land or sea, making them his legitimate captives. Nevertheless, he still considered freeing them until James of Palestrina and some of the other captured clergy denounced him as excommunicate to his face.[52]

After this verbal exchange, Thaddeus requested a postponement of the third session until the emperor could arrive personally to defend himself. Envoys from the imperial court had informed him that the emperor was at Turin, en route to the council and still hoping to "reform the bonds of peace" between him and the church. Innocent agreed to wait until 17 July to convoke the next session, a decision that did not sit well with many of the clergy and the members of the military orders in the city—not because of any desire to see Frederick judged, but because of the additional hassle and expenses accrued through a longer stay in the city.[53] Matthew Paris tells us that when first asked about a delay until Frederick could come personally, the pope absolutely refused, fearful that the emperor might come at arms and once again to ensnare him. He even said he would leave Lyons if Frederick approached because he was unwilling to be martyred or risk imprisonment. This portrayal of Innocent's cowardice fits nicely with Matthew's generally unfavorable view of the Roman pope. Innocent only agreed to allow the extension when proctors sent by the English and French crowns begged him to do so. When news reached Frederick of these events, Matthew writes, he denounced the entire council as loaded against him, mainly because the pope favored his native Genoese, pirates and enemies of the empire.[54]

During this protracted interval between sessions, someone favoring the papal position, perhaps sensing or worried about wavering among those attending the council, penned another polemical letter against emperor, *Confusa est mater*.[55] This diatribe, denouncing the enemy of the church, the "wolf" ravaging the Lord's flock, seemed to target those still favoring Frederick, or at least, those less committed to an adverse judgment against him. The voices of such men, the letter lamented, found more favor than "the voice of Christ or the voice of the blood shed by the brother bishops, the clergy, and the faithful laity." Lies and deceptions, excuses offered for the emperor by the "heralds of Antichrist," must not win the day. Those present at Lyons should rise up and fight for the church's liberty. "Know for certain," the letter declared, "that if the church is silent now and does not issue a sentence of deposition against the enemy, it will lose the supporters that it seems to have in Germany, Liguria, and elsewhere, and everyone will be subjected to his tyranny." This inflammatory address closed with a specific denunciation of the recent peace overtures by the patriarchs Albert of Antioch and Berthold of Aquileia, neither of whom had wrung concessions from Frederick. The emperor had done nothing good since Albert of Antioch arrived at the imperial court, lying about his willingness to spare the patrimony further assaults. As for Berthold, he had tried to arrange a marriage between Frederick and the duke of Austria's daughter that would strengthen the emperor's position. Even worse, like a "herald of Antichrist" the patriarch had preceded Frederick through lands subject to interdict, bearing a cross before him, blessing those places, and saying mass for the excommunicate ruler.[56]

Moderate voices still made their presence felt at Lyons, and not just among Frederick's representatives. During the deliberations, probably between the second and third sessions, Eudes of Châteauroux, cardinal bishop of Tusculanum, delivered a sermon on the "deposition of a king or emperor."[57] This address, until recently overlooked by historians of the council, did not mention Frederick by name but clearly had him in mind. The sermon begins with Jeremiah 51:25–26, " 'Behold, I am against you, O destroying mountain, who destroys the whole earth,' declares the Lord, 'And I will stretch out my hand against you, and roll you down from the crags, and I will make you a burnt-out mountain.' " Eudes then laid out for his listeners the nature of good and bad rulers, the former serving for the defense of their people like a ring of mountains, the latter bringing war, devastation, and depredation to their subjects like "sterile" mountains cursed by God. Such bad rulers should be deposed, not by men, but by God, who "extends his hand" against them and "changes the times and season, removes and sets up kingdoms." Deposition, Eudes also recognized, brought immense and irrevocable consequences, encouraging the deposed ruler to rebel against the sentence and refuse penance. "Since the door of mercy should be closed to no one," the cardinal bishop concluded his sermon, "and since the church wishes to bar no one from its flock who wants to return, therefore we pray to the Lord that he renders grace of lamentation to the tyrant, the grace of confessing his sins, making satisfaction for them, and returning to the church, so that his spirit might be saved."[58]

Between them, *Confusa est mater* and Eudes of Châteauroux's sermon speak to the controversial nature of the deliberations at Lyons, the former keeping up the attack on Frederick, the latter advocating a less extreme solution than deposition. Regardless of the precise reasons, Innocent's agreement to delay the proceedings indicated his desire to proceed cautiously toward the final stages of his public judgment against the emperor. Or perhaps it signaled the sheer necessity of doing so. Clearly, others besides Thaddeus of Suessa opposed any precipitous move to depose the Hohenstaufen ruler, while the pope wanted to present himself, unambiguously, as giving Frederick every chance of making amends with the church. Whatever Innocent intended, the weeks after the second session seem to have elevated the uncertainty surrounding the proceedings against the emperor, heightening rather than lessening the tension.

The Third Session

On 17 July, the *Account of the Council of Lyons* tells us, seeing that Frederick had no intention of coming to the council, Pope Innocent convened the third and final session. After performing the opening liturgical ceremonies, the pope had read aloud a series of "constitutions" for the "recovery of the Holy Land," for "assistance to the empire of Romania," and for the fight "against the Tatars."[59] These appeals signaled an ongoing papal commitment to the defense of Christendom, although they contained little in the way of new initiatives or ideas. The rhetorical means and fiscal mechanisms for marshaling Christians to action against "barbarians," "schismatics," and "infidels" ran in well-worn grooves familiar to those expected to take up arms or make financial contributions.[60] Although not mentioned by the anonymous account of the council, the pope also produced a set of constitutions making various reforms to judicial procedures, including rescripts, the power of judge-delegates and legates, the restitution of spoils, appeals, and the procedures for excommunication. Various versions of these constitutions circulated around Europe, making their way into chronicles and legal collections of decretals.[61]

After an open reading of the newly approved constitutions, Innocent presented another important set of documents to the council: copies of "all the privileges of the Roman church that had been granted by the princes of the world, emperors as well as kings." He had this collection of rolls "affixed with the seals of all the prelates present and wished them to have the same validity as the originals that they recorded."[62] The pope included a written preface to all of the Christian faithful that explained the need to preserve these "privileges and letters granted or sent in times past by emperors and kings and other noble princes and faithful Christians to the Apostolic See, some with golden seals, others with leaden or wax ones," lest they perish in the course of time. He also stressed their approval by the entire council as word-for-word copies, nothing added or changed, as attested by the prelates' signatures and seals appended to the documents in question.[63]

This memorialization of the Roman church's territorial possessions at the general council archived some key sources of grievance between the papacy and the emperor. The rolls did not exclusively highlight Frederick II's past guarantees and concessions to the Apostolic See, including letters and privileges from the kings of England, Bohemia, Hungary, Aragon, the Norman kings of Sicily, and others, yet the bulk of the collection focused on Frederick's previous agreements with Innocent III and Honorius III, which were made as the "king of the Romans and Sicily" and as emperor—the very same privileges that, according to the papacy and its supporters at Lyons, Frederick had repeatedly violated. The texts included materials directly relating to the church's conflict with the Hohenstaufen ruler, including materials from the Treaty of San Germano; the emperor's letter to Innocent IV, congratulating him on his election and informing him about his plan to send envoys for peace talks; and his formal commission for Raymond of Toulouse to swear on his behalf during the ceremony at Rome in March 1244. The signed and sealed documents thereby formed an archive that supported the soon-to-be issued sentence of deposition.[64]

As the *Account of the Council of Lyons* explains, the assembly next turned to the main business of the day. Thaddeus of Suessa stood and, seeing the "ax already placed at the root," appealed for a delay in judgment to a future pope or general council.[65] Innocent "humbly" and "gently" refused, reminding him that just such a council was happening at that very moment. Speaking about Frederick, "the pope began to recite how much he had favored him, before he became pope, and how much he withstood from him afterward even after the council was ordained, honoring him so marvelously with such words that scarcely anybody believed he would bring any sentence against him. Yet at once, he began verbally to utter everything and bring the sentence against him, depriving him of his every honor, and the empire, and his other kingdoms. And immediately, the sentence in written form was read before the synod."[66]

Judging by the written form of the sentence that remains, what did those attendees at Lyons hear when the pope's judgment was read to them? After opening the sentence with a proclamation of his apostolic duty to examine and care for all Christians, raising up the just and suppressing the guilty, Innocent presented them with a narrative of his relationship with Frederick. Seeing the "dire commotion of war" that disturbed the Christian provinces and desiring "tranquility and peace for the church and generally for the Christian people," soon after his election the pope had sent his envoys to the "author of the dissension and tribulation," Frederick, who had been excommunicated by his predecessor, Gregory IX. A summary of the peace proposed by the pope in August 1243 followed, requiring the emperor to release his captives from the destroyed Genoese fleet, to make satisfaction for the causes of his excommunication, and to restore stolen church lands. Like the "pharaoh," however, the obdurate ruler "hardened his heart." Innocent describes how Frederick's representatives swore an oath on his behalf before multiple witnesses in Rome in March 1244, although "afterward he did not fulfill what he swore, mocking rather than submitting" to the church. Unable to withstand such injuries to Christ any further and urged by his conscience, Innocent realized that he had to stand in judgment of the excommunicate emperor.[67]

Passing over Frederick's numerous other sins in suggestive silence, the pope charged him with four principle crimes: perjury, violating the peace between church and empire, sacrilege, and the suspicion of heresy, an accusation "demonstrated by weighty and clear arguments, not frivolous and doubtful ones." A detailed discussion of each accusation follows, revisiting the emperor's public misdeeds in the past and directly incorporating materials from previous documents, including the agreement from San Germano and the articles for peace drawn up by Innocent soon after his election as pope.[68] The charge of perjury highlighted his multiple oaths to honor and defend the territorial possessions of the Roman church before and after his imperial coronation and his violation of the fealty he owed to the papacy for the kingdom of Sicily. Not coincidently, these were some of the very same oaths reproduced in the "rolls" at the start of the council's third session. Through his acts of aggression, the charges continued, Frederick had committed treason against the church, attempting to defame the pope through his "threatening letters," seizing and despoiling the cardinals Otto and James, and showing his "contempt for the keys" by refusing to recognize Pope Gregory's sentence of excommunication and interdict.[69]

Frederick's violation of the peace turned mainly on his solemn agreement to the terms established by the peace of San Germano: his oath to obey the church's commands, to remit all rancor toward his former opponents who backed the church, to protect ecclesiastical liberties in the Regno, and to render satisfaction to the despoiled military orders. The emperor, Innocent charged, had refused to fulfill any of these obligations. To the contrary, he had assailed the church's followers in the Regno; abused, imprisoned, and killed members of the clergy, imposing tallages on them and forcing them to appear before secular courts; and failed to compensate the Templars or Hospitallers for any of their losses. The following accusation of sacrilege focused on the emperor's attack on the bishops and other clergy traveling to Rome with the Genoese fleet, including his seizure of the two cardinals. At Frederick's command, prelates were drowned, killed, and captured, robbed of their goods, and dragged off to harsh imprisonment.[70]

Finally, the pope accused the emperor of heresy, or rather, of the "deserved suspicion" that he stood guilty of "heretical depravity." Legally speaking, the accusation of heresy represented the gravest charge against Frederick and also the most difficult to prove. In this instance, the crimes imputed to the excommunicate ruler channeled the same sense of outrage that characterized the polemical letters circulating at the council before and during its deliberations. Frederick had "despised and despises the keys of the church," forcing the celebration of mass in his presence, profaning the divine offices, and declaring that he did not fear the papal ban. He enjoyed bonds of friendship with the Saracens, honoring their envoys in Sicily, sending their rulers gifts and embracing their rites, while allowing the "name of Muhammad" to be praised overseas in the Temple of the Lord "publicly, day and night." He joined himself in other bonds with infidels, employing Assassins to kill the duke of Bavaria and marrying his daughter to the schismatic Greek ruler, Vatzates, an "enemy of the church." He did not give alms to the poor, destroyed hospitals and churches, and compelled the subjects of the papal patrimony to violate their oaths of fidelity. "Surely," the sentence rhetorically asks, "these are not inconsequential but convincing arguments for the suspicion of heresy?"[71]

For these reasons and other unmentioned "nefarious acts," with the "counsel of the cardinals and sacred council," unworthy but acting as Christ's vicar on earth with the power to loosen and bind, Innocent passed his sentence: "We

Figure 5. Innocent IV deposes Frederick II. From Matthew Paris, *Historia Anglorum*. © The British Library Board, Royal MS 14 C VII.

demonstrate, denounce, and nonetheless deprive the aforesaid prince, who rendered himself unworthy of his empire and kingdoms and every honor and dignity, and who was cast down by God on account of his crimes lest he reign or command, cast down and bound by his sins, of every honor and dignity, as he was deprived of them by the Lord."[72] The papal judgment then absolved Frederick's subjects of their oaths of fidelity to him, excommunicating anyone who rendered Frederick "counsel, aid, or favor," calling upon those responsible to proceed with the election of a new emperor. As for the kingdom of Sicily, the pope would make arrangements as he saw fit.[73]

The pope's "thunderous" pronouncement against the emperor, Matthew Paris writes, "struck amazement and horror" among those listening. One deluxe manuscript of the *History of the English* includes an illustration of this powerful scene, featuring Innocent on the papal throne before the clergy gathered at the council, with Thaddeus of Suessa standing before him, brandishing a scroll bearing the words "this is a day of wrath, calamity, and misery." In the *Major Chronicle*, Matthew attributes similar words to the imperial judge as he watched the assembled prelates affirm Frederick's excommunicate status, holding and then extinguishing inverted candles: "Truly is this a day of wrath," Thaddeus lamented about the state of Christendom, "from this time, heretics shall sing, the Khwarezmians shall reign, and the Tartars rise up."[74] Others besides Thaddeus tried to postpone a final judgment, including the delegates of the French and English crowns, along with Berthold of Aquileia, who reminded the pope that "there are two columns propping up the world, namely the church and the empire." Innocent told him to be silent, or the pope would take away his bishop's ring.[75] After passing this judgment, according to Matthew Paris, Innocent declared, "I have done my part, now let God do and determine what he wills over these matters." The pope then pronounced the Council of Lyons to be at an end.[76]

Contesting the Deposition

In straightforward legal terms, Innocent IV's deposition of Frederick II might seem to stand as a landmark in the exercise of unfettered papal sovereignty. Upon closer consideration, however, clear signs emerge of the pope's sensitivity to the fact that he could not appear to act arbitrarily in his judgment of the emperor. Even if Innocent possessed the rightful jurisdiction to pass judgment on Frederick in the canonistic tradition, to make that sentence politically meaningful he needed to present a compelling case before the wider public of Christendom, demonstrating the reasons for his momentous decision. He had taken an extraordinary step, and he knew it, despite Nicholas of Carbio's assurances that other popes had judged secular rulers in the past, deposing them for lesser reasons.[77]

Even in the terms of the sentence, qualifiers on the pope's willingness or ability to act alone are evident, such as when Innocent called upon the electors in Germany to choose a new king, or when he declared that he would make plans for Sicily in consultation with the cardinals. There are other signs that the pope recognized the need to project a picture of consensus around the deposition, to avoid any sense of its arbitrary or capricious nature. The anonymous *Account of the Council of Lyons* does not conclude with the pope's issuing his judgment and the dissolution of the assembly but instead finishes by calling attention to the fact that Innocent, before judging Frederick, "sought the counsel of each and every prelate, whether or not he could or ought to proceed," asking "how much they all agreed to his deposition." The pope had each of the bishops "affix their own seals to the sentence, in written form, so that in the pronouncement of that judgment about one hundred and fifty seals were appended to the sentence."[78]

In his *Major Chronicle,* Matthew Paris transcribes another papal letter addressed to the Cistercian general chapter meeting in September 1245 and explaining Innocent's actions at Lyons in response to the "urgent cause" threatening "all of Christendom." The pope called upon the monks not to believe those who were spreading lies that he had deposed the emperor without consulting the cardinals and others at the general council. Indeed, Innocent claimed that he could not remember ever spending so much time and effort deliberating before making a decision, describing how before reaching the final verdict he and the cardinals staged a closed meeting—a mock trial with some of the clerics playing the role of Frederick's advocates and others representing the church, disputing just like schoolmen. When he realized that there was no other path forward without causing more offense to God and harm to the church, as well as to his own conscience, he reluctantly and sorrowfully proceeded with the deposition. According to Matthew, the letter worked. The brothers began to detest "Frederick's side" and miraculously turned toward the "pope's side," praying for God to protect his church from further stain.[79]

After the council of Lyons ended, the papal curia quickly began the process of getting the word out about Innocent's decision to depose Frederick. The sentence of deposition, as Albert of Stade describes it, "flew throughout the entire world."[80] Several original versions remain in European archives, some with the papal bull attached.[81] The full text was reproduced in chronicles and copied down on the spare folios of codices. Still other chroniclers provided detailed summaries of its contents, suggesting that they had read the document or heard detailed reports of its terms.[82] The *Chronicle of Erfurt* tells us that the pope relied especially on the Franciscans and Dominicans to spread news of his judgment.[83] In a letter sent directly to the Dominicans at Paris months later on 15 December 1245, Innocent instructed the friars to publicize the outcome of the legal proceeding against Frederick, informing the brothers about the just nature of his judgment at the general council and explaining how he had formally sentenced the emperor after a full exposition of his wicked deeds, acting with the "common counsel of the cardinals, as well as that of the council." To prevent the faithful from sparing Frederick out of ignorance and to demonstrate the "equity of the sentence for everyone," he called upon the friars to spread the news in the "right kind of places." Innocent acknowledged that the Dominicans engaged in public displays of this kind might suffer "abuse, exile, chains, imprisonment, lashings, or other sorts of bodily tortures or torments" and he promised them the indulgence of sins and an eternal reward for their actions.[84] In an accompanying letter sent to other prelates and clergy on 21 December, the pope celebrated the effort made by the Dominicans to spread the news of the proceeding against Frederick in "the right public places" following the tenor of the sentence sent by the pope throughout the entire world and authenticated by the papal seal. Again, Innocent recognized the possible burden placed upon the order for carrying out his instructions, assuring the brothers that they did not have to publicize the sentence in any other form than the official version forwarded to them by the pope.[85]

Resistance to his judgment, Innocent understood, would be impossible to avoid. He received a violent confirmation of that fact when a veritable riot broke out at Besançons due to the emperor's condemnation. As the pope described the scene in a letter to an unnamed judge, a group of citizens backing Frederick and his son had stormed into the Church of Mary Magdalene and had attacked its rector, who, following the "tenor of the sentence passed at Lyons," was celebrating mass and denouncing those who showed Frederick "aid, counsel, or favor." The mob tore the altar cloth and plundered the church before moving on to assault further holy sites in the city, ringing bells and carrying "martial banners" to more easily and quickly carry out their "premeditated iniquities." The assailants moved on to plunder the churches of Saint Peter and Saint Maurice before finally breaking into the nearby Dominican priory, smashing the doors that featured scenes from the Lord's Passion, and casting icons and crucifixes on the ground. Instructing the judge to investigate the matter personally, thereby assisting the church of Besançons with the "help of the secular arm," the pope gave explicit orders for those guilty to be deprived of any ecclesiastical benefices for up to four generations and banning anyone from commerce with them.[86]

In this public contest over the deposition, Frederick and his propagandists at the imperial court took a direct hand in countering the terms of the papal judgment. During the Council of Lyons, Thaddeus of Suessa already had produced a written rejection of the pope's right to judge his lord that denounced the proceedings on the grounds that the emperor did not receive a proper written summons, that the supposed judge was Frederick's enemy at war with him, and that Innocent, acting as both accuser and judge, already had made up his mind to issue a sentence against his lord. Thaddeus lodged an appeal to "a future Roman pontiff and universal council of kings, princes, and prelates, since the present council is not universal." At least one copy of this document made its way to England, included by the English delegation in their report to Henry III.[87] Just a week or so later, a letter written in Frederick's name, *Etsi causae*, spread these complaints about the papal miscarriage of justice more widely. Wishing to inform others about the truth of what happened at Lyons, this address directly attacked the pope's right to intervene in temporal judgments and deprive rulers of their kingdoms, an action unsupported by "divine or human law." The emperor's account of the proceedings against him offered a litany of legal malfeasance: the prejudiced witnesses called against him, the arbitrary labeling of the defendant as "notorious," the denial of his basic rights, the lack of a proper, written summons instead of the one given by the pope in a sermon, and more. The address ended with a warning to Frederick's fellow monarchs: kings should defend the emperor from the pope's juridical overreach, or else they might be the next to suffer such a miscarriage of justice.[88] In early 1246, another letter, *Illos felices*, followed, which denied the pope's rights of temporal judgment, again telling other rulers that they ought to fear Innocent, the supposed "prince of priests." This address also complained about the church's relentless financial exactions to fund the war against the emperor, unfavorably comparing the greedy clergy of the present with their apostolic predecessors and expressing the emperor's desire to return the church to its state of primitive poverty.[89]

These imperial letters, in turn, provoked a response from the papal curia. In 1246, someone in Innocent's circle replied to Fredrick's criticisms with *Eger cui lenia*, perhaps the most controversial document in the history of the thirteenth-century papal monarchy. Written in the pope's voice, this address opened by describing the "sick man" who, when milder medicine cannot cure him, heaps abuse upon the physician forced to cut or cauterize his wounds.[90] Frederick had reacted in this manner to the church's judgment against him at the recent general council, sending his own "little pamphlets" throughout the world denouncing the pope. Textured with layers of scriptural, theological, and historical argumentation, *Eger cui lenia* evocatively defended the pope's jurisdiction over everyone, which was granted to Saint Peter by God and not man. Whoever denied that authority tried to diminish God. "For we enjoy a general legation on earth of the King of kings," the pope declared in the text, "who attributed the fullness of power to both loosen and bind not just anyone, but anything on earth, to the prince of apostles and, through him, to us."[91] As for those who suggested that the Apostolic See gained its authority over the Roman Empire due to Constantine's donation to the Roman church, they missed the point entirely. The emperor had never legitimately possessed the power of empire in the first place. As prefigured by the biblical priest-king Melchisedek, temporal power ultimately belonged to Christ, the true King of kings, who committed "not just a pontifical but a royal monarchy to Saint Peter and his successors, who reigned over a terrestrial and earthy empire at once." By acknowledging his subordination to Sylvester, Constantine had donated nothing to the church. Rather, he had recognized the Vicar of Christ as the ultimate source of his sovereignty, surrendering his illegitimate imperial rule and receiving it back legitimately from the pope.[92]

Eger cui lenia projects the sort of uncompromising imagery that might be expected from the papal monarchy, endowing the pope with the fullness of power to judge anyone, absolutely. Given its lack of legalistic restraint and qualifications on the papal fullness of power, experts on canon law have long debated whether Innocent, trained as a canon lawyer, actually wrote the letter bearing his name or whether radicals at the curia produced the text.[93] Its tone is undeniably different from the more measured discussion of papal power found in Innocent's later legal commentary on the deposition. But this question about the provenance of the letter to some extent misses the point. The pope and his supporters did not strive for legal consistency above all else. They moved to shape public opinion and arouse emotions, acting within the wider legal culture of Christian Europe. In the theologically and historically inflected landscape of *Eger cui lenia*, which responds directly to Frederick's attacks, the pope stands as a priest-king, the rightful judge of both spiritual and temporal powers, the ultimate disposer of empire. Whoever wrote *Eger cui lenia*—most likely someone at the curia presumably acting with the pope's consent—deliberately evoked an awe-inspiring image of sacerdotal sovereignty, countering Frederick's denial of the papal right to judge him.[94]

As always, it remains difficult to gauge the impact of such letters on public attitudes toward the unresolved conflict between the pope and the prince. Matthew Paris, for one, claims that the two imperial letters had a mixed reception. *Etsi causae*, intended by Frederick to "restore his fame," turned the sentiments of many "against the pope." *Illos felices*, however, caused the emperor's reputation to suffer, seeming to confirm that he was a heretic bent on destroying the Roman church. Regardless, Matthew observes, other kings began to worry that the pope might move on to other targets after deposing Frederick, provoking princes everywhere to rise up against the papacy.[95] The English chronicler did not seem to be aware of *Eger cui lenia*. As for Frederick's personal reaction to the sentence of deposition, Matthew describes his rage at hearing about Innocent's actions. "This pope casts me aside at his synod, depriving me of my crown. From where does such audacity come? From where does such bold presumption arise?" the emperor fumed. "Where are my traveling coffers, containing my portable treasury?" When his belongings were brought before him, Frederick removed one of his crowns and placed it on his own head. "Now we'll see if I have lost my crown." Denouncing Innocent and his council, foreswearing any bonds of veneration for the pope, and renouncing any obligations to keep the peace, Frederick began to plan his revenge.[96]

Divine providence communicated its own messages, albeit mysterious as always, about the significance of what happened at the Council of Lyons. On the day and hour that the pope's sentence was passed against the emperor, Roland of Padua observes, many reported a "burning, fiery star" that appeared around dusk before the setting of the sun, rapidly shooting across the sky from east to west "like a flaming arrow or brand, as if tearing the heavens asunder." Roland claimed to have marveled at this apparition himself along with numerous others.[97] Many must have wondered what would come next as Innocent turned to other measures to raise the pressure on Frederick even more: electing an anti-king, calling for crusades against the Hohenstaufen ruler, funneling even more money to his military opponents. After all, as Matthew Paris let his readers know, the end of the conflict between the two powers lay nowhere in sight. The pope remained in self-imposed exile at Lyons, while the emperor stood unbowed, still possessing his crown along with the wealth, symbolic capital, and raw power that went with it. The war for Christendom, it turned out, was far from over.

Chapter 7

Christendom at War

During his years-long stay at Lyons after the general council had concluded its business, Innocent completed initial work on a project that would define his legacy in the Latin canon law tradition: his *Commentary on the Five Books of Decretals.*[1] This extensive gloss on Gregory IX's canonistic collection allowed the pope, who was trained in canon law, the chance to offer his opinions on almost every aspect of ecclesiastical governance. He also added and analyzed several decretals of his own, including *Ad apostolice sedis,* the sentence formally deposing Frederick II. In his gloss on that judgment and elsewhere in his commentary, Innocent defended the right of the pope, under certain circumstances, to act as the supreme judge in areas of civil jurisdiction, above all when facing a miscarriage of secular justice, even to the extent of deposing rulers. In no uncertain terms, Innocent stressed the sufficient authority of the pope—the pope alone with a council present only to solemnize the proceedings—to condemn the emperor based on his "fullness of power" and status as the singular heir to Christ. In one evocative passage, Innocent interpreted the progression of history as culminating with the pope's universal jurisdiction, starting with Noah as the first "rector" of God's people, passing down through the patriarchs, judges, kings, and priests of Israel until the time of Christ, the "natural lord and king" of creation, who left Peter and his heirs as his vicars.[2] In canonistic terms, Innocent's carefully delineated sovereign power over the spiritual and temporal realms stood on firm ground.

In the wider public, translating that judicial power into a political reality remained a far more contested process during the years after Innocent passed his judgment against the emperor. Historians sometimes claim that the deposition effectively did not matter, since Frederick maintained his position and retained the bulk of his supporters. This all-or-nothing evaluation of Innocent's sentence does not appreciate how the papal confrontation with the "former" emperor—as the pope commonly referred to him after the deposition—accelerated and intensified during the years after the Council of Lyons. To isolate and oppose Frederick, Innocent strategically deployed his apostolic fullness of power to his maximum advantage, assigning legates to war-torn regions with special privileges to reward the church's allies and punish its opponents through the papal oversight of church offices, properties, and even sacred vows. He widely publicized Frederick's banned and deposed status, threating his allies with spiritual and material penalties. He supported the election of "anti-kings" in Germany and called for crusades against Frederick and Conrad, attempting to raise armies and redistributing vast sums of money to sustain those doing the actual fighting against Hohenstaufen forces.

Innocent thereby mobilized the Roman church for what one scholar has aptly called a state of "total war."[3] After the Council of Lyons, one might reasonably claim that the pope committed himself to pushing Frederick from power by redesigning the political landscape of Europe with little to no room left for the Hohenstaufen dynasty. Charting this provocative course, Innocent wagered the reputation of his priestly office like never before, trying to convince Christians around Europe that the Apostolic See bore the responsibility to oppose Frederick by every means possible. While the emperor refused to recognize the legality of his supposed deposition, he could not easily disregard the pope's efforts to turn Christendom against him, still seeking ways of mitigating the damage done to his reputation by the sentence of judgment leveled against him. Innocent publicly and privately rebuffed the possibility of compromise with Frederick. While some contemporaries celebrated the pope's tireless defense of the church, others called him Antichrist, anticipating the imminent apocalypse. Meanwhile, rumors swirled about plots and assassination attempts on both sides, shady attempts by the pope to kill Frederick or vice versa. As the years passed, the scandalous political conditions of Christendom seemed greater than ever, with no clear end in sight.

The Fullness of Power

In his *Commentary on the Five Books of Decretals*, Innocent elaborated with legalistic precision the extent and nature of his ecclesiastical jurisdiction as the bishop of Rome, successor to Saint Peter, and Vicar of Christ. In canonistic terms, the pope stood as a "juridical person," one who embodied nothing less than the Christian "commonwealth." His priestly sovereignty not only included the authority to depose an emperor under extraordinary circumstances, but also encompassed more mundane privileges, such as the right to settle disputed clerical elections, grant dispensations for illegitimate births, transfer benefices, and commute vows. During the months and years after the Council of Lyons, Innocent leveraged such ordinary prerogatives to reassure the church's supporters and to ratchet up the pressure on Frederick's supporters. Although the apostolic "fullness of power" did not allow him to enforce his will upon those remaining loyal to Frederick, it did enable him to complicate their lives immensely.[4]

After the deposition, the pope delegated a series of war-time legates to communicate and implement his invigorated opposition to the deposed emperor. In Germany, he appointed Philip, bishop-elect of Ferrara, as his chief representative in 1245, followed by Peter Capocci, cardinal deacon of San Giorgio in Velabro.[5] In a similar manner, he assigned the cardinals Stephen Conti and Rainier of Viterbo to the Regno in 1246, empowering them with a full range of privileges and prerogatives.[6] Working through his representatives, the pope sought to reward those loyal to the church and punish imperial holdouts. Among other privileges, his legates possessed the right to provide benefices to worthy clerics, to remove ungrateful clerical office holders from their positions, to offer dispensations for illegitimate birth and acts of simony, and to wield ecclesiastical censure against lay people and clergy.[7] Taking advantage of his ultimate control over the disposition of clerical benefices, offices, and incomes, Innocent directly intervened in ecclesiastical appointments, rewarding clergy for their devotion to the church and revoking the positions of those who supported Frederick while instructing bishops to make financial provisions for churchmen displaced by Frederick and his allies. In the Papal States, where the pope possessed direct rights of temporal lordship, Innocent likewise transferred feudal holdings that pertained to the church, reassigning fiefs to loyalists and compensating persons who suffered from the service to the Apostolic See.[8]

The seesaw public relations battle between the two powers did not abate, as both sides tried to limit the effectiveness and reach of their opponents. Judging by Frederick's complaints, Philip of Ferrara had considerable success in "corrupting" his followers in Germany, while the emperor called upon his subjects to deny him and his envoys passage through their territories.[9] At another point, Innocent complained to the master general of the Templars about one of its members who, accompanied by a Hospitaller and Teutonic knight, was caught carrying letters from the emperor that spread sedition against the church.[10] Ecclesiastical bans continued to fly at a fast and furious pace. In areas under his authority, Frederick declared that any clerics repeating the ban should be deprived of their offices. Innocent called for the disciplining of clergy who favored Frederick and Conrad publicly and refused to publicize the anathema against them.[11] He granted his legates sweeping permission to reconcile repentant imperial supporters after they had rendered sufficient satisfaction.[12] Even when his envoys succeeded in turning Frederick's supporters against him, backsliding remained a constant concern for the pope. Writing to Peter Capocci, Innocent called upon him to perform excommunications in places "where people gather" against those who had renounced Fredrick and sworn obedience to the church but then returned to the former emperor's service.[13]

As seen at Ratisbonne, the lines drawn between the supporters of the church and empire persisted beyond the grave. Siding with Frederick, the citizens of

Ratisbonne had expelled their former bishop, Siegfried, defying his interdict by giving their deceased relatives Christian burial. After Siegfried died, they likewise expelled their new bishop, Albert, when he took up his office. When one dying citizen insisted upon burial outside of the city walls, faithfully observing the conditions of the interdict, his irate fellow burghers dug up his corpse and dragged it through the streets, finally tossing the body in a field for the birds and beasts to ravage. They also assaulted a priest who had remained loyal to Albert, spitting on him, beating him, and jailing him until he paid a fine for his release. Adding "sin upon sin," they issued an edict that anyone caught wearing the crusading sign of the cross would be executed. The pope told Albert to warn the citizens that they had until the Feast of the Assumption on 15 August to reconcile with the church or face the loss of all church properties that they held as fiefs and the revocation of all benefices held by their descendants, until the fourth generation.[14]

Through his fullness of power, Innocent wielded a unique source of persuasion in his campaign against the emperor: the ability to offer dispensations and absolve Christians from their vows. He did not hesitate to take advantage of it. Writing to King Bela of Hungary in August 1245, the pope assured him that he did not have to honor his oath of fealty to Frederick, which had been rendered in return for promised aid against the Tartars that did not arrive within the requisite amount of time. This was not the last time that Innocent would relieve a specific ruler from his sworn obligations to the emperor.[15] The pope increasingly intervened in another kind of public bond, marriage vows. Innocent tried to block marriages that would benefit the emperor, such as the proposed union between the marquis of Meissen's son Albert and one of Frederick II's daughters, Margaret.[16] On another occasion, he instructed Peter Capocci to summon several prelates for judgment at the papal curia after they helped to broker a marriage proposal between Frederick and the duke of Saxony's daughter, despite the fact that the union never happened. Innocent also worked to foster and enable other marriages for the benefit of the church. In January 1246, he gave his approval to a marriage between Louis IX's brother Charles d'Anjou and Beatrice, daughter and heiress of the recently deceased count of Provence, granting a dispensation for their relationship within the prohibited degree. This union helped to keep the contested region in more or less safe hands for the papacy.[17] The following year, the pope encouraged Margarita, daughter of the deceased duke of Austria and Henry VII's widow, to marry Henry, count of Henneberg, "to advance the interests of the church and empire." He did this despite Margarita's declared desire to live a life of chastity after her former husband died.[18]

Recognizing the pressures placed upon him, Frederick did not stop searching for some sort of strategic reconciliation with the pope. Innocent described one such attempt in a letter sent to the "all of the faithful" on 22 May 1246. After revisiting his decision to depose Frederick at the general council for "plainly evident and reasonable causes," Innocent related that the former emperor had sent a delegation to the papal curia including Bernard, archbishop of Palermo; Stephen, bishop of Pavia; the abbots of Cava and Casanova; and two unnamed Dominicans. The pope could have refused these churchmen an audience due to their excommunicate status as Frederick's representatives bearing his written documents and letters. But since they claimed to represent him as a "simple Christian," rather than as a king or emperor, Innocent gave them a hearing and assigned Otto, cardinal bishop of Porto; Peter, cardinal bishop of Albano; and Hugh, cardinal priest of Santa Sabina to consider their petitions. Frederick's envoys presented an official document produced by a *scriniarius* from the diocese of Lucano and letters sealed with the Hohenstaufen ruler's golden bull. These texts explained that Frederick, given the suspicion of heresy leveled against him, had submitted to questioning by Bernard, Stephen, and the others, who interrogated him about the Christian creed and articles of the faith. He firmly swore to his orthodox belief and assigned the churchmen in question to act as his proctors, who might give sworn testimony to his orthodoxy at the curia in the pope's presence. The envoys then declared aloud that were ready to take just such an oath.[19]

For Innocent, this represented a chance to spell out again the consequences of Frederick's banned status. When the cardinals informed him about the emperor's petition and passed along the relevant documents for the pope's inspection, he immediately determined that the envoys had no power to make such an expurgation and denounced their audacious and unauthorized examination of the excommunicate and deposed ruler. The written materials they had brought with them, affixed with the golden bull, still referred to Frederick as emperor. On this account, Innocent observed, the aforesaid *scriniarius* should be considered excommunicate. In his letter to the faithful informing them about these events, the pope reviewed the charges against Frederick that rendered him suspect of heresy, including, above all, his contempt for the keys, forcing the celebration of the divine offices in disregard of interdicts, and his detestable friendship with the Saracens that caused great harm to the cause of Christians in the Holy Land. "For these and other reasons contained in the aforesaid sentence," Innocent followed, "which we will pass over here, due to their excessive length, the above-named Frederick ought to be named a heretic, according to legitimate sanctions."[20] In closing, the pope indicated his willingness to receive such an act of expurgation if Frederick came personally before him in some appropriate place, within a reasonable amount of time, and unarmed and accompanied by a modest retinue. Frederick had no intention of taking up the pope's offer to appear before him in such a compromised state. Circulating a letter that described his unsuccessful appeal to the papal curia, he insisted that he was entirely ready to obey the mandates of the church, but the pope would not grant an audience to the emperor's envoys, not wishing to hear his petition or any other "word of peace."[21]

Sensing his advantage, Innocent had no plans to let his opponent off the hook. Over the following years, publicly and behind the scenes, certain interested parties still held out hope for some sort of mediated resolution to the conflict between the pope and the prince. Some of Frederick's "friends" at the papal curia apparently devised a plan for the pope to baptize his son Henry, King Henry III of England's nephew born from Frederick's marriage to Isabella, to symbolize the possible "reformation of the peace" between the emperor and the Roman church. This proposal never came to pass.[22] King Louis IX showed a particular interest in ending the division between the papacy and the empire, which he viewed as a dangerous diversion from his planned crusade overseas. Not long after the Council of Lyons, Innocent met with the French ruler personally to discuss his crusading plans. He spoke with Louis in a "most secret meeting," joined by the king's mother, Blanche, at Cluny before Christmas in 1245.[23] During this meeting, the pope and king addressed the ongoing war between the pope and the emperor that threatened to erode support for the upcoming French crusade. Dealing with the two "superpowers," as Jacques Le Goff aptly describes the situation, Louis tried to broker a reconciliation between them.[24] In a letter to the French monarch, Innocent explained that he and the cardinals had wanted peace with Frederick since the time of the pope's election through his flight to Lyons. The pope remained willing to pursue the matter with Louis but would not allow the church to be "fooled" again by the emperor. According to Matthew Paris, Innocent flatly rejected any accommodation with Frederick, who had explicitly asked the French ruler to intervene on his behalf.[25] The two met again in 1248 as Louis passed by Lyons on the start of his journey east on crusade. After this second encounter, Innocent sent a letter to an unnamed prince telling him not to believe any "false rumors" about a compromise between the pope and the emperor. There would be no peace agreement made that left Frederick or Conrad in their positions.[26]

Christians could not—would not—be allowed to forget the hard choices that they faced during the unresolved struggle between the two powers. On Maundy Thursday in April 1248, the pope solemnly renewed the anathema passed against Frederick, again reviewing all of the reasons for his deposition.[27] Writing to the archbishop of Canterbury a year later, Innocent lamented the challenges confronting the church in both the western and eastern regions of the world, including the emperor's machinations, the profanation of the holy places by the infidels, and the continued threat posed by the Tartars. He called upon the archbishop and his subordinates to offer their prayers to God in response and to celebrate masses dedicated to the liberation of Jerusalem, the peace of the church, and the strength of those opposing the Tartars. On the next feast day, the pope instructed, the archbishop should organize a solemn procession, after which the clergy and people would gather together to hear preachers speak about the dangers facing the faithful. During this ceremony, the preachers would exhort those gathered to strive for the liberation of the holy places, to provide for the fight against the Tartars, and to offer "no favor in word or deed, secretly or in public, for Frederick, for we command that he and all of his supporters be denounced by preaching of this kind, bound as they are by the chain of excommunication." Such processions and preaching should be staged throughout towns, castles, and villages in the diocese, especially in churches, with the offer of forty-days' indulgence for attendees. Four years and counting after the deposition, the papacy's effort to rally the faithful against Frederick showed no sign of abating.[28]

Anti-Kings and Crusades

Beyond such indirect means of influencing Christians or coercing them into opposing Frederick, during the years after the Council of Lyons Innocent employed more direct means of combating the emperor and his allies. In Germany, his battle against Frederick involved two overlapping strategies: encouraging the election of a new king of the Romans and declaring crusades against the Hohenstaufen ruler and his son Conrad. These initiatives created high-profile opportunities for Innocent to substantiate his public opposition to the emperor. But they also created fresh tensions and did not always comfortably align with the papacy's other stated goals, above all the need for a new crusade to the holy places. Raising "anti-kings" and channeling crusades against Frederick came at a price, rendering the pope and papal curia vulnerable to another round of criticism about their failure to meet Christendom's pastoral needs.

Hinted at or pursued behind the scenes by Gregory IX and Innocent before the Council of Lyons, elevating a ruler to replace Frederick became the papacy's openly stated goal after the deposition. As Innocent declared in the closing lines of *Ad apostolice sedis*, "Let those responsible in the empire for the election of a new emperor freely choose one."[29] Securing the election of a monarch to replace Frederick, however, was a process that Innocent could not easily influence or control, involving as it did the group of traditional electors—clerical and lay magnates, including the archbishops of Mainz, Trier, and Cologne, the king of Bohemia, the duke of Saxony, and the margrave of Brandenburg—that hardly formed a unified body of uncritical support for the pope or opposition to Frederick. After the emperor's deposition, Albert of Stade reports, the electors immediately cautioned Innocent that "it is not the pope's role to put in place or remove an emperor, but to crown the one elected by the princes."[30] They nevertheless moved forward with the choosing of a new king, identifying Henry Raspe, landgrave of Thuringia, as the leading candidate. There are signs that Henry remained reluctant to accept any such honor, not ready to risk the fortunes of war against the emperor.[31] In April 1246, Innocent, critical of such delays, addressed the electors directly, exhorting them in the remission of their sins to choose Henry as their new king, for the "praise and glory of our Lord Jesus Christ and the catholic faith, the growth of the church's liberty, and peace for the entire Christian people."[32]

A month later, the German princes and prelates elevated Henry as the new king of the Romans at Veitshöchheim outside of Cologne. The *Annals of Erford* tellingly says that they did so "by the authority of the pope," an apparently common impression, despite the insistence of the electors that they acted independently. Frederick and his allies derisively called Henry the "priests' king" for this reason.[33] After the election, as envoys moved back and forth between the papal curia and Henry's court, Innocent demonstrated his support for the new king, who faced skepticism or outright hostility from some German princes. As he often did, the pope relied in particular upon members of the mendicant orders to communicate his interests. Doing what he could to reverse resistance to Henry, Innocent repeatedly called for reluctant individuals and parties to back their rightful monarch, promising them the remission of sins for their support. In other instances, he instructed his legates to compel reluctant parties by ecclesiastical censure to swear oaths of fealty to Henry. When a number of bishops refused to attend an assembly called by Henry in July 1246, for example, the pope instructed Philip of Ferrara to excommunicate them and to suspend them from office until they presented themselves for judgment at the papal curia.[34]

Innocent's support for Henry also involved the transfer of vast sums of money. Nicholas of Carbio claims—in an approving way—that the pope diverted fifteen thousand silver marks to the new king to support his war efforts against Frederick and Conrad. Other chroniclers took note of the immense sums sent by the pope to the new German ruler.[35] Not everyone found the pope's financial contributions to the landgrave of Thuringia so laudable. In his *Major Chronicle*, Matthew Paris found repeated opportunities to complain about Innocent's recent round of financial exactions, including those intended for the fight against Frederick.[36] Such funds did not always arrive at their destination. Matthew also observed that the emperor managed to get his hands on some of the money sent to the upstart German ruler, turning the seized funds against the pope. According to his account, Innocent wrote a "consolatory letter" to the Franciscans and Dominicans charged with raising such monies, telling them to avoid Frederick's "snares" by putting off their habits and disguising themselves.[37]

During the months after his coronation, distributing "gifts" from the funds provided by the pope, or so the *Chronicle of Erford* tells us, Henry began to bring reluctant parties in Germany over to his side. According to histories friendly to the pope and the king, after his coronation Henry immediately took steps to defend the Roman church and republic, backed by the public call for a crusade against Frederick, Conrad, and their supporters.[38] A number of chronicles describe how thousands of lay nobles and clerics "took the cross" against the enemies of the church after the landgrave's coronation at Veitshöchheim. Over the following months, the archbishops of Mainz and Cologne likewise preached the cross against Frederick in their dioceses.[39] Writing to such prelates, his legates, and mendicant crusade preachers, Innocent publicized this crusading effort against the deposed ruler, denouncing Frederick as a tyrant and persecutor of the church and calling for churchmen in their cities and dioceses to preach the word of the cross against him and his allies, either themselves or through worthy men deputized for that purpose. The pope authorized the same indulgence of sins for such crusaders as those going to the Holy Land, creating an equivalency between the two theaters of holy war.[40] Over the following years, Innocent frequently repeated such calls for crusade preaching against the deposed emperor and Conrad, commuting crusade vows made for Jerusalem into ones against Frederick or Conrad and allowing noncombatants to pay for others sworn to fight in their stead.[41]

Historians often identify Innocent's preaching of the cross against Frederick after Lyons as the first full-blown "political crusades," insisting that these repeated calls for such a campaign somehow taxed the crusading spirit and disillusioned contemporaries, despite any short-term gains that the pope's policy might have achieved.[42] Measuring the decline of crusading in this way can be difficult, however, in part because it assumes that earlier crusades were somehow more genuine in their appeal and disregards the fact that Christians from the beginning of the crusading movement showed mixed motives for taking up the cross. Rather than wearying contemporaries through their heightened frequency, public calls for crusades against Frederick seemed in some cases to have elevated consumer demand for crusader status and the benefits that went with it. Clergy promoting the crusades enjoyed special privileges to absolve and reconcile those taking up the cross against Frederick, including those excommunicated for heinous acts such as arson or assaulting clergy that would normally require an appearance before their bishop or the papal curia. Sworn crusaders did not hesitate to take advantage of their special legal status. Writing to Philip of Ferrara in July 1246, for example, Innocent described an appeal by Gerbert, count of Stoltenbroke, who had been married for eight years to a woman within the prohibited fourth degree of relation. The two had a single child. Given the count's offer to support the church and Henry Raspe, along with his willingness "to be signed with the character of the cross," the pope granted him a dispensation for his illicit union.[43] Innocent did not dissimulate the nature of this quid pro quo and others like it, offering to noblemen similar dispensations for consanguineous marriages provided that they agreed to take up the cross against the deposed emperor.[44]

Innocent's deployment of crusading against Frederick continued to raise questions about the legitimacy of waging war against a Christian ruler—even an excommunicated and deposed one—under the sign of the crusade. The pope did not fail to recognize that his preaching of the cross against Christendom's "internal" enemies might create a conflict of interest and even a sense of public scandal, given the apparently existential threat posed to the Christian religion by the Tartars and the recent sack of Jerusalem by the Khwarezmian Turks. After Louis IX swore a crusading vow in 1246, the pope had to balance his commitment to crusading against Frederick with the church's support for the French king's planned crusade. When Innocent called for Eudes of Châteauroux to stop preachers from signing people with the cross for the holy places, prioritizing instead the fight against Frederick, he instructed the cardinal legate to "keep this secret, revealing it to no one." In other instances, the pope seemed to reverse course, wanting crusaders bound overseas to honor and not commute their vows into service in other regions of crusading, including at home in Germany against the emperor and his allies.[45]

Far from declining, crusading in its various iterations had assumed an unprecedented ubiquity, although managing the public face of crusading had become more complicated than ever before. Crusade fund-raising also opened the door to sensational cases of fraud. In his *Chronicle,* Menko describes how a friar named Renold showed up in Frisia bearing a letter from the pope authorizing him to collect crusade funds stored in the treasury boxes of local churches. The locals complained that the money was intended for local pilgrims, meaning Frisian crusaders bound for the Holy Land. They subsequently discovered that this friar was an imposter. When the real Renold had died, this con man took his letter so that he might abscond with the funds and use them to curry favor at the papal curia. Other indignant Franciscans jailed the false Renold. Menko also relates the story of the friar Wilbrand, who preached the cross against Frederick and proclaimed a fifteen-year truce among his enemies, drawing immense crowds due to the generous indulgences he offered at his sermons—or at least he did until Franciscan authorities arrived on the scene, branding him a disobedient rogue. Wilbrand eventually found his way to Lyons bearing the monies raised through his redemption of crusade vows, earning him a warm reception.[46]

Describing the violence in Germany and elsewhere, Matthew Paris writes that a "new custom" had arisen at the papal curia. When nobles waged war upon each other, the pope openly took sides, favoring one party and excommunicating the other.[47] Backed by the pope, the election of Henry Raspe and redirection of crusader energies against Frederick seemed poised to turn the political and military tables in Germany. Building upon his growing momentum, on 5 August 1246, Henry and his forces clashed with Conrad near Frankfurt, killing many of Conrad's followers, capturing many more, and seizing massive amounts of plunder.[48] Germany seemed to be slipping from the Hohenstaufen grasp when Henry suffered a mortal wound during a siege near Ulm in February 1247. After he died, not leaving a clear successor, a number of his neighbors, including the margrave of Meissen and the count of Anhalt, invaded his territories. The pope and cardinals, Matthew Paris informs us, immediately began to deliberate about what to do next. Panic seemed to set in. According to Salimbene of Adam, the papal legate Philip of Ferrara was so terrified when Henry died that he took refuge in a Franciscan convent, telling the friars what had happened but warning them not to discuss it except in his presence and only then to talk in Latin, not German. Borrowing a Franciscan habit, he tried to flee from town through a ditch, since the surrounding walls were barred against him. He was so fat, Salimbene remarks, that he got stuck squeezing through the hole in the city wall, and another friar had to shove him on his backside to push him through.[49]

Henry's death left the pope and those opposed to Hohenstaufen rule in Germany without a figure to rally around, publicly or privately. Under these circumstances, finding a replacement king became an immediate priority. In September 1247, with encouragement from Innocent and his current legate in Germany, Peter Capocci, the electors settled on William of Holland as their next ruler. As he had done for Henry Raspe, Innocent began to channel ecclesiastical funds from around the Roman church into the hands of the new king to shore up his support. He also maintained the church's crusading campaign against the emperor, commissioning another round of crusade preaching of the cross, offering crusaders against Frederick the same legal and spiritual benefits as those bound for the Holy Land and commuting other crusade vows into ones directed against the church's enemies at home.[50] Not everyone greeted William with open arms. Aachen shut its doors to the new monarch and emperor-elect, setting the stage for a months-long siege that began in April 1248.[51] A fresh round of violent conflict ensued. Numerous chronicles place crusaders on the scene, joined by Franciscans and Dominicans, some from Frisia diverted down the Rhine from their planned campaign overseas, others coming from surrounding regions. The *Annals of St. Pantaleon* describe how Peter Capocci preached the cross against Frederick at Cologne, gathering a considerable number of crusaders, "some by encouragement, others by threat," and excommunicating some of those who refused his summons.[52] On 18 October 1248, Aachen finally surrendered, the citizens swearing fealty to William and to the Roman church. Two weeks later, Peter Capocci and William, cardinal bishop of Santa Sabina, crowned William of Holland as king of the Romans in the city's cathedral church, where he sat on Charlemagne's throne.[53] William's symbolic victory, however, belied a loss of momentum in the fight against Frederick. After more than three years of fighting since the Council of Lyons, the situation in Germany remained more or less a stalemate.

The Battle for Italy

While papal legates, anti-kings, and crusaders battled against Frederick's forces in Germany, Innocent also tried to undermine the emperor in the Regno. In this regard, Innocent had made unmistakably clear his intentions after Lyons. As seen above, the formal sentence deposing Frederick specified, "As for the kingdom of Sicily, taking counsel with our same brothers, we will take care to make such plans as seem most expedient to us."[54] From the papacy's perspective, the situation in the Regno stood on different legal ground than that of Germany, where the pope had to rely upon the electors to choose a new king. In Sicily, by contrast, the pope acted as Frederick's direct feudal lord, who had the right to remove a malfeasant vassal. Despite this legalistic difference, the strategies for opposing Frederick on the Italian peninsula looked quite similar to those employed in Germany—a combination of hard and soft power, working through intermediaries, bringing military pressures to bear, and using incentives and penalties to sway local nobles over to the side of the church.

The Italian peninsula remained a region of intense, sometimes shocking, violence between the two powers and their allies. In many regions of Italy, the fighting had never stopped since the outbreak of hostilities between Frederick and the Lombard League in 1237. Shortly before the Council of Lyons, the church had suffered some high-profile defections from the ranks of its supporters, when the marquises of Montferrat, Cerva, and Correto had changed sides and had sworn allegiance to Frederick. Amadeus of Savoy, whose forces controlled many of the alpine routes leading into northwestern Italy, also remained loyal to the emperor.[55] On the papal side, Gregory of Monte Longo was still in the field, supporting Milan and its allies. In the Papal States, Innocent turned for assistance to his rectors, the governing officials who stayed in place when he had fled to Lyons, men such as the cardinals Stephen Conti and Rainier of Viterbo. As observed above, in 1246 the pope assigned Stephen and Rainier as his special legates to the Regno and tasked them with restoring the church's liberty in the kingdom by casting off the "boot heel" of Frederick's oppression. Much like in Germany, the pope granted the two cardinals exceptional privileges to absolve those excommunicated due to their past association with the emperor, undercutting his support. He also ordered them to "gather an army against Frederick and his supporters, and do whatever seemed expedient for the rescue of that region, for the honor of God and the church, in spiritualities as well as temporalities."[56]

The crusade against the Hohenstaufen prince had come to Italy. Throughout his letters to loyalists in the region, Innocent struck an evocative tone, calling Frederick a "new Nero" and "pharaoh," whose oppression of the church in Sicily "sounds forth into every land."[57] Corresponding with Stephen Conti, Innocent instructed him to "preach the cross" in Rome, Campagna, and Maritima, thereby summoning the faithful to defend the papal patrimony against Frederick's tyranny and granting such sworn crusaders the same indulgence as those serving overseas.[58] The pope likewise encouraged his legate in Lombardy, Ottaviano Ubaldini, to raise up crusading forces. Innocent specifically authorized Ottaviano to offer any troops he raised the same indulgence as those going to the Holy Land, instructing him to make sure that bishops in Lombardy and Romaniola likewise preached the cross against Fredrick.[59] The cardinals sometimes took a direct hand in military excursions, such as when Rainier of Viterbo led a group of Perugians signed with the cross against Foglino, a city favoring the emperor.[60]

In June 1247, the imperial city of Parma revolted against Frederick, rising up—as Nicholas of Carbio puts it—like "another Maccabees." News of this event quickly spread around Europe, becoming the latest sensational event in the ongoing struggle between the papacy and empire.[61] Pope Innocent personally heard details about the city's uprising from Salimbene of Adam, who was still present in Parma during the revolt. A faction of exiled citizens working with their allies on the inside had expelled the emperor's officials and installed their own podesta, Gerard de Corigia. Members of Innocent's own family, including his brother-in-law Bernard Roland Rossi, a former confidante of Frederick II, played a key role in turning the city against the so-called Ghibellines.[62] Salimbene offers numerous reasons for why Parma managed this coup, including the warm welcome the citizens gave the exiles as liberators, the aid rendered by the pope's relatives, and the flood of troops and other material support that arrived from other Lombard cities immediately afterward. The friar also credited Innocent's sentence of deposition as setting the conditions for Parma's uprising, since that judgment absolved the emperor's followers of the fealty they owed to him. Conditions at the city had reached a breaking point, Salimbene implies, as he describes the devastating impact of years of fighting in the region, which was plagued by bandits and wild animals. Farmers were afraid to sow or reap their fields and were able to work outside the city walls only when guarded by armed men.[63]

Parma soon emerged as ground zero in Lombardy for the wider conflict between church and empire. When the city turned against him, Frederick was at Turin, en route to Provence for a planned assembly of princes and barons in the region. At this point, apparently, he and the pope had made tentative plans for Frederick to meet with papal representatives near Lyons, where he might expurgate himself from the charges of heresy hanging over him.[64] Parma's uprising, the emperor lamented, put an end to that plan, because he immediately changed course and returned to deal with the rebellion. Frederick's forces and allies arrived on the scene, including his son Enzio and Ezzelino da Romano, the "son of devil," as Salimbene calls him, along with troops from Modena, Reggio, and Cremona plus Saracen soldiers from Lucera. Following these events from Lyons, Innocent instructed Ottaviano Ubaldini to relieve Parma with a large contingent of troops. Allied with Frederick, Amadeus of Savoy blocked the mountain passes leading into Italy, delaying Ottaviano until his funds ran out and his forces melted away. Some reinforcements, led by Gregory of Monte Longo, managed to reach Parma from Milan.

Determined to utterly reduce Parma, Frederick ordered the construction of a large encampment to cordon off the city, a veritable town unto itself that he named Victoria. A brutal siege followed. Every morning, in sight of Parma's walls, Frederick ordered the execution by hanging and decapitation of prisoners who supported the church, including two hundred knights from Parma and Ancona. Inside Parma, a group of women commissioned the construction of a detailed model of the entire city, made from silver, dedicating it to the Holy Virgin Mary as an offering.[65] Recalling the desperate situation in Parma, Salimbene offers a striking description of how Gregory of Monte Longo tried to alleviate the defenders' anxieties during the siege. As the citizens despaired, Gregory invited a number of prominent nobles to dinner at his lodgings. In the middle of the meal, a messenger burst into the room, dust on his sandals and a letter attached to his belt. The letter, Salimbene continues, "was read aloud for all of us present to hear, and it gave us good news that help was soon on the way." Everyone at dinner later spread these tidings around the city, giving people reason to rejoice. What Salimbene knew—and they did not—was that two of his fellow Franciscans, Jacob and Gregory, had forged the letter in Gregory of Monte Longo's chambers earlier that evening. The entire scene was staged to comfort the Parmese in their time of need.[66]

In February 1248, the "best rumors" reached Salimbene, by that time staying at Sens, outside of Paris. During Frederick's absence from camp while hunting, the citizens of Parma had burst out from their besieged position and assaulted Victoria, overrunning and thoroughly destroying the emperor's faux city. Much like the original news of Parma's revolt, word of this imperial reversal spread widely: thousands slaughtered, others taken captive, the Cremonese carroccio captured, and the imperial treasury seized, including Fredrick's scepter and war gear, the latter taken by his longtime foe, Gregory of Monte Longo. Thaddeus of Suessa numbered among the casualties.[67] Not content with a prose record of Parma's victory, Albert Beiham copied down a verse commemoration in his memorial book, rhapsodizing about the defeated Frederick:

> The pope with the council, as everyone knows
> removed the scepter from him, through his sentence
> but vengeful God passed his own sentence
> so He might punish the rebel, who returned His favor with ingratitude.[68]

Over the course of the spring, consolidating his position at Cremona, Frederick regained much of the territory he had lost after Victoria's destruction, although he did warn his followers to be on the lookout for letters bearing the seal from his golden bull that was lost during the scramble and was being used by his enemies to send out false communications. In March, Enzio captured and executed Bernard Roland Rossi, a ringleader of rebels from Parma. Salimbene claims that Frederick, enraged by Bernard's betrayal, explicitly wanted him taken alive so sport could be made of him. The devastating, back-and-forth warfare described earlier by the friar continued, leaving farmers afraid to till their fields and citizens unwilling to leave the safety of their city walls. A year later, the Bolognese captured Frederick's son, Enzio; in retaliation, the Ghibelline podesta of Reggio, Guido de Sesso, hanged twenty-five Guelf supporters of the church. Salimbene tells us that Guido denied them confession, sardonically declaring that, since they were on the "side of the church," they were already "holy men."[69]

Despite Frederick's overall recovery, the loss at Parma stung. Remembering the Parmese victory, Matthew Paris described how it brought "glory to the church" and "shame for Frederick," yet another moment of shifting fortunes in the pope and emperor's public reputations.[70] Coming on the heels of this defeat, Matthew tells us, Rainier of Viterbo crafted another (his final, since he died soon after) polemical letter, *Grande piaculum*, which detailed one of Frederick's most notorious deeds yet: his savage execution of Marcellinus, bishop of Arezzo, on 18 March 1248. The bishop, still acting as rector of the March of Ancona, had been captured in battle the previous December. According to Rainier, the "raging dragon" Frederick ordered Marcellinus's execution while he was staying at Victoria, just three days before that city's destruction. When the sentence reached the bishop's jailors at Saint Flaviano on the Adriatic coast, they tried to force Marcellino to excommunicate the pope in public and swear loyalty to Frederick. With the classic fortitude and constancy of a Christian martyr, he refused. Some Saracen troops on hand bound his hands and blindfolded him while he sang *Te deum laudamus* and then dragged him through the streets behind a horse with his head tied near its tail so that the horse's shit would fall in his mouth. After making his confession to some Franciscan friars, he was hanged on the first Sunday of Lent, around the same hour as the crucifixion. Three days later, the friars rescued his still sweet-smelling corpse, but Frederick's executioners got hold of his body again and strung it up a second time.[71]

For Rainier of Viterbo, this latest atrocity clearly revealed why Christians should take up the cross against this tyrant at home rather than crossing over the seas or traveling far away to fight the infidels or Tartars. Matthew Paris follows this letter by observing that its contents would have turned even more people against Frederick than they did, except for the papacy's ongoing greed and harassment of crusaders: first, the pope had urged those sworn with the cross to go to the aid of the Latin Empire in Greece and the Holy Land, but then he suggested that they might stay home and fight the emperor instead, while the mendicants continually fleeced them. Thus, as the admittedly ignominious Frederick continued his attacks on the church, he found "open" and "secret" supporters for his wicked crimes. As usual, for the English historian, the war between the papacy and the empire seemed like a zero-sum game for the vast majority of Christians.[72]

An Apocalyptic Mood

Confronting such relentless conflict between the two powers, some Christians began to suspect that they were living in nothing less than the end times. Rather than a sign of medieval hysteria or gullibility, apocalyptic speculation provided another venue for contemporaries to gauge the turmoil characterizing their community in the present. Generally speaking, purveyors of the apocalypse were not wild-eyed prophets on the fringes of society. They were sensational, sought-after prophetic celebrities. They constituted what might be called—to borrow from Brian Stock—a textual community, one that shared a kind of apocalyptic hermeneutics, writing, circulating, and conversing about the coming end of history and what it portended for the present.[73]

An apocalyptic mood gripped parts of Christendom, one that did not uniformly favor either of the two powers. Writing his short tract *On the Correction of the Church* in Germany in 1248, a Dominican friar named Arnold described a spiritual revelation in its pages, namely, his realization that God planned to reform and renew his church as the sixth age of history drew to a close, inaugurating the seventh and final age of justice and peace on earth. He rushed to see "the most serene emperor, the principle defender of the Church," who greeted this news with great joy. Arnold left no doubt about the one responsible for the degraded conditions among present-day Christians: "From that point forward, with the Lord assisting me, standing fast in the prospect of this sacred business, I summoned Christ's poor and all the faithful to the truth of the two Testaments and their gloss, on account of every injury borne against them in spiritual, bodily, and temporal matters by Pope Innocent IV and all of his members." Innocent stood "contrary to Christ" in all things.[74] In his *Annals* under the year 1248, Albert of Stade describes a group in Germany in Swabia with similar beliefs: preaching all sorts of deviant ideas "publicly," denying that the pope or bishops could pass a sentence of interdict, and declaring that clergy should celebrate mass regardless of such a ban. They would not even say the name of the pope, a man of such perversity, proving through a "learned gloss"—perhaps the same one described by Arnold—that the Roman pontiff did not truly possess the power to "loosen and bind." But they prayed for the emperor, Frederick, and his son Conrad, who were "perfect and just men."[75]

Salimbene of Adam describes how he encountered during his travels various Joachites, that is, clerics, monks, and friars who subscribed to views of history associated with Joachim of Fiore, the famous twelfth-century interpreter of Scripture and prophet from Calabria.[76] Joachim's exegesis offered contemporaries a guide to the totality of history, past, present, and future, by dividing time into two periods: that of the Old and New Testaments, each of which was subdivided into corresponding sets of seven seals. He also posited the Trinitarian nature of history, dividing time into three stages: that of the Father, the Son, and the Holy Spirit. The millennial Sabbath age of the Holy Spirit lay around the corner—an era when "spiritual men" would arise and transform the church, purifying the faithful and spreading the Gospels to every corner of the earth. Such predictions of new spiritual orders appearing in the church appealed especially to certain Dominicans and above all Franciscans, who associated their own ranks with those promised figures and ardently embraced Joachim's ideas.[77]

Not content with the abbot's genuine productions, including his *Concordance of the New and Old Testament, Exposition on the Apocalypse,* and *Psaltery in Ten Chords,* starting in the 1240s some of his devotees began to create new images and texts ascribed to Joachim, such as the popular *Commentary on Jeremiah.*[78] Such Joachite materials circulated alongside other prophetic traditions that were attributed to Merlin and the pagan Sibyls of the ancient world.[79] Such works commonly associated Frederick with apocalyptic evils, presenting him as a persecutor of the Latin church during a new "Babylonian captivity," dispersing the flock of the faithful, abusing clergy, plundering churches, and generally causing "scandal and ruin." One striking Joachite image, featuring the seven-headed dragon from Revelation, identified the seventh head as Frederick—the great Antichrist, the last in a series of historical persecutors.[80] Apocalypse-minded clerics, however, did not point fingers only at the empire but reserved some of their most intense criticism for the Roman church itself. This internal critique runs throughout the *Commentary on Jeremiah,* which excoriates negligent prelates, who acted more like "mercenaries than pastors." The day was coming when the "priests of Christ" would be submerged in the Red Sea like the pharaoh's chariots. In this regard, Frederick's despoiling of the "carnal" Roman church represented a just punishment, a scourge that would foster the coming of a spiritualized church in the future, one that observed apostolic poverty.[81]

In 1248, Pope Innocent personally heard the criticisms of one "great Joachite" at the papal curia when the Franciscan friar Hugh of Digne appeared before the pope and cardinals at Lyons and delivered a stinging rebuke of their sloth, avarice, and nepotism. Salimbene of Adam, an admirer of Joachim himself in his younger days, describes how he first met Hugh while passing through the Provençal port of Hyères in 1247. Hugh kept a salon of sorts at the Franciscan convent, where the brothers, notaries, judges, prominent townspeople, and passing travelers might gather and listen to him talk about Scripture and Joachim's ideas.[82] Salimbene also describes Hugh's dramatic appearance before the pope and cardinals at Lyons. Although Hugh's address to the assembled churchmen did not dwell on apocalyptic ideas, he did invoke Joachim at one point: "Abbot Joachim of Fiore correctly

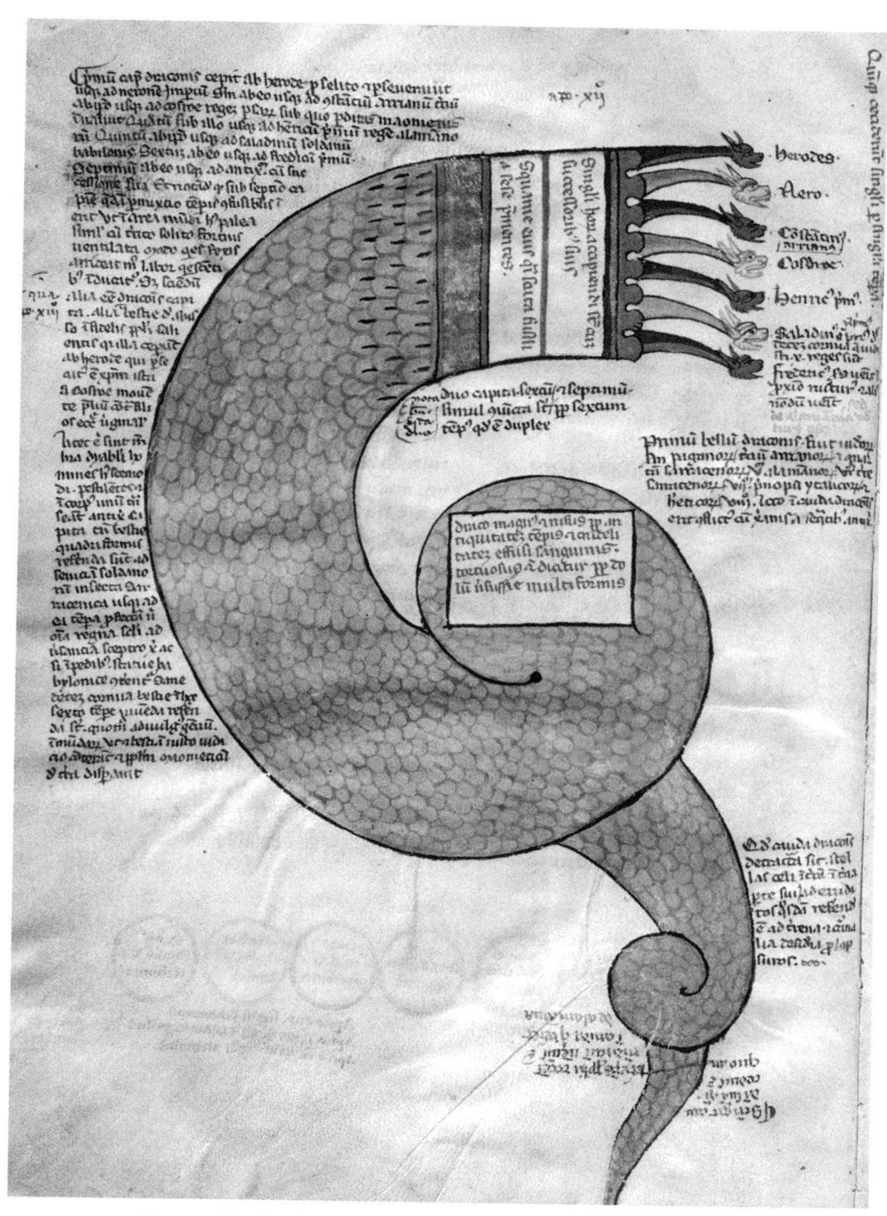

Figure 6. The Joachite seven-headed dragon (with Frederick II as the seventh head). From Joachim of Fiore's *Book of Figures*. Getty Images.

called you 'graspers' and not 'cardinals,'" he proclaimed, in a play on the Latin words *carpinales* and *cardinales*, "for truly your highest art is stealing and cheating and emptying purses." The fearless Franciscan friar complained that their symbolic red hats, recently given to them by Pope Innocent, were an outward sign of their puffed-up self-importance. How, Salimbene wonders, did Hugh dare to say such things before those powerful churchmen? In part, due to his stellar reputation as a thinker, exegete, and prophet. Assuring him that he could speak his mind before the cardinals, Innocent told Hugh, "We have heard that you are a great scholar and a fine, spiritual man, but we have also heard that you are the successor to Abbot Joachim in prophecy, and that you are a great Joachite." Even the pope, apparently, was not immune to the contemporary fascination with Joachim's ideas, despite their hard edge of clerical criticism.[83]

Two years later, Innocent faced yet another ecclesiastical personality who rebuked the pope and cardinals in apocalyptic terms when Robert Grosseteste, bishop of Lincoln, appeared before the consistory.[84] Grosseteste, who had appealed to the curia on multiple occasions when he encountered resistance to the exercise of episcopal authority over his own diocese, hardly rejected the pope's fullness of power. But he did insist that each bishop enjoyed the same "pastoral power" over souls in his own diocese as the pope did in the universal church, power granted to every prelate directly by God, including the right to supervise and correct his clerical subordinates. The only difference lay in the extent of that power—the bishop's confined to his diocese, the pope's extending over all churches. This pastoral system, however, had begun in recent times to break down due to the lack of "good pastors" and the proliferation of "bad" ones—Antichrists who killed the souls they were supposed to protect. The bishop of Lincoln expressly blamed the growing number of bad pastors on the failing leadership of the pope and the cardinals, who were supposed to embody Christ's teachings. "Let it not come to pass," he warned, "that this most sacred see and those presiding over it, whose every command and mandate ought commonly to be obeyed, order anything contrary to the commands and will of Christ." Such a turn of events would represent a sign that the "falling away" foreseen in Paul's second letter to the Thessalonians had come to pass, presaging *the* final Antichrist. Grosseteste called for his listeners to recover their sense of pastoral purpose before it was too late.[85]

Looking into the course of history, not everyone saw unremitting gloom and doom or imminent millennial transformations on the horizon. In his commentary on the Book of Revelation, which he started around 1247 or 1248, another Franciscan friar, Alexander Minorita, viewed current events as apocalyptic signs but ultimately offered a reassuring view of the church's place in history.[86] Inspired by divine revelation and familiar with Joachim's works, Alexander interpreted the Apocalypse as a continuous, symbolic narrative revealing the entirety of time from the Bible through the church of the martyrs, the conversion of Constantine, the time of Charlemagne, and the start of the crusades right up until the present day. The problem of the two powers, the conflict between church and empire, formed a central concern for his view of history. Alexander emphasized Constantine's surrender of imperial power to the popes of Rome as an especially crucial point when a new era of history had begun, in which bishops and priests ruled "like kings" over those who were subordinate to them, as promised by Revelation 5:10: "You have made them to be a kingdom and priests to serve our God, and they will reign on the earth." That period of sacerdotal rule, he stressed, would last one thousand years, the period of Satan's binding, while the saints reign and live with Christ.[87]

Undeniably, recent events showed signs of apocalyptic turbulence between the two powers. The "tyrant Frederick," Alexander declared, had shown by his many deeds that he possessed the image of that beast. The "dragon," meaning the Devil, had given Frederick great strength; the beast's head, which looked "as if it were slain," indicated the sentence of judgment delivered against the emperor by Pope Innocent IV at the First Council of Lyons in 1245, which had deprived him of his imperial dignity. And yet that head appeared healed, as Frederick continued his onslaught against the church. Some asked, "Who shall be able to fight with him?" since he possessed such a great multitude of warriors, enough that he could conquer as he willed, even if the whole world opposed him. He spoke "blasphemies" against his excommunication by the pope. His "power to act for forty months" indicated the growing evils he caused during the four years following his deposition. Those worshipping the beast were the ones who continued to proclaim him emperor, despite the many ills he and his son Enzio caused for the faithful, such as the capture of clergy en route to Rome in 1241 and the slaughter of countless men during a battle outside Parma years later.[88]

And yet, putting the brakes on transformative millennialism, the Franciscan exegete cautioned seeing current events as a sign of the imminent end times. The millennium that had started in the time of Pope Sylvester and Constantine still had seven decades to go, meaning that the church would endure and continue to rule on earth for at least another seventy years, and perhaps even more. A cautious apocalyptic commentator, Alexander noted that God reserved the right to add time to that one thousand years to give men further opportunities for penance. Despite recent apocalyptic signs, the devil could not exercise his full power until that millennium or more was complete. Antichrist had not yet been born, as some claimed. Frederick was not *the* Antichrist, nor would the Antichrist come in the year 1260, as some Joachites predicted. Rather, the pope would continue to reign and rule with other priests until the one thousand years since Constantine were fulfilled. The church would not be subject to any other people or tyrant but would continue to spread around the world before the end times. The "royal priesthood" of the Roman papacy would endure, even if its present tribulations seemed so dire as to suggest the imminent apocalypse.[89]

Unsavory Plots and Foul Conspiracies

As the years passed after the Council of Lyons, while armies marched, crusade preachers delivered their sermons, and prophets speculated about the end times, Innocent and Frederick waged a "shadow campaign" of sorts, one of plots and conspiracies and furtive attempts at assassination—or so Christians heard rumored from various quarters. Despite their ostensibly secret nature, such stories of treachery and mayhem entered into the shared pool of gossip around Christian Europe. As always, Matthew Paris showed a particular fascination with lurid episodes that seemed to confirm the dire conditions in Christendom. But he was not the only one. Stressing the public nature of Frederick's crimes in his legal gloss on the sentence of deposition, Innocent himself commented about his machinations: "A man can scarcely narrate how many dangers on land and sea, assassins and traitors and all sorts of other things were suffered by the pope who issued this sentence, although they are nevertheless written down in the chronicles of the Roman church."[90]

The first such conspiracy took shape in the Regno in the spring of 1246, when a group of nobles with close ties to the emperor, including Theobald Francis, James de Morra, Pandulf de Fasanella, and William of Saint Severino, turned against him. In letters sent to rulers around Europe, trying explicitly to combat the spread of rumors that might upset his friends and comfort his enemies, Frederick described how these traitors plotted to murder him. When word of their scheme leaked, however, the perpetrators fled—some to Rome, others taking refuge with their supporters in nearby fortresses at Capaccio and Scala. During the following months, Frederick laid siege to these castles, capturing them both in turn and seizing, mutilating, and executing the traitors who did not take their own lives by the sword or by throwing themselves off cliffs.[91] In his subsequent correspondence on the matter, the emperor left no doubt about who stood behind this wicked plan: the pope and his allies, including Bernard Roland Rossi and Cardinal Rainier. After their flight, the plotters were accompanied by several Franciscans who had signed them with the cross. The friars also pretended to bear "apostolic letters" and revealed that they were "acting in this matter on behalf of the holy Roman church, their mother, declaring that the supreme pontiff was the promoter of this attempt on our life as well as the attempt to disinherit us." The prisoners taken at Scala freely confessed to something similar before dying, while the bishop of Bamberg, recently captured while returning home from the papal curia, had been publicly preaching beforehand that Frederick would soon meet his demise at the hands of his friends. Writing to Henry III, Walter d'Orca told him that the emperor had planned to capture and send the principal traitors around Europe "with the impression of the papal bull, discovered in their possession, stamped on their foreheads as form public testimony to their treachery."[92]

Whether Innocent, Bernard, or Rainier had any direct role in this conspiracy is anyone's guess. By deposing Frederick, the pope had absolved his vassals from their bonds of fealty to the Hohenstaufen ruler and, as seen above, he circulated numerous letters around the Regno calling upon the former emperor's followers to desert and oppose him, presenting him as a tyrant, a "new pharaoh," and a "herald of Antichrist." After the plotters were exposed, in April 1246 the pope wrote directly to several of them, praising them for their resistance to the deposed emperor that their transformation from "soldiers of the tyrant into fighters for our Lord Jesus Christ," and promising them his support in the future. Their names, Innocent told them, had become famous for their deeds. Whether these letters represented an endorsement of attempted murder was in the eye of the beholder. In some ways, the question of whether Innocent actively fostered an attempt on Frederick's life is beside the point. The accusation of such wrongdoing took on a life of its own, regardless.[93]

Turnabout is fair play, or so Matthew Paris seemed to suggest when describing some similar attempts on the pope's life at Lyons. At one point, he had heard, two men tried to sneak into the curia in the manner of "assassins," meaning actual Assassins, the mysterious Saracen killers. Others suggested that this story was made up with the intentions to defame Frederick even further.[94] Matthew later describes an elaborate plot wherein a knight named Ralph, who left the emperor's service when he was not paid on time, went to Lyons, presumably seeking a new patron. His host, Reginald, arranged for him to meet Walter d'Orca, who convinced him to return to Frederick's service by killing Innocent. Walter promised him three hundred talents, ten times what Judas received, advising him that such an act would not be a sin since the pope "who ought to be a model and exemplar of all religion, is an evident usurer, a furnace of simony, thirsting after and grabbing all of the money he can, while his curia is a marketplace for con men, or rather, a brothel for whores." The conspirators moved forward with their plan until Reginald took ill and revealed the entire plot to his confessor, who told the pope. Questioned under torture, Ralph likewise confessed. Innocent detailed the plot in a written bull so that Frederick might be "more gravely condemned and scandalized." Soon after, the pope caught wind of another plot by two soldiers from Italy planning with forty other knights to kill him, since even if Frederick were dead, Innocent would remain a "disrupter of the world, a defiler of churches." After this happened, the pope surrounded himself with guards and refused to leave his chambers, not even to celebrate mass.[95]

Such plots and conspiracies did not stop at the borders of Christendom. In 1246, according to Matthew's description of events, when Innocent proposed a peace treaty with the Egyptian sultan as-Salih Ayyub, the Muslim ruler declared in a letter to the pope that he could not come to any accord with him unless the emperor assented. Albert of Stade, who transcribes a version of the same letter, claims that the pope sent his envoys to the sultan in the first place to "draw him away from his friendship and closeness with the former emperor, Frederick." When Innocent received the sultan's reply, Matthew Paris reports, he suspected that Frederick had forged the letter in question, despite the fact that his own trusted and familiar envoy had brought the news back to the curia.[96] Later, the *Major Chronicle* describes people's fears that the emperor would call upon the Tartars to come from Russia or seek help from his friend, the Egyptian sultan, to fight against the pope and his allies, causing "confusion throughout Christendom." In the *Major Chronicle* and the *History of the English*, Matthew claims that Innocent in fact received envoys from the Tartars and proposed alliances with them, first against the "schismatic" Greek ruler Vatatzes, and then against Frederick. Repulsed by such hatred between Christians and speaking through their interpreters, the Tartar representatives would not agree to such plans. Years later, when Frederick heard news that Vatatzes had allowed several mendicant emissaries from the pope to speak at the Byzantine court, the emperor warned him not to be fooled by the pope's apparently pastoral aims. In reality, the pope was conspiring against Frederick and could not be trusted.[97]

Public accusations and counteraccusations of conspiratorial wrongdoing on the home front persisted. In March 1249, Frederick informed his loyal followers about another attempt on his life: a doctor treating him for various ailments instead tried to poison him. A papal legate had approached the physician with this scheme at Parma, where he was jailed after the city's revolt. Once released, he traveled to the imperial court, promising all sorts of medicinal cures for the ailing emperor. Frederick uncovered the plot just in time through some intercepted letters. And again, Frederick told his readers and listeners who lay behind this plot: the pope, trying to destroy the empire, not content with all of the harm he had publicly caused the Hohenstaufen ruler.[98] "Behold how our most dear father loves us!" he sarcastically declared. "Behold his praiseworthy zeal and pastoral diligence! Behold the honest works of this prince of priests!" This time, Innocent dragged one of Frederick's oldest confidantes into the scheme, Peter de Vinea. Matthew Paris observes that this act of betrayal greatly upset the emperor, who had Peter blinded and dragged through the streets before handing him over to some Pisans for execution.[99] In a letter to an unnamed official instructing him to proceed with the capital sentence, Frederick said nothing about his own state of mind or feelings, but he did write that Peter, arrested for the crime of treason, suffered "many and different kinds of torture, so that the penalty of one might strike fear into many." The pope's reputation, Matthew goes on to write, began to suffer from these accusations, although, he concludes once again after telling such a scandalous story, only God knew the truth of the matter.[100]

~

On 13 December 1250, nature managed what supposed plots, assassins, and poisons had not. After a period of worsening illness, Frederick II died at Castel Fiorentino in Apulia. Matthew Paris tells us that he passed away peacefully, wearing a humble Cistercian habit. In his *Life of Innocent IV*, Nicholas of Carbio declares that Frederick finally reaped his just rewards, dying excommunicate and deposed after a lifetime spent persecuting the church.[101] In his last will and testament, the emperor left his son Conrad as heir to his various royal titles, including Jerusalem and the Regno. For as long as Conrad remained in Germany, Frederick's son Manfred, born from his relationship out of wedlock with Bianca Lancia, would act as his bailiff with full power in Sicily. Frederick's young son Henry would inherit the kingdom of Arles and the crown of Jerusalem if Conrad wished to cede it to him. In addition, the deceased ruler left one thousand gold ounces to support the Christian presence in the Holy Land. Frederick made no specific mention of his conflict with the papacy, but his last will and testament declared that any contested ecclesiastical rights, properties, and offices should be restored to the Roman church, as long as the church first recognized the full rights of the empire.[102]

When Salimbene of Adam heard the news, he did not—could not—believe it. "For I was a Joachite," he wrote, "and utterly convinced and still hoping that Frederick would do even greater wicked deeds in the future than he had already done, as numerous as his past evils were."[103] By weaving numerous prophecies and predictions into his chronicle about Frederick's role in the future, based on Scripture and the works of Joachim, Merlin, and more, Salimbene exposed prophecy's not uncommon tendency to disappoint its consumers rather than to enlighten them. Others, even those not jolted by the failure of Joachite expectations, must have shared his uncertainties. Right up to the end of his life, Matthew Paris observed, the emperor had continued to reach out to the pope, seeking a compromise that might end their conflict. Innocent, who hoped to crush the "great dragon" Frederick and then to overcome all the "adders and serpents," that is, the rulers of England, France, and other kings, refused his entreaties.[104] With the "herald of Antichrist" dead, Christians must have wondered what would come next for the apparently victorious pope: peace—or more war, scandal, and discord.

Chapter 8

The Price of Victory

On 11 October 1254, Pope Innocent met with Frederick II's illegitimate son, Manfred, at a bridge across the Garigliano River on the border between the Papal States and the Regno. Over the preceding months, the two had exchanged frequent letters and legates, negotiating the terms of papal support for Manfred's contested claim to the kingdom of Sicily as his rightful inheritance. From Innocent's perspective, the Regno remained Saint Peter's "special patrimony," which should be held only by a loyal vassal of the Roman church. A plan took shape for Manfred and local allies to surrender their territories to the pope, recognizing him as their feudal lord, who would then bestow the lands back to their holders. These exchanges had grown tense at points. In early September, Innocent had excommunicated Manfred and other prominent nobles from Apulia when they failed to render him homage by the Feast of the Nativity of the Blessed Virgin. Over the ensuing weeks, the two sides nevertheless came to terms, setting the stage for their October meeting. One chronicle, written by a member of Manfred's court, describes how the Hohenstaufen prince received Innocent with great devotion, prostrating himself at the pope's feet and playing the role of his groom by taking the reins of his horse and ceremonially leading him across the bridge into the Regno.[1]

Life imitated art. Innocent had found the Constantine to his Sylvester, so to speak, performing a scene with Manfred similar to the one featured in the Church of Santi Quattro Coronati, as described in the opening to this book. This apparently impressive display, however, elided the diminished nature of Innocent's supposed triumph. Manfred was hardly an august figure—not an emperor and still struggling for recognition as the ruler of the Regno. The pope's display of sovereignty did not so much manifest his supreme priestly authority over Christendom as his immediate lordship of the Papal States, the bishop of Rome acknowledging the service and subordination of his vassal. And even that limited submission did not last long. With deliberate foreshadowing, the chronicler close to Manfred's circle told of a "marvelous event" just after Innocent crossed the bridge over the Garigliano, when the man bearing the ceremonial cross customarily carried before the pope dropped it to the ground: a sign of Innocent's tough road ahead. Indeed, news soon reached the pope that one of Manfred's followers had murdered Burello d'Angione, a noble with close ties to the papal curia. When Innocent demanded that Manfred submit to judgment for this crime, he fled to Apulia and took refuge at Lucera with his deceased father's Saracen mercenaries. From that point forward, Manfred began to raise forces to oppose the pope, while Innocent oversaw the assembly of a papal army to subdue his enemy. War had returned once again to the Regno.[2]

Modern historians typically pay little attention to Innocent IV after Frederick II's death, viewing the last four years of his papacy as an unremarkable coda of sorts to the epic struggle between the two powers. The battles between papacy and empire that had shocked and scandalized Christendom for a generation end not with a bang but with a whimper.[3] Upon closer inspection, a more complex picture emerges of Innocent's remaining years as pope, marked by a growing tension between the Roman church's broader public commitments and a new parochialism. On the one hand, the papacy's projects for the common good of Christendom—creating peace between the church and empire, enabling the crusades, and wiping out heresy among them—continued to occupy a high profile. On the other, after a seven-year absence from Italy, Innocent devoted more and more of his sacerdotal office's political, financial, and symbolic capital to the immediate demands of securing and protecting the territorial integrity of the Papal States, reasserting the pope's presence and direct lordship on the Italian peninsula. By outlasting Frederick, Innocent undeniably benefited from the lack a strong imperial rival; by the same token, perhaps ironically, he no longer enjoyed an imperial nemesis that cast his priestly sovereignty into the starkest relief.

The Empire Undone

During the first few months after the news of Frederick's death reached him, Innocent repeatedly proclaimed his intentions to make arrangements for the empire before he returned to Italy. Bringing peace and stability to the territories of Germany ruled by the king of the Romans and the prospective next emperor represented a crucial step in shaping the post-Hohenstaufen political order. With Frederick gone, Innocent saw an opportunity to unite German elites under William of Holland, who had continued to struggle for support during the years after his coronation at Aachen. Among other problems, Frederick's son Conrad remained at large as a rallying point for Hohenstaufen loyalists, although the pope denied him any legitimate claim to the kingship of the Germans, an elected, not hereditary, office. From a legal perspective, Frederick's condemnation at the Council of Lyons had rendered his sons ineligible for that position. Innocent repeatedly made this point clear: no descendant of the Hohenstaufen line would ever sit upon the German and imperial thrones.[4]

The pope did what he could to spread the message that the time had come to end the divisive conflict in Germany. Deputizing new envoys for this purpose, including James, archdeacon of Lodi and also a papal chaplain, Innocent summoned important lay nobles and prelates from the region to a meeting at Lyons during Holy Week in 1251. Writing to James in February, the pope instructed to him to travel in the company of Theodoric, master general of the Teutonic knights, who might act as his translator for the German-speaking dukes, margraves, counts, and others who should return to the devotion of the church and to swear fidelity to William, who was about to be crowned emperor.[5] He specifically reached out to Frederick's former allies and uncommitted nobles like Albert of Saxony, Otto II of Bavaria, Godfrey of Hohenlohe, and Philip of Valkesten, asking them to render homage to William and make plain their "affection" for the Roman church. Turning to the wives of such highly placed nobles, Innocent called upon them to assure their husbands' goodwill. Much as he did before Frederick's death, the pope looked to marriage as a means to broker alliances between supporters of the church, encouraging certain unions and offering dispensations for consanguineous marriages where needed.[6] Dealing with excommunicate individuals and communities, he empowered his envoys to grant absolution to the deceased emperor's allies after they rendered sufficient penance and committed themselves to the side of the church. After years under interdict, reconciled communities might again sound their church bells and give their dead a proper burial. For those who persisted in their loyalty to the lost Hohenstaufen cause, such as the city of Worms, Innocent threatened still more sentences of excommunication and interdict.[7]

If anyone imagined that Fredrick's passing would bring peace to the territories of the empire, they must have been disappointed. More than a decade of partisan warfare had left difficult-to-heal divisions in the church, creating unexpected winners and losers. Innocent intervened in one dispute involving two canons from Mainz, Gerard and Berthold, who had joined Conrad's army and had taken up arms against their own archbishop, Siegfried. Years earlier, in 1244, Siegfried had excommunicated both of them, depriving them of their benefices and degrading them from clerical status. Writing to Siegfried, the pope had assured him that he would not receive or consider any letters from the excommunicate canons that did not acknowledge their degraded status. According to later reports that reached Innocent, after making amends for their crimes the two had been on the verge of reconciling with the archbishop when he died. In April 1251, "inclined toward their supplications," the pope finally restored them to their offices and benefices.[8] By then, Siegfried's successor, Christian, faced his own detractors at the papal curia, who accused him of being "useless" for the church because he fought unwillingly for William of Holland. Seeing the fires, destroyed vineyards, and wasted fields, Christian asserted that it did not behoove a priest to fight in worldly battles, although he stood ready to wield the "spiritual sword," that is, "the word of God." When his critics insisted that he should follow in the footsteps of his warlike predecessor, he replied by quoting John 18:11, "Put up your sword in its sheath." Hated by the king and his followers, Christian did not last long in his position. His accusers at the papal curia secured his removal from office by the pope, who appointed none other than the bellicose canon Gerard in his place.[9] Certainly, there was no end in sight to the violence in Germany, as the crusade against the Hohenstaufen continued. To keep up the pressure on Conrad, Innocent called upon the mendicants and others to preach the word of the cross in the "German tongue" against him and his allies, the "persecutors of the church," promising the same indulgences for such crusaders as those enjoyed by soldiers heading overseas along with a forty-day remission of sins for those attending crusade sermons. The pope specifically tasked William of Holland's chaplains, William de Eyka and John de Dist, with such rallying of crusaders, allowing them to repurpose the apostolic letters granted for the crusade against Frederick toward one against his son.[10]

Despite such disruptions, Innocent's overall plans to address the business of the empire moved forward. On Maundy Thursday in 1251, in a field on the edge of Lyons, he delivered a sermon before the throngs of people seeking indulgences from the Roman pontiff, so many—as Nicholas of Carbio described the scene—that the city could scarcely contain them. Among the other princes and magnates present, King William joined the pope, called to Lyons by "solemn envoys and letters." The Roman pontiff, who spoke to the crowd with wisdom and eloquence, blessed everyone and offered them the forgiveness of their sins. The *Deeds of the Bishops of Trier* offers a similar account of this gathering where the pope delivered his address. Innocent spoke in Latin, while the archbishop of Trier, Arnold, translated his words into German. Neither account tells us the topic of Innocent's sermon, but one can imagine its celebratory tone, in light of the pope's recent letters to the faithful rejoicing over the death of Frederick, whom he compared to "Nero" or the "pharaoh." After speaking to the gathering, Innocent returned to the Church of Saint Just with a small group of notables and cardinals, celebrating mass and dining with them.[11]

Through such public displays and private conversations, Innocent projected the promise of peace after years of struggle between the two powers. Yet, there are signs that not everyone entirely supported the pope's designs. While the *Deeds of the Bishops of Trier* reports that Arnold received a warm welcome at Lyons, greeted with honor by the pope and given the kiss of peace, other notable bishops summoned to the curia, including the archbishops of Bremen and Cologne, did not come. In a letter to William of Holland before they met,

Innocent encouraged him to remain steadfast and to ignore those unspecified voices who wished to "erode" the bonds of love between him and the Roman church.[12] Although the pope declared more than once that the time for William's coronation as emperor was coming soon, Innocent did not crown him at Lyons. It seems likely that Innocent did not intend to easily give away his greatest source of leverage over the king of the Germans, namely consecration and the ceremonial bestowing of the imperial crown. They might have planned for the crowning to happen at Rome after the pope returned to the city. Regardless, William of Holland began his return journey to Germany four days after Easter accompanied by the archbishop of Trier and the cardinal bishop of Santa Sabina, Hugh, both of them sent by the pope to help him stabilize his rule. He and the pope would never meet again.[13]

No one knew that there would not be another emperor for over thirty years, the period of the so-called Interregnum, a misleading label since there were in fact kings crowned in Germany, just none strong enough to claim the imperial title. In his *Major Chronicle*, keeping up his relentless complaints about the pope's pastoral failings, Matthew Paris described how Innocent could barely find anyone willing to take up the imperial crown, until William of Holland agreed to try. William drove himself into poverty seeking to make good on that claim. Finally, the pope encouraged Haakon, king of Norway, to become the next emperor. After considering the idea, Haakon decided against it, telling Matthew—who was present at the Norwegian court during one of his rare journeys away from Saint Albans—that he wished to fight against the enemies of the church, but not against the pope's enemies. "Thus, our father the pope," the English monk observed about Innocent, "who followed in the footsteps of Constantine rather than Peter, caused many disasters in the world."[14] After years of battling against one emperor, Innocent sought to create another one but could not find any takers.

Crusading Disillusionments

During the final months of his stay at Lyons, Innocent had to face the latest blow to the long-held goal of overcoming the infidels overseas: the capture of Louis IX at the battle of Fariskur in April 1250. This disastrous outcome for the saintly king's crusade reopened far-reaching questions and criticisms about the papal commitment to the crusades as a means of freeing the holy places. By the middle of the thirteenth century, crusading had become the hallmark of the pope's spiritual and worldly sovereignty: the priestly leader of Christendom calling for armies to fight in God's name. The decades-long struggle between papacy and empire had served to enhance the profile of crusading, placing the "business of the cross" at the center of debates over the rightful disposition of the two powers. Across the span of Gregory IX and Innocent IV's papacies, crusading had become ubiquitous, the "word of the cross" preached against infidels, pagans, Tartars, heretics, and, of course, the Antichrists Frederick and Conrad. As an investment of spiritual, material, and political capital, however, the crusades came at a public cost to the Apostolic See. As the most recent disaster in Egypt demonstrated, each and every crusading failure could be laid at the pope's doorstep.

Not everyone was surprised by Louis IX's losses, or so Salimbene of Adam would have his readers believe. Describing his stay at a Franciscan convent outside of Paris two years earlier, he encountered two Joachites—a native of Parma named Bartholomew Guisculo and a Sicilian called Gerard of Borgo San Donnino—who openly mocked Louis's upcoming expedition, confidently predicting that the king would not only fail in his goals but also would be captured by the infidels. Salimbene's friend Maurice told him to ignore the two troublesome friars.[15] After Louis's defeat, capture, and ransom by the Egyptian sultan, Christians could not so easily disregard the news that came back to Europe in letters and eyewitness reports.[16] As Matthew Paris observed, the dismal failure of Louis's crusade, coming after the collapse of the Fifth Crusade, the disastrous losses at Gaza during the Baron's Crusade, and the sack of Jerusalem Khwarezmian Turks raised doubts about crusading like never before. "It's like God has become our enemy," Christians worried, as the English chronicler described reactions to all these setbacks. "Surely the law of Muhammad is not better than that of Christ?" News of the French king's capture made the pope so depressed that he suspended the issuing of papal bulls for several days, although Matthew goes on to suggest that Innocent was less upset by outcome of the crusade and more anxious about the growing infamy attached to his name because of the latest crusading debacle.[17]

In his historical works, Matthew devotes a great deal of attention to the fallout from Louis's crusade, providing a capstone to his complaints about the abuse of trust and financial chicanery linked to crusading, which he saw as manipulated by kings and their advisers, by the mendicants, and, above all, by the papacy. The recent disaster in Egypt revealed God's displeasure at the exploitation of the poor and needy in Jerusalem's name for dubious ends, including Innocent's unrelenting fight with Frederick. As a warning for the kings of England, Matthew described how Louis had cut a deal with the pope that allowed the French ruler to collect a crusade tithe from the churches of his kingdom for three years. Innocent would then gather the same tithe over the next three years for his war against Frederick. But after the first year's collection, Louis changed his mind, telling the pope that he would not allow money that ought to go toward the fight against the unbelievers to be spent by a priest for attacking fellow Christians. Exploiting papal tax collectors nevertheless, Louis continued to make unreasonable financial demands. Matthew tells the sad story of a poor French clerk forced to sell his school books to meet the demands of one such avaricious Roman tax man.[18]

As news spread of the French king's defeat, the English chronicler continues, complaints emerged on all sides that the pope's refusal to reconcile with Frederick represented a major reason for the collapse of the crusade. The comparison between Innocent's spilling of Christian blood in Italy and Germany and the emperor's bloodless recovery of Jerusalem years earlier was a stark one. Considering all of the misfortunes experienced by the church on his watch, Pope Innocent, who called himself the Vicar of Christ, must have been born under a bad sign.[19] Even Louis's own brothers laid the blame for French defeat squarely at the pope's feet. After his ransom and release, Louis had indicated his intention to remain in Syria so that he might ransom crusaders still in captivity and protect the Christian holdings around Jerusalem. Charles d'Anjou and Alphonse of Poitiers, however, "secretly" set sail for Europe on his orders, eventually meeting with the pope at Lyons. Joined by the duke of Burgundy, Charles and Alphonse demanded that Innocent make peace with Frederick, the only Christian ruler with the power and resources to aid their beleaguered brother. Otherwise, they would expel him from his seat at Lyons.[20]

Judging by his correspondence, Innocent openly acknowledged the trauma shared by the French king, the people of his kingdom, and Christians everywhere. In August 1250, six months before Frederick died, the pope had written directly to Louis at Acre, where he had taken up residence after his release from captivity. He also wrote to Louis's mother, Blanche, offering his consolation for the pious ruler's sufferings and setbacks, part of God's mysterious design. Addressing the archbishop of Rouen and aware that rumors about the bitter defeat on the Nile might have outpaced his letter, Innocent called upon him to make sure that the cities, dioceses, clergy, and people under his authority rendered general prayers for God to console the church, to safeguard the king, and to preserve the glory of Christendom by giving strength to his followers so that they might finally liberate Jerusalem.[21] But the pope did not just rely on prayers and other forms of spiritual assistance. In November, he authorized a new round of financial measures to gather funds for Louis's ongoing defense of the holy places by collecting outstanding tithes and monies raised by the redemption of crusade vows. He sent additional instructions for bishops and members of the mendicant orders to assure that delayed crusaders or those who had "laid aside their crosses" without the church's approval in Provence, Toulouse, Frisia, Norway, and Germany prepare to set out overseas by the next general passage, following the orders of the French queen.[22]

Innocent pinned much of his hope for crusading reinforcements on the French king's longtime rival, Henry III. Encouraged by the pope, the English ruler had sworn a crusade vow in March 1250, when he received the sign of the cross from the archbishop of Canterbury. As news of the disaster at Fariskur spread, Henry began to lay the groundwork for his upcoming crusade: raising money, proposing a sixteen-year truce with the French crown, and reaching out to rulers overseas, such as the king of Cyprus.[23] In Ireland, he instructed various bishops, who were working with the mendicants, to publicize Innocent's letters authorizing his crusade and appointed worthy persons to deliver crusade sermons. He added careful instructions for the recipients of the papal letters to deposit them somewhere for safekeeping in case they were needed for later reference. Over the following year, corresponding directly with the king and with leading prelates in England, Innocent gave explicit instructions for the raising of funds through the redemption of crusade vows, and he authorized a new tithe on ecclesiastical incomes for two years, anticipating the launch of the English king's expedition.[24]

The question of how to fund the next crusade caused more controversy. As Matthew Paris related, from the moment Henry took the cross, some suspected that he did so for nefarious reasons, using the crusade as an excuse to extort money from the barons of the realm, with backing from the pope.[25] Complaints about such collusion between the English crown and papal curia would continue for years to come, prompting the fearless Robert Grosseteste, bishop of Lincoln, to deliver a stinging rebuke of the king to his face. The precise departure plans for the campaign caused additional tensions. Initially, Innocent seems to have favored an early departure for some of the sworn crusaders in England, instructing Robert and the bishop of Chichester to ensure that one large group would depart in June 1250 en masse rather than in small parties. Henry, however, rejected the English nobles' desire to form an advanced wave that would serve to intimidate the infidels before his arrival. He insisted that the crusaders wait for him and obtained letters from the pope that forbade them from leaving without their ruler. He even set guards on the port at Dover to prevent anyone from setting sail. Once again, for arguably sound logistical reasons, the papacy found itself in the unpopular position of calling for a crusade and then preventing crusaders from setting out on their sworn pilgrimage.[26]

During the spring of 1251, discontent with the crusading status quo revealed itself in a dramatic and unsettling way during the so-called Shepherds' Crusade. Numerous chroniclers took note of this popular movement by bands of mostly French *pastoureaux*—poor men and women of rural origins—who had the declared intention of embarking on a crusade and rescuing King Louis.[27] Most of those historians presented the shepherds' supposed devotion as a dangerous delirium. Led by an elderly, charismatic Hungarian preacher bearing a letter from the Virgin Mary, these meek and humble crusaders declared that they would succeed where great princes had failed. They marched under multiple banners, including the sign of a lamb, which was a mark of their humility and innocence, and a cross as the standard of their victory. Initially, Queen Blanche greeted the apparent outpouring of piety and support for her son with favor and support.

When the *pastoureaux* grew violent, however, attacking Jews, clergy, and mendicants and assaulting churches in cities that included Paris and Orléans, the French queen mobilized local authorities to attack and disperse the would-be crusaders. The Shepherds' Crusade seemed to fall apart as quickly as it formed, its leader slain by a disgruntled follower and the bulk of its participants scattered and killed "like rabid dogs." Some of the survivors set aside their illicit crosses, did penance, and took an official crusading vow at the hands of legitimate authorities.[28]

Innocent never directly addressed the Shepherds' Crusade in his letters, and Nicholas of Carbio passes over the event in conspicuous silence. But his response can be readily imagined. By critiquing the rich and mighty who had repeatedly failed in their efforts to recover Jerusalem, the *pastoureaux* publicly challenged the crusades, a project managed by popes and prelates, kings and other nobles. Matthew Paris, who specifies that the movement's leader preached "without papal authority or the support of any prelate," records that he learned about this "pestilence" from Boniface, archbishop of Canterbury, who had returned from Lyons to England early in the summer of 1251. Boniface related to him that the movement began around Easter, just before Innocent left Lyons for Italy under the protection of the city's bishop-elect, Philip, who spent three thousand marks on the pope's escort. Such wasteful spending, this story seems to imply, represented precisely the kind of extravagance that provoked the crusading rabble in the first place. Continuing his account, Matthew explicitly declares that the pope's absence from Lyons encouraged the uprising, not exactly blaming Innocent for the Shepherds' Crusade, but coming close.[29]

Whatever Innocent felt about Louis's defeat and the provocative crusade of the *pastoureaux,* he made no significant changes to the curia's crusading policy toward the holy places. He continued to offer consolation and support to Louis's mother, instructing the bishop of Paris to absolve her for the sin of corresponding in the past with the excommunicate and deposed emperor. But his sympathy had clear limits, as seen when he informed Blanche that he would not wait for her at Lyons for a proposed meeting to discuss her son's stalled crusade.[30] The pope likewise told Henry III that he would be leaving Lyons soon and could not meet with him before he set out on his planned journey overseas, as the king had requested. He promised instead to meet with the English ruler in Italy during his journey to the Holy Land or during his return from his crusade. Henry, it turned out, would never actually leave on his crusade. Despite all of the public lamentations about Louis IX's defeat, no substantial crusading force came to the French king's aid before he returned to Europe in the spring of 1254.[31]

Indeed, Louis's invasion of Egypt proved to be the last major crusade campaign in the Eastern Mediterranean during the Middle Ages. By that time, crusading had become part of the fabric of European society in ways that previous generations of crusaders could have scarcely imagined, being imbricated in the financial, legal, and devotional life of the Roman church. The more that the bishops of Rome owned the crusades, however, the more they owned their failures and were accountable for the waste, loss, and disillusionment that the expeditions overseas seemed unerringly to produce. By the closing years of Innocent's papacy, the crusades remained one of the Apostolic See's greatest instruments to intervene in European public life, and one of its greatest liabilities.

The Return to Italy

In April 1251, even as the *pastoureaux* began their crusading protests, Innocent left Lyons for Italy, after seven years in exile. Heading back to the Italian peninsula represented a logical next step after Frederick's demise, a high-profile demonstration of the Roman church's victory now that the "herald of Antichrist" had been swept from the board. On Easter, just days before he left Lyons, the pope sent a purposely dramatic message to those who continued to oppose the Roman church and serve the Hohenstaufen cause. As Matthew Paris relates, sharing news he heard from the archbishop of Canterbury, Innocent "horribly" excommunicated Frederick's bones, taking one last spiritual shot at his deceased enemy. He also excommunicated the emperor's son Conrad, who had "violently" seized power in parts of Germany and the Regno, and Thomas of Savoy, who years earlier had blocked the papal troops from crossing the Alps as they were headed to relieve Parma. The enemies of the church were being put on notice before the bishop of Rome returned home.[32]

Innocent carefully laid the groundwork for his journey. In February, he announced the coming of his chaplain Stephen, a Dominican friar, "in the name of peace" to Marseilles, Arles, and Avignon, centers of imperial resistance that had "wandered from the path" of the church in recent years. In separate communications with Stephen, the pope advised him to work with Charles d'Anjou's seneschal and bailiffs in the region in order to coordinate the transfer of power to the French king's brother.[33] Innocent also dispatched a new round of letters to Ghibelline cities, including Cremona, Pavia, Padua, and Bergamo, calling upon them to return to the obedience of the church and seize the opportunity provided by Frederick's death to renew their bonds with the church rather than further "scandalizing" those Christian provinces.[34] He gave additional instructions for civic authorities and bishops in Lombardy to prepare for his arrival, summoning them to an assembly at Genoa on the Feast of the Ascension in May, where they would deliberate about how to restore "concord" and "tranquility" to Italy after decades of war. Cooperating with the papal legate Ottaviano Ubaldini and Gregory of Monte Longo, bishops in the region were expected to issue letters of safe conduct for envoys attending the planned meeting at Genoa.[35] Before departing from Lyons, the pope announced to the faithful that he was taking the city under the "special protection" of the Apostolic See, a sign of his gratitude toward the place that had protected him when he fled from Italy.[36] Supposedly, when Cardinal Hugh of Santa Sabina departed from Lyons around the same time, he observed that the curia had accomplished a great deal there. When they arrived, they found only three or four brothels, but now there was only one—the entire city. He offended a number of women who overheard him, but the joke "spread like wildfire."[37]

Unlike during his flight to Lyons years earlier, Innocent traveled back to Italy with great fanfare, accompanied by an apparently expensive entourage of armed guards provided by the archbishop-elect of Lyons and joined by a number of cardinals and other officials from the curia. Nicholas of Carbio, Innocent's Franciscan confessor and biographer, accompanied the pope on his return journey. More or less reversing his path from years earlier, Innocent headed down the Rhone by ship, passing through various smaller communities until he reached Marseilles, where throngs of well-wishers greeted him with hymns and praises, hoping to catch a glimpse of the pope. The pope next made his way overland to Genoa, drawing large crowds wherever he went. When the Genoese heard that their native son was returning home, they ordered all of the coastal roads cleared and bridges repaired, at considerable expense. In late May, Innocent reached the city. Much as they did for the pope's arrival in 1244 en route to Lyons, the Genoese celebrated his arrival with a public procession, festooning the roads along the seashore with silk banners. The podesta went out to greet the Roman pontiff, leading him into the city on a large palanquin under a sunshade, accompanied by an honor guard and onlookers who were singing hymns and playing instruments. Innocent installed himself at the archbishop's palace, where he would remain over the following month.[38]

By the time that Innocent reached Genoa, the Fieschi family had managed to more or less secure the city for the "party of the church." During the year before Frederick's death, Innocent's relatives had worked to reconcile the imperial party of the commune, the so-called Mascarati, drafting a public instrument that its adherents would obey the pope's mandates. Frederick's death solidified the Fieschi grasp on Genoa. Both the *Genoese Annals* and Nicholas of Carbio describe how Innocent received numerous podestas, envoys, and ambassadors from cities around Lombardy that remained loyal to the church, holding a daily general audience in the archbishop's palace.[39] After his arrival, the pope continued to rely on his family for support in the effort to turn the tables on Hohenstaufen loyalists and holdouts. Resorting yet again to the ties of marriage, he arranged a union between the repentant Count of Flanders, Thomas of Savoy, and his richly endowed Fieschi niece, Beatrice, while marrying another one of his nieces to a nobleman identified by Matthew Paris as Tur de Pin. Innocent also staged a wedding for one of his nephews, which was described by Salimbene of Adam with a hint of disapproval as so lavish that the queen of Sheba would have been amazed.[40]

Uncertainty surrounded Innocent's next moves. According to Nicholas of Carbio, he intended to go immediately to Rome, but Ottaviano and Gregory of Monte Longo convinced him first to make an urgently needed detour through the cities of Lombardy. The pope's biographer offers a detailed account of Innocent's route, starting from Genoa and heading to Milan, where eager crowds of men, women, and children greeted him with pageantry and singing. More than fifteen thousand people lined the road into the city, a "procession the likes of which has never been seen."[41] From Milan, Innocent headed to Novara in late June, where he met personally with Thomas of Savoy, reconciling him and his brother Amadeus with the church along with some of the other nobles excommunicated at Lyons the previous Easter.[42] He next traveled to Brescia, Mantua, and Padua. While staying near Brescia, he visited the tomb of Mathilda of Tuscany, performing a blessing in memory of her "good deeds for the Roman church and popes," including her donation of the so-called Mathildine lands to the papal patrimony, a donation contested by generations of emperors, including Frederick II.[43] Leaving Padua, the pope stayed at Ferrara, where Salimbene of Adam listened to him preach from a window in the bishop's palace. Innocent took Psalm 32:12 for his theme, "Blessed is the nation whose God is the Lord: the people whom he has chosen for his inheritance." After finishing, the pope proclaimed, "The Lord has watched over me during my travel from the lands of Italy, my stay at Lyons, and now my return. May he be blessed forever! This is my city, I call on you to live in peace, for, I say, that emperor who persecuted the church is dead." At this point, Salimbene finally had to accept the fact of Frederick's death, prompting a friend on hand to chide him gently about abandoning his misguided belief in Joachim of Fiore's prophecies.[44] Leaving Ferrara, Innocent visited Bologna and Faenza before finally reaching Perugia on 5 November. He would remain there for the next year and a half, receiving envoys from foreign powers, favor seekers, and penitent supporters of the deceased emperor, while letters sent out from the curia called for the cities of Italy to embrace the peace.[45]

Nicholas's triumphalist presentation of the pope's itinerary papered over the considerable challenges that Innocent faced as he crossed through war-torn territories held by allies of the deceased emperor. Lombardy and Tuscany remained in a volatile state, their communes divided internally into competing factions, while imperial communities such as Cremona, Pavia, and Vercelli continued to fight with papal allies like Milan and Parma. The immediate reasons for such conflicts often had little to do with the overarching politics of the struggle between the church and empire. Nevertheless, as Salimbene of Adam observed, around this time people in Tuscany began to use the labels "Guelf" and "Ghibelline" to denote two such factions, respectively. Years of fighting had left a bloody legacy of exiles driven from their homes, fortunes destroyed, captives abused, executions, and other acts of violence. In his chronicle, Salimbene spends considerable time describing the divisive conditions in his native Parma after Frederick's demise, the city split between those loyal to the church and members of the imperial party that had returned from exile. The Franciscan chronicler relates in particular how an obscure tailor named John Barisello rose up to lead the church party, moving through Parma with a cross and the gospels and compelling "imperialists" to swear an oath of allegiance to the "Roman pontiff" and "the side of the church." Over the following years, control of the city would continue to seesaw between the two sides, marked by continued fighting and reprisals.[46]

Innocent faced a similar situation in Piacenza, where fighting had once again broken out between the city's Guelf militia and the Ghibelline popular party. Writing to the bishop-elect of Bobbio and the abbot of Mezano, Innocent instructed them to revoke any benefices held by clergy, monks, or lay people offering support to the *popolo* and to warn the city's podesta that he would be publicly excommunicated and that Piacenza would be placed under interdict if the rebellious citizens refused to reconcile with the church by the given deadline.[47] In other instances, Innocent's arrival in the name of peace triggered warfare. As a favor to him, the Milanese attacked and captured Lodi, an imperial city allied with Cremona and Pavia. To counter this assault, the podesta of Cremona, Ubertino da Pellavincio, arrived to reinforce the city's garrison, which was still in imperial hands. For weeks, the Cremonese, joined by allies from Piacenza and Pavia, burned the outskirts of the city and assailed its walls before withdrawing. Innocent later restored Lodi's status as a bishopric, passing over the fact that the citizens of the city, while siding with Frederick, had once burned a number of Franciscan friars.[48]

Innocent's return to Italy also drew attention to an inescapable consequence of this years-long battle with Frederick: massive debt. During the pope's stay in Milan, according to Matthew Paris, the Milanese demanded compensation for the money they had spent for "his honor and that of the church against Frederick." Pleading poverty after his long exile from Rome and knowing that "his hand was placed in the lion's mouth," Innocent mollified them with gifts and promises of future restitution. When the time came to leave their city, he even managed to convince the Milanese to provide him with an expensive armed escort to protect him from the "Fredericians" on his route.[49] Worries over debts, Matthew asserted, contributed to his long stay at Perugia, since he did not dare return to Rome, where his creditors awaited him. The Perugians, on the other hand, were delighted by Innocent's presence, which assured a flood of visitors to the curia on church business with their open wallets.[50]

Fleeing from Italy seven years earlier, Innocent had demonstrated his resolve to fight against Frederick regardless of the costs. Coming back from self-imposed exile, he began to face the consequences of that long absence. The pope's personal presence in Lombardy might have reminded Christians about the Roman church's mandate to create conditions of peace, but it did not alter the violent political and social dynamics that characterized the region. By the same token, the emperor's demise did nothing to defuse the endemic conflict within and between various communes. In this sense, Innocent's return to Italy brought him into closer proximity with challenges that he did not have the resources, capabilities, or support to meet effectively, despite the apparent latitude that Frederick's death allowed him.

An Inquisitorial Turn

Upon his return to Italy, Innocent pursued a particular strategy for extending and deepening papal oversight over civil authorities, nobles, and clergy on the Italian peninsula, identifying inquisition into the "heretical depravity" as a key means for the papacy to intervene in local communities and target individuals who defied catholic authorities. This intensified crackdown on heretics would persist for the remainder of his time as pope, as he reinforced the inquisitorial powers of the mendicants, assigning each order its own territories of responsibility for rooting out heresy in Lombardy and the Papal States, while calling for Christians to take up the cross against heretics of every kind. In effect, Innocent proposed an endless crusade of sorts in the Roman church's own backyard. Among the policies that Innocent pursued following Frederick's death and his return to Italy, this vigorous turn toward inquisition marked one of the most important and lasting changes in the public face of papal authority.[51]

The pope made his priorities clear soon after reaching Genoa, writing to the Dominican inquisitor Peter of Verona and his companion Viviano on 8 June 1251. By that time, Peter had a long history of preaching the peace and denouncing heretics in Ghibelline strongholds like Florence, harkening back to the days of the Great Devotion in 1233.[52] In his letter to the Dominican friar, the pope spelled out his hopes that the end of conflict between the church and the deceased Frederick would enable an intensified effort to wipe out heresy throughout the world, but above all in Lombardy. "Formerly, while that perfidious tyrant lived, due to his interference, it was not possible to take action freely against the pestilence of this kind, especially in Italy," Innocent wrote to Peter, "for he favored rather than opposed that pestilence, evidently held suspect of heresy himself, even if on account of his sins and many other enormous transgressions he was nonetheless condemned by us at Lyons." The pope instructed Peter to head to Cremona, which was still refusing to submit to the church and failing to take action against heretics and their supporters. If local leaders opposed this effort, the pope continued, he would not hesitate to turn the "sword of ecclesiastical power" against them, summoning armed assistance from "kings, princes and other faithful, marked with the sign of the cross for aid to the Holy Land or some other service to Christ, and other catholics besides." Desiring to avoid such a dire outcome, the pope called upon Peter to explain the situation to the Cremonans, advising them to aid his anti-heretical efforts rather than impeding them.[53]

Just over a week later, Innocent sent another letter to the bishop of Treviso and the Dominican prior at Mantua, giving them instructions on how to deal with Ezzelino da Romano, who was still at large as a "public enemy" of the church. The Veronese lord's reputation for savagery had only grown since his support for the emperor during and after the bitter siege of Parma, revealing him to be crueler even than Frederick. At least, one gets this sense from Salimbene of Adam's descriptions of Ezzelino as the devil's "special friend," a sort of anti–Saint Francis, who joked and cavorted with his men while burning eleven thousand Paduan prisoners alive.[54] Innocent had formally charged Ezzelino with suspicion of heresy and cited him to appear before the papal curia three years earlier, in 1248. Much like Frederick, Ezzelino had sent his proctors to Lyons to expurgate him from the charges. The pope had assigned the cardinal bishop of Sabina to give them a hearing, but he ultimately rejected Ezzelino's appeal. The seriousness of the crimes demanded a personal appearance before the Apostolic See. On the Maundy Thursday before departing from Lyons, when he excommunicated Frederick's bones, Innocent had also anathematized the Lombard warlord, informing him that he must appear before the curia by the next June or face more serious consequences. Raising the matter again at Genoa, Innocent extended the deadline to the first of August. If Ezzelino failed to appear, Innocent called upon the bishop of Treviso and Dominican prior to denounce him as a "manifest heretic" and to preach the cross against him and his supporters.[55]

Such letters marked the beginning of an intensified inquisitorial program that was closely linked to papal policy on the Italian peninsula after the pope's return from Lyons. Much like Gregory IX after his peace with the emperor in 1230, following Frederick's death Innocent almost immediately linked the intensified suppression of heresy to the reassertion of papal authority after years of war and political disruption due to conflict between the two powers. Not surprisingly, he turned in particular to the Franciscans and Dominicans—his workers in the Lord's vineyard—as enforcers for this coordinated campaign against heretics on the Italian peninsula: the so-called Cathars and other heretical groups, real or imagined, along with disruptors of the peace.[56] In addition to issuing and reissuing a now standard set of inquisitorial privileges and mandates for the mendicants, the Roman pontiff called upon civic leaders in Lombardy to support their efforts by passing a public ban on known heretics and their supporters, while instructing the friars to pressure magistrates to pass and observe anti-heretical statutes, variants of the ones issued by Frederick decades earlier.[57] The pope's threat against

Cremona, which called for sworn crusaders to take action against the city if its leaders did not prosecute heretics, did not represent an isolated example of such intensifying pressures. Repeatedly, Innocent enjoined the mendicants to preach the cross publicly against heretics in Lombardy and the papal patrimony, offering would-be crusaders the same indulgence as those heading to Jerusalem.

As always, it remains difficult to determine what sort of reaction these sermons occasioned or how many recruits they gathered. Judging by the fate of Peter of Verona, however, those determined to resist the growth of the inquisitorial enterprise took the threat to their interests quite seriously. According to later reports from Peter's own hagiographical dossier, in April 1252 an assassin named Carino da Balsano, hired by Cathar conspirators, ambushed the Dominican friar and one of his companions on a back road approaching Milan. Carino hacked Peter to death with a machete-like weapon. After the news of this sacrilegious murder reached the papal court at Perugia, Innocent fast-tracked Peter for sainthood, celebrating the mass for his canonization at the Dominican convent in Perugia just under a year later.[58] Others continued to resist, contest, or disregard the inquisitors. Ezzelino da Romano refused to appear before the papal curia despite Innocent's best efforts to force his hand. So too did Robert, lord of Giussano, a small town north of Milan with a reputation for harboring heretics. Cited publicly to appear before the pope on the accusation of abjuring his heresy but then backsliding, Robert failed to answer the summons. Supposedly, Peter of Verona had foreseen the sack of Giussano in a vision before his martyrdom. Writing to the Dominicans in Lombardy years later, Innocent tried to make that prophecy come true, calling for the burning of Giussano, including the bones of the deceased heretics buried there. The pope saw no rest for the remains of such heretical evil dead, no escape from earthly or spiritual retribution.[59]

While the papacy had valorized the fight against heresy for generations, during the years after Frederick II's death, Innocent cemented the papal commitment to inquisition as the primary means of policing orthodoxy. Shortly after Peter of Verona's martyrdom, the pope issued the bull *Ad extirpanda de*, which formulated the most comprehensive guidelines yet for the institutionalizing of the inquisition in Italy's urban communities, where the "tares of heresy" were growing like never before. In addition to publishing the church's anti-heretical statutes, Innocent instructed the civil authorities to hold public assemblies announcing the ban of suspected heretics. Newly elected podestas would coordinate the election of twelve additional men, including two notaries, two Franciscans, and two Dominicans, to a panel tasked with arresting the accused and impounding their goods. The guilty, branded with infamy, would be consigned to jails built especially for this purpose, their homes and those of their supporters destroyed. A registry would be kept of the names of such heretics, copies of which would be held by the commune, by the bishop of the diocese, by the local Dominican convent, and by

Franciscan authorities. The business of rooting up and destroying heresy as a public threat would no longer be left to hearsay and imperfect memory but would instead rely on such systematic technologies overseen by the Apostolic See.[60]

The Sicilian Business

As Innocent reoriented the priorities of his papacy after Frederick's death, he remained fixated on one issue before all others: what to do about the rulership of the Regno. Dealing with the so-called Sicilian business would consume much of Innocent's remaining time and energies in office, highlighting the fact that the removal of the strong Hohenstaufen presence on the southern borders of the Papal States represented a mixed blessing. For decades, the bishops of Rome had struggled against the perceived dangers posed by a sovereign who might combine the kingdom of Sicily with the iron crown of Lombardy and the imperial title, hemming in the Papal States. That threat was more or less gone. In its place, however, emerged a new source of insecurity—the possibility that the Roman church's special patrimony could remain in unfriendly hands, starting with either of Frederick's sons, Conrad or Manfred.

From the moment that he learned about the emperor's death, Innocent had begun to advertize his intentions to reassert papal authority over the Regno, restoring the pristine liberty of its churches after years of bondage. The pope declared that he would come himself as soon as possible to evaluate conditions there "with his own eyes." During his return journey from Lyons, his passage through Lombardy, and his long stay in Perugia, the pope continued to monitor the situation in the kingdom of Sicily, declaring as null and void all of Frederick's past decrees that were prejudicial to the church in the Regno. Sending his directives to local clergy such as the archbishop of Bari, to mendicant envoys, and to an assigned legate, Peter of San Giorgio in Velabro, Innocent called for crusade preaching against Frederick's heirs and allies in "public places," while seeking to reconcile repentant imperial supporters with the church.[61]

In January 1252, a few months after Innocent settled at Perugia, Frederick's more likely successor, Conrad, had traveled from Germany to Apulia to take up rulership of the Regno. During his passage by boat down the Dalmatian coast, he was reminded about the legacy of Innocent's deposition of his father and legal dispossession of Frederick's excommunicate heirs when the archbishop of Split, Roger, refused to receive him in the city, closing its churches and suspending the celebration of mass. The citizens nevertheless greeted Conrad warmly and housed him in the archbishop's palace after Roger went elsewhere. Angered by Roger's refusal, Conrad ordered a search of the episcopal archives during his stay there, seeking any letters or other documentation that might expose him as guilty of treason against his king and thereby brand him with infamy.[62]

Although the pope had proclaimed on previous occasions that he would never settle for one of Frederick's sons remaining on the throne in Germany, Conrad must have sensed an opening for negotiations about the status of the Regno. According to Nicholas of Carbio, the following spring the Hohenstaufen prince sent his solemn envoys to the curia at Perugia. They included Berthold, marquis of Hohenberg, a leading magnate in southern Italy; the archbishop of Trani; and Walter d'Orca, the last man standing from among Frederick's old advisers. Conrad, who desired to "succeed in the place of his father to both the empire as well as the Regno," humbly proclaimed his willingness to "obey the church's commands." To avoid appearing harsh, Innocent received his messengers kindly.[63] Looking back, Nicholas claims that Frederick's son acted deceitfully from the start, making his father look like a saint by comparison. At the time, however, Innocent seemed receptive to some sort of agreement with Conrad. In September 1252, writing to the podesta of Ascoli Piceno, he authorized the commune to sign a truce with Conrad, who was described in that instance as a "noble man."[64] Matthew Paris, who continued to follow the twists and turns of the pope's relationship with Conrad, insists that the cardinals pushed Innocent to make peace with Frederick's heir, fearful that further conflict would destroy the church, if not the entirety of Christendom. The pope seemed willing to explore a compromise and even considered marrying one of his nieces to Conrad. Around this time, however, the Hohenstaufen ruler unexpectedly took ill, leading some to suspect that Innocent had poisoned him just as he had Frederick, fearful that the emperor's son would seek revenge for his deceased father. Others wondered if someone had acted on Innocent's behalf without his knowledge. Regardless, when he recovered, Conrad blamed the pope for the deed, and their negotiations for peace came to an abrupt end.[65]

Even as he kept channels open with Conrad, Innocent pursued an ambitious plan to settle the question of who ruled the Regno once and for all. Acting as the temporal lord of the kingdom, he would bestow it upon an outside ruler invited by the papacy to occupy that position as a vassal of the Apostolic See. Apparently, Innocent's first choice for the position was Richard of Cornwall. Matthew Paris, again, tracks the details of this proposal, which was supposedly first made to Richard in 1250 during a visit to Lyons. Two years later, according to Matthew and Nicholas of Carbio, the pope sent his notary Master Albert of Parma to England to pursue the "Sicilian business" with Richard. Matthew found this whole scheme ludicrous and possibly dangerous, comparing Innocent's offer to the devil's temptation of Christ. In effect, Richard would do the pope's dirty work at his own expense. He writes that Richard did not make the mistake of falling for Innocent's ploy and demanded hostages to assure the pope's support, along with money up front and control of certain fortified points bordering the Regno. Otherwise, Innocent might as well have said, "I will sell you or give you the moon, rise up and take it."[66]

Although the exact timing of the negotiations remains unclear, by the spring of 1252, Innocent also began to consider Charles d'Anjou as a possible contender for the Sicilian crown.[67] Nicholas of Carbio writes that Charles expressed his interest in the crown of the Regno after he got wind of the pope's offer to Richard of Cornwall; he then sent envoys to the curia to place himself at the "service of the Roman church." As seen above, the pope already had connections to Charles, supporting his marriage to Beatrice of Provence. By June 1253, acting on Innocent's instructions, Albert of Parma placed a formal offer on the table to bestow the kingdom of Sicily upon Louis IX's brother.[68] The terms of this agreement reveal a great deal about Innocent's hopes for the disposition of the Regno. Among other promises, as a sworn vassal of the pope, Charles would agree to protect and promote the church's liberties, assuring free clerical elections, restoring exiled bishops to their sees, and refraining from bringing clergy before civil judges or imposing tallages on church persons and properties—the reverse of Frederick's "tyrannous" policies during the previous years. Charles and his successors would also commit to never marrying an enemy of the church or a relative of the deceased Hohenstaufen emperor, to never combine the Sicilian crown with the imperial dignity, and to never enter into any agreements beyond the Regno that would be prejudicial to the church—not with any king, prince, or baron, be they Christian, "Greek," or "Saracen." In addition to symbolically giving the pope a suitable palfrey once a year, Charles would also pay one thousand gold ounces for his investiture, an annual census of one thousand silver marks, and funds for five knights to serve six months in the papal patrimony.[69] Much like Richard of Cornwall, however, Charles began to have second thoughts. According to Nicholas of Carbio, he sadly listened to the "wicked counsel" of bad men, who dissuaded him from accepting the pope's "magnificent gift." Albert told the pope that Charles remained open to the proposal but wanted changes to the document outlining its terms. Innocent agreed to further negotiations, instructing Charles to send his envoys to the curia to receive the investiture of the Regno. Nevertheless, over the following months, it became clear that the French ruler would not follow through on the plan.[70]

With Richard of Cornwall and Charles d'Anjou out of the running, Innocent turned to yet another possibility: Henry III's young son, Edmund. By March 1254, Master Albert, now representing the papacy's interests for the third time in the Sicilian business, conferred the kingdom of Sicily to Edmund, presumably under similar terms as those offered to Charles d' Anjou the previous summer. According to Matthew Paris, Conrad had already warned Richard not to accept the Sicilian crown from the pope. When he heard the news that Henry III had agreed to receive the Regno on behalf of his son, Conrad knew that Innocent had duped the king. Matthew agreed, strongly suggesting that Henry had wasted his time and money on this scheme. In retrospect, the English monarch's willingness to embrace the pope's proposal might have made perfect sense, given Henry's anticipating his own crusade to Jerusalem within a few years and wider ambitions to extend his influence into the Mediterranean. Whatever Henry intended, however, he did not rush to commit any forces to subduing the Regno, despite Innocent's eagerness for him to do so. In the short term, facing uncertainty on the southern border of the Papal States, the pope was on his own.[71]

Innocent's Last Stand

In the middle of his effort to find a new ruler for the kingdom of Sicily, Innocent decided that the time had finally come for the long-absent bishop of Rome to return to his city. As seen at various points throughout this book, thirteenth-century popes ironically faced some of the most relentless opposition to their immediate sovereignty over the papal patrimony from the Roman commune and citizenry. Nicholas of Carbio gives us some sense of why Innocent might have avoided returning to the city sooner, describing how the Romans schemed to undermine the pope's position by electing a new senator, Brancaleone, who was on friendly terms with the heretical Ezzelino and was corrupted by Conrad's bribes. As securing control of the Regno moved to the center of his priorities, however, Innocent apparently decided that the risks of a move to Rome were worth taking and headed south to reassert his authority over the city.[72]

The pope departed from Perugia in April 1253, stopping first at Assisi, where he remained for the rest of the summer while waiting for the heat to pass and no doubt laying the groundwork for his safe arrival in Rome. During his stay, Innocent maintained a high profile, as he and cardinals consecrated the city's newly completed cathedral church. The ceremony drew large crowds of clergy and lay people, who were attracted by the offer of indulgences for their attendance. Nicholas of Carbio must have taken special pride in that event. Four years earlier, the pope had named him bishop of Assisi, a fitting reward for his faithful Franciscan confessor. The pope also canonized Saint Stanislaus, famous for his resistance to the wicked king of Portugal, and he visited the ailing Clare of Assisi on her deathbed, confirming the rule of her order just days before her passing.[73] After celebrating the Feast of Saint Francis on 4 October, Innocent left Assisi, passing through Narni and Sabina before reaching the outskirts of Rome. Fortunately, Nicholas observes, God did not allow the conspirators in league with Ezzelino and Conrad to stop the pope from entering the city. Instead, large crowds of clergy and lay people led by the Roman senator greeted the Roman pontiff, who took up residence at the Lateran palace.[74] Resuming his theme of how outstanding debt dictated the pope's movements, Matthew Paris claims that the Romans wanted

Innocent back in their city due to all of the lost revenues from his long absence. They had even written to the Perugians and to the citizens of Assisi, threatening them if they delayed the pope's return any longer. While the Romans greeted Innocent joyfully, according to the English chronicler, Innocent entered the city in an anxious state of mind, worried that his creditors would demand the money he owed them for the long and expensive war against Frederick. Nicholas, to the contrary, emphasized Innocent's generosity to everyone in the city, restoring the run-down Church of Saint Lawrence and the Basilica of Saint Peter and supporting destitute clergy and nobles exiled from the Regno.[75]

Whatever local troubles he faced, Innocent's attention remained fixed on conditions in the Regno and the challenge posed by Conrad, who had attacked Capua and besieged Naples the previous October.[76] In February 1254, in a letter to all the faithful, the pope explained how he had issued a public summons for Conrad to appear before him and answer to a series of charges. Conrad's proctors came to the curia and responded publicly to the articles in the pope's hearing.[77] Matthew Paris somehow got his hands on a transcript of Conrad's replies to the charges made against him. The accusations against Conrad echoed those made against his father: that he forced clergy to celebrate mass in the Regno, despite the papal interdict; that he supported those who publicly preached heresy in Lombardy; that he showed favor toward Ezzelino da Romano, a known heretic; that he conspired to murder his own relatives; and that he occupied church properties in Sicily, despoiled the military orders, and kept ecclesiastical offices vacant for his own material gain. Above all else, the pope charged him with unlawfully occupying the Regno, claiming it as his inheritance even though the right to the kingdom "pertained to the Apostolic See." Likewise, by wrongfully claiming the imperial dignity, Conrad damaged the dignity of the empire.[78]

Echoing his father's defense against similar charges years earlier, Conrad denied or tried to explain away these supposed crimes, attributing many of them to lies spread by his enemies. He did not show "contempt for the keys," having never received a formal notice of his excommunication. When he arrived in the Regno years earlier, he had found clergy there celebrating the divine offices and merely allowed them to continue doing so: he himself attended mass only from an excess of piety, as a "true Christian and catholic prince." Letters presented as proof of his wrong doing were not in fact written by him. To the contrary, he could provide letters that he sent to his officials showing that he did not compel anyone to celebrate mass. As for his supposed support of heretics, Conrad emphasized his efforts to destroy heretics in Germany and his unfulfilled desire to do so in Lombardy, where it was "public knowledge" that civic authorities allowed heretics to preach openly. As for Ezzelino da Romano, Conrad had no awareness of his heretical status and would never knowingly associate with a known heretic. In the Regno, his lawful inheritance, he governed peacefully and exercised his time-honored prerogatives, causing no harm to the Roman church or clergy and rendering justice indifferently to all. He acted as emperor because, as the king of the Romans, he possessed the right to do so. In closing, Conrad opposed any further investigation into the charges against him because they amounted to hearsay, which was inadmissible according to canon and civil law.[79]

Such a response must not have pleased the pope, but Innocent, acting with "paternal affection" toward Conrad, extended the deadline for a resolution to their disagreements to the middle of Lent.[80] Their differences remained unbridgeable, however. On Maundy Thursday in April 1254, Innocent formally renewed the sentence of excommunication leveled against Conrad in the Lateran church. Before the crowds gathered for the Holy Week, he also anathematized Ezzelino da Romano—"not a man, but a public enemy of mankind." After two years of refusing to answer for the charges against him, Ezzelino stood condemned as a manifest heretic and supporter of heretics, having turned aside the minds of the faithful from orthodox belief, despised the sacrament of marriage, and slaughtered men, women, and children. Summoning Ezzelino to appear before the curia by 21 May, the pope instructed bishops in Lombardy to announce the sentence with full and public ceremony, depriving him and his followers of any ecclesiastical fiefs and benefices.[81]

Just over a month after the pope anathematized Conrad, however, the Hohenstaufen prince died from illness or—some claimed—from poison. Salimbene of Adam writes that a doctor gave him a purgative enema secretly intended to kill him. While his followers were carrying his bones to Palermo for burial, Salimbene continues, the citizens of Messina grabbed them and cast them into the sea, in revenge for his father's abuse of the city. Innocent had once again won a reprieve in his battle with the Hohenstaufen dynasty by outliving his opponent. Describing Conrad on his deathbed, Matthew Paris attributed words of grief to him, lamenting that the empire that had flourished since the days of Christ had begun to slide into oblivion. The pope rejoiced, seeing that his two principal enemies had died: Conrad, and also the outspoken bishop of Lincoln, Robert Grosseteste, who had passed away the previous October.[82]

Conrad's death left Frederick's son Manfred, designated in the emperor's will as prince of Taranto and regent in the Regno, as the last significant Hohenstaufen contender for the crown of Sicily. Conrad's son, Conradin, was just a child. As early as June 1252, Innocent had indicated his willingness to negotiate with Manfred and Conrad's bailiff in Sicily, Berthold of Hohenberg, over the terms for their return to the obedience of the church. As a sign of his good faith, the pope instructed Peter of San Giorgio in Velabro to invest Manfred and Berthold with their holdings of Taranto and Anadria, respectively, as fiefs held by the pope's authority. Nothing came of these initial negotiations, mainly because Manfred lined up behind his brother Conrad after he arrived in the Regno, resisting any expansion of the pope's influence in the region. With Conrad's demise, Innocent again opened the door to striking an agreement with Manfred, provided that he and the nobles supporting him recognize papal sovereignty over the Regno. Saba Malaspina, a chronicler with close ties to the papal curia, suggests that Manfred desired the pope's support to shore up his claims to the throne, above all against some of Conrad's former allies who favored Conradin.[83]

When news of Conrad's demise reached Innocent, he was at Assisi, escaping the early summer heat in Rome. In June, he moved the curia to Anagni because, according to Nicholas of Carbio, it represented a more suitable location for dealing with the business of the Regno. On 15 August, the pope convoked an assembly at Anagni to promote "peace and concord" in the Regno, joined by Manfred, Berthold of Hohenberg, Frederick of Antioch, Walter d'Orca, and many other former officials from Frederick's court, along with a number of cardinals and "public multitude of the faithful."[84] After two weeks of discussion, an accord was reached. By the Feast of the Nativity of the Blessed Virgin on 8 September, the nobles in attendance from the Regno would surrender all of their towns, fortifications, and other holdings to the pope, promising not to interfere with the papal rectors who would be sent to oversee church governance in the region. In return, the pope would invest them with the territories that they had surrendered, to be held by them as papal vassals. Those who refused would be held as "rebels and enemies of the Roman church."[85]

For reasons that are unclear, this whole plan suddenly broke down, as Manfred, Berthold, and others refused to commit to such unfavorable terms and left Anagni. On 8 September, Innocent excommunicated all of the nobles who had walked away from the talks. Preparing once again for war, Innocent summoned the faithful in Lombardy, Genoa, Tuscany, the March of Ancona, and Spoleto to take up arms on the church's behalf. He also appointed his nephew William, cardinal deacon of Sant'Eustachio, as his legate to the Regno, putting him in charge of the papal army gathering at Capua.[86] The nobles of the Regno splintered, Nicholas of Carbio claimed, with some of them returning to the side of the church, at first "secretly" and then "openly," while others favored continued opposition to the pope. In yet another turnabout, however, Manfred and Innocent just as suddenly settled their differences. On 20 September, the pope absolved Manfred, praising him as a "noble" and "faithful son" of the church, confirming his title as prince of Taranto and recognizing his position as the "captain" of Apulia until Conradin reached his majority. This agreement between them set the stage for their meeting on 11 October at the bridge over the Garigliano, where the pope ceremoniously entered the Regno, seated on his horse, while Manfred acted as his groomsman, performing a scene of iconic deference to the pope of Rome.[87]

Innocent did not have long to enjoy this apparent triumph. According to Saba Malaspina, nobles in Apulia favoring Manfred began to work behind the scenes to turn him against the pope, murmuring, "The dominion of clergy is not right for us. Let spiritual things be enough for the Roman church, and let the church freely relinquish temporal things to the prince, son of the emperor."[88] In early October, Manfred and a group of his soldiers stumbled across Burello d'Angione, a noble with ties to the pope, en route to the curia. Precisely what happened next depends upon which chronicle one reads. Those favorable to Innocent recorded that Manfred savagely ordered his men to murder Burrello, who had contested some of Manfred's claims in the Regno. Others blamed Manfred's overeager soldiers, insisting that he did everything he could to stop Burello's slaughter by the side of the road. Manfred protested his innocence to the pope, while the Roman pontiff suspended any agreements with him until he rendered satisfaction for his "grave crime." Sources friendly to Manfred reported that he feared to go to the curia to expurgate himself because it might give his enemies a chance to imprison, exile, or kill him. Yet if he refused to go, the pope would invade the Regno. Facing such undesirable outcomes, Manfred opted for the lesser of evils and took flight.[89]

By late October, showing signs of illness, Pope Innocent had settled at Naples. During the following weeks, a papal army assembled in Capua under the command of William of Sant'Eustachio and other Fieschi relatives of the pope. Reconciled with the pope, Manfred's former ally Berthold of Hohenberg joined the side of the Roman church, as did a number of other nobles from the Regno. Manfred gathered support from his deceased father's allies, including some German soldiers, but also from the Muslim mercenaries at Lucera, who supposedly feared that papal lordship over the Regno would mean their destruction. After some inconclusive negotiations for a peaceful resolution to this conflict, Manfred and his forces moved toward the papal army gathered at Foggia.[90] The ensuing battle turned against the church's troops after some of them, perhaps treacherously or perhaps from fear, abandoned their position. Some of the survivors, including several of Innocent's family members, took refuge in the main palace at Foggia when Manfred's soldiers captured the outskirts of the city. When news of this defeat reached William of Sant'Eustachio at nearby Troia, he also withdrew his forces. Eventually the garrison holding out at Foggia slipped away, leaving the suddenly exposed citizens to beg Frederick's son's forgiveness for their decision to side with the pope's allies. Perhaps not surprisingly, Matthew Paris blamed the defeat of the papal army on its preoccupation with "worldly things" and the pope's refusal to heed God's warnings. Whether Innocent learned about the outcome of the battle remains unclear. Within a few days of his army's defeat at Foggia, on 7 December 1254, this particular Vicar of Christ had breathed his last.[91]

POSTLUDE

The Afterworld

Like almost every other aspect of Innocent IV's papacy, his death polarized contemporaries—or at least they left divergent kinds of memorials to him. At the end of the pope's vita, Nicholas of Carbio describes how Innocent gracefully spent his final hours, making confession, taking the Eucharist, and receiving last rites. An outpouring of grief followed as the Franciscans and Dominicans present, joined by a crowd of monks and clerics, bore his body for burial to the cathedral church in Naples. Generally positive toward Innocent, Salimbene of Adam expressed his disappointment that the pope had issued a letter revoking many of the mendicant orders' privileges not long before he died, yielding to complaints by the secular clergy about the friars' infringement upon their pastoral prerogatives. As the pope lay sick on a bed of straw with no one to attend him, as was customary for dying Roman pontiffs, two Franciscans nevertheless promised Innocent they would wash his body and prepare him for burial.[1]

Others were less kind. After years of cataloguing Innocent's abuses of the English church, Matthew Paris seemed to relish the news of his demise. In his *Major Chronicle*, the Benedictine chronicler describes how the bishop of Lincoln, Robert Grosseteste, posthumously appeared before the pope in a dream. As he had done in life, Robert rebuked him for his failings and struck him in the side with his episcopal staff. When Innocent awoke, he felt a persistent pain in the spot where the bishop had landed his blow. "I will never be restored to my previous state of health," he told his chamberlains before dying soon after. Matthew followed with the story of an unnamed cardinal who in a dream saw the deceased pope standing before Christ, the Virgin Mary, and a woman representing the church. That woman accused Innocent of making her into a slave and turning her into a money changer's table, overthrowing her foundations built on justice, faith, and truth. "Go," the Lord said to Innocent, "and receive your reward according to your deserts." The cardinal awoke, terrified by this vision of the pope's posthumous fate.[2]

Eudes of Châteauroux offered some less one-sided thoughts on Innocent's demise in a sermon, apparently written for his fellow cardinals on the one-year anniversary of the pontiff's death.[3] Eudes took Numbers 20:30 as his theme: "And the whole multitude, seeing that Aaron was dead, mourned him for twenty-one days." Like Aaron, who reached the Promised Land but died before entering it, Innocent had passed away on the edges of the Regno trying to capture that kingdom, struck down by divine judgment as a punishment for his sins. Eudes praised Innocent in his sermon, extolling his immense erudition and knowledge of the law. He also celebrated the authority of the papal office that Innocent had occupied: the rights to define Christian belief, to act as the supreme judge, to summon the secular arm in defense of the church, and to call for crusades. And yet, Innocent had made his mistakes, financially oppressing churches for the sake of acquiring the Regno and wrongly striving for a victory that the Lord had plainly reserved for another. Eudes reminded his listeners about the fleeting nature of power, recalling how Aaron after his death was stripped of his garments that were given to his successor, Eleazar. "Let us, therefore, exert ourselves so that when we are stripped of our dignities, honors, riches, and power, we may not be found naked without the clothing of virtues, the clothing of good works and the nuptial garment," he advised his brothers. "For those who are naked without these garments will not be admitted to the wedding of eternal joy."[4]

Eudes seemed to appreciate the mixed blessings of Innocent's legacy. The fight between the Roman church and the Hohenstaufen dynasty did not end with the pope's passing but continued on a reduced scale, focused on the question of who would rule the Regno. Presumably mindful of the long vacancy preceding Innocent's election, the cardinals in Naples moved quickly to elect his successor, choosing the elderly Raynald da Jenne, cardinal bishop of Ostia, as the next bishop of Rome. Taking the name Alexander IV, he continued to pursue the same vision of the "Sicilian business" as his predecessor, opposing Manfred and seeking an outside ruler for the kingdom of Sicily. Elected in 1261, Pope Urban IV finally convinced Charles d'Anjou to take charge of the Regno. Under Pope Clement IV, Charles defeated and killed Manfred at the battle of Benevento in 1266, marking the "end of an era in Italian history."[5] Despite this apparent victory, the kingdom of Sicily would remain a political quagmire for decades to come, absorbing a great deal of the papacy's time, energy, and resources. Whatever arrangements Innocent had envisioned for the Regno after Frederick's demise, one suspects that this was not it.

Beyond the Regno, consequential and challenging developments loomed on the horizon for papal claims to wield authority over Christendom, including Pope Boniface VIII's humiliation at Anagni, where agents of the French king Philip IV arrested and abused him to the point of causing his death; the Avignon papacy, the protracted and controversial installation of the papal curia in southern France; and the Great Schism, when two lines of popes at Avignon and Rome claimed the papal office. Drawing upon newly influential Aristotelian ideas about the nature of human governance, fourteenth-century critics of the Roman papacy such as Marsilius of Padua and William of Ockham leveled unprecedented attacks on the pope's right to intervene in matters of earthly governance and temporalities, publicly questioning the scriptural basis of papal authority.[6] Among other proof texts for his attack on the papacy, Ockham highlighted *Eger cui lenia* as an example of everything wrong with the Apostolic See, above all its claims to wield both spiritual and secular power, which denied temporal rulers their legitimate sovereignty. Thus, that polemical tract written in the heat of the papal conflict with Frederick first began to haunt Innocent's afterlife, marking him out an aspirational theocrat who tried to depose an emperor with little regard for the limits of his priestly office.[7]

As the years passed following Innocent's death, succeeding generations seemed largely to forget him, beyond remembering his contributions to the canon law tradition. He did not, for example, merit a spot in Dante's masterpiece *The Divine Comedy,* that poetic who's who of politics and religious life written at the turn of the fourteenth century. But Frederick did appear. At one point in his life part of the White Guelf faction in Florence, Dante came to believe that only the reemergence of strong imperial rule could hope to restore order in Italy. Nevertheless, he made space for Frederick among the damned in the sixth circle of the Inferno, where the poet's dead friend Cavalcante tells him, "More than a thousand lie with me: the second Frederick is but one among them." An admirer of Peter de Vinea's rhetorical style, the Italian poet placed him in the seventh circle with other suicides, his soul trapped in a tree ravaged by Harpies and broken into pieces, before growing back and starting all over again. "I am the one who guarded both the keys of Frederick's heart and turned them, locking and unlocking them with such dexterity that none but I could share his confidence," he confides. Envious enemies nevertheless turned the emperor against Peter and caused him to take his own life. If we consider Matthew Paris and Dante together, it seems that Innocent and Frederick, joined by the Hohenstaufen ruler's favorite public relations specialist, finally wound up on the same page—together in hell.[8]

Epilogue

> *Temporal* and *spiritual* government are but two words brought into the world, to make men see double, and mistake their *lawful sovereign.*
>
> —Thomas Hobbes, *Leviathan* (1651)

> The authority of the Popes was the power chosen and constituted in the middle ages for balancing temporal sovereignty and rendering it supportable to mankind.
>
> —Joseph de Maistre, *On the Popes* (1819)

In *Leviathan,* which is widely recognized as a foundational work of modern political philosophy, Thomas Hobbes famously described the Roman papacy as "not other than the Ghost of the deceased Roman Empire, sitting crowned upon the grave thereof." People often seem to forget that fact that the English philosopher devoted a great deal of attention in that famous book to the problem posed by the popes of Rome and their claims to "universal monarchy over all Christendom." For Hobbes, the fundamental question of Scripture boiled down to the issue of whether "Christian kings, and the sovereign assemblies in Christian commonwealths, be absolute in their territories, immediately under God; or subject to one Vicar of Christ, constituted of the universal church." He answered that question emphatically in favor of the former position, denouncing the papal notion of Christendom as the antithesis of the true sovereign: the uncontested, underived, and absolute ruler of the commonwealth. Although Hobbes stopped short of calling the pope of Rome Antichrist, as some of his Protestant contemporaries did, he associated the Roman papacy and Christendom with the "kingdom of darkness," a "confederacy of deceivers" trying to "obtain dominion over men in the present world."[1]

Hobbes articulated his criticisms of Christendom as a response to contemporary Catholic apologists like the Jesuit intellectual Robert Bellarmine, who defended the papacy's "indirect power" over secular governance, which was linked to the spiritual ends of human life. "Authority over Christian princes and kings," Bellarmine declared, "not properly a temporal authority, but one that extends to temporal matters, is attributed to the Supreme Pontiff as the Vicar of Christ by divine law."[2] Among other historical examples of the pope's ultimate sovereign right to judge rulers, Bellarmine pointed to Innocent IV's deposition of Frederick II.[3] This line of argumentation would persist among Catholic conservatives and counterrevolutionaries for centuries to come. Writing in the aftermath of the "satanical" French Revolution, for example, Joseph de Maistre likewise located ultimate sovereignty in the person of the pope. For de Maistre, every law made by man required an "exception," since men could not foresee all things. The exception, in turn, needed a "dispensing power" to avoid violations of the law. Only the pope, he insisted, possessed that power of dispensation, which was delegated by divine mandate. At the same time, the papacy acted as a brake upon the unstrained authority of princes, protecting the people from their tyranny, as evident when medieval popes had rightly deposed overreaching emperors.[4] In Joseph de Maistre's view, simply put, the pope "made Europe."[5]

Hobbes, Bellarmine, and Joseph de Maistre provide just a few instances of how early modern intellectuals constructed their formulations of sovereignty, negatively or positively, in part by invoking Christendom, the two powers, and the papal monarchy. They did so not as an academic enterprise but in response to the pressing political and religious controversies of their own day, including the Protestant Reformation, the Catholic Reformation, the Wars of Religion, the English Civil War, and the French Revolution. In the nineteenth century, the question of the two powers and the role played by the medieval papacy in the formation of the European political order took root in the modern discipline of history. To name just one example, Leopold von Ranke, the "father" of positivist historiography, argued that the popes of Rome had played a key role in binding the Western nations of the Middle Ages into "a single state, temporal and spiritual." That success, however, formed only "one stage in the great progress of things," as such "universality" gave way to the "individuality" of independent nations.[6]

The Christian theological and juridical division of sovereignty into spiritual and temporal realms thereby came to feature prominently in what Mary Anne Perkins calls the "Christendom narrative," that is, the assertion that modern European identity derives in large part from its medieval Christian roots.[7] As political thinkers, philosophers, and historians wrestled with the dilemma of modern sovereignty—its origins and nature as supreme, undivided authority—they invariably looked back to the dual sovereignty of the Middle Ages. By doing so, they shaped how we remember the medieval papacy and its relationship with secular rulers, above all the famous struggles between popes and emperors. Indeed, writing this book on Gregory IX and Innocent IV's confrontations with Frederick II, I have come to the conclusion that the history of medieval Christendom and the two powers cannot be understood in isolation from this highly politicized, often polemical, trajectory of claims, counterclaims, and debates over sovereignty.

Needless to say, a full discussion of this problem would require far more space than this brief epilogue. But a few points can be raised here. From one perspective, the medieval era stood as an age of faith in Christian Europe, a "feudal" society characterized by porous or nonexistent boundaries between religion and politics, which was manifest in the rule of sacral kings, judicial ordeals, holy wars, and other arenas of human governance influenced by convictions about God's will. Popes meddled in politics, calling for crusades and excommunicating rulers. "Sovereignty," as Harold Laski puts it, "in the sense of an ultimate territorial organ which knows no superior, was to the Middle Ages an unthinkable thing." The medieval world represented the antithesis of the conditions required for modern political life, including the concept of sovereignty as self-sufficient and underived power. With the coming of the modern age, among other radical changes the bishops of Rome lost their ability to dictate to emperors, kings, and princes. As Laski continues, "From the time of the Reformation, the sovereignty of the universal Church, vested in the papacy, began to diminish and the preeminence of the popes gradually gave way to the sovereignty of nations, embodied in the person of the monarch."[8]

Rather than seeing a political rupture between the medieval and modern eras, other scholars have located critical contributions to the development of sovereignty in medieval theories of governance. In his influential work *Political Traditions of the Middle Age*, Otto von Gierke viewed the medieval political tradition as an interlude between the consonant "antique" and "modern" concepts of politics, although he stressed that certain "kernels" of antique thought survived inside medieval "husks" to reemerge later. For Gierke, the idea of Christendom and the two powers elaborated a critical sense of unity, but one counterintuitively based on duality. "In all centuries of the Middle Age, Christendom, which in destiny is identical with Mankind, is set before us as a single, universal Community, founded and governed by God Himself," he observes. "Then, however, along with this idea of a single Community comprehensive of Mankind, the severance of this Community between two organized Orders of Life, the spiritual and the temporal, is accepted by the Middle Age as an eternal counsel of God." In this framework, the pope stood as "Christ's Vice-Regent," "the earthly Head of the Church," and "the only Head of all Mankind." The pope was the "wielder of what is in principle an Empire (*principatus*) over the Community of Mortals. He is their Priest and their King; their spiritual and temporal Monarch; their law-giver and Judge in all causes supreme." Conflict between the medieval sense of "Duplicity" and the "requisite Unity," Gierke declares, eventually became "the starting-point for speculative discussions of the relation between Church and State."[9]

From this perspective, as the chief representative of priestly authority presiding over the universal Christian community and claiming the "fullness of power" over the church, the bishop of Rome represented the closest thing to a true sovereign known in the Middle Ages. As Maurice de Wulf describes the "society of nations in the thirteenth century," the "true agents of international action were the Popes, the representatives of the Theocracy, which attained during the thirteenth century, the greatest potency of its authority. The kind of internationalism imposed by the Popes upon Christian nations, which were indistinguishable from the civilized world, was based upon the Catholicity of the Christian faith and morality, and upon the discipline of the Roman Church. Catholicity means universality. One head recognized by all is the guardian of the great ideal by which the society of the time lived."[10] Revisiting the ideas of Hobbes and de Maistre, the controversial German philosopher Carl Schmitt, an avowed Catholic, isolated the sovereign as the one who "decides" and determines the "state of exception," rather than the rule. Although Schmitt did not dwell on the figure of the pope in his 1922 work *Political Theology*, he famously identified "all significant concepts of the modern theory of the state" as "secularized theological concepts," creating a bridge between medieval theology and modern political ideas. Elsewhere, Schmitt pointed to the Roman Catholic Church of the Middle Ages under the pope as representing supreme, universal authority. Acting as "Christ's commissar," the pope liberated the church from the limitations of the "feudal" state. The papal "fullness power" (*plentitudo potestatis*) represented precisely the sort of theological concept that, in secularized form, enabled modern sovereignty.[11]

Catholics of a liberal bent have likewise looked back to medieval Christendom for political inspiration, viewing the papacy as a source of universalism, peace, and stability. For scholars writing around the time of Europe's devastating world wars or confronting postwar totalitarianism, medieval Christendom appeared as an antidote to the divisive ills of the present, almost like a League of Nations or United Nations in the Middle Ages with the pope of Rome at its head. Christendom, as Christopher Dawson observed, "was rooted in the medieval belief that the whole Christian people formed a single body with a twofold organization—the Regnum and the Sacerdotium, the Empire and the Papacy." Although "the former never succeeded in making good its claim to universal authority," he continues, "the latter gave Western Europe a real international organization, which was far more powerful than the local and partial authority of the secular state." The medieval papacy, Dawson asserted elsewhere, was "a genuinely international power that made its authority felt in every corner of Christendom. For the medieval Church was not only a much more universal and comprehensive body than the Empire or feudal state, it exercised many functions which we regard as essentially political."[12]

Battles between popes and secular rulers, moreover, had an unintended consequence: neither of the powers could achieve complete dominance. As Lord Acton stated about the Middle Ages in his 1877 essay "The History of Freedom in

Christianity," if "the Church had continued to buttress the thrones of the Kings whom it anointed, or if the struggle had terminated speedily in an undivided victory, all Europe would have sunk down under a Byzantine or Muscovite despotism."[13] Self-consciously echoing Acton, Brian Tierney later claimed about the two powers that this "unusual duality of structure" in European political and religious life prevented "medieval society from congealing into a single monolithic theocracy."[14] With exceptional erudition, Tierney and other experts in canon law have sought to rehabilitate the papal monarchy of the Middle Ages, highlighting elements of the canonistic tradition that placed restraints on the apparent absolutism of the pope, finding nothing less than the origins of constitutional governance and human rights in the medieval church.[15]

Christendom and its popes, battling against emperors, have thereby come to form what might be called—to borrow from Kathleen Davis's important book *Periodization and Sovereignty*—a "privileged origin and condemned past" for the modern West.[16] Privileged, as the site of Europe's unique genius, differentiating between spiritual and temporal spheres of human activity; condemned, as a past in which the popes of Rome tried without success to transgress those very same boundaries as they aspired to theocratic rule. Viewed from this vantage point, Gregory IX and Innocent IV's confrontations with Frederick II might seem to constitute one especially dramatic stage in an inexorable clash between rival sovereigns. At the height of their prestige in the thirteenth century, the popes of Rome made their bid to stand as the ultimate masters of Christendom in the spiritual and temporal realms. Standing in the way of that goal, the Hohenstaufen emperor had to be opposed, if not destroyed. By throwing the full weight of the papacy against the empire, Gregory and above all Innocent damaged both institutions, helping to create the conditions for their eventual decline and setting the stage for the emergence of a new political order based upon the primacy of the sovereign state and the extrication of religion from public life. Without the medieval concept of the two powers, therefore, the modern separation of church and state, a key characteristic of modernity, might never have come to pass. Without popes like Gregory and Innocent battling for sovereignty against Frederick, one of the two powers might have won too soon and derailed Western civilization from its special destiny.

Yet there are, I would submit in closing, several problems with such linkages between the medieval past and modern iteration of sovereignty. First, these historical interpretations of the two powers rely upon some dubious generalizations about the uniqueness of the West in relation to the rest of the world. As Dawson put it, "Even in the Middle Ages the religious unity imposed by the Church never constituted a true theocracy of the *oriental type*, since it involved a dualism between the spiritual and the temporal powers, which produced an internal tension in Western society and was a fertile source of criticism and change." Or, consider Tierney's observation about the interplay between the medieval two powers: "It is these areas of interaction that we need to study—the interplay between religious and secular ideas and, more subtly, the interplay between medieval present and classical past—if we want to understand why the Western tradition of constitutional thought developed in its unique way, differently from that of China, say, or ancient Peru, or Japan, or the lands of Islam." Christendom in the Middle Ages, with its delineation between the two powers, thereby laid the seeds for the separation of church and state, while other parts of the world, still mired down in medieval attitudes, have not transcended their theocratic impulses, have not yet achieved the proper clarity of distinction between religion and politics. Needless to say, there are deeply embedded Orientalist sensibilities in such views of the European Middle Ages.[17]

Second, and not unrelated, whether celebrating or condemning medieval Christendom, these views of the two powers assume secularization as the dominant trend of historical progress. That is to say, whether they see continuity or rupture between the political traditions of the Middle Ages and the modern era, scholars have taken for granted an increasingly secular world, historically progressing from the imbrication of religion and politics to their modern separation. Over the last several decades, however, the so-called return of religion seems to have thrown such certainties about secularization into doubt. Political theology survives, not just in a secularized garb, but in rawer forms. In the public realm, religious values, identities, and authorities—if they ever even went away—are back with a sometime startling vengeance. Commenting on the role of present-day religion in the "public square," José Casanova observes that Catholicism in the era of globalization looks something like it did before the "straightjacket of the territorial national-state" constrained the Roman Church:

> Progressively, from the end of the nineteenth century to the present, one can witness the reconstruction, reemergence, or reinforcement of all those transnational characteristics of medieval Christendom that had nearly disappeared or been significantly weakened since the sixteenth century: papal supremacy and the centralization and internationalization of the church's government; the convocation of ecumenical councils; transnational religious cadres; missionary activity; transnational schools, centers of learning, and intellectual networks; shrines as centers of pilgrimage and international encounters; and transnational religious movements.[18]

Other religions, he adds, are undergoing "their own particular transformations as a response to the same global issues."

In this regard, it might be said that the papal monarchy of the Middle Ages has indeed been a ghost haunting the Western political tradition—although not in the way that Hobbes imagined. Rather, set within a narrative of progressive secularization, medieval popes such as Gregory IX and Innocent IV are still with us, whether remembered as theocratic boogeymen, embodying the West's safely transcended medieval backwardness, or as the guardians of an ecumenical spirit, imbuing the West with a unique identity and destiny. This immense historical burden placed upon the medieval papacy explains, I think, some of the strong feelings shown toward Gregory and Innocent in past scholarship by Frederick's biographers and others who blame them for ruining Christendom, as well as by those who try to exculpate them from the accusation that they abused their sacerdotal office. The stakes are immeasurably high.

Reconsidered from a "post-secular" perspective, the battles between the two powers examined in this book seem less like a distant mirror and more like a close reflection that is suggestive of how religious identities take shape in the public realm and shape it in turn. Instead of viewing Gregory and Innocent as architects of papal absolutism or enablers of a harmonious premodern international order, we find them as self-consciously public figures, pursing the aims of the moment, balancing competing interests, and scrambling to keep up with fast-moving events. Although the two popes laid claim to the perfect "fullness of power" over the church, their practical abilities to intervene in European political life depended upon decidedly imperfect means of communication and representation through their legates, their letters, word-of-mouth instructions, and rumors that they did not control. Gregory and Innocent faced constant pushback on their intentions to act beyond the spiritual realm, not just from Frederick but also from Christians everywhere who questioned the Apostolic See's right to wage war, to deploy the resources of the church for worldly ends, or to stand in judgment of temporal rulers. In this sense, the crisis between papacy and empire demonstrated that the popes of Rome could not appear to act arbitrarily but rather had to publicize their rightful authority, seeking consensus and canvassing for support. Their struggle for sovereignty was less one against Frederick and his imperial power than a never completely successful effort to realize the papacy's spiritual and sacramental authority as a means of governing Christian lives in the here and now.

Rather than a stage in the secularizing development of the modern political order, the contests between the two powers in the thirteenth century might serve as a reminder about the negotiations required between spiritual and temporal commitments, and about the abilities and limits of religious authorities to take public action while motivating their followers to act publicly. Indeed, every time the pope or any other representative of the Apostolic See invoked the power of the keys, the fullness of power, or the pope's status as the Vicar of Christ, they created an opportunity for contemporaries to question and critique the papacy's political interventions, based on their own interpretation of what those concepts meant. From conservative voices like Matthew Paris to radical Joachite prophets, from clergy who refused to pay their tithes in support of papal armies to parishioners who rioted rather than listen to an illegitimate sentence of excommunication, the inhabitants of medieval Christendom stood ready to make their own judgments about the reasonableness and limits of what sacred authorities could rightly demand of them. In this regard, the citizens of the modern world still have something in common with the denizens of the medieval past.

Abbreviations

Acta Inn.	*Acta Innocentii PP. (1243–1254). Pontificia commissio ad redigendum codicem iuris canonici orientalis, fontes, III.* Edited by Theodosius Halushchyn'skyi and Meletius Voinar. 4 vols. Rome, 1962.
AII	*Acta imperii inedita seculi XIII: Urkunden und Briefe zur Geschichte des Kaiserreichs und den Königsreichs Sicilien in den Jahren 1198 bis 1273.* Edited by Edward Winkelmann. 2 vols. Innsbruck: Wagner'schen Universitäts-Buchhalndlung, 1880.
AM	*Annales monastici.* Edited by Henry Richard Luard. Rerum Britannicarum medii aevi scriptores. 5 vols. London, 1825–91.
ASV	Archivio Segreto Vaticano
Bagliani, *CCFC*	Agostino Paravicini Bagliani, *Cardinali di curia e 'familiae' cardinalizie al 1227 al 1254.* Italia Sacra: Studi e documenti di storia ecclesiastica. 2 vols. Padua: Editrice Antenore, 1972.
BAV	Biblioteca Apostolica Vaticana
BF	*Bullarium Franciscanum Romanorum Pontificum constitutiones, epistolas, ac diplomata continens.* Edited by J. H. Sbaralea. 4 vols. Santa Maria degli Angeli: Edizioni Porziuncola, 1983. First published 1768.
BL	British Library
BNF	Bibliothèque National de France
BOP	*Bullarium ordinis FF. Prædicatorum: sub auspiciis SS. D.N.D. Benedicti XIII, pontificis maximi, ejusdem Ordinis.* Edited by Thomas Ripoll. 8 vols. Rome, 1729–40.
CCQL	*Constitutiones concilii quarti Lateranensis una cum commentariis glossatorum.* Edited by Antonius García y García, vol. 2, series A: Monumenta iuris canonici. Vatican City: Biblioteca Apostolica Vaticana, 1981.
CDSR	*Codice diplomatico del Senato romano dal MCXLIV al MCCCXLVII.* Edited by Franco Bartolini. Fonti per la storia d'Italia pubblicate dall' Istituto storico italiano per il Medio Evo, no. 87. Rome: Tip. del Senato, 1948.
CIC	*Corpus iuris canonici.* Edited by Aemelius Friedberg. 2 vols. Graz: Akademische Druck-U. Verlagsanstalt, 1955.
COD	*Conciliorum oecumenicorum decreta.* Edited by Joseph Alberigo et al. Basilae: Herder, 1962.

CQD	*Commentaria Innocentii quarti pontificis maximi super libros quinque decretalium.* Frankfurt, 1570.
CRH	*Close Rolls for the Reign of Henry III Preserved in the Public Record Office.* 14 vols. London, 1916–64.
DN	*Diplomatarium Norvegicum: Oldbreve til Kundskab om Norges Indre og Ydre Forholde, Sprog, Slaegter, Saeder, Lovgivning og Retterhand i Midelalderen.* Edited by Christian C. A. Lange and Carl R. Unger. 22 vols. Christiana: P. T. Mallings Forlagshandel, 1847.
HB	*Historia diplomatica Friderici secundi Romanorum imperatoris, Jerusalem et Siciliae regis.* Edited by J.-L.-A. Huillard-Bréholles. 6 vols. Paris, 1854–55.
LTC	*Layettes du trésor des chartes.* Edited by Alexandre Teulet et al. 4 vols. Paris: Henri Plon, 1863–1902.
Lupprian, *BPHB*	Karl Ernst-Lupprian, *Die Beziehungen der Päpste zu islamischen und mongolischen Herrschern im 13. Jahrhundert anhand ihres Briefwechsels.* Studi e testi, vol. 291. Vatican City: Biblioteca Apostolica Vaticana, 1981.
Matthew Paris, *CM*	Matthew Paris, *Chronica majora.* Edited by Henry Richard Luard. 7 vols. Rerum Britannicarum medii aevi scriptores. London, 1872–83.
Matthew Paris, *HA*	Matthew Paris, *Historia Anglorum.* Edited by Frederic Madden. 3 vols. London: Longmans, Green, Reader, and Dyer, 1866–69.
MGH	*Monumenta Germaniae Historica*
Const.	*Constitutiones et acta publica imperatorum et regum.* Edited by Ludwig Weiland. Legum, section IV. 4 vols. Hannover, 1893–1911.
epp. saec. XIII	*Epistolae saeculi XIII e regestis pontificum Romanorum selectae.* Edited by Carl Rodenburg. 3 vols. Berlin, 1883–87.
SRG	*Scriptores rerum Germanicarum in usum scholarum seperatim*
SS	*Scriptores*
Nicholas of Carbio, *VI*	Nicholas of Carbio, *Vita Innocentii IV.* In Alberto Melloni, *Innocenzo IV: La concezione e l'esperienza della cristianità come regimen unius personae,* 259–93. Genoa: Marietti, 1990.
Reg. Greg.	*Les registres de Grégoire IX, recueil des bulles de ce pape publiées ou analysées d'après les manuscrits originaux du Vatican.* Edited by Lucien Auvray. 4 vols. Paris: Ernest Thorin, 1890–1955.
Reg. Inn.	*Les registres d'Innocent IV, publiées ou analysées d'après les manuscrits originaux du Vatican et de la Bibliothèque Nationale.* Edited by Élie Berger. 4 vols. Paris: Ernest Thorin, 1884–1911.
RHC	*Recueil des historiens des croisades, historiens occidentaux.* 5 vols. Paris, 1844–1895.
RIS	*Rerum Italicarum scriptores,* n.s. Edited by G. Carducci and V. Fiorini. 34 vols. Città di Castello, 1900–75.
Roger of Wendover, *FH*	Roger of Wendover, *Chronica, sive Flores historiarum.* Edited by Henry O. Coxe. 4 vols. London, 1841.

Rymer and Sanderson, *Foedera* — *Foedera, conventiones, literae et cujuscunque generis act et publica inter reges Angliae et alios imperatores, reges, pontifices, principes, vel communitates*. Edited by Thomas Rymer and Robert Sanderson, 3rd ed. Hague: Apud Joannem Neaulme, 1845.

Salimbene of Adam, *CA* — Salimbene of Adam, *Chronica*. Edited by Guiseppe Scalia. 2 vols. Corpus Christianorum, Continuatio Mediaevalis, 125–125A. Turnhout: Brepols, 1998.

VG — *Vita Gregorii*. In *Le Liber censuum de l'église Romaine*, edited by Paul Fabre, 18–36. Bibliothèque des écoles française d'Athènes et de Rome, vol. 3. Paris: Thorin et fils, 1905.

VMHHS — *Vetera monumenta historica Hungariam sacram illustrantia*. Edited by Augustin Theiner. 2 vols. Rome: Typis Vaticanis, 1859–60.

Notes

Introduction

1. On this programmatic cycle of frescoes, see Sohn, "Bilder als Zeichen der Herrschaft"; Marcone, "Gli affreschi Constantiniani"; and Thumser, "Perfekte Harmonie."

2. Among such biographers, see the influential if controversial Kantorowicz, *Frederick the Second* (originally published as *Kaiser Friedrich der Zweite* in 1927), which is accompanied by a supplementary volume of source citations, *Kaiser Friedrich der Zweite: Ergänzungsband*. On the anti-Catholic themes running throughout Kantorowicz's book, see Ruehl, "In This Time Without Emperors," especially 200–201, 211–12. See also Schaller, *Kaiser Friedrich II*; Van Cleve, *Emperor Frederick II*; Abulafia, *Frederick II*; Stürner, *Friedrich II*; Rader, *Friedrich II*; and Gouguenheim, *Frédéric II*. Although the more recent works on Frederick's imperial reign starting with Abulafia show more restraint in their treatment of the papacy, they have continued to present Gregory IX and Innocent IV as somewhat dubious figures of secondary historical importance. For example, Abulafia (*Frederick II*, 4–5) opens with the statement "I have not set out to write a denunciation of the medieval popes. But (like Frederick) I remain deeply suspicious of religious leaders who bend truth to serve what they believe to be a higher purpose." Others in the past have critiqued such one-sided views: see Powell, "Frederick II and the Church," along with Powell's review of Van Cleve's *Emperor Frederick II*, in *Speculum* 49 (1974): 161, where Powell observes that the author "adopts a Ghibelline position not merely in his sympathy for Frederick but also his attitude toward the Papacy."

3. Recent monographs on Gregory IX and Innocent IV are virtually non-existent, above all in English. Previous books on Gregory IX include Felten, *Papst Gregory IX*; Brem, *Papst Gregor IX*; and Sibilia, *Gregorio IX*; on Innocent IV, see Rodenberg, *Innocenz IV*; Berger, *Saint Louis et Innocent IV*; Weber, *Der Kampf*; Dehio, *Innocenz IV. und England*; and Melloni, *Innocenzo IV*.

4. On the Papal States (Map 1), see Waley, *The Papal State*; and Partner, *Lands of St. Peter*. Others besides Frederick's biographers have identified Gregory IX and Innocent IV's papacies as the beginning of the end for the medieval papal monarchy, e.g., Barry, *Papal Monarchy*, 347; Smith, *Church and State*, 244–45; Throop, *Criticism of the Crusade*, 49–60; Runciman, *Sicilian Vespers*, 22; Barraclough, *Medieval Papacy*, 118; and Kennan, "Innocent III."

5. See the unabashedly apologetical Mann, *Honorius III to Celestine IV*; and Mann, *Innocent IV*.

6. As observed by Zutschi ("Roman Curia," 226): "Communications have relatively seldom received explicit attention from historians of the papacy, although of course, they lie behind all accounts of relations between the papacy and the various parts of Latin Christendom." For some general observations on the subject of medieval communications, see Morris, *Medieval Media*; and Menache, *Vox Dei*. Even a glance at Mostert, *New Approaches*; and Mostert, *Bibliography of Works* reveals the relative lack of attention to the papacy in the field.

7. In nineteenth- and twentieth-century scholarship, the concept of the medieval papal monarchy, more or less envisioned as a form of papal absolutism, has a long pedigree. See Gierke, *Political Theories*, 9–21; Carlyle and Carlyle, *History of Mediaeval Political Theory*, vol. 5; and Ullmann, *Medieval Papalism*, 114–37. For a more cautious view, attuned to the legal complexities of the canonistic tradition, see Watt, "Theory of Papal Monarchy"; and Watt, "Spiritual and Temporal Powers." See also Morris,

Papal Monarchy (559–60), who cautions against viewing the "bitter quarrels" between the papacy and Frederick as "the result of some inevitable law of nature."

8. On the papal "fullness of power" and juridical authority over the Roman church, in fact subject to constitutional limits and constraints, see Benson, "*Plenitudo Potestatis*"; Ladner, "Concepts of 'Ecclesia' and 'Christianitas' "; and Pennington, *Popes and Bishops.*

9. More than anyone else, Walter Ullmann popularized this notion of the hierocratic papacy, linked to his model of "ascending" and "descending" themes in medieval political theory. In addition to *Medieval Papalism,* see Ullmann, "Some Reflections"; Ullman, *Growth of Papal Government*; and Ullman, *Principles of Government and Politics.* Others, however, long ago criticized Ullmann's selective and schematic reading of the medieval canonistic tradition, including Stickler, "Concerning the Political Theories"; Tierney, "Some Recent Works"; and Oakley, "Celestial Hierarchies Revisited." See also Tierney ("Continuity of Papal Political Theory"), who already cautioned against the blanket use of the labels "dualistic" and "hierocratic," or "monistic." More recently, see Harris, *Papal Monarchy,* who considers the hierocratic papacy as a Kuhnian "paradigm," reaching the conclusion that (ibid., 127) "There was, then, a plurality of beliefs concerning papal monarchy in the thirteenth century. Terms such as 'paradigm' and 'hierocratic theory' disguise such variety."

10. On the development of the pope's title "Vicar of Christ," see Maccarrone, *Vicarius Christi.*

11. Smail, *Consumption of Justice,* 213. On the "performative" nature of legal practices in the Middle Ages, see also the introduction to Mostert and Barnwell, *Medieval Legal Process,* 1–10.

12. Smail, *Consumption of Justice,* 207–41. Scholars have called previous attention to "propaganda" generated by the conflict between the papacy and Frederick II. See Graefe, *Die Publizistik*; Schaller, *Politische Propaganda*; Herde, "Literary Activities"; and Shepard, *Courting Power.* See also Lomax, "*Ingratus* or *Indignus,*" which explores how papal and imperial antagonists deployed legal language and concepts to build their case against the other before the wider audiences of the period.

13. Moos, "Das Öffentliche und das Private"; Moos, *"Öffentlich" und "privat"*; and Kintzinger and Schneidmüller, "Politische Öffentlichkeit."

14. Goering, "Internal Forum," 380.

15. See Constable, *Letters and Letter-Collections*; and Boureau, "Letter-Writing Norm." On papal letters and their production at the chancery in the thirteenth century, see Sayers, *Papal Government,* 15–49; Zutschi, "Innocent III"; Zutschi, "Personal Role of the Pope"; and Thumser, "Kuriale Briefkultur."

16. Works on the historical significance of scandal include Adut, *On Scandal*; and Szabari, *Less Rightly Said.* See also the introduction to Fenster and Smail, *Fama,* 1–11.

17. See Vaughan, *Matthew Paris*; Weiler, "Matthew Paris"; and Lewin, "Salimbene de Adam."

18. When invoking ritual as described in texts, one must consider the cautionary observations of Buc, *Dangers of Ritual.*

19. My first book, *Dominion of God,* explored the formulation and significance of Christendom within apocalyptic frameworks of history. In retrospect, among other possible shortcomings, this study did not pay nearly enough attention to *how* such ideas circulated, either in material form or verbally. On the development and significance of medieval Christendom, among numerous other titles, see Rupp, *L'idée de chrétienté*; Laarhoven, " 'Christianitas' et réforme grégorienne"; and Araujo and Lucal, "Forerunner for International Organizations."

20. The well-known formulation of M. T. Clanchy in *From Memory to Written Record.*

21. For these developments, see Robinson, *Papacy 1073–1198.* See also the still unmatched Lunt, *Papal Revenues.*

22. See Habermas, *Structural Transformation,* originally published as *Strukturwandel der Öffentlichkeit.* In this influential work on the "bourgeois public sphere" (*Öffentlichkeit*), Habermas (*Public Sphere,* 7) observes, "Sociologically, that is to say by reference to institutional criteria, a public sphere in the sense of a separate realm distinguished from the private sphere cannot be shown to have existed in the feudal society of the High Middle Ages."

23. Anderson, *Imagined Communities,* 12–17.

24. For a critique of Habermas and emphasis on the dynamic nature of premodern publics, see especially Symes, *Common Stage*, 1–20, 127–30. See also Sawyer, *Printed Poison*; Zaret, *Origins of Democratic Culture*; Hobbins, *Authorship and Publicity*; Pardue, *Printing, Power, and Piety*; and Novikoff, *Medieval Culture of Disputation*.

25. Pardue, *Printing, Power, and Piety*, 8; and Mah, "Phantasies of the Public Sphere," 166. See also Warner, *Publics and Counterpublics*; and Taylor, *Modern Social Imaginaries*, 83–99.

26. Such confrontations included the first great "clash" between popes and emperors during the Investiture Contest in the eleventh and early twelfth centuries. See Mirbt, *Die Publizistik*; Leyser, "Polemics of the Papal Revolution"; Robinson, *Authority and Resistance*; and, directly engaging Habermas' model of the public sphere, Melve, *Inventing the Public Sphere*; see also Melve, "Assembly Politics"; and Melve, " 'Even the Very Laymen Are Chatting.' " See, however, the thoughtful review of Melve's book by Carol Symes in *American Historical Review* 114 (2009): 68–69; and Symes, "Out in the Open."

27. Oakley, *Mortgage of the Past*, 41.

28. Casanova, "What Is a Public Religion?" See also de Vries and Sullivan, *Political Theologies*, 1–88.

Prelude

1. April, November–December 1220, nos. 82–87, *MGH Const.*, vol. 2, 106, 103–11. Many of these constitutions reiterated previous made agreements between Frederick and the papacy, including the Golden Bull of Eger, 12 July 1213, nos. 46–50, ibid., 57–63; and his promise to maintain a separation between the Regno and the empire, 1 July 1216, no. 58, ibid., 72. Pope Innocent III had defended Frederick's claim to the kingdom of Sicily since his minority, adopting him as a ward after the unexpected death of his father in 1197, which was soon followed by his mother's in 1198. After Frederick came of age, Innocent offered him further support in 1212 when he journeyed to Germany to assert his royal rights against his rival and former papal ally, Otto of Brunswick. See Arnold, "Emperor Frederick II."

2. Richard of San Germano, *Cronica*, 340: "Tunc ipse imperator per manus Otiensis episcopi, qui postmodum in papam Gregorium est promotus, resumpsit crucem, votum publice innovavit."

3. Hugolino acted as Innocent III's legate in 1208 during negotiations between Otto IV of Brunswick and Philip of Swabia, rival claimants to the German crown, e.g. Kempf, *Regestum Innocentii III*, 335, 338–48, 385–94. He also served as Honorius's legate to Lombardy in 1217, promoting the Fifth Crusade, 23 January 1217, no. 12, *MGH epp. saec. XIII*, vol. 1, 9–10. He was apparently supposed to go Hungary that same year to assure the fulfillment of King Andrew II's crusade vow but never did. See Brem, *Papst Gregor IX*, 4–24; and Sibilia, *Gregorio IX*, 42–51.

4. 10 February 1221, nos. 91–93, *MGH Const.*, vol. 2, 114–17.

5. Thouzellier, "La légation en Lombardie"; and Alberzoni, "Le legazioni di Ugo d'Ostia." Generally, on papal legation, see Zimmermann, *Die päpstliche Legation*; Schmutz, "Medieval Papal Representatives"; Figuerira, "*Legatus Apostolicae Sedis*"; Figuerira, "Papal Reserved Powers"; and Rennie, *Foundations of Papal Legation*.

6. Levi, *Registri dei cardinali Ugolino d'Ostia*, 3–154. For Hugolino's appointment, see 4 March 1221, no. 111, 138–40. The edition is based on a fourteenth-century manuscript, Paris, BNF, Lat. 5152A. As noted in Sayers, *Papal Judges Delegate*, 30–31, the material in Hugolino's register represents "probably as complete" an example of such a record "as can be found."

7. As discussed in Miller, *Bishop's Palace*.

8. Nos. 4, 9, 17, 37, 41, Levi, *Registri dei cardinali Ugolino*, 7–8 (at the bishop's palace in Siena on 26 March), 11 (at the bishop's palace in Florence on 4 April), 19 (at the communal palace in Milan on 9 May), 33 (at the palace of the lord advocate in Mantua on 22 July).

9. 4 March 1221, no. 111, Levi, *Registri dei cardinali Ugolino*, 138–40.

10. Canon no. 71, *CCQL*, 110–18. The most comprehensive study of the Fifth Crusade remains Powell, *Anatomy of a Crusade*. See also Cassidy-Welch, " 'O Damietta.' " On Honorius's crusading plans and policies, see Claverie, *Honorius III et l'orient*; Smith, "Role of Honorius III"; and Smith, *Curia and Crusade*.

11. As captured most memorably in the letters of James of Vitry, crusade-preacher, missionary, and participant on the Fifth Crusade (Jacques de Vitry, *Lettres de Jacques de Vitry*).

12. On Frederick's protected status as a crusader, see Honorius's letter to Frederick, 11 February 1219, no. 90, *MGH epp. saec. XIII*, vol. 1, 67; and to the archbishops of Salzburg, Cologne, and Trier, no. 94, ibid., 67–68, calling upon them to enforce those protections in Germany. On the deadlines for Frederick's departure, see 11 February 1219, no. 95, ibid., 68–69 (setting the departure date for 24 June 1220); 18 May 1219, no. 97, ibid., 70 (extending the deadline to 29 September); and 1 October 1219, no. 106, ibid., 75–76 (resetting the deadline again for 21 March 1221). See also Honorius III's letter to Pelagius of Albano, 24 July 1220, no. 124, ibid., 88–91; and the pope's instructions to his legates making plans for the coronation, 10 November 1220, no. 83, *MGH Const.*, vol. 2, 104–5.

13. Nos. 4–6, 9, 17–28, 77, 105, 111, Levi, *Registri dei cardinali Ugolino*, 7–9, 11–13, 19–24, 101, 128–33, 138–40.

14. *CCQL*, 116–17. The link between internal peace among Christians and exported crusading against unbelievers represented a longstanding one. See Mastnak, *Crusading Peace*.

15. At the very start of his papacy, Honorius leveled sentences of excommunication and interdict against Milan and Piacenza (August 1216, nos. 2–3, *MGH epp. saec. XIII*, vol. 1, 1–4), insisting that the two cities cease their attacks on Pavia that violated the general truce established for the upcoming crusade. On the social and political conditions of thirteenth-century Italy, Waley, *Italian City Republics*; Jones, *Italian City-State*; and Thompson, *Cities of God*.

16. Nos. 1, 3, 7, 14, 33–35, 38–39, 42–43, 45, 48, 56, 65–66, 69–71, 73, Levi, *Registri dei cardinali Ugolino*, 3–4, 6, 10, 16–17, 29–31, 34–38, 43–50, 52–58, 77–78, 88–90, 92–94, 96–98.

17. English scholarship on medieval excommunication and interdict is strangely limited, considering their importance. See Vodola, *Excommunication*; and Clarke, *Interdict*.

18. As made clear in Frederick's "Privilege in Favor of Ecclesiastical Princes," 26 April 1220, no. 73, *MGH Const.*, vol. 2, 90; and confirmed at his imperial coronation, ibid., 108.

19. Levi, *Registri dei cardinali Ugolino*, 13–14, 14–15, 26–27, 31, 76–77, 79–80, 43–46.

20. Hugolino gave such instructions to Berthold of Aquileia, telling him to "publish" (*publicari*) the excommunication and imperial ban leveled against Ferrara (Levi, *Registri dei cardinali Ugolino*, 45). See also his letter to the commune at Milan (ibid., 37–38), notifying the podesta about his plans to publicize the interdict leveled against their city if they did not recall the banned archbishop, Henry. On the ritual performance of excommunication in canon law, *CIC*, C. 11 q.3 c. 106, vol. 1, 674.

21. Levi, *Registri dei cardinali Ugolino*, 10, 12, 16, 27, 29–30, 52–58, 65–66, 77.

22. 14 August 1221, no. 44, Levi, *Registri dei cardinali Ugolino*, 48–50. See also Honorius's letter to the bishop of Vercelli calling upon him to publicize and observe Hugolino's excommunication of the Milanese, 14 January 1222, no. 188, *MGH epp. saec. XIII*, vol. 1, 132.

23. Moorman, *History of the Franciscan Order*, 46–49; and Powell, "Papacy and the Early Franciscans."

24. The bibliography on medieval heresy is massive. For a recent overview, Moore, *War on Heresy*. On the Cathars, see Pegg, *Most Holy War*, which focuses on the region of Provence and views the existence of a "Cathar church" as the product of the inquisitorial imagination; and Lansing, *Power and Purity*, which focuses on the social make-up, beliefs, and behaviors of what Lansing sees as substantial Cathar communities in the urban areas of northern Italy.

25. *CCQL*, 47–51. The legislation passed at the Fourth Lateran Council drew in turn upon earlier canons dating back to the Third Lateran Council in 1179 and the Council of Verona in 1184 (*COD*, 200–201); also, Peters, *Heresy and Authority*, 168–73.

26. Honorius III to Hugolino, 25 March 1221, no. 169, *MGH epp. saec. XIII*, vol. 1, 118. Hugolino secured a similar agreement from the commune at Bergamo: Levi, *Registri dei cardinali Ugolino*, 54, 86–88, 94–96, 109–110.

Chapter 1

1. 23 March 1227, nos. 1–4, *Reg. Greg.*, vol. 1, 1–4; no. 343, *MGH epp. saec. XIII*, vol. 1, 261–62. The edition of Gregory's Vatican register by Lucien Auvray, based on ASV, Reg. 14–20, includes an important contemporary collection of the pope's letters held by the municipal library at Perugia, ms. 302, *Reg.*

Greg., vol. 3, 562–616. See also Auvray, "Le registre de Grégoire IX." On the letter announcing Gregory's election, see Richard of San Germano, *Cronica*, 347.

2. Kantorowicz, *Frederick the Second*, 171; Van Cleve, *Emperor Frederick II*, 190; and Abulafia, *Frederick II*, 164. See also Mayer, *Crusades*, 233; and Tyerman, *God's War*, 747.

3. See the pope's letters to Frederick on 13 June 1221, no. 175, *MGH epp. saec. XIII*, vol. 1, 121–22 and on 19 November 1221, no. 183, ibid., 128–30; to Pelagius of Albano, 25 April 1222, no. 196, ibid., 137–38; to the French King Philip, 27 April 1223, no. 225, ibid., 152–55; and to Frederick, 18 July 1225, no. 276, ibid., 198–99. The concept of "clamor" possessed a legal resonance, denoting grounds for inquiry into accusations of wrongdoing or the neglect of one's duties (*CCQL*, 54–57).

4. Shepard, *Courting Power*, 33–48, 115–23.

5. Hiestand, "Friedrich II. und der Kreuzzug"; and Caumanns, "Kreuzzugsmotivation Friedrichs II."

6. Smith, *Crusade and Curia*, 173–99.

7. Perry, *John of Brienne*, 135–49; and Smith, "Between Two Kings."

8. See Honorius's letter introducing the cardinal legates, 18 July 1225, no. 276, *MGH epp. saec. XIII*, vol. 1, 198–99; Frederick's written confirmation of his oath, no. 102, *MGH Const.*, vol. 2, 129–31; and Richard of San Germano, *Cronica*, 344. The emperor also committed to providing one thousand soldiers for two years' service in the Holy Land, to furnishing ships for the transportation of two thousand armed men with horses and supplies, and to a deposit of one hundred thousand gold ounces for aid to the crusader kingdoms.

9. This second Lombard League (*societas Lombardorum*) was modeled after a similar coalition that formed against Frederick II's grandfather, Frederick I. See Raccagni, *Lombard League*; Chiodi, "Istituzioni e attività"; and Smith, *Crusade and Curia*, 200–208.

10. See Frederick's encyclical summoning the assembly, March 1226, HB, vol. 2/1, 548–49; along with Richard of San Germano, *Cronica*, 345; and *Breve chronicon de rebus Siculis*, 78. In a letter to Honorius, Frederick complained about the "illicit Lombard conspiracy" against him: 29 August 1226, HB, vol. 2/2, 675–77.

11. On 10 June 1226, a group of prelates who had gathered at Parma issued a sentence of excommunication against the Lombard cities assaulting Frederick, a sworn crusader under papal protection. For the assembly's written record of the deliberations, see no. 105, *MGH Const.*, vol. 2, 132–34. See also Frederick's imperial ban of the Lombard League, 12 July 1226, no. 107, ibid., 136–39. Not everyone viewed Honorius as an honest broker; e.g., see the accusations about his double-crossing the emperor, *Chronica regia Coloniensis*, 258.

12. September–October 1226, no. 309, *MGH epp. saec. XIII*, vol. 1, 234–35; and January 5 1227, nos. 327–30, ibid., 246–50. For the legal connotations of rancor, Hyams, *Rancor and Reconciliation*.

13. 10 March 1227, no. 342, *MGH epp. saec. XIII*, vol. 1, 259–60.

14. See Gregory IX's letter to the Lombards on 27 March 1227: no. 345, *MGH epp. saec. XIII*, vol. 1, 263; and his letter complaining about the missing seals: 16 April 1227, no. 349, ibid., 265–67. Always ready to view Gregory's actions in a negative light, Van Cleve (*Emperor Frederick II*, 193) writes that the pope ignored the "deficiencies" in the letters missing the signatures and seals, forwarding a "brief abstract" of the documents to Frederick and thereby obliviously provoking the emperor's suspicion that a "secret understanding" existed between the papal curia and Lombards. Abulafia (*Frederick II*, 164) makes a similar observation that Gregory "sent an abbreviated version of the agreement to Frederick, hardly adequate after the long months of negotiation." Yet the pope did no such thing. Writing to Frederick on 16 April (no. 351, ibid., 267–68), Gregory explicitly informed the emperor that he would be sending the complete letters with a future envoy, while repeating his insistence to the Lombards that they send the documents with the proper seals (no. 350, ibid., 267).

15. *Waverley Annals*, 303; Roger of Wendover, *FH*, vol. 4, 144–45. On Honorius's plans, see his letters to Ugrin, archbishop of Cologne, 11 January 1227, no. 334, *MGH epp. saec. XIII*, vol. 1, 252–53; and 11 January 1227, no. 335, ibid., 253–54. For Gregory's follow-up letters on the preaching campaign, see nos. 352–54, ibid., 268–69. Also *Tewksbury Annals*, 69–70; and *Dunstable Annals*, 112. Two prominent English bishops, Peter of Winchester and William of Exeter, took the cross: 5 April 1227, no. 18, *Reg.*

Greg., vol. 1, 12; and 6 April 1227, no. 24, ibid., 13. On Peter of Winchester's role in the crusade, Vincent, *Peter des Roches*, 229–58.

16. 22 July 1227, no. 365, *MGH epp. saec. XIII*, vol. 1, 278–80.

17. *Waverley Annals*, 304; and *Annales Scheftlarienses maiores*, 338. Also, Richard of San Germano, *Cronica*, 348; Alberic of Trois-Fontaines, *Chronicon*, 919; *Annales et notae Sancti Emmerammi*, *MGH SS*, vol. 17, 574; *Breve chronicon de rebus Siculis*, 78; *Tewksbury Annals*, 69–70; *Dunstable Annals*, 107; William of Andres, *Chronica*, 767; and Roger of Wendover, *FH*, vol. 4, 149. For Gerold's appointment as legate to the Holy Land, 24 April 1227, no. 55, *Reg. Greg.*, vol. 1, 30; and no. 57, ibid., 30–31.

18. Abulafia, *Frederick II*, 167. On Frederick's excommunication, see Lomax, "Crusade of Frederick II," wherein he claims—based upon a close reading of the events from a legalistic perspective—that Gregory planned from the start of his conflict over the emperor's crusade vow to deprive him of his various titles.

19. See, however, the exceptional Mierau, "Exkommunikation und Macht."

20. *VG*, 19–20; and Marx, *Die Vita Gregorii IX*.

21. *VG*, 19–20; and Bagliani, *CCFC*, vol. 1, 19–97.

22. *VG*, 20. For the procedures of excommunication, see *CIC*, C. 11 q.3 c. 106, vol. 1, 674.

23. *CIC*, C. 11 q.3 c. 106, vol. 1, 674. See Vodola, *Excommunication*, 44–69; and Beaulande, "La force de le censure."

24. *In maris amplitudine*, 10 October, no. 368, *MGH epp. saec. XIII*, vol. 1, 281–85. See also Gregory's letter two days earlier to the princes of Germany about the emperor's abandonment of the crusade, 8 October 1227, no. 367, ibid., 280–81.

25. Roger of Wendover, *FH*, vol. 4, 157–65; Albert of Stade, *Annales*, 359; Richard of San Germano, *Cronica*, 348; and *Tewksbury Annals*, 73. See also Shepard, *Courting Power*, 123.

26. *In admiratione vertimur*, 6 December 1227, no. 116, *MGH Const.*, vol. 2, 148–56. On the circulation of this "exculpatory" letter, see Richard of San Germano, *Cronica*, 348; Burchard of Ursburg, *Chronicon*, 382; and Alberic of Trois-Fontaines, *Chronicon*, 920. See also Shepard, *Courting Power*, 137.

27. Roger of Wendover, *FH*, vol. 4, 165. For Henry's replies to the pope and emperor, 20 February 1228, *CRH*, vol. 1, 93–94. Discussion in Weiler, *Henry III*, 39–44.

28. *Annales Placentini Guelfi*, 443. The Guelf *Annals of Piacenza* are attributed to a notary named Giovanni Codagnello (ca. 1226–36) and designated as such to distinguish them from the later, pro-imperial Ghibelline continuation, *Annales Placentini Gibellini*. See also *Annales Scheftlarienses maiores*, 338; Burchard of Ursburg, *Chronicon*, 382; *Waverley Annals*, 303; and *Notae Sancti Emmerammi*, 574.

29. Richard of San Germano, *Cronica*, 348; *MGH Const.*, vol. 2, 154.

30. *Breve chronicon de rebus Siculis*, 79; and Richard of San Germano, *Cronica*, 348–49.

31. *Annales S. Rudberti Salisburgenses*, 784.

32. March 1228, no. 371, *MGH epp. saec. XIII*, vol. 1, 288–89. The pope's threat to proceed against Frederick as if against a "heretic and despiser of the keys" could imply legal grounds to depose him from office. As far as I can tell, Gregory never actually accused Frederick of heresy. As for depriving Frederick of his feudal right in the Regno (ibid., 289), the pope—acting as Frederick's temporal lord—did not mention his other titles at this stage.

33. December 1227, HB, vol. 3, 50–51. See Clarke, *Interdict*, 59–85. On the limited impact of the anathema in Germany, see Freed, *Friars and German Society*, 91–93.

34. *VG*, 20. See also Roger of Wendover, *FH*, vol. 4, 169; Burchard of Ursburg, *Chronicon*, 382 (who attributes the assault to the Frangipani family); *Waverley Annals*, 303–4; and the *Annales et notae Sancti Emmerammi*, 575.

35. Mayer, *Crusades*, 234.

36. April 1228, HB, vol. 3, 57–60; June 1228, no. 119, *MGH Const.*, vol. 2, 158–59. On Frederick's departure from Brindisi, Richard of San Germano, *Cronica*, 350; and *Breve chronicon de rebus Siculis*, 350. Mayer (*Crusades*, 234–35), Van Cleve (*Emperor Frederick II*, 205), and Abulafia (*Frederick II*, 170) emphasize political control of the crusade as central to Frederick's decision to depart in defiance of the pope. Lomax ("Crusade of Frederick II," 218–24) argues that Frederick went on crusade to rob Gregory of his justification for deposing him as ruler of the Regno.

37. Van Cleve, "Crusade of Frederick II"; Powell, "Church and Crusade"; Stürner, *Friedrich II*, vol. 1, 143–69; and Tyerman, *God's War*, 739–55. See also Takayama, "Frederick II's Crusade."

38. *VG*, 576. See also Gregory's letter *Ad vestram et*, 30 August 1228, no. 6117, *Reg. Greg.*, vol. 3, 568–72.

39. Roger of Wendover, *FH*, vol. 4, 174–76. On the "viral" nature of excommunication, *CIC*, C. 11 q.3 c. 110, vol. 1, 675. On Frederick's arrival in Syria, Albert of Stade, *Annales*, 359–60; Richard of San Germano, *Cronica*, 354; and Alberic of Trois-Fontaines, *Chronicon*, 925.

40. *Estoire de Eracles*, *RHC*, vol. 2, 370. On the complicated authorship and manuscript tradition of the *Estoire de Eracles*, see Edbury, "Lyon *Eracles*."

41. *Estoire de Eracles*, *RHC*, vol. 2, 372.

42. 26 March 1229, no. 384, *MGH epp. saec. XIII*, vol. 1, 299–304.

43. No. 380, *MGH epp. saec. XIII*, vol. 1, 296–98. For Gerold's description of how he obtained a copy of the treaty, ibid., 302. Another letter featured in the *Waverley Annals* (305–7) describes the treaty in favorable terms.

44. *MGH epp. saec. XIII*, vol. 1, 300–302. Gerold also objected to the accord because it made no arrangements regarding the possession of ecclesiastical properties (*casalia*) outside of Jerusalem. On how these local concerns shaped his presentation of Frederick's crusade, see Hamilton, *Latin Church*, 258–59.

45. *MGH epp. saec. XIII*, vol. 1, 279.

46. *MGH epp. saec. XIII*, vol. 1, 303–4. Gregory's biographer (*VG*, 20) accuses Frederick of handing the Temple of God over to the "worshippers of Magometti."

47. 18 March 1229, no. 122, *MGH Const.*, vol. 2, 162–67. For Hermann's two letters, both dated March 1228, see no. 121, ibid., 161–62; and no. 123, ibid., 167–68.

48. Roger of Wendover, *FH*, vol. 4, 174–76. For the archbishop of Caesarea's declaration of the interdict in Jerusalem, see also Richard of San Germano, *Cronica*, 355. On 23 July 1229, the pope wrote to the archbishop of Caesarea, confirming the excommunication, no. 398, *MGH epp. saec. XIII*, vol. 1, 318–19.

49. *MGH epp. saec. XIII*, vol. 1, 303. This represented a legally questionable move, since canon law made explicit accommodations for crusaders to travel with excommunicate parties while on campaign. See Brundage, *Medieval Canon Law*, 155–56.

50. *MGH Const.*, vol. 2, 165–66, 168.

51. Hermann describes this address in his letter "to a friend," *MGH Const.*, vol. 2, 167–68. See also Gerold's comments on this address, *MGH epp. saec. XIII*, vol. 1, 303.

52. *Quam mirabiliter immo*, featured in Matthew Paris, *CM*, vol. 3, 177–84. Based on stylistic differences from Gerold's first letter and the fact that the second letter does not appear in Roger of Wendover's *Flowers of History*, Powell ("Patriarch Gerold," 19–26) argues that the "letter to the faithful" represents a later forgery or perhaps a heavily interpolated version of a genuine letter by the patriarch, most likely produced in Dominican circles ca. 1237–38, when Gregory and Frederick's relations were again beginning to deteriorate. Apparently unnoticed by Powell, in his letter *Inter alia flagitia* (no. 397, *MGH epp. saec. XIII*, vol. 1, 316–17) Gregory indicates that he received two letters from Gerold, on 29 June and on 7 July. Judging by Gregory's description of the second letter's contents, it seems to match some version of the letter attributed to Gerold by Matthew Paris. See also the notice about the patriarch's multiple letters in Alberic of Trois-Fontaines, *Chronicon*, 925.

53. Matthew Paris, *CM*, vol. 3, 179–84.

54. Matthew Paris began work on his chronicle around 1236. For the preceding years, he relied heavily upon—but also modified in key ways—Roger of Wendover's *Flowers of History*.

55. Matthew Paris, *CM*, vol. 3, 177–79.

56. *Annales Scheftlarienses maiores*, 339; Burchard of Ursburg, *Chronicon*, 383; Richard of San Germano, *Cronica*, 354; *Breve chronicon de rebus Siculis*, 90; and Roger of Wendover, *FH*, vol. 4, 180–82, 188, 194–95.

57. 13 June 1229, no. 390, *MGH epp. saec. XIII*, vol. 1, 308–9, 315–17.

58. *MGH epp. saec. XIII*, vol. 1, 315.

59. *MGH epp. saec. XIII*, vol. 1, 315.

60. For Gregory's complains about the Regno, see his letter to Frederick, late 1227, no. 370, *MGH epp. saec. XIII*, vol. 1, 286–87; his March 1228 letter to the bishops of Apulia, ibid., 288–89; and his letter to Frederick, 23 September 1228, no. 372, ibid., 289–90. For Honorius's earlier complaints to Frederick, see *Miranda tuis sensibus*, May 1226, no. 296, ibid., 216–22, written in response to a no longer extant letter from the emperor to the pope and protesting the Roman church's inadequate measures on his behalf in the past. As pointed out by Lomax ("Crusade of Frederick II," 213–18), the charge of "ingratitude" possessed a legal resonance, one that might justify deposing a ruler from their office. Thus, he views Gregory's accusations of ingratitude as "essentially a threat of deposition." Evidence for the pope's plan to depose Frederick, however, remains ambiguous.

61. Lomax, "Frederick II."

62. 30 August 1228, *Ad vestram et*, no. 6117, *Reg. Greg.*, vol. 3, 568–72; and *Attendite quesumus et*, 6 August 1228, no. 6118, ibid., 572–75 (transcribed in Roger of Wendover, *FH*, vol. 4, 166–69). On the pope's decision to absolve Frederick's followers of their oaths, *Dunstable Annals*, 113.

63. The pope described this situation in a letter to his vassal Azzo VII, marquis d'Este (23 September 1228, no. 373, *MGH epp. saec. XIII*, vol. 1, 290–91), insisting that Azzo return to defend Ancona from Raynald's assault as soon as possible. Also, *VG*, 20–21.

64. 7 November 1228, no. 375, *MGH epp. saec. XIII*, vol. 1, 291–92. See also Richard of San Germano, *Cronica*, 350.

65. Gregory IX to the Genoese, 20 November 1228, no. 376, *MGH epp. saec. XIII*, vol. 1, 293–94; and to bishops in Tuscany, 3 December 1228, no. 377, ibid., 294–95.

66. On the expulsion of the friars, Richard of San Germano, *Cronica*, 353. See also Freed, *Friars and German Society*, 91–93; Maier, *Preaching the Crusades*, 26–31; and Voci, "Federico II imperatore." For the canonization of Saint Francis, 16–19 July 1228, *BF*, vol. 1, 42–44; and *VG*, 21. See also Goodich, "Politics of Canonization," especially pp. 300–302; and Vauchez, "Grégoire IX."

67. *VG*, 577.

68. Isabella of Brienne had died in April 1228. Before her death, John had already broken with Frederick over his perceived attempt to usurp the kingship of Jerusalem. See Smith, "Between Two Kings," 52–58.

69. Loud ("Papal 'Crusade,'" 103) calls the War of the Keys the "crusade that never was," pointing out that Gregory did not promise the equivalent remission of sins for the army's soldiers as those going to the Holy Land, nor did his troops march under the crusader sign of the cross. See also Strayer, "Political Crusades"; Abulafia, "Kingdom of Sicily"; and Raccagni, "Crusade against Frederick II."

70. Richard of San Germano, *Cronica*, 355. Also, *Breve chronicon de rebus Siculis*, 92; and Alberic of Trois-Fontaines, *Chronicon*, 923.

71. Chodorow, *Christian Political Theory*, 223–46.

72. Roger of Wendover, *FH*, vol. 4, 184, 200–202. Roger adds that as a condition for his support of Gregory's campaign against the emperor, Henry III secured the pope's favorable judgment in a disputed election over the archbishopric of Canterbury. See also William of Andres, *Chronica*, *MGH SS*, vol. 24, 768.

73. W. H. R. Jones, ed., *Vetus registrum Sarisberiense*, vol. 2, 144–46. See also Powicke and Cheney, *Councils and Synods*, vol. 2/1, 167–69.

74. Gregory to Erik, king of Sweden, 21 December 1228, no. 378, *MGH epp. saec. XIII*, vol. 1, 295–96; to the Lombards, 15 May 1229, no. 385, ibid., 304–5; to Peter of Portugal, June 1229, no. 389, ibid., 308; and to the archbishop of Lyons, 28 September 1229, no. 403, ibid., 322–23, at which point, the pope offered the remission of sins for those fighting on behalf of the church.

75. Tyerman, *How to Plan a Crusade*, 129–38. There are differing opinions about the success of Gregory's appeals. Strayer ("Political Crusades," 349) observes that "for the first time, the papacy could afford a first-class war," while Abulafia ("Kingdom of Sicily," 73) expresses skepticism about outcome of the papal drive for funds and troops.

76. Gregory to the Lombards, 26 June 1229, no. 395, *MGH epp. saec. XIII*, vol. 1, 313–14; and 13 July 1229, no. 396, ibid., 314–15. The *Dunstable Annals* (114) report that the Lombards indeed supplied one thousand soldiers as instructed.

77. Roger of Wendover, *FH*, vol. 4, 202–3. See also the additional materials collected relating to the collection of the funds in the *Vetus registrum Sarisberiense* (Jones, ed.), vol. 2, 148–54. See the discussion in Lunt, *Financial Relations*, vol. 1, 145–46.

78. February–March 1229, HB, vol. 3, 110–12; Roger of Wendover, *FH*, vol. 4, 182–84.

79. See the description of the papal army's depredations in Richard of San Germano, *Cronica*, 350–53. Also, Burchard of Ursburg, *Chronicon*, 382–83; *Annales Sancti Rudberti Salisburgenses*, 784; and *Annales Scheftlarienses maiores*, 339.

80. Lavaud, no. 19, *Poésies complètes*, 170–77; and Bartholomaeis, no. 115, *Poesie Provenzali*, vol. 2, 98–106 (stanzas 8–9, 19); and no. 116, ibid., 106–14 (stanzas 7, 13). See Throop, *Criticism of the Crusade*, 49–50; and Siberry, *Criticism of Crusading*, 4–11, 175–77.

81. *Annales Placentini Guelfi*, 444.

82. *VG*, 21.

83. 19 May 1229, no. 386, *MGH epp. saec. XIII*, vol. 1, 305–6.

84. Kantorowicz, *Frederick the Second*, 206–8; Van Cleve, *Emperor Frederick II*, 231–32; Abulafia, *Frederick II*, 199–201; Mayer, *Crusades*, 238; and Lomax, "Crusade of Frederick II," 173–74.

85. Benham, *Peacemaking in the Middle Ages*, 209.

86. On this quick military reversal in the Regno, see Richard of San Germano, *Cronica*, 353–55; Roger of Wendover, *FH*, vol. 4, 207; Burchard of Ursburg, *Chronicon*, 383; William of Andres, *Chronica*, 768–69; and Frederick's letter to the faithful in Lombardy, 5 October 1229, HB, vol. 3, 165–66. Gregory's biographer (*VG*, 22) passes over Frederick's victories in conspicuous silence. For Gregory's renewed sentence of excommunication, see August 1229, no. 399, *MGH epp. saec. XIII*, vol. 1, 318–20. See also Raccagni, "Crusade Against Frederick II," 723, which misdates this reissuing of the sentence to August 1228. On Frederick's "excusatory letters," see Richard of San Germano, *Cronica*, 357.

87. For the final terms of the Treaty of San Germano, see July–October 1230, nos. 126–49, *MGH Const.*, vol. 2, 170–83. In Gregory's Vatican register, the documents relating to the agreement feature separately from the main body of letters, set off by a blank folio from the preceding third year, ASV, Reg. 14, fols. 161r–167r (*Reg. Greg.*, 58–68).

88. Starting with the pope's commission for Thomas of Capua to absolve Frederick, 10 November 1229, no. 6148, *Reg. Greg.*, 590–91, the Perugian Register includes a series of letters and documents relating to the proposed peace that do not feature in the Vatican register (nor the *MGH Const.* edition). For other relevant and often over looked documents, see also Rodenberg, "Verhandlugen"; and Hampe, *Aktenstücke*.

89. Rodenberg, "Verhandlugen," 181–82.

90. Rodenberg, "Verhandlugen," 180–83; and no. 6150, *Reg. Greg.*, 592. Thomas describes another letter from "a friend" that he edited, "removing things that I thought should be removed" before forwarding a copy to the emperor.

91. Nos. 6154, 6171, *Reg. Greg.*, 597, 608–9. On this dispute, Richard of San Germano, *Cronica*, 359.

92. Thomas to an unnamed cardinal, December 1229, Rodenberg, "Verhandlugen," 183–85. For Pope Gregory's report to Thomas about the arrival of the Lombard delegation at curia, 4 February 1230, no. 6157, *Reg. Greg.*, 598.

93. Nos. 6154, *Reg. Greg.*, 596–97. These securities included Frederick's temporary surrender of various castles and fortifications for eight months: nos. 133–36, *MGH Const.*, vol. 2, 175–76.

94. Early July 1230, nos. 6168–69, *Reg. Greg.*, 605–7. At this point, the fighting in the Regno had still not entirely stopped. See Gregory's letter to Frederick, 28 August 1230, no. 146, *MGH Const.*, vol. 2, 180–81.

95. Rodenberg, "Verhandlugen," 182–83, 185–86.

96. No. 130, *MGH Const.*, vol. 2, 172–73. Also, Richard of San Germano, *Cronica*, 359–61; *Breve chronicon de rebus Siculis*, 94–96; *Annales Scheftlarienses maiores*, 339; and Burchard of Ursburg, *Chronicon*, 383.

97. For the princes' fiduciary oaths on Frederick's behalf and other written statements relating to the peace, see July 24–August 28, nos. 131–45, *MGH Const.*, vol. 2, 173–80. See also Richard of San Germano, *Cronica*, 361.

98. *VG*, 22; also, Richard of San Germano, *Cronica*, 362.

Chapter 2

1. As Pennington ("Constitutions of Melfi," 54) aptly summarizes previous views on the matter. For the text of the constitutions, HB, vol. 4/1, 1–178; translation and analysis by James Powell, *Liber Augustalis*.

2. 5 July 1231, no. 443, *MGH epp. saec. XIII*, vol. 1, 357–58. For the letter to Jacob of Capua rejecting his "frivolous excuse" that he was just "the scribe, not the issuer" of the law, HB, vol. 3, 290. Pennington, "Constitutions of Melfi," 60–61, provides a critical edition of both letters.

3. Pennington, "Constitutions of Melfi," 59.

4. 27 July 1230, no. 447, *MGH epp. saec. XIII*, vol. 1, 360.

5. 11 July 1231, no. 445, *MGH epp. saec. XIII*, vol. 1, 359. See also Gregory's letter to Frederick, 7 June 1231, no. 441, ibid., 355–56.

6. Historians typically disregard or try to explain away these years of cooperation between the pope and emperor, which are seen—in retrospect—as an interlude between Frederick's excommunications. See, for example, Kantorowicz, *Frederick the Second*, 388; Sibilia, *Gregorio IX*, 133–59; Van Cleve, *Emperor Frederick II*, 349–64; and Abulafia, *Frederick II*, 202–89. In recent years, however, this neglect has started to change. See Weiler, "Gregory IX"; and Lomax, "*Negotium Terrae Sanctae*."

7. On theologies of peace and peacemaking, see Malegam, *Sleep of Behemoth*.

8. Powell, *Liber Augustalis*, 7–11. In this context, the word "public" suggests a close affiliation with the monarch. As a public crime, heresy was also treason.

9. 15 October 1230, no. 421, *MGH epp. saec. XIII*, vol. 1, 340–41; 3 December 1230, no. 422, ibid., 341. On 10 January 1231, HB, vol. 3, 253–54, the pope wrote to his fellow prelates around Italy and Germany, instructing them to make sure that the guarantors of the peace swear the requisite oaths as stipulated by the Treaty of San Germano. On 19 January 1231 (HB, vol. 3, 257), Gregory addressed Frederick again, reminding him to fulfill certain obligations from the agreement before the eight-month deadline expired.

10. Alberic of Trois-Fontaines, *Chronicon*, 927.

11. Richard of San Germano, *Chronica*, 362–65, 369. See also Gregory's letters to Frederick, 12 July 1232, no. 469, *MGH epp. saec. XIII*, vol. 1, 379; and 24 July 1232, no. 473, ibid., 381. Gregory responded to Frederick's complaints about Città di Castellana in his letter on 10 December 1230, no. 423, ibid., 341–42. On the settlement at Gaeta, see the letters on 23 June 1233, HB, vol. 4/1, 439–41.

12. 10 October 1230, no. 420, *MGH epp. saec. XIII*, vol. 1, 339–40; and 18 May 1231, no. 440, ibid., 355. Also, no. 128, *MGH Const.*, vol. 2, 171.

13. No. 155, *MGH Const.*, vol. 2, 190–91. As described in Bartholomew the Scribe, *Annales*, 177–78, Frederick announced the assembly with letters sent "to the faithful throughout various parts of the empire." On this important source for the history of Genoa, see Dotson, "Genoese Civic Annals."

14. HB, 4/1, 937–38.

15. 4 September 1231, no. 452, *MGH epp. saec. XIII*, vol. 1, 365; 27 September 1231, no. 454, ibid., 366–67; 27 September 1231, no. 455, ibid., 367–68; and 27 September 1231, nos. 456 and 457, ibid., 368–69. Also, Richard of San Germano, *Cronica*, 364.

16. Bartholomew the Scribe, *Annales*, 177–78, provides a detailed account of the Genoese involvement with the general assembly. Also, *Annales Placentini Guelfi*, 53; *Annales Placentini Gibellini*, 470; and *Chronica regia Coloniensis*, 263. Gregory appointed the two cardinal legates in January 1232: Richard of San Germano, *Cronica*, 365; and no. 166, *MGH Const.*, vol. 2, 204. See also Bagliani, *CCFC*, vol. 1, 76–97, 114–29.

17. Nos. 161–64, *MGH Const.*, vol. 2, 199–203, present a series of documents from March 1232, including the imperial petitions and replies.

18. No. 165, *MGH Const.*, vol. 2, 203.

19. No. 166, *MGH Const.*, vol. 2, 204.

20. HB, 4/1, 937–38; *Annales Placentini Guelfi*, 453; and *Annales Placentini Gibellini*, 470. The Guelf annals present the emperor's departure as an insult to the honor of the pope and his legates, while the later Ghibelline version of the chronicle asserts that Frederick merely wanted to make a pilgrimage to the basilica of Saint Mark.

21. No. 167, *MGH Const.*, vol. 2, 204–5.

22. No. 168–69, *MGH Const.*, vol. 2, 205–9. Both parties also agreed to pay a twenty-thousand-mark penalty if they contravened the terms of this agreement.

23. HB, vol. 4/1, 366–67; and Richard of San Germano, *Cronica*, 369. In his letters to the rectors of the Lombard League, 12 July 1232, no. 470, *MGH epp. seac. XIII*, vol. 1, 379; and to Frederick, 26 January 1233, no. 505, ibid., 404–5, Gregory declared that an insufficient number of the league's envoys had come to the curia, forcing him to defer the meeting until fifteen days after Easter. He warned the emperor and the Lombards that they would face a three-thousand-mark penalty for missing the new deadline, announcing a six-thousand-mark fine if they violated the peace in the meanwhile.

24. For the documents relating to these negotiations, May–14 August 1233, nos. 176–82, *MGH Const.*, vol. 2, 225; also, no. 531, *MGH epp. saec. XIII*, vol. 1, 426–28.

25. No. 178, *MGH Const.*, vol. 2, 221–22.

26. No. 179, *MGH Const.*, vol. 2, 222.

27. No. 180, *MGH Const.*, vol. 2, 222–23.

28. 12 August 1233, no. 553, *MGH epp. saec. XIII*, vol. 1, 446–47.

29. Nos. 181–182, *MGH Const.*, vol. 2, 223–25.

30. *Dunstable Annals*, 132.

31. Salimbene of Adam, *CA*, vol. 1, 102–113. Salimbene finished revising his *Chronica* in the 1280s. See Lewin, "Salimbene de Adam."

32. Kantorowicz, *Frederick the Second*, 398; and Thompson, *Revival Preachers*, 210–11.

33. Thompson, *Revival Preachers*, 1–25. See also Brown, "Alleluia."

34. *Annales Placentini Guelfi*, 454–55. See Thompson, *Revival Preachers*, 36–38. Leo was promoted to the archbishopric of Milan in 1244. Salimbene of Adam, *CA*, vol. 1, 107–8, describes an episode where Leo rallied Milanese troops in battle against Frederick's forces, but this undated story refers to much later events.

35. Salimbene of Adam, *CA*, vol. 1, 102–4, 109–111. Also, *Annales Parmenses Maiores*, 608. Salimbene notes that Gerard later became known for being "inclined" toward the "imperial party," although he nevertheless "walked with God in 'peace, and inequity, and turned many away from iniquity' (cf. Mal. 2:6)."

36. Manselli, "Ezzelino da Romano."

37. 12–15 July 1231, HB, vol. 3, 290–93. On the fighting at Verona, see *Annales Veronenses*, 7–8; *Annales Mantuani*, 21; *Annales S. Justinae Patavini*, 153–54; Roland of Padua, *Chronica*, 55–58; and the eyewitness account by a notary and chronicler from Vincenza, Gerard Maurisius, *Cronica*.

38. On the October 1231 meeting at Bologna, *Annales Placentini Guelfi*, 453. See also the near contemporary account in HB, 4/1, 937–38. In his *Cronica*, 29–30, Gerard Maurisius transcribes two letters—obtained at his own initiative and expense, he stresses, without compensation—of protection issued by the imperial chancery for the Romano brothers. Ezzelino and Alberic both met with Frederick ca. 1231–32 (HB, vol. 4/1, 406–7; and *Annales S. Justinae Patavini*, 154).

39. *Annales Veronenses*, 7–8; *Annales Mantuani*, 21; Roland of Padua, *Chronica*, 58–59; *Annales S. Justinae Patavini*, 154; and Gerard Maurisius, *Cronica*, 31–32. See Thompson, *Revival Preachers*, 39–62.

40. As noted by Thompson (*Revival Preachers*, 210), a "papal mandate did not create a charismatic preacher." For Gregory IX's disregarded instructions to John, 20 April and 28 June 1233, nos. 1268–69, 1436, *Reg. Greg.*, vol. 1, 713, 801–2. For the account given (ca. 1260) by Thomas of Cantimpré, *Bonum universal de apibus*, 424.

41. Thompson, *Revival Preachers*, 61, 73, calls Guala and William "John's collaborators in the revival and peace-making" without fully considering the close ties between the two bishops and the papal curia.

42. 28 June and 13 July 1233, nos. 1437, 1461, *Reg. Greg.*, vol. 1, 802, 813; and 6 August 1233, HB, vol. 4/1, 446–47. See also *Annales Veronenses*, 8; and Roland of Padua, *Chronica*, 59.

43. *Annales Placentini Guelfi*, 454–55. See also Gregory's series of letters addressing the attack on Roland, 15 and 22 October 1233, nos. 556, 559, *MGH epp. saec. XIII*, vol. 1, 449–50, 452–53; and from December 1233 and February 1234, nos. 1606–7, 1795, *Reg. Greg.*, vol. 1, 883–84, 963.

44. Gerard Maurisius, *Cronica*, 34; *Annales S. Justinae Patavini*, 154; and *Annales Veronenses*, 9. John was arrested on 3 September and released on 22 September. See Thompson, *Revival Preachers*, 76–79.

45. Thompson, *Revival Preachers*, 111. Salimbene of Adam (*CA*, vol. 1, 113), while clearly admiring some of the revivalist preachers, seemed to regard John of Vicenza as something of a fraud. He tells a particularly pungent story about a Franciscan "prankster" named Detesalve of Florence, who demanded a piece of John's robe as a sacred relic from a Dominican convent—and then used it to wipe his ass after defecating, tossing it in the privy and asking the Dominicans to help him fish it out.

46. On Frederick's renewed commitment to papal mediation, HB, vol. 4/1, 465–66. See also Pope Gregory's letters to the rectors of the Lombard League, nos. 581, 583, and 587, *MGH epp. saec. XIII*, vol. 1, 472–74, 476–77.

47. Thompson, *Revival Preachers*, 58–59, 96, 111.

48. See especially Weiler, "Gregory IX," 192, in which he observes that the tendency of historians to treat Gregory and Frederick's acts of cooperation after San Germano as a mere interlude before resuming inevitable hostilities "does justice neither to Gregory nor his imperial adversary."

49. *Ille humani generis*, 28 February 1231, no. 433, *MGH epp. saec. XIII*, vol. 1, 438–39. In his earlier letter to Frederick on conditions in Jerusalem, 19 January, no. 425, ibid., 343–45, the pope refers to another widely sent letter about new threats to the Holy Land.

50. By the "king of the Persians," the pope might have been referring to al-Ashraf Musa, al-Kamil's brother, who captured Damascus an-Nasir Da'ud in June 1229.

51. 25 April 1231, no. 438, *MGH epp. saec. XIII*, vol. 1, 353; 14 August 1231, no. 425, ibid., 343–45; and 14 August 1231, no. 450, ibid., 363–64.

52. 26 February 1231, no. 427, *MGH epp. saec. XIII*, vol. 1, 345–46.

53. Lupprian, *BPHB*, nos. 6–19, 118–39. See Whalen, "Corresponding with Infidels."

54. Richard of San Germano, *Cronica*, 368–69; and *Chronica regia Coloniensis*, 263. See also Edbury, *John of Ibelin*, 24–57.

55. Gregory to Frederick, 26 February 1231, no. 428, *MGH epp. saec. XIII*, vol. 1, 346; and same date, no. 429, ibid., 347. Also, Richard of San Germano, *Cronica*, 364.

56. Gregory to Gerold, 17 June 1232, *MGH epp. saec. XIII*, vol. 1, 376–77; and 7 July 1232, ibid., 377–78. See also the pope's letters to Frederick, 12 July 1232, no. 469, ibid., 378–79; and two further letters to Gerold, 25 July 1232, no. 474, ibid., 382; and 26 July 1232, no. 475, ibid., 383.

57. For Gregory's instructions to Albert, 26 July 1232, no. 476, *MGH epp. saec. XIII*, vol. 1, 383–84. Shortly before her death in 1228, Isabella of Brienne had given birth to Conrad, heir to the crown of Jerusalem. See also the pope's letter to the Hospitallers, 26 July 1232, no. 477, ibid., 384–85.

58. 22 March 1232, no. 578, *MGH epp. saec. XIII*, vol. 1, 471; and 8 Augustus 1234, no. 594, ibid., 481–83.

59. *Rachael suum videns*, 17 November 1234, no. 605, *MGH epp. saec. XIII*, vol. 1, 491–95. See also the pope's letter to Louis IX, 12 February 1234, no. 2269, *LTC*, vol. 2, 259–60, calling for a three-year truce between the kingdoms of France and England. On Gregory's plans and preparations for crusade, see Lower, *Baron's Crusade*, 13–36.

60. 15 May 1235, no. 640, *MGH epp. saec. XIII*, vol. 1, 532–33; and 28 June 1235, no. 646, ibid., 542–43. See also Matthew Paris, *CM*, vol. 3, 279–88, 309–12. Matthew was far from the only one to view the popularity of the new mendicant orders as a threat to traditional religious orders and the secular clergy. See Szittya, *Antifraternal Tradition*.

61. In April 1234, Frederick recommitted himself to papal arbitration with the Lombards, HB, vol. 4/1, 465–66. See the pope's letter to the Lombard rectors about the upcoming crusade, 27 October 1234, *MGH epp. saec. XIII*, vol. 1, 488–91, which refers to earlier exchanges with the League, nos. 581, 383; and 587, ibid., 472–74, 476–77.

62. See Peters, *Inquisition*, 122–54; Ames, *Righteous Persecution*; and Sullivan, *Inner Lives*. For a tour-de-force study emphasizing the local dynamics and "technologies" of medieval inquisition, see Given, *Inquisition and Medieval Society*.

63. *VG*, 23; and Richard of San Germano, *Cronica*, 363–64.

64. February 1231, no. 539, *Reg. Greg.*, 351–52. Legislation passed at the Third Lateran Council in 1179, *COD*, 200–201 (canon 27), and the Fourth Lateran Council in 1215 (canon 3), *CQL*, 47–51, along with papal bulls such as *Ad abolendam* (1184) and *Vergentis in senium* (1199), had created systematic guidelines for dealing with the "infamous" and "treasonous" crime of heresy. See Diehl, "'Ad Abolendam.'"

65. For the statutes issued by the Roman senator, February 1231, no. 74, *CDSR*, vol. 1, 118–20; also nos. 540–41, *Reg. Greg.*, vol. 1, 352–54.

66. *VG*, 24; and Richard of San Germano, *Cronica*, 365. See also the record of Miranda's submission to Alatrin in the *Liber censuum*, 4 April 1234, no. 271, ed. Fabre, *Le Liber censuum*, vol. 1, 537–41, a contemporary collection of charters, privileges, deeds, and other documents relating to the papal patrimony.

67. 1 September 1231, no. 451, *MGH epp. saec. XIII*, vol. 1, 364–65. See also Gregory's letter to the podesta and people of Padua, encouraging them to action against Ezzelino, and his other letter to the younger Ezzelino and his brother Alberico, informing them about the sanctions placed on their father and encouraging them to reconcile their father with the church, 1–2 September 1231, nos. 705–6, *Reg. Greg.*, vol. 1, 441–42.

68. The *Annales Veronenses* (8) report that John of Vicenza burned sixty-one heretics in the city's public amphitheater on 21 July 1233. Gerard Maurisius (*Cronica*, 33) numbers only four burned. The *Annales Placentini Guelfi* (454) say that a mob of heretics attacked the Dominican friar Roland when he delivered his anti-heretical message. See also Housley, "Politics and Heresy"; and Diehl, "Overcoming the Reluctance."

69. Gregory to the archbishop of Trier, 25 June 1231, no. 81, *CDIHPN*, vol. 1, 80–81.

70. *Illi humani generis*, 20 October 1232, no. 490, *MGH epp. saec. XIII*, vol. 1, 394–96; *Vox in Rama*, June 1233, ibid., 432–35.

71. For the Dominican involvement in medieval inquisition, see Ames, *Righteous Persecution*; for the Franciscans, see Grieco, "Pastoral Care."

72. For the authorizing of anti-heretical measures, see Gregory's letters to the bishop of Strasburg, 19 October 1232, no. 485, *MGH epp. Saec. XIII*, vol. 1, 390; to John, bishop of Liège, July 1232, no. 87, *CDIHPN*, vol. 1, 86–88; to the bishops of Germany, 26 February 1233, no. 514, *MGH epp. saec. XIII*, vol. 1, 414; to the Dominican friar Robert Bulgarus, 19 April 1233, no. 90, *CDIHPN*, vol. 1, 91–93; and to Conrad of Marburg, no. 537, *MGH epp. saec. XIII*, vol. 1, 432–34, sending him a version of *Vox in Rama*. For some chroniclers' descriptions of how papal letters or "mandates" from the Apostolic See authorized local anti-heretical activities, see *Annales Erphordenses*, 27; Alberic of Trois-Fontaines, *Chronicon*, 931; and *Gesta Treverorum Continuata*, 400–401.

73. See the sixth and seventh articles of Frederick's coronation oath, no. 85, *MGH Const.*, vol. 2, 107–8; Powell, *Liber Augustalis*, 7–10; Richard of San Germano, *Cronica*, 363–64; and Frederick's edicts against heresy, 22 February 1232, no. 157, *MGH Const.*, vol. 2, 194–95, and March 1232, no. 158, ibid., 195–97.

74. 26 February 1231, HB, vol. 3, 268–69; and 16 June 1233, HB, vol. 4/1, 435–36.

75. For the pope's call to action against the Stedingers, which was addressed to the bishops of Minden, Lübeck, and Ratzeburg, see his two letters on 29 October 1232, no. 489, *MGH epp. saec. XIII*, vol. 1, 393–94, and on 17 June 1233, no. 539, ibid., 436–37. See also his address to Sigfried, archbishop of Mainz, and Conrad, bishop of Hildesheim, 10 June 1233, no. 533, 429–30; and his letter to Henry, landgrave of Thuringia, who had taken up the sign of the cross against heretics, 11 February 1234, no. 572, ibid., 466–67. Numerous chronicles took note of the "crusade" against the Stendingers, which was fought with papal authorization. See Albert of Stade, *Annales*, 361–62; *Annales Erphordenses*, 28; *Chronica regia Coloniensis*, 265; and *Tewksbury Annals*, 93.

76. No. 537 (III), *MGH epp. saec. XIII*, vol. 1, 435.

77. 15 July 1233, no. 550, *MGH epp. saec. XIII*, vol. 1, 444–45.

78. In addition to Sibilia, *Gregorio IX*, 133–59, see Gregorovius, *City of Rome*, 153–80; Waley, *Papal State*, 141–43; and Partner, *Lands of St. Peter*, 250–51. Also, Kantorowicz, *Frederick the Second*, 399–400; and Van Cleve, *Emperor Frederick II*, 372–73.

79. Partner, *Lands of St. Peter*, 249.

80. *VG*, 22–25; and Richard of San Germano, *Cronica*, 364–65, 369.

81. For Gregory's letters to Frederick, 24 July 1232, no. 473, *MGH epp. saec. XIII*, vol. 1, 381; 21 October 1232, no. 485, ibid., 390–91; 27 October 1232, no. 488, ibid., 392–93; and 7 December 1232, no. 497, ibid., 400–401.

82. For Frederick's letter to the pope, 3 December 1232, HB, vol. 4/1, 408–11. Also, Richard of San Germano, *Cronica*, 365.

83. 3 February 1233, no. 508, *MGH epp. saec. XIII*, vol. 1, 407; and 10 February 1233, no. 510, ibid, 408–9.

84. *VG*, 24–25.

85. *VG*, 23–25. Also, Richard of San Germano, *Cronica*, 369. For the terms of the peace agreement, no. 75, *CDSR*, 121–23. The senator at this time was Giovanni di Poli. In a letter to the rectors of Rome, 10 August 1233, no. 551, *MGH epp. saec. XIII*, vol. 1, 445, the pope excommunicated "disturbers" of the peace that had begun to refortify Castel Monastero, violating the terms of the recent agreement.

86. *VG*, 25.

87. May–June 1234, no. 591, *MGH epp. saec. XIII*, vol. 1, 479.

88. Richard of San Germano, *Cronica*, 372; and *Breve chronicon de rebus Siculis*, 100.

89. 6 July 1234, HB, vol. 4/1 743–76. For Henry's earlier agreement with his father, July 1232, ibid., 525–26.

90. *VG*, 25–26.

91. 3 July 1234, no. 587, *MGH epp. saec. XIII*, vol. 1, 476–77.

92. Gregory to the barons, podestas, and other leaders in Tuscany, 1 August 1234, no. 592, *MGH epp. saec. XIII*, vol. 1, 480; and to the archbishop of Mainz, 24 October 1234, no. 602, ibid., 488. See also the pope's letter to William, Count of Tuscany, 26 July 1234, no. 590, ibid., 478–79, thanking him for his promised aid to the Roman church and taking him under the "special protection" of the Apostolic See.

93. Roger of Wendover, *FH*, vol. 4, 322–24; and Matthew Paris, *HA*, vol. 2, 373–74. Also, *Dunstable Annals*, 142; and Richard of San Germano, *Cronica*, 372.

94. Nos. 78–80, *CDSR*, vol. 1, 125–30.

95. 25 November 1234, no. 607, *MGH epp. saec. XIII*, vol. 1, 496–97; and 5 December 1234, no. 612, ibid., 501–2, sent to the archbishop of Rouen, as well to King Sancho II of Portugal and the duke of Austria among others.

96. 2 January 1235, no. 617, *MGH epp. saec. XIII*, vol. 1, 505. In accompanying letters, nos. 618–19, ibid., 506–7, the pope absolved the people of Velltri from oaths owed to the Romans and confirmed a number of long-standing privileges from the Roman church.

97. 9 December 1234, no. 614, *MGH epp. saec. XIII*, vol. 1, 503; and *Tewksbury Annals*, 94. Also, *VG*, 26.

98. April–May 1235, no. 636, *MGH epp. saec. XIII*, vol. 1, 520–30. See also Frederick's letter to Gregory, 7 March 1235, no. 635, ibid., 520.

99. Around 20 July 1235, HB, vol. 4/2, 729–30.

100. For the marriage arrangements between Frederick and Isabella, see 15 November 1234–3 May 1235, nos. 188–92, *MGH Const.*, vol. 2, 230–36; and Rymer and Sanderson, *Foedera*, pt. 1, vol. 1, 114–16, 120–21. See also Weiler, *Henry III*, 65–67.

Chapter 3

1. 20 September 1235, no. 655, *MGH epp. saec. XIII*, vol. 1, 552–53.

2. Kantorowicz (*Frederick the Second*, 468) describes these exchanges as "petty accusations," underlying the "inevitability of struggle" between the two sides. See also Van Cleve, *Emperor Frederick II*, 391–409; and Abulafia, *Frederick II*, 290–320.

3. 28 July 1235, no. 194, *MGH Const.*, vol. 2, 239.

4. For the constitutions issued at the Diet of Mainz (the so-called *Mainzer Landfriede*), 15 August 1235, no. 196, *MGH Const.*, vol. 2, 241–63. See also Stürner, *Friedrich II*, vol. 2, 313–16.

5. 24 August 1235, *MGH Const.*, vol. 2, 239–40.

6. No. 195, *MGH Const.*, vol. 2, 239–40.

7. 2 March 1235, no. 628, *MGH epp. saec. XIII*, vol. 1, 513–14; 21 May 1235, no. 641, ibid., 533–34; and 26 September 1235, no. 661, ibid., 559–60.

8. Gregory to Hermann of Salza, 22 September 1235, *MGH epp. saec. XIII*, vol. 1, 556–57; to Frederick, 23 September 1235, no. 658, ibid., 557–58; and to rectors of the Lombard League, 26 September 1235, no. 662, ibid., 560–61.

9. 5–7 November 1235, HB, vol. 4/2, 796–98.

10. Gregory to Frederick, 21 March 1236, no. 678, *MGH epp. saec. XIII*, vol. 1, 576–78. Versions of this letter were also sent to Hermann of Salza, the imperial chancellor Siegfried, the bishop of Ratisbonne, the archbishops of Mainz and Trier, and the bishop of Hildesheim. See also Gregory's letters to Hermann of Salza (27 March 1236, no. 681, ibid., 579), instructing him to return to the papal curia as soon as possible, and to the rectors of the Lombard League (1 April 1236, no. 682, ibid., 580), informing them about his request for Hermann's return to the negotiating table.

11. *Annales Placentini Gibellini*, 471–72. See Massimo, "Pier della Vigna e Federico."

12. *Annales Placentini Gibellini*, 471.

13. For the series of letters relating to Marcellino's legation, 24 March–5 April, nos. 679, 682–685, *MGH epp. saec. XIII*, vol. 1, 578, 580–83.

14. May 1236, no. 200, *MGH Const.*, vol. 2, 266–69.

15. Gregory to Frederick, 10 June 1236, no. 691, *MGH epp. saec. XIII*, vol. 1, 588; and the bishops in Lombardy, same date, no. 693, ibid., 589–91.

16. *Annales Placentini Gibellini*, 473–74; and Bartholomew the Scribe, *Annales*, 185.

17. Van Cleve (*Emperor Frederick II*, 394–95) calls the appointment of James a "hostile act." See also Abulafia, *Frederick II*, 294–96.

18. June 1236, HB, vol. 4/2, 872–80.

19. Matthew Paris, *CM*, vol. 3, 361–62, 375–76. The sentiments attributed to Frederick, June 1236 in HB, vol. 4/2, 880–81, appear only in the *Major Chronicle*.

20. For Matthew's ongoing complaints, this time about Thomas, a Templar master, bearing a "warrant" from the pope to commute crusader vows for cash, *CM*, vol. 3, 373.

21. Matthew Paris, *CM*, vol. 3, 396–403, 446–47. On the planned diversion of the Baron's Crusade, see Spence, "Gregory IX's Attempted Expeditions"; and Lower, *Baron's Crusade*, 58–73.

22. 20 March 1235, no. 634, *MGH epp. saec. XIII*, 518–20; also nos. 15–17, Lupprian, *BPHB*, 132–38. See Richard, "L'attitude du pape Grégoire IX."

23. Gregory to the Hospitaller, Templar, and Teutonic orders in the Holy Land, 28 July 1235, no. 649, *MGH epp. saec. XIII*, vol. 1, 548–49; and to John of Ibelin, same date, no. 650, ibid., 549. See also Edbury, *John of Ibelin*, 45–57. As seen above, Albert was acting as a papal legate in Lombardy, but his deacon remained in Syria, continuing to act as a mediator on the pope's behalf.

24. 22 September 1235, no. 656, *MGH epp. saec. XIII*, vol. 1, 554–56.

25. 21 February 1236, no. 674, *MGH epp. saec. XIII*, vol. 1, 571–72 (cf. Matt. 13:41).

26. In addition to no. 674, *MGH epp. saec. XIII*, vol. 1, 571–72, see Gregory's letter to the Teutonic Order at Acre, 19 February 1236, no. 673, ibid., 570–71; and 23 February 1236, no. 675, ibid., 573. This plan specified that the Teutonic Knights would maintain control of Tyre's garrison on Frederick's behalf.

27. *Estoire de Eracles*, *RHC*, vol. 2, 406–7.

28. *Chronica regia Coloniensis*, 268.

29. *Annales Veronenses*, 9–10; and Gerard Maurisius, *Cronica*, 35.

30. *Annales Veronenses*, *MGH SS*, vol. 19, 10.

31. Numerous chroniclers noted of Frederick's arrival in Lombardy and subsequent campaign, including *Annales Placentini Gibellini*, 474; *Annales Veronenses*, 10; Gerard Maurisius, *Cronica*, 39; *Annales Mantuani*, 21; *Chronica regia Coloniensis*, 269–70; *Annales S. Justinae Patavini*, 155; Bartholomew the Scribe, *Annales*, 185; and Roland of Padua, *Chronica*, 60.

32. Matthew Paris, *CM*, vol. 3, 376–78. On Frederick's Lombard campaign in 1236, see also Salimbene of Adam, *CA*, vol. 1, 135.

33. *Dum preteritorum consideratione*, 29 February 1236, no. 676, *MGH epp. saec. XIII*, vol. 1, 573–74.

34. 3 December 1232, no. 494, *MGH epp. saec. XIII*, vol. 1, 388–89; and 27 August 1233, no. 553, ibid., 447–48. Responding to the pope on 3 December 1233 (HB vol. 4/1, 457–58), Frederick indicated his willingness to allow the friars to preach to his Muslim soldiers and presumably their families. See Lomax, "Frederick II."

35. HB, vol. 4/2, 828–32. Lomax ("*Ingratus* or *Indignus*," 55–60, 286–90) argues that *Dum preteritorum consideration* represented the first of the three written warnings required by canon law before the pope could legally excommunicate Frederick. If the letter did serve this purpose, the threat of censure was oblique not explicit, and the pope's follow-through a long time coming.

36. For this series of letters, see 17 August 1236, nos. 695–99, *MGH epp. saec. XIII*, vol. 1, 592–94.

37. 19 August 1236, no. 699, *MGH epp. saec. XIII*, vol. 1, 594–96.

38. 19 June 1236, no. 692, *MGH epp. saec. XIII*, vol. 1, 588–89.

39. No. 700, *MGH epp. saec. XIII*, vol. 1, 596–98. This list is not dated in the papal register but precedes the first folio of the ninth year of Gregory's papacy (March 1235–March 1236). Lomax ("Ingratus *or* Indignus," 319–22) considers this list the second of three warnings by the pope, anticipating Frederick's eventual excommunication.

40. Gregory had raised the issue of the missing prince previously, in 23 June 1236, no. 694, *MGH epp. saec. XIII*, vol. 1, 591.

41. 20 September, HB, vol. 4/2, 905–13.

42. No. 702, *MGH epp. saec. XIII*, vol. 1, 598–99. The list is undated but appears with no. 700 before the start of the ninth year of Gregory's papacy.

43. 23 October 1236, *Si memoriam beneficiorum*, no. 703, *MGH epp. saec. XIII*, vol. 1, 599–605.

44. Van Cleve, *Emperor Frederick II*, 395. On Gregory's invocation of the *Donation of Constantine*, see also Kantorowicz, *Frederick II*, 429; Abulafia, *Frederick II*, 296; Tierney, *Crisis of Church and State*, 143–44; and Morris, *Papal Monarchy*, 565.

45. Fuhrmann, "Konstantinische Schenkung." On the historical "transfer of empire," see Goez, *Translatio Imperii*.

46. *Si memoriam beneficiorum*, *MGH epp. saec. XIII*, vol. 1, 605: "Non attendens quod sacerdotes Christi regum et principum omnium fidelium patres et magistri censentur." Cf. *CIC*, D. 96 c. 9, 342–45.

47. *Si memoriam beneficiorum*, *MGH epp. saec. XIII*, vol. 1, 605.

48. Gregory first announced this appointment to the Lombards, 29 November 1236, no. 704, *MGH epp. saec. XIII*, 605–6. See also his letter to Frederick, 23 May 1237, no. 707, ibid., 609–10.

49. Matthew Paris, *CM*, vol. 3, 377–78. On the duke of Austria's "public temerity" and rebellion, see Frederick's widely circulating letter, June 1236, no. 201, *MGH Const.*, vol. 2, 269–71; and Richard of San Germano, *Cronica*, 373.

50. *Annales S. Justinae Patavini*, 155; and *Annales Placentini Gibellini*, 475. Gerard Maurisius (*Cronica*, 41–43) ends his chronicle on this note of triumph for the Romano brothers in 1237.

51. July 1237, HB, vol. 5/1, 93–95.

52. *Annales Placentini Gibellini*, 476.

53. *Annales Veronenses*, 10; *Annales Placentini Gibellini*, *MGH SS*, vol. 18, 476; and Salimbene of Adam, *CA*, vol. 1, 136–38. On the Milanese carrocio, see Webb, "Cities of God," especially pp. 115–18.

54. Matthew Paris, *CM*, vol. 3, 406–10, includes the letter to Richard of Cornwall. For other imperial letters on the battle sent to the archbishop of York, to the duke of Lotharingia, to "all the faithful" of the empire, to Gregory and the cardinals, to the princes of Germany, and to the citizens of Rome, HB, vol. 5/1, 132–39, 142–45, 161–63. On the battle of Cortenuova and its aftermath, see also *Annales Placentini Gibellini*, 477; Bartholomew the Scribe, *Annales*, 186; *Annales S. Rudberti Salisburgenses*, 787; *Chronica regia Coloniensis*, 271–72; and Richard of San Germano, *Cronica*, 375. In the year 1237, Richard (ibid., 374) describes how the emperor sent letters about another victory at Vincenza that were read aloud to an audience at San Germano.

55. *Annales Placentini Gibellini*, 478; and Salimbene of Adam, *CA*, vol. 1, 139.

56. *Annales Placentini Gibellini*, 478.

57. *Encyclica de curia Placentiae celebranda,* May 1236, no. 200, *MGH Const.,* vol. 206–8. The assembly did not meet until 23 May. In September 1232 and December 1235, Frederick had renewed and confirmed Raymond's rights and status as a loyal vassal: HB, vol. 4/2, 486, 799–800.

58. 28 April 1236, no. 688, *MGH epp. saec. XIII*, vol. 1, 584–86.

59. For the notification of James's legatine status, sent to the bishop of Toulouse and other inquisitors in the region, see Gregory's letter, 13 May 1238, no. 2711, *LTC*, vol. 2, 377; for the instructions given to James to absolve Raymond, 9 June 1238, no. 731, *MGH epp. saec. XIII*, vol. 1, 630–31.

60. May 1238, HB 5/1, 201–2. Similar statutes were issued at Verona, HB 5/1, 215–16; at Cremona, *CDIHPN*, no. 111, 107–9; and Padua, *CDIHPN*, no. 118, 113. See Merlo, "Federico II."

61. *VG*, 32. Frederick addressed his complaints about James to a faithful representative, perhaps at the papal curia, HB, vol. 5/1, 269–71. See also his letter to the pope, June 1238, *AII*, no 349 vol. 1, 310–11. As noted by Richard of San Germano (*Cronica*, 376), when Gregory realized that James would not be able to fulfill his assignment, in August he commissioned Guido, the bishop of Sorano, in James's place, leading to revisions of the legatine letters in the papal register. See Spence, "Impact of Historical Events."

62. September 1238, HB, vol. 5/1, 237–38.

63. Bartholomew the Scribe, *Annales*, 187–89.

64. Pope Gregory to Adelasia (misidentified as Agnes here), April/May 1238, no. 726, *MGH epp. saec. XIII*, vol. 1, 624–25; and 31 May 1238, no. 729. On Adelasia's marriage to Enzio, see Richard of San Germano, *Cronica*, 376.

65. On the initial 1238 departure deadline, see the letters issued on 2 and 4 November 1237, nos. 713–14, *MGH epp. saec. XIII*, vol. 1, 613–14 (specifying that a monk named Theodosius acted as the go-between bearing these letters from the pope to Frederick); and to Lando, archbishop of Messina, no. 715, ibid., 614–15. For Frederick's extension of the deadline for departure, no. 716, ibid., 615; and HB, vol. 5/1, 164–65.

66. Matthew Paris, *CM*, vol. 3, 471–72, describes Gregory's increasing hard line toward the Greeks. In his letters to Frederick on 12 March and 17 March 1238, no. 724–25, *MGH epp. saec. XIII*, vol. 1, 622–23, the pope emphasized his decision to attack the Greeks after his unsuccessful negotiations with the Greek patriarch at Nympha in 1234, which had been carried out by members of the mendicant orders. See Doran, "Rites and Wrongs."

67. On the long and violent nature of this siege, see *Annales Placentini Gibellini*, 479–80; *Annales S. Justinae Patavini*, 156; *Annales Veronenses*, 10; *Annales S. Pantaleonis Coloniensis*, 531; and Matthew Paris, *CM*, vol. 3, 491–92, which specifies that Henry III sent one hundred soldiers to serve in Frederick's forces.

68. Albert of Stade, *Annales*, 363; *VG*, 29–32.

69. *VG*, 29–32.

70. Matthew Paris, vol. 3, 444–46. Otto's time in England was marked by controversy, including a brawl and riot in Oxford between his entourage and members of the university. See Williamson, "Some Aspects of the Legation."

71. 28 October 1238, HB, vol. 5/1, 249–58. Lomax ("*Ingratus* or *Indignus*," 345–48) views this as the final of the three written warnings required by canon law.

72. *Chronica regia Coloniensis*, 273.

73. Gregory also wrote directly to Frederick to complain about the emperor's arrest of Peter Saracen, 3 June 1238, no. 730, ibid., 629–30.

74. Gregory's biographer (*VG*, 29) describes these plots in Rome in 1238, when some of the citizens marked themselves with the "sign of Antichrist."

75. HB, vol. 5/1, 249–50.

76. *Chronica regia Coloniensis*, 273: "que litteras postea per Teuthoniam sunt transmisse et audite." Matthew Paris (*CM*, vol. 3, 551–62) wrongly inserts his copy of the document in 1239, after Gregory excommunicated Frederick for the second time.

77. February 1239, no. 213, *MGH Const.*, vol. 2, 286–89.

78. *Cum Christus sit*, 10 March 1239, HB, vol. 5/1, 282–84; and Richard of San Germano, *Cronica*, 376. On this letter, see Rader, *Friedrich II*, 450.

79. Matthew Paris, *CM*, vol. 3, 488–89; and *Gesta Treverorum Continuata*, 404.

80. Matthew Paris, *CM*, vol. 3, 520–21; and Matthew Paris, *HA*, vol. 2, 415.

Chapter 4

1. *VG*, 32. For the sentence of excommunication, see HB, vol. 5/1, 286–89.

2. Kantorowicz, *Frederick the Second*, 468; Van Cleve, *Emperor Frederick II*, 427–41; and Abulafia, *Frederick II*, 313–20.

3. Matthew Paris, *HA*, vol. 2, 421, 424, 443–44; Matthew Paris, *CM*, vol. 3, 550–51; Salimbene of Adam, *CA*, vol. 1, 252–53; and *Annales S. Pantaleonis Coloniensis*, 536.

4. Gregory to the archbishop of Rouen, *Sedes apostolica*, 7 April, 1239, no. 741, *MGH epp. saec. XIII*, vol. 1, 637–39; and to the archbishop of Reims, *Cum nuper in Fredericum*, 7 April, 1239, no. 742, ibid., vol. 1, 640–41. Both letters were sent "in the same way" to "archbishops and bishops, kings, dukes, counts, and nobles." In Gregory's register, ASV, Reg. Lat. 19, fols. 155r–156v, the letters relating to Frederick's excommunication are together, set off by a blank folio (nos. 5092–5152, *Reg. Greg.*, vol. 3).

5. Matthew Paris, *CM*, vol. 3, 532–36, 569–73; Albert of Stade, *Annales*, 363–64; and *Annales Placentini Gibellini*, 480–81. See also *Tewksbury Annals*, 113; *Waverley Annals*, 322; *Dunstable Annals*, 148; and *Osney-Thomas Wykes Annals*, 86; Albert of Stade, *Annales*, 363–65; Alberic of Trois-Fontaines, *Chronicon*, 944; *Annales S. Justinae Patavini*, 156; *Annales Erphordenses*, 33 (entered under the wrong year in 1238); and *Annales S. Pantaleonis Coloniensis*, 531.

6. See Maleczek, "La propaganda antiimperiale."

7. *MGH epp. saec. XIII*, vol. 1, 639.

8. Matthew Paris, *CM*, vol. 3, 537–38, 545, 562–63, 568–73; and Matthew Paris, *HA*, vol. 2, 423. On the monks expelled from Monte Cassino, Richard of San Germano (*Cronica*, 377–388) observes that Frederick fortified the monastery as part of his preparations for war, leaving only eight monks at the site.

9. Albert of Stade, *Annales*, 365 ("ut pro scandalo ecclesiae evitando").

10. Most of our information about Albert Behaim's activities comes from a series of notes and transcriptions made in the sixteenth century, based on now missing manuscript materials, published in Höfler, *Albert von Beham*. See also the critical edition of Albert's "memorial book," Frenz and Herde, *Das Brief- und Memorialbuch*. This volume collects letters, tracts, prophetic texts, and other materials belonging to the legate. On Albert's activities c. 1239–41, see Höfler, *Albert von Beham*, 5–17; and Zimmermann, *Die päpstliche Legation*, 132.

11. Höfler, *Albert von Beham*, 10–16.

12. 21 October 1239, nos. 2835–36, *LTC*, vol. 2, 17–19.

13. Matthew Paris, *CM*, vol. 3, 624–28. This letter does not appear in any other contemporary sources besides the *Major Chronicle*. Even Van Cleve (*Emperor Frederick II*, 437) admits that this letter's "authenticity may be seriously questioned." On James of Palestrina's legation to France, see Zimmermann, *Die päpstliche Legation*, 113–14.

14. Höfler, *Albert von Beham*, 5; *Annales Erphordenses*, 33; and Albert of Stade, *Annales*, 365. See also the pope's communications with Albert and the king of Bohemia, September 1240, HB, vol. 5/1, 1035–37.

15. Richard of San Germano, *Cronica*, 379; and Höfler, *Albert von Beham*, 10–16.

16. Salimbene of Adam, *CA*, vol. 1, 140. On Salimbene's treatment of Frederick in his chronicle, see Gatto, "Federico II."

17. Salimbene of Adam, *CA*, vol. 1, 140–252 (especially pp. 247–48); and Matthew Paris, *CM*, vol. 3, 628. See also the account of Elias's deposition given by the contemporary Franciscan friar Thomas of Eccleston, *De adventu fratrum*, 44–48; along with Richard of San Germano, *Cronica*, 379; *Dunstable Annals*, 155; and Frederick's letter on June 1239, HB, vol. 5/1, 346–48. On Elias's controversial tenure as minister general, see Moorman, *History of the Franciscan Order*, 96–104.

18. 19 December 1239, no. 763, *MGH epp. saec. XIII*, 662–63; 7 July 1240, no. 780, *MGH epp. saec. XIII*, 678–79; and Salimbene of Adam, *CA*, vol. 2, 888.

19. Roland of Padua, *Chronica*, 71.

20. Richard of San Germano, *Cronica*, 377; Albert of Stade, *Annales*, 364–65; and Matthew Paris, *CM*, vol. 3, 546–47 (transcribing Frederick's letter to the Roman senate, *Cum Roma sit*), 548–50 (transcribing *Cum Christus sit*). Albert and Matthew present *Cum Christus sit*—written before the pope anathematized Frederick—as being a response to Gregory's passage of the ban.

21. MGH epp. saec. XIII, vol. 1, 639.

22. Matthew Paris, *CM*, vol. 3, 545. See Frederick's letters to Henry III, *Cum inter reges*, 29 October 1239, HB, v. 5/1, 464–66 (also in Matthew Paris, *CM*, vol. 4, 16–190); and to the English barons, HB, v. 5/1, 467–69.

23. *Annales S. Pantaleonis Coloniensis*, 531; Frederick to the cathedral chapter at Passau, May–June 1241, HB, vol. 5/2, 1130–32; and Richard of San Germano, *Cronica*, 378. The *Breve chronicon de rebus Siculis*, 104, says that James traveled *privatim non publice*.

24. For Frederick's letters, HB, vol. 5/2, 903, 1089–90. Richard of San Germano, *Cronica*, 377, 380, claims that the expulsion of the mendicants happened late in 1240 and adds that two native-born friars remained in the Regno under house arrest. See also *Osney-Wykes Annals*, *AM*, vol. 4, 86; and *Gesta Treverorum Continuata*, 403, which describes how Frederick ordered the borders of Germany sealed to intercept papal envoys and letters.

25. Salimbene of Adam, *CA*, vol. 1, 264–65.

26. *Levate in circuitu*, 20 April 1239, HB, vol. 5/1, 295–307; *Ascendit de mari*, 1 July 1239, *MGH epp. saec. XIII*, no. 750, vol. 1, 645–54; *In exordio nascentis*, July 1239, HB, vol. 5/1, 348–51; *Triplex doloris*, 16 March 1240, HB, vol. 5/2, 840–46; *Collegerunt pontifices*, June 1240, HB, vol. 1/5, 309–12; and *Convenerunt in unum*, June 1240, in Schaller, "Die Antwort Gregors IX," 160–65. HB, vol. 5/1, 309, dates *Collegerunt pontifices* to April 1239, but see Schaller, "Die Antwort Gregors IX," 143–45, for the revised dating. On these polemical exchanges ca. 1239–40, see Graefe, *Die Publiszistik*; Schaller, *Politische Propaganda*; Schaller, "Endzeit-Erwartung"; Herde, "Literary Activities"; and Shepard, *Courting Power*, 189–209.

27. In addition to Maleczek, "La propaganda antiimperiale," 292–96, see Westenholz, *Kardinal Rainer von Viterbo*; and Thumser, "Kardinal Rainer von Viterbo."

28. See, for example, BAV, Pal. Lat. 953, fols. 29r–78v. Based on its contents, this letter collection is associated with Rainier of Viterbo or his circle (e.g., Maleczek, "La propaganda antiimperiale," 294–95; Thumser, "Kardinal Rainer von Viterbo," 194–95). It includes a number of the letters under discussion here—e.g., *Levate in circuitu* (fols. 36r–39v), *Cum sit Cristus* (fols. 43r–43v), *Collergerunt pontifices et* (fols. 49r–50v)—with other materials relating to the Lombard League and its struggles with Frederick. On Peter de Vinea's letter collection, preserved in well over two hundred manuscripts, see Schaller, "Briefsammlung des Petrus de Vinea."

29. *Ascendit de mari*, *MGH epp. saec. XIII*, no. 750, vol. 1, 647, 650–52. Maleczek ("La propaganda antiimperiale," 299) links *Ascendit de mari* with Rainier's circle. Although Thumser does not question Rainier's role as a polemicist, he insists that Rainier's role in producing *Ascendit de mari* remains "speculative" ("Kardinal Rainer von Viterbo," 188n2).

30. *In exordio nascentis*, HB, vol. 5/1, 348–49.

31. *Collegerunt pontifices*, HB, vol. 5/1, 310; and *Convenerunt in unum*, in Schaller, "Die Antwort Gregors IX," 161–62.

32. *In exordio nascentis*, HB, vol. 5/1, 348.

33. HB, vol. 5/1, 304 (*Levate in circuitu*), 309; (*Collegerunt pontifices*), 350 (*In exordio nascentis*).

34. *Convenerunt in unum*, in Schaller, "Die Antwort Gregors IX," 162.

35. Smail, *Consumption of Justice*, 211.

36. For these examples, see HB, vol. 5/1, 297 (*litteras latenter*), 301 (*impedimenta clandestina*); HB, vol. 5/2, 842–43 (*furtivas legationes*); and *MGH epp. saec. XIII*, vol. 1, 645, 649.

37. For these characteristic examples, see *Levate in circuitu*, HB, vol. 5/1, 295–96 (*generale orbis scandalum*); *In exordio nascentis*, July 1239, HB, vol. 5/1, 48–49; *Ascendit de mari*, *MGH epp. saec. XIII*, no. 750, vol. 1, 646–48, 650; and *Triplex doloris*, HB, vol. 5/2, 845. Also, *VG*, 32–33.

38. *VG*, 32–33; and Matthew Paris, *CM*, vol. 3, 520–21. Albert of Stade, *Annales*, 363, also describes the pope's suspicions of the emperor since he showed "too much affection" toward Muslims.

39. Matthew Paris, *CM*, vol. 3, 578–89 (*Levate in circuitu*); 590–608 (*Ascendit de mari*); and 631–38 (*Triplex doloris*). On Matthew's deployment and sometimes modification of imperial and papal letters throughout his chronicle, see Hilpert, *Kaiser- und Papstbriefe*, 62–119. Hilpert plausibly argues that Richard of Cornwall and his household represented an important source of information for Matthew and probably provided him with copies of many such letters coming from the imperial chancery.

40. Matthew Paris, *CM*, vol. 3, 562–63, 608–9, 621; and Matthew Paris, *HA*, vol. 2, 415, 428.

41. On Gregory's military actions against Frederick, revisiting the question of whether the pope organized a genuine crusade against him or not, see Raccagni, "Crusade Against Frederick II," especially pp. 728–40. Based mainly on Italian chronicles, Raccagni argues that the crusade against Frederick—the first full-blown crusade against a secular Christian ruler—did not take shape until 1240.

42. Albert of Stade, *Annales*, 365; Gregory to Alberic da Romano, June 1239, HB, vol. 5/1, 317; and Bartholomew the Scribe, *Annales*, 192.

43. Verga, "Gregorio de Monte Longo"; and Zimmermann, *Die päpstliche Legation*, 130–31.

44. *Annales Placentini Gibellini*, 481; *Annales S. Justinae Patavini*, 156–67; Roland of Padua, *Chronica*, 75–76; Salimbene of Adam, *CA*, vol. 1, 254–55; and Bartholomew the Scribe, *Annales*, 192. On the siege of Ferrara, see Raccagni, "Crusade Against Frederick II," 731–33.

45. Salimbene of Adam, *CA*, vol. 2, 586–93; and Matthew Paris, *CM*, vol. 3, 573–75.

46. HB, vol. 5/1, 301, and vol. 5/2, 843–45; *MGH epp. saec. XIII*, 650, 652. See also *Annales Placentini Gibellini*, 483.

47. *Annales S. Pantaleonis Coloniensis*, 531.

48. *Triplex doloris*, HB, vol. 5/2, 84. See also Frederick's letter to the citizens of Ravenna, August 1239, HB, vol. 5/1, 371–73, expressing his "scandalized" reaction to their revolt; and the pope's letter to the citizens of Bologna, August 1239, HB, vol. 5/1, 373–74, calling upon them to work with Paul Traversario to support Ravenna. Frederick recaptured the city in August 1240.

49. See Gregory's letter to Sinibaldo, 4 July 1240, no. 779, *MGH epp. saec. XIII*, vol. 1, 677–78.

50. HB, vol. 5/1, 390–94; HB, vol. 5/2, 1012–13.

51. Matthew Paris, *CM*, vol. 4, 20–22.

52. On the fighting between Raymond Berengar and Raymond of Toulouse, see Matthew Paris, *CM*, vol. 4, 22–24; the letter from James of Palestrina to Raymond Berengar, 10 November 1239, no. 662, *AII*, vol. 1, 528–29; the count's promise of "service to the church," same date, HB, vol. 5/1, 488–89; James of Palestrina's letter to the archbishop of Narbonne, calling upon him to oppose Raymond Berengar's enemies, 10 May 1240, no. 663, *AII*, vol. 1, 529–30; and Zöen's declaration of the ban against Raymond of Toulouse, 15 July 1240, no. 665, *AII*, vol. 1, 530–32. Frederick cited the count of Provence to appear at the imperial court after Raymond Berengar expelled the imperial vicar from the city of Arles, September 1239, HB, vol. 5/1, 401–2. Zöen, it is worth noting, was a former chaplain to Rainier of Viterbo (Maleczek, "La propaganda antiimperiale," 299).

53. 10 January 1240, no. 764, *MGH epp. saec. XIII*, vol. 1, 664.

54. Matthew Paris, *CM*, vol. 3, 627; vol. 4, 4–7, 10–11; and *Annales S. Pantaleonis Coloniensis*, 531. On these exactions in England, see Lunt, *Financial Relations*, 197–205.

55. Matthew Paris, *CM*, vol. 4, 4–7, 16–19.

56. Matthew Paris, *CM*, vol. 4, 9, 15, 35–43 The meeting at Northampton took place on 24 June 1240. See Powicke and Cheney, *Councils and Synods*, vol. 2/1, 285–93.

57. Matthew Paris, *CM*, vol. 4, 42. In their protests, the bishops also pointed out that clergy who had sworn a crusading vow enjoyed a special privilege to keep all of their ecclesiastical revenues for three years to pay for related costs. The pope's planned subsidy contravened that preexisting exemption.

58. Matthew Paris, *CM*, vol. 3, vol. 3, 620, 627–28.

59. Writing to the bishop of Madyte, Gregory complained about such backsliding crusaders, 5 October 1240, no. 5296, *Reg. Greg.*, vol. 3, 317–18.

60. Matthew Paris, *CM*, vol. 3, 614–15, 620.

61. Frederick to the crusader army, July 1239, HB, vol. 5/1, 359; and to Theobald of Navarre, January 1240, HB, vol. 5/2, 646–47. Matthew Paris (*CM*, 620, 627–28) writes that Frederick told the crusader armies in France that he would join them personally if they delayed their departure until the pope's "spirit of wrath" had settled. When they rejected his overtures, the emperor angrily denied their forces any supplies from his lands.

62. *Attendite ad petram*, February 1240, HB, vol. 5/2, 776–79. On this procession, see *VG*, 35–36 (the text breaks off and ends with this episode); *Annales Placentini Gibellini*, 483; and *Dunstable Annals*, 153, which describe how Gregory "publicly" preached to the people of Rome, calling upon them to defend Saints Peter and Paul. The reference to Frederick desiring to "sit" in the "Temple of the Lord" plays on 2 Thess. 2:4, long associated with the figure of Antichrist.

63. See the September 1239 letter of the German prelates, HB, vol. 5/1, 398–400; King Ferdinand of Castile's letter to Gregory IX, 4 December 1239, no. 760, *MGH epp. saec. XIII*, 569–71; and the German archbishops Conrad of Cologne, Landolf of Worms, Ludolf of Münster, and Engelbert of Innsbruck's letter to the pope, 8 April 1240, no. 225, *MGH Const.*, vol. 2, 313–14 (cf. nos. 226–32 for similar letters sent to the pope by various parties involved in the proposed negotiations, including Siegfried, archbishop of Mainz, Otto II, duke of Brunswick, and Albert, duke of Saxony).

64. Matthew Paris, *CM*, vol. 4, 25–26, includes two such letters, one anonymously addressed "to a friend," the other written by Count Henry II of Montfort to his wife, Beatrice. On the battle of Gaza on 13 November, see Painter, "Crusade of Theobald."

65. 25 April 1240, HB, vol. 5/2, 920–23. Matthew Paris, *CM*, vol. 4, 26–29, includes a version of this letter addressed to Henry III, following the two letters that describe the recent crusader defeat at Gaza. See also Matthew Paris, *HA*, vol. 2, 433–34; and *Annales S. Pantaleonis Coloniensis*, 533.

66. Matthew Paris, *CM*, vol. 4, 26, 29.

67. Gregory to Russudana and her son King David of Georgia, 13 January 1240, no. 765, *MGH epp. saec. XIII*, vol. 1, 664–66. Also, Matthew Paris, *CM*, vol. 4, 119.

68. In addition to *Cum Christus sit*, HB, vol. 5/1, 282–84, see Frederick's letter to the cardinals on March 1239, no. 214, *MGH Const.*, vol. 2, 289–90.

69. Tierney, *Foundations of the Conciliar Theory*, 43–61.

70. Matthew Paris, *CM*, vol. 4, 58–61; and Richard of San Germano, *Cronica*, 81.

71. Gregory to Raymond Berengar, 20 June 1240, no. 664, *AII*, vol. 1, 530.

72. See Congar, "Quod omnes tangit."

73. 9 August 1240, no. 781–82, *MGH epp. saec. XIII*, vol. 1, 679–84. Marginal notations in Gregory's register identify excommunicated bishops receiving the summons to the council. On the legal concept of the *pars sollicitudinis*, which is linked to the pope's "fullness of power" in the canonistic tradition, see Benson, "*Plenitudo Potestatis*."

74. Matthew Paris, *CM*, vol. 4, 30; and Gregory's letter to Raymond Berengar, 20 June 1240, no. 664, *AII*, vol. 1, 530.

75. See Frederick's letters to Henry III, 13 September, 1240, HB, vol. 5/2, 1037–41 (portions of this letter are featured in Matthew Paris, *CM*, vol. 4, 65–68); and to Louis IX, ibid., 1075–77; and to the Dominicans at Paris, 27 February 1241, ibid., 1098–1100. For the anonymous letter on the perils of sea-travel, see HB, v. 5/2, 1077–58. Matthew Paris, *CM*, vol. 4, 95–96, presents a speech attributed to Frederick, decrying the pope as his "open enemy" and forbidding any prelates from attending the council.

76. February 1241, HB, vol. 5/2, 1089–90.

77. *Petri navicula matris*, 15 October 1240, no. 785, *MGH epp. saec. XIII*, vol. 1, 688–92 (transcribed in Matthew Paris, *CM*, vol. 4, 95–98).

78. On 12 December 1240 (no. 794, *MGH epp. saec. XIII*, vol. 1, 702), the pope recalled Sinibaldo and replaced him with Marcellino of Arrezzo; on 19 March 1241 (no. 808, ibid., vol. 1, 711), he recalled Gregory of Monte Longo, who never returned to Rome.

79. These instructions are included in series of letters about the Roman church's massive debts and the funds needed for the fleet: 5–6 November 1240, no. 787, *MGH epp. saec. XIII*, 692–95. These materials feature separately in Gregory's register, ASV, Reg. 20, fols. 53r–v (with the rubric "Super

pecunia mutuanda ecclesie Romane a prelatis subscriptis" added later). For an additional set of letters about financial arrangements for the fleet, see nos. 784, 791–93, *MGH epp. saec. XIII*, 684–88, 697–702. These letters are likewise set off in Gregory's register, ASV, Reg. 20, fols. 56r–59v (with the rubric "Littere super apparatu navigii" added later).

80. Bartholomew the Scribe, *Annales*, 194–96.

81. 15 March 1241, no. 806, *MGH epp. saec. XIII*, vol. 1, 710.

82. 10 May 1241, no. 812, *MGH epp. saec. XIII*, vol. 1, 713–14.

83. Matthew Paris, *CM*, vol. 4, 123–30; *HA*, vol. 2, 449–50; Albert of Stade, *Annales*, 367; *Gesta Treverorum Continuata*, 404; *Annales S. Pantaleonis Coloniensis*, 534–35; *Annales Placentini Gibellini*, 484–85; and *Annales S. Justinae Patavini*, 158.

84. 18 May 1241, HB, vol. 5/2, 1123–25. This letter is transcribed in Matthew Paris, *CM*, vol. 4, 126–29. For a similar, widely circulated letter, see HB, vol. 5/2, 1126–28.

85. Matthew Paris, *CM*, vol. 4, 129.

86. 14 June 1241, no. 820, *MGH epp. saec. XIII*, 720–21.

87. 10 May 1241, no. 813, *MGH epp. saec. XIII*, 714–16.

88. As reported in Richard of San Germano, *Cronica*, 381, Frederick issued a number of "general letters" regarding the Tartar invasions to the "princes of the west" in the summer of 1241, including his letters to the Roman senate, HB, vol. 5/2, 1139–43; to King Bela IV of Hungary, ibid., 1143–46; and to Henry III, ibid., 1148–54. See also the letter to the bishop and canons at Brescia from a Dominican friar named Bartholomew calling for them to pray for Christian unity in the face of the barbarians, HB, vol. 5/2, 1146–48. On Conrad's swearing of the cross in May 1241, HB, 5/2, 1214. See Jackson, "Crusade Against the Mongols."

89. 18 June 1241, no. 821–22, *MGH epp. saec. XIII*, vol. 1, 721–23. See Berend, *Gate of Christendom*, 34–41, 163–71.

90. Edited in Schaller, "Das letzte Rundschreiben Gregors IX."

91. Gregory to Bernhard II, duke of Carinthia, 19 June 1241, no. 823, *MGH epp. saec. XIII*, 723–24. On Richard of Cornwall's visit to Rome, see Matthew Paris, *CM*, vol. 4, 147–48; and *Tewksbury Annals*, 120. For the pope's letter to the Genoese, see no. 828, *MGH epp. saec. XIII*, 727–28.

92. Matthew Paris, *CM*, vol. 4, 162–63; and HB, vol. 5/2, 1165–67.

Interlude

1. For the text of this letter, see Hampe, *Ein ungedruckter Bericht*, 26–31. See also Wenck, "Das erste Konklave."

2. As discussed in Tierney, *Foundations of the Conciliar Theory*, 68–84.

3. Matthew Paris, *CM*, vol. 4, 164–65, 168, 170–74, 194, 239–41, 250–52.

4. Bagliani, *CCFC*, vol. 1, 32–71, 130–59. Giles de Torres was the cardinal deacon of Santi Cosma e Damiano; Robert Somercotes, cardinal deacon of Sant'Eustachio; and Richard Annibaldi, cardinal deacon of San Angelo in Pescheria.

5. As required since reforms to the election process in 1179. See Robinson, *Papacy 1073–1198*, 84–85.

6. Matthew Paris, *CM*, vol. 4, 164–65, 168.

7. Matthew Paris (*CM*, vol. 4, 164–65) writes that Frederick freed Otto before Celestine's election in August 1241. Other sources (e.g., Richard of San Germano, *Cronica*, 383) accurately report that the emperor first released him in August 1242.

8. Matthew Paris, *CM*, vol. 4, 194.

9. Matthew Paris, *CM*, vol. 4, 173–74. Later in his chronicle (ibid., 250–52), Matthew addresses an example of more mundane ecclesiastical business caught up in the vacancy, transcribing a letter to the abbot of Wardon from a number of the cardinals who responded to an appeal by a certain Master Peter, a Roman cleric who had been denied his rights to the revenues of the church at Guilden Morden by bishop of Ely. According to the letter, under false pretenses the bishop had received permission from the deceased Pope Gregory. The cardinals instructed the abbot, who had been previously ordered by the bishop to withhold the revenues from a certain farm pertaining to the church, to restore control of

the property to Peter and to give full accounting of its revenues. Mathew included a copy of this letter, he said, because some wondered if the "papal power" devolved upon the "university of the cardinals" during the vacancy. This letter suggested that it did.

10. *Gesta Treverorum Continuata (Deeds of the Bishop of Trier)*, 404; Albert of Stade, *Annales*, 367; and Menko, *Chronica*, 536: "Frederico imperatore electionem tam occulte quam manifeste impediente, et maximos per quosdam cardinals, quos in captivitate detinuit, sine quibus electio non poterat celebrari. Et sic accidit illud prophete: 'Vidi Israel sicut oves sine pastore.'" Cf. 2 Chron. 18:16.

11. Salimbene of Adam, *CA*, vol. 1, 265.

12. HB, vol. 6/1, 68–70.

13. Matthew Paris, *CM*, vol. 4, 249.

14. Fall 1241, HB, vol. 5/2, 1165–67.

15. See Frederick's three letters to the cardinals: March 1242, HB, vol. 6/1, 35–36; May 1242, ibid., 44; and July 1242, ibid., 59–61; to an unidentified supporter, May 1243, ibid., 87–88; to the emperor of Constantinople with a similar version sent to an unspecified king, June 1243, ibid., 90–95; and to Louis IX, June 1243, ibid., 95–98. See also the letter of an unidentified imperial sympathizer, writing to cardinals and berating them for their failure to elect a new pope, late 1242, HB, vol. 6/1, 70–72.

16. As Frederick explained to Louis IX (HB, vol. 1, 6/1, 95–98). On 14 June 1242 (no. 100, *CDSR*, vol. 1, 166–68), Matteo Rosso issued a call for assistance from neighboring communes for a campaign against the emperor's forces, to "safeguard the liberty of the church of God," marching under the "protection of Saints Peter and Paul."

17. Matthew Paris, *CM*, vol. 4, 239–41.

18. Bartholomew the Scribe, *Annales*, 200–202, 208–9; and *Annales Placentini Gibellini*, 486.

19. *Annales S. Pantaleonis Coloniensis*, 536.

20. Fall 1241, HB, vol. 5/2, 1165–67.

21. Matthew Paris, *CM*, vol. 6, 75–84.

22. The *Annales Placentini Gibellini*, 486, record that the emperor freed the two cardinals and gave them "many gifts." Frederick's release of James and Otto also features in *Annales S. Pantaleonis Coloniensis*, 538; and Richard of San Germano, *Cronica*, 383–84.

23. HB, vol. 6/1, 35–36, 93–95.

24. Menko, *Chronica*, 537.

25. Including among others, Albert of Stade, *Annales*, 368; *Annales S. Pantaleonis Coloniensis*, 538; Roland of Padua, *Chronica*, 78; *Annales S. Justinae Patavini*, 158; Bartholomew the Scribe, *Annales*, 212; and the *Annales Placentini Gibellini*, 486.

Chapter 5

1. Nicholas of Carbio, *VI*, 259–62. See Pagnotti, "Niccolò da Calvi."

2. As Van Cleve (*Emperor Frederick II*, 454) puts it, "The die was cast with no hope of stopping the fight unto the death between the *sacerdotium* and the *imperium*, the spiritual rule of priests and the temporal rule of monarchs." For similar appraisals, see Kantorowicz, *Frederick the Second*, 623; and Abulafia, *Frederick II*, 294. For a more balanced take on Innocent's papacy, see Melloni, *Innocenzo IV*. On Innocent's training as a canon lawyer, see Piergiovanni, "Sinibaldo dei Fieschi decretalista"; Le Bras, "Innocent IV Romaniste"; and Orallo, *Persona jurídica y ficción*; and Melloni, *Innocenzo IV*, 26–55.

3. Innocent's registers are preserved at the Vatican ASV, Reg. 21–23. These manuscripts cover only the first through the fifth and the eighth through the eleventh years of his papacy: years six and seven were lost, although a portion of year six survives in a later copy, in Paris, BNF, Lat. 4039. See Berger, *Les registres d'Innocent IV*. During Innocent's papacy, the practice began of grouping some letters together at the end of each year as "curial letters" of special importance for the curia and Roman church as a whole. See Berger, ibid., vol. 1, v–lxxix, along with Bock, "Studien zu den Registern Innocenz' IV." An additional collection of letters from Innocent's papacy, featuring materials not included in the Vatican register, survives in a manuscript at the Biblioteca Antoniana, Padua, no. 79, fols. 41r–62r, inventoried by Abate, "Lettere 'secretae' d'Innocenzo IV." For a selective edition of these letters, see Sambin, *Problemi politici*.

4. Innocent IV to the archbishop of Reims, 2 July 1243, no. 1, *MGH epp. saec. XIII*, vol. 2, 1–3. Other recipients named in the register include the Cistercian abbot, William III; the abbess and convent at Iovarre, near Meaux; the king of Castile-Leon; and the podesta and commune of Milan (for the letter to the Milanese, no. 754, *MGH epp. saec. XIII*, vol. 2, 558–59).

5. Van Cleve, *Frederick II*, 463; he adds that the letter shows the pope's "true intentions" by its lack of specifics with regard to the emperor and "ominous" appeal to the Milanese.

6. Matthew Paris, *CM*, vol. 4, 256, 278; Menko, *Chronica*, *MGH SS*, vol. 23, 537; and *Annales S. Justinae Patavini*, *MGH SS*, vol. 19, 158.

7. See Innocent's letters to Berthold of Aquileia, 21 July 1243, no. 2, *MGH epp. saec. XIII*, vol. 2, 3–4; to the Dominican prior at Nandoralben (modern Belgrade), 13 July 1243, *VMHHS*, no. 345, 186–87; and to the Cistercian and Premonstratensian abbots in Dubrovnik, soliciting information about the Mongols' whereabouts, 22 July 1243, no. 3, *MGH epp. saec. XIII*, vol. 2, 4.

8. 2 August 1243, no. 27, *DN*, vol. 1, 21–22.

9. On the appointment of these three legates, on 10, 15, and 18 July 1243 respectively, nos. 10, 13, 27, *Reg. Inn.*, vol. 1, 3–4, 7. For the authorization of a ten-thousand hyperpyron subsidy in defense of the Latin Empire, 13 July 1243, no. 22, ibid., 6; on the rebuilding of Jerusalem's walls, 5 August 1243, no. 3, *Acta Inn.*, 4–5.

10. Salimbene of Adam, *CA*, vol. 1, 256; and Menko, *Chronica*, *MGH SS*, vol. 23, 537.

11. Frederick to Henry II, duke of Brabant, 28 June 1243, HB, vol. 6/1, 98–99. See also the letter attributed to the emperor and addressed to "all the faithful," June 1243, ibid., 101–3, that celebrates Innocent's election in similar terms. As noted by Huillard-Bréholles, the fact that the letter refers to Gregory IX as a "worthy rector of blessed memory" raises doubts about its attribution to Frederick. On the singing of hymns in the Regno, see Richard of San Germano, *Cronica*, 384.

12. 26 July, HB, vol. 6/1, 104–6. On this initial legation, see Richard of San Germano, *Cronica*, *MGH SS*, vol. 19, 384. The commonly told story of Frederick's reaction to Sinibaldo's election—claiming "I have lost my best friend, since he has become pope"—comes from a much later thirteenth-century source, Jacob de Aquis, *Chronicon*, 1583.

13. Nicholas of Carbio, *VI*, 262–63. On these negotiations, in addition to Melloni, *Innocenzo IV*, 71–74, see Rodenburg, "Friedensverhandlungen," 165–204. Rodenburg represents a rare exception to those who see immediate antagonism between the two sides, arguing that both the pope (facing Frederick's military dominance on the Italian peninsula) and the emperor (still excommunicate and dealing with the rebellion in Lombardy) had legitimate reasons for seeking an accommodation.

14. No. 7, *MGH epp. saec. XIII*, vol. 2, 112–13; also no. 240, *MGH Const.*, vol. 2, 239–40. Nicholas of Carbio, *VI*, 262, gives a similar list of demands from the pope, including the freeing of the captives from the destroyed Genoese fleet and the opening of blocked-off roadways.

15. 26 August 1243, no. 9, *MGH epp. saec. XIII*, vol. 2, 8–11 (also no. 241, *MGH Const.*, vol. 2, 330–31). On Zoën's activities in Provence, see Berger, *Saint Louis et Innocent IV*, 65–67, 71–72.

16. *MGH epp. saec. XIII*, vol. 2, 10.

17. 2 September 1243, no. 20, *MGH epp. saec. XIII*, vol. 2, 16; also no. 242, *MGH Const.*, vol. 2, 331–32.

18. Nicholas of Carbio, *VI*, 263. See Rodenburg, "Friedensverhandlungen," 169–70.

19. See Innocent's letter appointing an unnamed Perugian archpriest as the new rector of Spoleto and the papal patrimony in Tuscany, 26 August 1243, no. 10, *MGH epp. saec. XIII*, vol. 2, 11, with a series of related letters, nos. 11–13, ibid., 11–13. By early September, however, Innocent had appointed two different rectors, Philip, bishop of Camerino, and the abbot of Saint Severin in Orvieto (no. 18, ibid., 15–16). See also Innocent's letters confirming Marcellino as rector of Ancona, 26 August 1243, nos. 16–17, ibid., 14–15.

20. Innocent to the Perugians, 26 August 1243, no. 13, *MGH epp. saec. XIII*, vol. 2, 12–13; to Brescians, 7 November, no. 38, *MGH epp. saec. XIII*, vol. 2, 30; and to Alberic da Romano and Biaquino de Camino, 27 September 1243, no. 30, ibid., 21.

21. Writing to Marcellino of Arezzo (no. 16, *MGH epp. saec. XIII*, vol. 2, 14), Innocent confirmed his position as rector of Ancona and included instructions about absolving repentant imperial supporters in the march. Writing to the bishop of Arborea in Sardina (23 October 1243, no. 35, *MGH epp. saec.*

XIII, vol. 2, 28–29), the pope gave similar instructions regarding Adelasia di Torres, who had been excommunicated on account of her marriage to Enzio.

22. Innocent to the commune of Radicofani, 2 October 1243, no. 26, *MGH epp. saec. XIII*, vol. 2, 21–22, promising 740 Sienese pounds for the upkeep of the hostages; and to Assisi, 26 August, 6 October, and 7 November 1243, nos. 14, 28, and 37, ibid., 13–14, 23, 29–30.

23. 23 September 1243, no. 22, *MGH epp. saec. XIII*, vol. 2, 18, also no. 243, *MGH Const.*, vol. 2, 332; and 12 November 1243, no. 39, *MGH epp. saec. XIII*, vol. 2, 30–31.

24. BAV, Pal. Lat. 953, fols. 29r–78r. For this narrative about Viterbo's revolt and subsequent siege, see *AII*, vol. 1, 546–54. See also Nicholas of Carbio, *VI*, 263–64; Matthew Paris, *CM*, vol. 4, 266–67; *Annales S. Pantaleonis Coloniensis*, 538; and *Annales Placentini Gibellini*, 487.

25. September 1243, HB, vol. 6.1, 127–30. For additional letters about the siege, HB, vol. 6/1, 124–26.

26. *AII*, vol. 1, 147–48.

27. 7 October 1243, no. 30, *MGH epp. saec. XIII*, vol. 2, 24–25. Rainier and the envoys initially asked for funds to support five mounted soldiers and one thousand foot soldiers for a period of eight or fifteenth days. Innocent specified that the allocated funds should go toward foot soldiers, exclusively, which was more appropriate for defending a city under siege.

28. 11 October 1243, no. 32, *MGH epp. saec. XIII*, vol. 2, 26–27.

29. *AII*, vol. 1, 147–51.

30. HB, vol. 6/1, 140–42, 142–45.

31. For some general observations about the military roles of the Franciscans and Dominicans, see Bachrach, "Friars Go to War."

32. HB, vol. 6/1, 143–44.

33. *AII*, vol. 1, 552–53.

34. Matthew Paris, *CM*, vol. 4, 269.

35. Nicholas of Carbio, *VI*, 263.

36. Nicholas of Carbio, *VI*, 263.

37. The problem of debt from the fighting between the Roman church and Frederick emerged early in Innocent's papacy. In a letter to the prelates and clergy in the province of Bordeaux (30 July 1243, no. 62, *Reg. Inn.*, vol. 1, 16), Innocent authorized a one-twentieth tithe to help pay for expenses stemming from the "hardship of war," incurred when the archbishop of Bordeaux was captured during the attack on the Genoese fleet in May 1241. The archbishop later made a personal appearance before Innocent, begging for financial relief.

38. On Raymond's arrival at the imperial court in Melfi, Richard of San Germano, *Cronica*, 383–84. See also Innocent's letter to the archbishop of Bari, 2 December 1243, no. 40, *MGH epp. saec. XIII*, vol. 2, 31–32, and to Louis IX, 1 January 1244, no. 45, ibid., 35–36, telling the French king—who had labored to reconcile Raymond with the church—about the count's absolution.

39. January 1244, no. 244, *MGH Const.*, vol. 2, 332–33.

40. 12 and 28 March, nos. 245, 247–48, *MGH Const.*, vol. 2, 334, 337–38; also transcribed in *Annales Placentini Gibellini*, 487.

41. Nicholas of Carbio, *VI*, 264–65; *Annales S. Pantaleonis Coloniensis*, 538; *Annales Placentini Gibellini*, 487; and *Encyclica imperatoris de pace inita et de curia Veronae habenda*, April 1244, no. 249, *MGH Const.*, vol. 2, 338–40. Similar versions of the call for an assembly at Verona were circulated to individual prelates and "all the faithful throughout Italy." On Innocent's sermon, ibid., 339.

42. *Forma satisfactionis imperatoris*, no. 246, *MGH Const.*, vol. 2, 334–37, consisting of fifteen separate points.

43. Specifically, see nos. 5 and 15, no. 246, *MGH Const.*, vol. 2, 336–37. Matthew Paris, *CM*, vol. 4, 331–36, includes the first twelve points of these articles.

44. Matthew Paris, *CM*, vol. 4, 331–36; and Nicholas of Carbio, *VI*, 264–65.

45. *MGH Const.*, vol. 2, 33; and Frederick's letter to Bergamo, May 1244, HB, vol. 6/1, 192–95.

46. April 1244, HB, vol. 6/1, 183–84.

47. April 1244, HB, vol. 6/1, 185.

48. HB, vol. 6/1, 186.

49. 30 April 1244, no. 63, *MGH epp. saec. XIII*, vol. 2, 346.

50. 23 January 1244, no. 49, *MGH epp. saec. XIII*, vol. 2, 38.

51. See Innocent's marriage dispensations to Henry of Thuringia, 12 April 1244, Fredrick II, duke of Austria, 6 May 1244, and Albert, duke of Saxony, 15 May 1244, nos. 55, 67, 68, *MGH epp. saec. XIII*, vol. 2, 41–42, 48–49, 49; and Henry of Thuringia's three-year exemption from excommunication, 12 April, no. 58, ibid., 43.

52. Early June, HB, vol. 6/1, 197–99.

53. Nicholas of Carbio (*VI*, 265), writes that Innocent created twelve new cardinals: three bishops; three priests; and three deacons; Matthew Paris, *CM*, vol. 4, 354, records ten new cardinals on 29 May. The discrepancy relates to the fact that Innocent, en route to Genoa, met with and promoted Odo of Châteauroux, cardinal bishop of Tusculanum, and Hugh of St. Cher, cardinal priest of S. Sabina. See Bagliani, *CCFC*, vol. 2, 163–67.

54. Nicholas of Carbio, *VI*, 263.

55. Bartholomew the Scribe, *Annales*, 213–14.

56. Bartholomew the Scribe, *Annales*, 214–15; and Nicholas of Carbio, *VI*, 265–67.

57. Matthew Paris, *CM*, vol. 4, 353–56.

58. *Annales S. Justinae Patavini*, 158; and *Annales Placentini Gibellini*, 487–88.

59. Prov. 28:1.

60. August 1244, no. 251, *MGH Const.*, vol. 2, 341–52. See also Frederick's letter to the king of Hungary, August 1244, ibid., 352–53, which briefly relates his troubles with Pope Gregory and failed hopes for peace with Pope Innocent, referring the reader to the longer, accompanying encyclical letter for more details.

61. *MGH Const.*, vol. 2, 342.

62. *MGH Const.*, vol. 2, 345–46.

63. *MGH Const.*, vol. 2, 350.

64. *MGH Const.*, vol. 2, 350–51. In his letter sent to Louis IX in June (HB, vol. 6/1, 198), Frederick mentions his request to the pope for a meeting with an unnamed cardinal, presumably Otto, to discuss the restoration of church properties in Campagna.

65. Matthew Paris, *CM*, vol. 4, 356–57.

66. Matthew Paris, *CM*, vol. 4, 391–93, 409–10. See also Berger, *Saint Louis et Innocent IV*, 25–29.

67. Bartholomew the Scribe, *Annales*, 215.

68. Nicholas of Carbio, *VI*, 268–69. See also Melloni, *Innocenzo IV*, 77–80.

69. For reports on the Khwarezmian attacks, see Matthew Paris, *CM*, vol. 4, 306–11; *Waverly Annals*, 334–35; Bartholomew the Scribe, *Annales*, 216; and Albert of Stade, *Annales*, 369. See also Runciman, "Crusader States, 1243–1291," especially pp. 561–64.

70. Salimbene of Adam, *CA*, vol. 1, 268–69.

71. Matthew Paris, *CM*, vol. 4, 337–45. A version of Robert's letter features in a thirteenth-century cartulary from the Benedictine abbey of Saint Augustine, BL, add. 46352, fols. 50v–52v.

72. Matthew Paris, *CM*, vol. 4, 298–99, 345–36.

Chapter 6

1. Nicholas of Carbio, *VI*, 271.

2. *Dei virtus et*, 3 January 1245, no. 78, *MGH epp. saec. XIII*, vol. 2, 56–58.

3. For the pope's sentence, *COD*, 278–83; no. 124, *MGH epp. saec. XIII*, 88–94; and no. 400, *MGH Const.*, vol. 2, 508–12. On the council of Lyons and Innocent's deposition of the emperor, see Kempf, "La deposizione di Federico II"; Melloni, *Innocenzo IV*, 88–91; Baaken, *Ius Imperii ad Regnum*, 295–340; and Werzstein, "Deposition of Frederick."

4. Ullmann, "Frederick II's Opponent," 53. For similar appraisals, see Carlyle and Carlyle, *History of Mediaeval Political Theory*, 300–301; Berger, *Saint Louis et Innocent IV*, 115–38; and Kempf, "La deposizione di Federico II."

5. On the figure of Melchizedek (Gen. 14:18–20) in thirteenth-century papal ideology, see Pennington, "Pope Innocent III's Views."

6. See Kantorowicz, *Frederick the Second*, 596, which describes the gathering as a "court of hostile priests"; Van Cleve, *Frederick II*, 484, where he observes "From the outset it was apparent that the Council would act in obedience to the desires of the Pope and the Curia"; and Rader, *Friedrich II*, 476, where he opines "Juristisch betrachtet war das Shauspiel ein Farce." Others have insisted that the trial, regardless of its political or moral dubiousness, did more or less follow existing judicial procedures, including Marazzato, "L'appello di Federico II"; and Werzstein, "Deposition of Frederick II."

7. For a discussion of church councils in the later Middle Ages as a "forum for public opinion," Miethke, "Die Konzilien als Forum der öffentlichen Meinung."

8. Such as when Innocent II fled to French kingdom during the papal schism with Anacletus II in the 1130s. See Montaubin, "Innocent II and Capetian France."

9. Maccarrone, "*Ubi est papa, ibi est Roma.*" This formulation, with its roots in the twelfth century, developed in part due to Innocent IV's long stay at Lyons and achieved juridical codification in the works of Innocent's contemporary, Hostiensis, in the 1250s.

10. Nicholas of Carbio, *VI*, 269.

11. *Annales S. Pantaleonis Coloniensis*, 539.

12. Matthew Paris (*CM*, vol. 4, 390) writes that Grosseteste went to Lyons for "secret negotiations" with the pope. See also Matthew Paris, *HA*, vol. 2, 498, 505; and *Waverly Annals*, 335.

13. Lambeth Palace Library, *Illam de vestre*, 20 December 1244, no. 37, preserves an original copy of one version of this letter sent to Bury St. Edmunds, demanding payment of the tithe in arrears and commissioning Master Martin to make the collection. The text more or less repeats the version found in Matthew Paris, *CM*, vol. 4, 369–70.

14. Matthew Paris, *CM*, vol. 4, 429.

15. Matthew Paris, *CM*, vol. 4, 418; and Matthew Paris, *HA*, vol. 2, 501. In the deluxe manuscript of the *Historia Anglorum*, Royal 14 C VIII, fol. 138r, this modified account of the fire was inserted later, on a small piece of parchment sewn over the original folio (from the word *noctium* to *feliciter*). According to the Roll Series edition of the *HA*, vol. 2, 501n6, the original wording is legible underneath and closely follows the description of the fire found in the *Major Chronicle*. Presumably, Matthew heard rumors about the fire later and changed his account accordingly.

16. Matthew Paris, *CM*, vol. 4, 417–18.

17. *Relatio de concilio Lugdunensi*, *MGH Const.*, vol. 2, 515. Lunt, in "Sources for the First Council of Lyons," identifies the anonymous author of the *Relatio* as a member of the curia, present at the council for its deliberations. Lunt (ibid., 75–76) describes the text as "dry" and compares it unfavorably to Matthew Paris's rambling but "exceptionally good" story. See also Tangl, "Die soganannte *Brevis nota*."

18. Matthew Paris, *CM*, vol. 4, 386–89; and *Burton Annals*, *AM*, vol. 1, 271–75.

19. Nicholas of Carbio, *VI*, 269. During the spring of 1245, Innocent renewed several of Gregory IX's missionary bulls for the mendicants, including the apocalyptically themed *Cum hora undecima*, 22 March 1245, no. 119, *Acta Inn.*, 36–42. See Whalen, *Dominion of God*, 159–70.

20. 5 March 1245, no. 102, *MGH epp. saec. XIII*, vol. 2, 72–73; and 13 March 1245, no. 105, ibid., 74–77. See Richard, *La papauté et les missions d'Orient*, 65–120.

21. These materials sent to the pope, nos. 52–56, *Acta Inn.*, 95–108, are undated but included in the curial letters for 1247 (nos. 3035–39, *Reg. Inn.*, 455–56). For Simon's letter to Frederick and his address to Louis IX, see Claverie, "Deux lettres."

22. Salimbene of Adam, *CA*, vol. 1, 111–18. See also John of Plano Carpini, *Itinera et relationes fratrum minorum*, 3–130; for a Latin translation of Güyük's letter, included in the travel account by John's companion, see Benedict the Pole, ibid., 142–43. See also Legassie, *Medieval Invention of Travel*, 21–58.

23. The papal curia faced mundane reminders of the recent devastation caused by the barbarians, and granted permission for clergy to retain additional or multiple benefices if the invaders had

destroyed the ones they already possessed, e.g., 21 December 1244, no. 824, *Reg. Inn.*, vol. 1, 139; and 22 February, 1245, no. 1068, ibid., 168–69.

24. *Annales S. Pantaleonis Coloniensis*, 538. Matthew Paris, *CM*, vol. 4, 337–45, transcribes one such letter, bearing "twelve seals" and sent in the name of Robert, patriarch of Jerusalem, along with various bishops, abbots, and members of the military orders. See also *Burton Annals*, 257–63. Salimbene of Adam, *CA*, vol. 1, 268–69, includes another version of a much shorter letter about the Khwarezmian Turks, also attributed to Robert.

25. Bartholomew the Scribe, *Annales*, 217; and *Annales Placentini Gibellini*, 488–89.

26. Nicholas of Carbio, *VI*, 271. On the requirement for a written summons (*legitima inscriptio*) to legal judgment, see canon no. 8, *CCQL*, 54–57.

27. Boos, *Chronicon Wormatiense*, 180. Also, Bachrach, "Making Peace and War." On the renewal of the emperor's ban, *Annales Placentini Gibellini*, 489.

28. See Innocent's letter to Conrad, bishop of Cologne, 9 May 1245, *Reg. Inn.*, vol. 1, 192, which was sent in the "same way" to eighteen other bishops and clergy in the region.

29. Boos, *Chronicon Wormatiense*, 180; and Matthew Paris, *CM*, vol. 4, 406–7.

30. See Albert's letter to Cardinal Rainier, March 1245, no. 255, *MGH Const.*, vol. 2, 565–66; and Innocent IV's letter to Albert, reviewing the circumstances of his presence at the imperial court, 30 April 1245, no. 258, ibid., 355.

31. April 1245, no. 256, *MGH Const.*, vol. 2, 354–55.

32. 6 May 1245, no. 259, ibid., 357. Innocent granted permission for Albert to absolve the emperor if he met all of the pope's conditions.

33. April 1245, no. 57, *MGH Const.*, vol. 2, 355–56; after 8 May 1245, no. 720, *AII*, vol. 1, 566–67; and May 1245, no. 721, ibid., 567.

34. For Henry III's letters, 8 June, Rymer and Sanderson, *Foedera*, vol. 1, pt.1, 152–83. See also Cole, *Documents Illustrative of English History*, 351–57, for a series of documents relating to the English delegation at Lyons, including a brief description of the council's opening session; details on the English delegation; Thaddeus of Suessa's written appeal on Frederick's behalf; a letter sent from the English barons to the cardinals (cf. Matthew Paris, *CM*, vol. 4, 441–42); and a list of "grievances and oppressions" suffered by the English church with replies from the curia (cf. Matthew Paris, *CM*, vol. 4, 527–29). Cole bases his edition of these materials on an original manuscript briefly described as a "roll" (the first of three) dating to the period of Henry III and Edward I and haphazardly deposited in the Queen's Remembrancer department of the Exchequer. See also Lunt ("Sources for the First Council of Lyons," 73), who relies on the Cole edition. Apparently unknown to Cole or Lunt, London, BL, Cotton Cleopatra E 1, vol. 1, fols. 183r–185r, includes a near contemporary copy of the same series of documents for the first council of Lyons in a codex containing miscellaneous royal and papal charters and letters from the twelfth to fourteenth centuries.

35. On the council's attendees, see Nicholas of Carbio, *VI*, 271–73; Matthew Paris, *CM*, vol. 4, 430–31; *Relatio de concilio Lugdunensi*, *MGH Const.*, vol. 2, 513; Bartholomew the Scribe, *Annales*, 216; Menko, *Chronica*, 538 (who numbers three hundred bishops and abbots); *Annales Erphordenses*, 34 (250 bishops); *Annales S. Pantaleonis Coloniensis*, 539 (150 bishops); and William de Puylaurens, *Chronique*, 176, 178.

36. Matthew Paris, *CM*, vol. 4, 431–34; and Matthew Paris, *HA*, vol. 2, 507.

37. See Schaller, "Endzeit-Erwartungen und Antichrist-Vorstellungen," especially p. 938.

38. On Rainier's central role in such propagandistic productions, see Maleczek, "La propaganda antiimperiale," 292–96; Thumser, "Kardinal Rainer von Viterbo"; and Hampe, "Über die Flugschriften."

39. *Iuxta vatacinium Ysaie*, June 1245, no. 51, in Frenz and Herde, *Das Brief- und Memorialbuch*, 191–212. Also no. 1037a, *AII*, vol. 2, 709–15. Cf. Isa. 28:17.

40. *Iuxta vatacinium Ysaie*, Frenz and Herde, *Das Brief- und Memorialbuch*, 209.

41. *Aspidis ova reperant*, June 1245, no. 54, Frenz and Herde, *Das Brief- und Memorialbuch*, 215–26; also no. 1037 (II), *AII*, vol. 2, 717–21. Cf. Isa. 59:5.

42. *Aspidis ova reperant*, Frenz and Herde, *Das Brief- und Memorialbuch*, 220. Cf. 2 Chron. 26:18.

43. Frenz and Herde, *Das Brief- und Memorialbuch*, 224, seems to be referring to Frederick's widely circulating letter *Levate in circuitu*. For good measure, *Aspidis ova reperunt*, ibid., 225–26, ends by suggesting that foul play might have been involved with the death of the emperor's three wives.

44. June 1245, HB, vol. 6/1, 275–77.

45. *Relatio de concilio Lugdunensi*, *MGH Const.*, vol. 2, 513.

46. *Relatio de concilio Lugdunensi*, *MGH Const.*, vol. 2, 514.

47. Matthew Paris, *CM*, vol. 4, 434–35, offers a slightly different version of the pope's sermon: one based on Lamentations 1:12 and comparing the five wounds of Christ on the cross to the Christian people's five sources of grief—the Tartars, the Greeks, the rise of "new heresies," the sack of Jerusalem, and Frederick, who was "supposed to be the protector and defender of the church" but had become its "powerful enemy." The documents produced by the returning English delegation (Cole, *Documents Illustrative of English History*, 381) align more closely with the *Relatio de concilio Lugdunensi*, saying that the pope proposed "five articles," the first being a set of "rules and constitutions for the entire general church" followed by aid to the Holy Land; assistance for the Latin Empire; placing the "arm of the church" against the Tartars; and "for making peace between the church and emperor." Cf. London, BL, Cotton Cleopatra E 1, fol. 183r.

48. *Relatio de concilio Lugdunensi*, *MGH Const.*, vol. 2, 514.

49. *Relatio de concilio Lugdunensi*, *MGH Const.*, vol. 2, 515.

50. Matthew Paris, *CM*, vol. 4, 434–35.

51. *Relatio de concilio Lugdunensi*, *MGH Const.*, vol. 2, 515.

52. Matthew Paris, *CM*, vol. 4, 437–39.

53. *Relatio de concilio Lugdunensi*, *MGH Const.*, vol. 2, 515; and Matthew Paris, *CM*, vol. 4, 437.

54. Matthew Paris, *CM*, vol. 4, 437. At Pisa around June 1245, according to Bartholomew the Scribe, *Annales*, 216, Frederick had denounced the Genoese as "traitors" to the empire, declaring his intention to destroy them and transfer their privileges to the Pisans.

55. *Confusa est mater*, late June 1245, no. 723, *AII*, vol. 1, 568–79.

56. Matthew Paris (*CM*, vol. 4, 440) writes that Thaddeus of Suessa expressed concerns at the council of Lyons that the duke of Austria's niece would refuse to marry Frederick due to his impending judgment. Bartholomew the Scribe (*Annales*, 217) asserts that when the duke received a letter from the pope instructing him to put off the marriage for as long as Frederick remained disobedient to the church, he ended the nuptial negotiations, angering Frederick even more against the pope.

57. For an edition of this sermon and a convincing argument for its deliverance at Lyons, Charansonnet, *L'université, l'eglise et l'etate*, vol. 1, 119–29; and vol. 2, 708–13.

58. Charansonnet, *L'université, l'eglise et l'etate*, 713.

59. *Relatio de concilio Lugdunensi*, *MGH Const.*, vol. 2, 516.

60. *COD*, 295–301. The constitution on the crusade more or less repeats canon 71 from the Fourth Lateran Council, *CCQL*, 110–18. See Purcell, *Papal Crusading Policy*, 187–99.

61. *COD*, 283–93. The initial twenty-two constitutions issued at Lyons, along with those calling for action in the Holy Land, in the Latin Empire, and against the Tartars, are copied into Innocent's Register, Vat. Lat. 21, fols. 210r–212v (no. 1368, *Reg. Inn.*). Multiple versions of the twenty-two constitutions, transmitted and added to canonical legal collections, appear in various recensions. Innocent formally issued the first version of twenty-two constitutions from Lyons on 25 May 1245; a second version followed, featuring twelve more constitutions added to the initial group on 21 April 1246; and a third, consisting of the prior constitutions with another eight added on 2 September 1253. See Kuttner, "Die Konstitutionen." Nineteen of the original twenty-two constitutions—plus the decree for a new expedition to the Holy Land—feature in Matthew Paris, *CM*, vol. 4, 456–72. The call for aid to the Holy Land features also in *Burton Annals*, 267–71. Noticing the lack of general "reformist" canons issued at Lyons, scholars have sometimes sensed the waning of the "Gregorian" spirit, the beginnings of malaise in the papal monarchy, e.g., *COD*, 274; and Morris, *Papal Monarchy*, 567–68. Yet the need for overall pastoral and disciplinary reforms, just thirty years after the comprehensive canons issued at the Fourth Lateran Council, might have seemed less than pressing. The necessity for judicial reforms no

doubt seemed a high priority for the legally trained pope. See Longère, "Le concile oecuménique Lyon."

62. *Relatio de concilio Lugdunensi*, *MGH Const.*, vol. 2, 516.

63. The resulting documents possess a fascinating history in their own right. Innocent subsequently deposited the original seventeen rolls at the monastery of Cluny, where they remained until the destruction of the monastic house in the eighteenth century, when they were hidden, lost, or most likely destroyed, except for one. For the surviving roll, see Paris, BNF Lat. 8989. Not long before the rolls were lost, copies were made by Lambert de Barive, including illustrations of the various seals appended, also held at the BNF, Lat. 8990; and Lat. nouv. acq. 2128. For the Vatican Library manuscript, the one consulted for this study, see Rome, BAV, Ottob. Lat. 2546. See also the brief entry in HB, vol. 1, 6/1, 316–17. On the "Transcripts of Cluny" or "Rouleaux de Cluny," Huillard-Bréholles, "Examen des chartes"; Battelli, "I transunti di Lione"; and Clementi, "Further Notes."

64. As observed by Clementi ("Further Notes," 190), it "would appear that the Transcripts of Lyons of 1245' served a double purpose: they were in the first place a collection of documents of the title deeds of the temporal rights of the Apostolic See and secondly they were intended to justify the papal sentence of deposition pronounced against the emperor Frederick in 1245." As he notes, there has been some debate about this claim, due to the inclusion of documents that have nothing to do with papal-Hohenstaufen relations. Clementi takes seriously the stated purpose of collection in its preamble to preserve materials that might otherwise be lost, pointing out that Innocent's flight to Lyons and the ongoing threat posed by Frederick might have jeopardized the condition of the papal archives. He also observes that other royal powers besides Frederick with representatives at Lyons, such as the English crown, took issue with certain papal privileges.

65. Cf. Matt. 3:9.

66. *Annales Placentini Gibellini*, 489.

67. *Relatio de concilio Lugdunensi*, 508–9.

68. For a comparison between the sentence of deposition and some of its textual sources, see Baaken, *Ius Imperii ad Regnum*, 319–31.

69. *Relatio de concilio Lugdunensi*, *MGH Const.*, vol. 2, 509–10.

70. *Relatio de concilio Lugdunensi*, *MGH Const.*, vol. 2, 511.

71. *Relatio de concilio Lugdunensi*, *MGH Const.*, vol. 2, 510–11.

72. *Relatio de concilio Lugdunensi*, *MGH Const.*, vol. 2, 512.

73. *Relatio de concilio Lugdunensi*, *MGH Const.*, vol. 2, 512.

74. London, BL, Royal ms. 14 C V II, fol. 138v. See Matthew Paris, *HA*, vol. 2, 506; and Matthew Paris, *CM*, vol. 4, 446.

75. *Relatio de concilio Lugdunensi*, *MGH Const.*, vol. 2, 516.

76. Matthew Paris, *CM*, vol. 4, 473; *Relatio de concilio Lugdunensi*, *MGH Const.*, vol. 2, 512.

77. Nicholas of Carbio (*VI*, 272–73) points to the example of Alexander III excommunicating Frederick I; and to Innocent III excommunicating and deposing Otto IV of Brunswick. Innocent III, however, never formally issued a sentence deposing Otto, although he did excommunicate him and absolve his followers from their vows of fidelity. See Tillmann, "Datierungsfragen." Perhaps to reinforce this point, just days after the council of Lyons, the pope issued *Grandi non immerito*, calling upon the ruling elite of Portugal to remove their "imbecile" king, Sancho II, from office and to replace him with his brother, Alfonso. Nicholas of Carbio, *VI*, 273–74; and 24 July 1245, no. 1389, *Reg. Inn.*, vol. 1, 212. On this under-studied episode, see Peters, "Rex Inutilis."

78. *Relatio de concilio Lugdunensi*, *MGH Const.*, vol. 2, 516.

79. Mathew Paris, *CM*, vol. 4, 479–80. This letter does not feature in Innocent's register.

80. Albert of Stade, *Annales*, 369. See also Matthew Paris (*CM*, vol. 4, 610–13), who writes that the pope sent cardinals out to the "four corners of the world" to denounce Frederick.

81. E.g., Paris, Archives Nationales, L 245, no. 84. The National Archives, London, 7/64/47, preserve a contemporary transcription of the sentence. See also Baaken, *Ius Imperii ad Regnum*, 336.

82. See Matthew Paris, *CM*, vol. 4, 445–55; *Annales Placentini Gibellini*, 489–91; and *Annales S. Justinae Patavini*, 159. The *Annales S. Pantaleonis Coloniensis*, 540, refer the reader to another volume in

his monastery's collection where one might could read the full sentence. See also Menko, *Chronica*, 538–39; the *Burton Annals*, 267; the *Dunstable Annals*, 168; and the *Osney-Wykes Annals*, 93.

83. *Chronica S. Petri Erfordensis*, 34.

84. See Baaken, "Die Verhandlungen von Cluny," including pp. 578–79 for an edition of the letter *Dei filii qui*, 13 December 1245.

85. 21 December 1245, *BOP*, vol. 1, 158. The pope continued to rely upon the Dominicans to broadcast the terms of the deposition. During the general chapter meetings at Paris in 1246, 1247, and 1248 (Reichert, *Acta capitulorum*, vol. 3, 37, 39 and 42), the assembled friars codified their commitment to support the church and pope in "word and deed," avoiding any impression that they favored the deposed emperor.

86. Sambin, no. 50, *Problemi politici*, 67–68. Innocent sent a similar letter to the duke of Burgundy, no. 51, ibid., 68.

87. No. 399, *MGH Const.*, vol. 2, 508; and Cole, *Documents Illustrative of English History*, 351.

88. 31 July 1245, HB, vol. 6/1, 331–37.

89. February 1246, HB, vol. 6/1, 390–93.

90. No. 32, Frenz and Herde, *Das Brief- und Memorialbuch*, 102–11, presents *Eger cui lenia* after *Etsi causae* and *Illos felices* as a response to those letters. Edition also no. 1035, *AII*, vol. 2, 696–703.

91. Frenz and Herde, *Das Brief- und Memorialbuch*, 104–5.

92. Frenz and Herde, *Das Brief- und Memorialbuch*, 105–6.

93. *Eger cui lenia* does not appear in Innocent's official register, thereby contributing to the debates over its authenticity and authorship. For some scholars, the entire trajectory of the "papal monarchy" seems to hang on this text, which is linked to the question of whether Innocent IV was a "hierocratic" or "dualistic" thinker. For an extended discussion and critical edition of the letter, see Herde, "Ein Pamphlet." See also the important contribution by Cantini, "De autonomia judicis saecularis," which defends Innocent IV as a "dualist" against earlier scholars who portray him—rather than Innocent III—as an aspirational papal absolutist. Cantini rejects Innocent's authorship of the text, since its strident "monistic" opinions do not square with the overall "dualist" nature of Innocent IV's legal thought. Watt ("Theory of Papal Monarchy," 241–42n14), by contrast, sees *Eger cui lenia* as authentic, even though the letter was not included in the papal register. Critiquing Cantini's forced efforts to make Innocent IV into a "dualist," Tierney ("Continuity of Papal Political Theory") suggests that *Eger cui lenia* emerged from the papal curia and reflected the pope's position, even if he did not personally compose the text. For Tierney, who distinguishes between papal claims to power in "actual" and "potential" terms, the text itself represents a less absolutist view than many have argued in the past. Herde offers a similar analysis to that of Tierney, arguing that the letter reflects the sentiments of the pope and his curia, even if Innocent did not personally write the text.

94. Even in this provocative letter, one finds distinctions between the pope's "potential" possession of the "material sword" and the emperor's actual wielding of its power. See Tierney, "Continuity of Papal Political Theory," 236–42.

95. Matthew Paris, *CM*, vol. 4, 475–77, 538–44, wrongly places *Etsi causae* in 1246.

96. Matthew Paris, *CM*, vol. 4, 474.

97. Roland of Padua, *Chronica*, 82.

Chapter 7

1. In terms of accessibility, the early modern print edition of Innocent's *Commentaria Innocentii quarti pontificis maximi super libros quinque decretalium* (Frankfurt, 1570) remains the most widely available version of the text, although it contains sometimes significant errors. While I cite the Frankfurt edition, I have also checked my readings of important passages against an early manuscript of the *Commentaria* or *Apparatus*, BAV, Lat. Ross. 957. On Innocent's place in the canon law tradition and juridical formulation of the papal monarchy, see Pacaut, "L'autorité pontificale"; Hageneder, "Das päpstliche Recht der Fürstenabsetzung"; Watt, "Theory of Papal Monarchy," especially pp. 236–50; and Le Bras, "Innocent IV Romaniste."

2. *CQD*, 2.2.10, fols. 197va–198rb, fols. 316vb–317va. See Martin, "Biblical Authority." Around 1250–51, the influential canon law commentator Henry of Segusio, cardinal bishop of Ostia (typically known as Hostiensis), offered a similar appraisal of the proceedings at Lyon. Present at the council, he later included his legal opinion about the deposition in his canon law commentaries, the *Apparatus* and *Summa aurea*. For an analysis and edition of the relevant excerpts, see Watt, "Medieval Deposition Theory."

3. Morris, *Papal Monarchy*, 566.

4. See Melloni, "Ecclesiologia ed institutioni"; and Melloni, *Innocenzo IV*, 101–31.

5. On Philip's assignment to Germany, Nicholas of Carbio, *VI*, 275; *Annales S. Justinae Patavini*, 159; and the papal commission for his legation, 5 July 1246, and same date, nos. 203–4, *MGH epp. saec. XIII*, vol. 2, 154–56, plus nos. 204–5, ibid., 154–57. Innocent replaced Philip with Peter Capocci in March 1247 (no. 303, ibid., 303, 226–30).

6. 26 April 1246, no. 168, *MGH epp. saec. XIII*, vol. 2, 126–27.

7. Among other examples, nos. 256, 295, 360, 381, 454, 500, 668, and 699, *MGH epp. saec. XIII*, vol. 2, 191, 220, 266, 280–81, 326–27, 353, 478–79, 519. As Innocent acknowledged, granting the privilege to confer benefices upon non-cardinal legates ran counter to the new rules established at the council of Lyons.

8. For typical examples of such measures, nos. 252, 285, 400, 528, 698, 702, *MGH epp. saec. XIII*, vol. 2, 188–89, 213, 295–96, 370, 512, 520.

9. February–March 1246, HB, vol. 6/1, 393–94.

10. This letter features in the collection of Innocent's letters at the Biblioteca Antoniana at Padua (cod. 79) edited in no. 17, Sambin, *Problemi politici*, 48. Like most of the letters in the collection, its specific date is unknown but seems to be ca. 1246–47.

11. HB, vol. 6/2, 580–81.

12. Nos. 233, 266, 417, 451, 530, 638, *MGH epp. saec. XIII*, vol. 2, 172, 197–98, 302–3, 325, 371, 455.

13. 15 March 1247, no. 303, *MGH epp. saec. XIII*, vol. 2, 280; and 4 June 1247, no. 380, ibid., vol. 2, 280.

14. 13 May 1248, no. 554, *MGH epp. saec. XIII*, vol. 2, 392–93.

15. 21 August 1245, no. 131, *MGH epp. saec. XIII*, vol. 2, 98–99. See also Innocent's response to an appeal from King Henry of Cyprus, asking for assurances about his release from his oaths to the Hohenstaufen ruler, 5 March 1247, no. 291, ibid., 218–19.

16. Albert eventually married Margaret in 1255.

17. On these marriage negotiations, see Marc-Bonnet, "Le saint-siège."

18. 13–15 April 1247, no. 322, *MGH epp. saec. XIII*, vol. 2, 242–43. The pope did not always get what he wanted from the marriage bed. Despite his best efforts to prevent the union, in 1246, Frederick's son Conrad married Otto II's daughter, Elizabeth, cementing the duke of Bavaria's new alliance with the emperor. See the *Annales Augustani minores*, 9. In July 1246, Albert Beiham had written to Otto, forbidding this proposed marriage (HB, vol. 6/1, 446–47).

19. 22 May 1246, no. 187, *MGH epp. saec. XIII*, vol. 2, 141–43. In his description of Frederick's letter *Etsi causae*, Matthew Paris (*CM*, vol. 4, 544) claims that the emperor wrote the epistle to restore the damage done to his reputation by the charges of heresy.

20. *MGH epp. saec. XIII*, vol. 2, 142.

21. Late May 1246, HB, vol. 1, 6/1, 428–29.

22. As Frederick explained in a letter to Henry, February or March 1247, HB, vol. 6/1, 502–3. On Henry III's possible interest in brokering a peace between Innocent and Frederick, see Weiler, *Henry III*, 112–15.

23. On Louis's crusade plans and attempts to mediate between the pope and emperor, see Richard, *Saint Louis*, 99–112; Jordan, *Louis IX*, 26–30; and Le Goff, *Saint Louis*, 128–50.

24. Le Goff, *Saint Louis*, 114. On his side, Frederick tried to appeal to Louis by promising support for his upcoming crusade. See Frederick's letter to his officials in Italy, November 1246, instructing them to provide supplies to Louis' forces, and Louis's letter to Frederick thanking him for his aid, February–March 1247, HB, vol. 6/2, 500–502.

25. Matthew Paris, *CM*, vol. 4, 484–85, and vol. 5, 22–23.

26. August 1248, HB, vol. 6/2, 643–44. See also Frederick's letter to Henry III telling him about the failure of Louis' efforts with the pope, HB, vol. 2, 644–46. During this period, Innocent apparently faced resistance in the kingdom of France from the so-called Baron's League due in part to his calls for increased taxes and subsiding to fund the crusading effort against the emperor. According to some sources, the pope suspected that Frederick lay behind the protests. See the various reports and documents in Matthew Paris, *CM*, vol. 4, 561–62, and vol. 6, 99–112, 131. See also Campbell, "Protest of St. Louis."

27. Innocent relayed news of the repeated sentence to the prelates and other clergy in Germany, 18 April 1248, no. 541, *MGH epp. saec. XIII*, vol. 2, 378–80.

28. Matthew Paris, *CM*, vol. 5, 171–74. This letter does not appear in the papal register.

29. *MGH Const.*, vol. 2, 512.

30. Albert of Stade, *Annales*, 369. See the essays in Werner, *Heinrich Raspe*.

31. Matthew Paris, *CM*, vol. 4, 268–69, 495–96.

32. 16 Aril 1246, no. 159, *MGH epp. saec. XIII*, vol. 2, 120–21; and nos. 160–62, ibid., 121–23. On Henry's election, see Nicholas of Carbio, *VI*, 275.

33. Albert of Stade, *Annales*, 370.

34. On these activities, among other examples, see Innocent's letters to the nobles of Germany, 5 July 1246, no. 206, *MGH epp. saec. XIII*, vol. 2, 158; and to Philip of Ferrara and Henry Raspe, nos. 208–9, ibid., 159–60. On the bishops who refused to attend Henry's assembly, see 13 August 1246, no. 39, Frenz and Herde, *Das Brief- und Memorialbuch*, 126–30. For examples of Innocent's communications with the Franciscans, see nos. 131, 181, *BF*, vol. 1, 411, 447.

35. Nicholas of Carbio, *VI*, 275; *Annales S. Pantaleonis Coloniensis*, 541; and *Annales Erphordenses*, 35.

36. Mathew Paris, *CM*, vol. 4, 536–37, 544–45, 561–66, 617–19.

37. Matthew Paris, *CM*, vol. 4, 544–45, 551. See also Frederick's letter in September 1245 (HB, vol. 6/1, 359–61) calling for a subsidy to fund his war efforts after the pope rejected his appeals for peace, along with a similar letter sent to his son Enzio, HB, vol. 6/1, 361–62.

38. *Annales Erphordenses*, 34–35; and *Annales S. Justinae Patavini*, 159.

39. Albert of Stade, *Annales*, 369; *Annales Erphordenses*, 35; and *Annales maximi Coloniensis*, 540–41.

40. Innocent to the archbishop of Mainz and his suffragans, 27 June 1246, no. 199, *MGH epp. saec. XIII*, vol. 2, 150–51.

41. See Innocent's instructions for Peter Capocci to preach the cross against Frederick, given on 19 November 1247, no. 465, *MGH epp. saec. XIII*, vol. 2, 327–28, which refers to Frederick as the "devil's member, minister of Satan, and herald of Antichrist."

42. The sentiments of Abulafia, *Frederick II*, 386, are typical: "The decision of Pope Innocent IV to take much further Gregory IX's appeals for a crusade against Frederick was of momentous importance. It represents the first large-scale attempt to use the crusade as an instrument for the defeat of the papacy's political enemies within western Europe."

43. 7 July 1246, no. 222, *MGH epp. saec. XIII*, vol. 2, 166.

44. 31 August 1247, no. 425, *MGH epp. saec. XIII*, vol. 2, 309.

45. 5 July 1246, no. 214, *MGH epp. saec. XIII*, 161–62. Anticipating Louis IX's crusading expedition, in a separate letter to the cardinal bishop of Tusculum, 5 July 1247, no. 408, ibid., 296–97, the pope instructed him to enforce crusade vows for the Holy Land, not allowing their commutation into other forms of service. Examples of papal calls for crusade preaching against Frederick ca. 1246–49 include nos. 309, 453, 465, 504, 547, 589, and 630, *MGH epp. saec. XIII*, vol. 2, 234–35, 326, 332, 355–56, 385–86, 418, and 448–49.

46. Menko, *Chronica*, 539–40.

47. Matthew Paris, *CM*, vol. 4, 548.

48. Nicholas of Carbio, *VI*, 275, describes how the captives swore loyalty to Henry. See also Albert of Stade, *Annales*, 370; *Annales S. Pantaleonis Coloniensis*, 541; *Annales Erphordenses*, 35; *Gesta*

Treverorum Continuata, 412; and Henry Raspe's letter to Milan about his victory over Conrad, August 1246, HB, vol. 6/1, 451–52.

49. Salimbene of Adam, *CA*, vol. 2, 600–601.

50. On 20 November 1247, Innocent authorized Peter Capocci to commute the crusade vows of five unnamed soldiers from France and fifteen from Germany to fight for William of Holland, 20 November 1247, no. 4060, *Reg, Inn.*, vol. 1, 617. See also the pope's calls for crusade preaching on William's behalf, January and February 1249, nos. 630–31, 655, *MGH epp. saec. XIII*, vol. 2, 448–50, 469–70.

51. On William of Holland's election, including the involvement of Peter Capocci, see Nicholas of Carbio, *VI*, 275–76; Albert of Stade, *Annales*, 371; Bartholomew the Scribe, *Annales*, 223; *Annales S. Pantaleonis Coloniensis*, 541–42; *Annales Erphordenses*, 35; *Annales S. Justinae Patavini*, 160; and Matthew Paris, *CM*, vol. 4, 624–25, 639–40, 653–54. On the siege of Aachen, see Matthew Paris, *CM*, vol. 5, 25–27; *Annales S. Pantaleonis Coloniensis*, 543; and Menko, *Chronica*, 541. On 8 December 1248, Innocent wrote the citizens of Aachen (HB, vol. 6/2, 681–89), calling upon them to return to the obedience of the church and recognize the sentence passed against Frederick at Lyons.

52. *Annales S. Pantaleonis Coloniensis*, 543. The archbishop of Cologne, the chronicler tells us, later relaxed Peter's ill-advised excommunications.

53. Nicholas of Carbio, *VI*, 275; *Annales S. Pantaleonis Coloniensis*, 545; *Annales Erphordenses*, 35; and Menko, *Chronica*, 541–42.

54. *MGH Const.*, vol. 2, 512.

55. Bartholomew the Scribe, *Annales*, 217; and Nicholas of Carbio, *VI*, 276. Nicholas describes a plot hatched by Frederick and Amadeus of Savoy to seize pope at Lyons. In November 1248, Frederick delegated authority for Amadeus of Savoy and his brother Thomas to act as his representatives at the papal curia (no. 271, *MGH Const.*, vol. 2, 379). See also his letter "remitting all rancor" toward Boniface of Montferrat, HB, vol. 6/1, 329–31. In the winter 1247–48, Boniface changed sides again, returning to the side of the church: *Annales Placentini Gibellini*, 494.

56. No. 168, *MGH epp. saec. XIII*, vol. 2, 126–27. Weiler (*Henry III*, 114) misconstrues this particular episode as an overture for peace between Innocent and Frederick, claiming that the pope gave the cardinals permission to absolve Frederick, rather than his followers as an incentive for their return to the side of the church.

57. In addition to no. 168, *MGH epp. saec. XIII*, vol. 2, 126–27, see the series of letters relating to Stephen Conti and Rainier of Viterbo's legation to the Regno, nos. 170–73, ibid., vol. 2, 128–30; Innocent's letter to the Roman senate and people, late April 1246, no. 174, ibid., 131; and his letter to the prelates and lay persons in the papal patrimony, same date, no. 175, ibid., 134–35.

58. 11 October 1246, no. 247, *MGH epp. saec. XIII*, vol. 2, 184–85.

59. 8 March 1247, no. 292, *MGH epp. saec. XIII*, vol. 2, 219; and no. 296, ibid., 221. According to Nicholas of Carbio, *VI*, 275, the pope allocated fourteen thousand silver marks to the cardinal deacon to pay for military stipends.

60. *Annales S. Pantaleonis Coloniensis*, 540. This particular expedition did not end well for the cardinal, as forces from Foglino and Spoleto reinforced by German troops routed the Perugians. See Innocent's consolatory letters to the Perugians and Rainier, in nos. 13–14, Sambin, *Problemi politici*, 45–46.

61. On Parma's revolt, see Nicholas of Carbio, *VI*, 276–77; *Annales Placentini Gibellini*, 494; Bartholomew the Scribe, *Annales*, 219, 221–22; Matthew Paris, *CM*, vol. 4, 637–38, 648–49; *Annales S. Justinae Patavini*, 160; *Annales S. Pantaleonis Coloniensis*, 541.

62. Salimbene of Adam, *CA*, vol. 1, 78, 88–89, 286–301.

63. Salimbene of Adam, *CA*, vol. 1, 289.

64. Writing to the bishop of Winchester (30 May 1247, HB, vol. 6/1, 536–37), Innocent described Frederick's proposal to come to the curia, raising the pope's suspicions, since Frederick had not consulted the church about the terms of expurgation and insisted upon entering the region under arms. Writing to Louis IX in early June 1247 (HB, vol. 6/1, 553–55), Frederick described his plans to meet with the pope and how Parma's revolt forced him to turn back. A number of chronicles place Frederick at

Turin on his way to the papal curia when news of the uprising reached him, including Matthew Paris, *CM*, vol. 4, 637–38; and *Annales Placentini Gibellini*, 494.

65. Salimbene of Adam, *CA*, vol. 1, 297–98.

66. Salimbene of Adam, *CA*, vol. 1, 587–89.

67. Salimbene of Adam, *CA*, vol. 1, 320. Numerous chronicles took note of this one-sided battle, including Nicholas of Carbio, *VI*, 276–77; *Annales Placentini Gibellini*, 496; Bartholomew the Scribe, *Annales*, 224–25; *Annales S. Justinae Patavini*, 160; and *Annales S. Pantaleonis Coloniensis*, 544. Matthew Paris (*CM*, vol. 4, 637–38, 648–49, and vol. 5, 13–15) attributes Parma's suffering to divine wrath occasioned by their mistreatment of Robert, bishop of London, when he passed through the city returning home from Rome years earlier. After the Parmese repented for this act and promised to build a church in London, they sallied forth and destroyed Victoria. See also the letter attributed to the podesta of Parma, in Matthew Paris, *CM*, vol. 6, 146–47.

68. Nos. 97–100, Frenz and Herde, *Das Brief- und Memorialbuch*, 388–407.

69. Salimbene of Adam, *CA*, vol. 1, 486–87, 502–3. See also Frederick's letter to the faithful, late June 1248, HB, vol. 6/2, 634–36.

70. Matthew Paris, *HA*, vol. 3, 34.

71. Matthew Paris, *CM*, vol. 5, 60–67. On this polemical letter, see Thumser, "Antistaufische Propaganda"; who includes (pp. 27–34) a critical edition of the text based on two additional manuscripts besides the version found in Matthew Paris. See also Hechelhammer, "Zwischen Martyrermord und Todesstrafe."

72. Matthew Paris, *CM*, vol. 5, 67; and Matthew Paris, *HA*, vol. 3, 45. See also Loud, who in "The Case of the Missing Martyrs" argues that the fighting between the papacy and empire produced a surprising *lack* of martyrs, making Marcellinus the exception to the rule. Note that Loud (ibid., 150) erroneously dates Marcellinus's hanging to 21 February at Victoria, when and where Frederick rendered the death sentence against the bishop.

73. Stock, *Implications of Literacy.*

74. Winkelmann, *Fratris Arnoldi Ord. Praed.*, 9–19. Discussion is in Töpfer, *Das kommende Reich*, 156–60.

75. Albert of Stade, *Annales*, 371. Around this same time and place, someone wrote a tract showing, by assigning number values to letters, that "Pope Innocent IV" equals the number of the beast: 666. See Winkelmann, *Fratris Arnoldi Ord. Praed.*, 20–22. Cf. Rev. 13:18. See also Donne, "Il Papa e l'anticristo."

76. The bibliography on Joachim of Fiore is vast. Overviews of his life and apocalyptic ideas include Reeves, *Influence of Prophecy*; McGinn, *Calabrian Abbot*; Potestà, *Il Tempo dell'Apocalisse*; and Whalen, "Joachim."

77. Bloomfield and Reeves, "Penetration of Joachimism"; Reeves, *Influence of Prophecy*, 37–44; and McGinn, "Apocalyptic Traditions."

78. The manuscript tradition of the commentary *Super Hieremiam* remains a puzzle with no critical edition of the text. See Moynihan, "Development of the 'Pseudo-Joachim'." This being the case, one must still cite one of the widely available but flawed early modern editions, Pseudo-Joachim of Fiore, *Super Jeremiam Prophetam*. I have checked the printed text against the selective edition in Moynihan, "Joachim of Fiore," vol. 2, 537–764; and against BAV, Lat. 4860, a mid- to late thirteenth-century exemplar of the text.

79. See Jostmann, *Sibilla Erithea Babilonica*.

80. Tondelli, *Il libro delle figure*, tavola XIV. See also Lerner, "Frederick II"; and Patschovsky, "Holy Emperor."

81. Pseudo-Joachim of Fiore, *Super Jeremiam Prophetam*, 23r–27r, 30v–33v.

82. Salimbene of Adam, *CA*, vol. 1, 353–56, 358–59, 360–61, 451. See West, "Education of Fra Salimbene."

83. Salimbene of Adam, *CA*, vol. 1, 340–51.

84. Grosseteste appeared before the curia on 13 May 1250. See Gieben, "Robert Grosseteste"; for the memorandum, ibid., 350–69. Also, Southern, *Robert Grosseteste*, 272–95.

85. Gieben, "Robert Grosseteste," 353, 355, 361.

86. Alexander Minorita, *Expositio in Apocalysim*. On Alexander and his apocalypse commentary, see Schmolinsky, *Der Apokalypsenkommentar*; and Schmolinsky, "Prophezeite Geschichte."

87. Alexander Minorita, *Expositio in Apocalysim*, 110–21, 431–33, 441–50. Cf. Rev. 20:1–4.

88. Alexander Minorita, *Expositio in Apocalysim*, 430, 507–9. Cf. Rev. 13:3.

89. Alexander Minorita, *Expositio in Apocalysim*, 509–10.

90. *CQD*, 317ra: "quot enim periculis et maris et terrae et proditionum et assassinorum et aliis infinitis subiecit se Papa qui hanc tulit sententiam vix homo enarrare posset, quaedam tamen scripta sunt in chronicis ecclesiae romanae." Melloni (*Innocenzo IV*, 162) includes a transcription of this important section of Innocent's gloss but misreads the abbreviation for *homo* as *non*, thereby obscuring the passage's meaning (cf. Vat Ross. 957, fol. 148r).

91. On this plot, *Annales Placentini Gibellini*, 492–93; *Annales S. Pantaleonis Coloniensis*, 540; Matthew Paris, *HA*, vol. 3, 11–12; and Matthew Paris, *CM*, vol. 4, 569–77. Frederick sent out numerous letters describing this conspiracy in April 1246 (HB, vol. 6/1, 402–6, 438–44, 514–16).

92. For Walter d'Orca's letter to Henry III, HB, vol. 6/1, 457–59. The *Annales Placentini Gibellini*, 493, describe how Frederick's son Enzio made sure that news of the plot was shared aloud at Parma "publicly."

93. See Innocent's letters dated 26 April 1246, no. 166, *MGH epp. saec. XIII*, vol. 2, 125; late April 1248, no. 178, ibid., 135; and several undated curial letters for the year 1246 addressed to Theobaldo Francisco; to Panfulf de Fasanella and Jacob de Morr; and to Giles, lord of Gaeta, nos. 1982–84, *Reg. Inn.*.

94. Matthew Paris, *CM*, vol. 4, 585.

95. Matthew Paris, *CM*, vol. 4, 605–7.

96. This letter from the sultan to the pope is included in the curial letters for 1245, undated, although Berger, no. 296, suggests May 1246. For an edition of the text, see Lupprian, no. 22, *BPHB*, 150–54, which dates the letter 4 June 1245. See also Matthew Paris, *CM*, vol. 4, 655–68; Matthew Paris, *HA*, vol. 3, 11; and Albert of Stade, *Annales*, 370.

97. Matthew Paris, *CM*, vol. 4, 634–35; *CM*, vol. 5, 37–38; and Matthew Paris, *HA*, vol. 3, 38–39. For Frederick's letter to the Byzantine emperor, see May–June 1250, HB, vol. 6/2, 771–75.

98. Frederick to the faithful, March 1249, HB, vol. 6/2, 705–7.

99. Matthew Paris (*CM*, vol. 5, 68–69) writes that Frederick asked the doctor to drink some the proffered cure first, which he promptly spat out, revealing his complicity in the crime.

100. March 1249, HB, vol. 6/2, 708–9; Matthew Paris, *CM*, vol. 5, 69.

101. See Matthew Paris, *CM*, vol. 5, 190; Nicholas of Carbio, *VI*, 278–79; and Roland of Padua, *Chronica*, 92.

102. December 1250, no. 274, *MGH Const.*, vol. 2, 382–89. Versions of Frederick's testament are transcribed in Matthew Paris, *CM*, vol. 5, 216–18; and *Annales Placentini Gibellini*, 502.

103. Salimbene of Adam, *CA*, vol. 2, 263–64.

104. Matthew Paris, *CM*, vol. 5, 99–100.

Chapter 8

1. Nicholas of Jamsilla [pseud.], *Historia de rebus gestis Friderici II*, 30. The authorship of this chronicle, traditionally attributed to Nicholas of Jamsilla, remains unclear, although its production by someone close to Manfred seems beyond doubt. See the discussion in the edition translated by Louis Mendola as *Frederick, Conrad, and Manfred of Hohenstaufen*, 1–18. On Innocent's negotiations with Manfred, see also Nicholas of Carbio, *VI*, 290–91.

2. Nicholas of Jamsilla [pseud.], *Historia de rebus gestis Friderici II*, 31.

3. The most detailed study of Innocent's papacy after Frederick's death remains Rodenberg, *Innocenz IV*. See also Melloni, *Innocenzo IV*, 166–74; and Housley, *Italian Crusades*, although his book mainly covers the decades starting after Innocent died in 1254. Abulafia, *Frederick II*, 408–35, includes the chapter "Ghosts of the Hohenstaufen," covering the later decades of the thirteenth century.

4. Innocent to Gerhard II, bishop of Bremen, 27 January 1251, no. 41, *MGH epp. saec. XIII*, vol. 3, 31; to Conrad, archbishop of Cologne, 18 February 1251, ibid., 52; to the pro-imperial citizens of Worms,

19 February 1251, no. 74, ibid., 59–60, which was sent "in the same way" to Speyer, Oppenheim, Frankfurt, Gelnhausen, and other German communities; and to the nobles of Swabia siding with the church, 29 March 1251, no. 100, ibid., 79–80.

5. 18 February 1251, no. 66, *MGH epp. saec. XIII*, vol. 3, 52–53; and 20 February 1251, no. 78, *MGH epp. saec. XIII*, vol. 3, 62–63.

6. Among other examples, see Innocent's letters to Gertrude, duchess of Austria, urging her to marry William of Holland's cousin, 18 February 1251, no. 63, *MGH epp. saec. XIII*, vol. 3, 50–51; to Albert, duke of Saxony, encouraging the marriage of his daughter to King William, 18 February 1251, no. 64, ibid., 51; to Agnes, wife of Otto II, duke of Bavaria, instructing her to foster her husband's return to the church, 19 February 1251, no. 70, ibid., 56–57, with similar letters sent to the duke and duchess of Brunswick, and 19 February 1251, nos. 71–72, ibid., 57–58. See also the pope's letters to Godfrey of Hoenloch, 19 February 1251, no. 73, ibid., 58–59; and to Philip de Valkesten, 6 March 1251, no. 84, ibid., 66–67.

7. 1 December 1251, no. 124, no. 124, *MGH epp. saec. XIII*, vol. 3, 104–5; and no. 130, ibid., 110–11.

8. Innocent addressed this situation in a letter sent to Gerard and Berthold, 1 April 1251, no. 103, *MGH epp. saec. XIII*, vol. 3, 82–83. See also his earlier address to Siegfried, 5 May 1245, no. 113, ibid., 80–81. Siegfried had defrocked the two canons in conjunction with the council of Fritzlar on 30 May 1244.

9. Christian of Mainz, *Liber de calamitate*, 248.

10. Innocent to William de Eyka, Dominican prior and William of Holland's chaplain, 5 February 1251, no. 48, *MGH epp. saec. XIII*, vol. 3, 35–36; to the nobles in Swabia, 31 March 1251, no. 101, ibid., 80–81; and to the Franciscans in Germany, 10 February 1251, nos. 361–62, *BF*, vol. 1, 567–68, specifying preaching *usu Teitonicum idioma*. Papal calls for crusading against Conrad and his allies in Germany include nos. 187, 189, 194, *MGH epp. saec. XIII*, vol. 3, 156–58, 160–61.

11. Nicholas of Carbio, *VI*, 279. The *Gesta Treverorum Continuata*, 412, describes the sermon as happening on Easter Sunday (presumably, there might have been two such sermons on Thursday and Sunday). Innocent deployed the "Nero" and "pharaoh" comparisons to the deceased Frederick repeatedly, e.g., *Regnum Sicilie sedis*, 7 February 1251, no. 50, *MGH epp. saec. XIII*, vol. 3, 37. For a discussion of the political scene in Germany after 1250, see Weiler, *Henry III*, 134–40.

12. *Gesta Treverorum Continuata*, 412. See also Innocent's letter to William, king of the Romans, 15 February 1251, no. 60, *MGH epp. saec. XIII*, vol. 3, 47.

13. Nicholas of Carbio, *VI*, 279. In a letter to the nobles of Swabia, Innocent announced William's imminent arrival to resume the battle against Conrad, 31 March 1251, no. 101, *MGH epp. saec. XIII*, vol. 3, 80–81.

14. Matthew Paris, *CM*, vol. 5, 200–201.

15. Salimbene of Adam, *CA*, vol. 1, 356–57. The two friars tried to convince Salimbene to study Joachim's *Commentary on Jeremiah*, the source of their prognostications.

16. For two such letters, one attributed to Robert, patriarch of Jerusalem, and the other members of the military orders, *Burton Annals*, 285–89; and Matthew Paris, *CM*, vol. 6, 191–97.

17. Matthew Paris, *CM*, vol. 5, 108–9.

18. Matthew Paris, *CM*, vol. 5, 170–72. In fact, Innocent had granted a two-year collection. See his letter to the bishops of Paris, Évreux, and Senlis, 29 November 1250, no. 4928, *Reg. Inn.*, vol. 2, 161; also sent to Queen Blanche, no. 3924, *LTC*, vol. 3, 118–19.

19. Matthew Paris, *CM*, vol. 5, 172–73.

20. Matthew Paris, *CM*, vol. 5, 174–75.

21. Innocent raised these themes in his letters on 12 August 1250 to Queen Blanche, Duchesne, *Historiae Francorum scriptores coaetani*, vol. 5, 412–13; to Louis IX, ibid., 413–15; and to the archbishop of Rouen, ibid., 415–17.

22. For example, the series of letters on 29 November 1250, nos. 4926–30, *Reg. Inn.*, vol. 2, 160–61.

23. Weiler, *Henry III*, 140–46.

24. *CRH*, vol. 6 (1247–51), 134–36, 358, 522, 528.

25. Matthew Paris (*CM*, vol. 5, 101–3, 274) took a dim view of Henry's III crusade plans and related financial actions, including papal mandates for the collection of taxes still owed from Richard of Cornwall's crusade. See also the letters from Innocent to the bishops of Lincoln and Chichester, ordering the crusaders to set sail by the deadline of the Feast of St. John the Baptist, in Matthew Paris, *CM*, vol. 6, 200–202, along with letters relating to tithes for Henry III's crusade, in ibid., 296–98.

26. Matthew Paris, *CM*, vol. 5, 101–3, 134–36, 281–82, 324–28.

27. Matthew Paris, *CM*, vol. 5, 246–54; and *Burton Annals*, 290–93.

28. On the Shepherds' Crusade, see Barber, "Crusade of the Shepherds." The movement still does not enjoy a very positive reputation. See Le Goff, *Saint Louis*, 141.

29. Matthew Paris, *HA*, vol. 3, 111–12, repeats this claim that Philip, archbishop of Lyons, paid three thousand marks for the bodyguards accompanying the pope.

30. Innocent to Queen Blanche, 18 March 1251, no. 95, *MGH epp. saec. XIII*, vol. 3, 75–77; and to Reginald of Paris, 24 March, no. 98, ibid., 79.

31. 2 April 1251, no. 104, *MGH epp. saec. XIII*, vol. 3, 83–84.

32. Matthew Paris, *CM*, vol. 5, 248, 255–56.

33. 16 February 1251, nos. 61–62, *MGH epp. saec. XIII*, vol. 3, 48–50. Arles submitted to Charles d'Anjou on 30 April 1251; Avignon did so on 10 May.

34. 7 February 1251, no. 52, *MGH epp. saec. XIII*, vol. 3, 39–41.

35. Innocent to Algisio, bishop of Bergamo, 15 March 1251, no. 94, ibid., 73–75; and to William, bishop-elect of Arrezo, 26 March 1251, no. 99, ibid., 77. The pope reiterated that local authorities should strip Frederick's rectors and other officials in Tuscany and elsewhere of their authority and not allow them to exercise public office.

36. 13 February 1251, no. 58, *MGH epp. saec. XIII*, vol. 3, 45–46.

37. Matthew Paris, *CM*, vol. 5, 237–38.

38. Nicholas of Carbio, *VI*, 280.

39. *Annales Ianuenses*, 229; and Nicholas of Carbio, *VI*, 280.

40. Nicholas of Carbio, *VI*, 280; *Annales Ianuenses*, 228–29; and Salimbene of Adam, *CA*, vol. 2, 673–74. Matthew Paris, *CM*, vol. 5, 255, says the wedding cost twenty thousand marks.

41. *Annales Placentini Gibellini*, 504–5.

42. Nicholas of Carbio, *VI*, 280; and Matthew Paris, *CM*, vol. 5, 255–56. Innocent's letters provide signs of his ongoing rapprochement with the two brothers. On 9 June 1251 (no. 111, *MGH epp. saec. XIII*, vol. 3, 90–91), the pope gave instructions to the archbishop of Vienna and bishop of Grenoble to give Amadeus a two-month deadline for reconciling with the Roman church or face additional censure. On 29 November 1251 (no. 122, ibid., 102–3), he made provisions for monies collected in Burgundy from repentant sinners to be handed over to Thomas.

43. Nicholas of Carbio, *VI*, 281; Salimbene of Adam, *CA*, vol. 2, 673–74; and Matthew Paris, *CM*, vol. 5, 255–56.

44. Salimbene of Adam, *CA*, vol. 2, 675.

45. Among other examples, see Innocent's letters to William of Tuscany, 9 January 1251, no. 129, *MGH epp. saec. XIII*, vol. 3, 110; to the citizens of Viterbo, April 1252, no. 138, ibid., 119–20; to the bishop of Mantua, 30 May 1252, no. 142, ibid., 124–25; to a group of nobles in Ancona, 30 July 1252, no. 151, ibid., 131; to Azzo d'Este, 9 July 1252, no. 145, ibid., 126; and to the citizens of Florence, 26 August 1252, no. 158, ibid., 135–37.

46. Salimbene of Adam, *CA*, vol. 2, 574–75, 564–70.

47. 15 July 1251, no. 117, *MGH epp. saec. XIII*, vol. 3, 97–98. On 25 August 1252 (no. 157, ibid., 134), the pope instructed the Milanese to release a security of four thousand imperial marks to the "militia" at Piacenza, which had been deposited years earlier at Pope Gregory IX's instructions.

48. Nicholas of Carbio, *VI*, 281; and Salimbene of Adam, *CA*, vol. 2, 674–77. On the restoration of Lodi's episcopal status, see 9 January 1252, no. 128, *MGH epp. saec. XIII*, vol. 3, 109.

49. Matthew Paris, *CM*, vol. 5, 237–38. The pope's financial woes at Milan did not end there. See his letter to Leo, archbishop of Milan, instructing him to lift a sentence of excommunication leveled

against the city's podesta and commune for not paying debts they owed to the Roman church, giving them until Lent 1253 to settle, 4 September 1252, no. 162, *MGH epp. saec. XIII*, vol. 3, 139.

50. Matthew Paris, *CM*, vol. 5, 206–7, 237–38.

51. Among other examples, see 30 May 1254, *BOP*, vol. 1, 247; 23 March 1254, no. 532, *BF*, vol. 1, 714; and, dividing Italy into Franciscan and Dominican inquisitorial provinces, *Licet ex omnibus*, 30 May 1254, no. 558, *BF*, vol. 1, 742. On the early stages of the inquisition in Italy, with a focus on the Franciscan order, see d'Alatri, *L'inquisizione francesana*; and Grieco, "Pastoral Care."

52. Prudlo, *Martyred Inquisitor*, 57–67, 71–88.

53. 8 June 1251, no. 110, *MGH epp. saec. XIII*, vol. 3, 87–89.

54. Salimbene of Adam, *CA*, vol. 2, 295–96, 559–60, 889.

55. 16 June 1251, no. 113, *MGH epp. saec. XIII*, vol. 3, 93–95. On Innocent's earlier actions against Ezzelino at Lyons, see 18 April 1248, no. 542, *MGH epp. saec. XII*, vol. 2, 381; and 27 April 1248, no. 545, ibid., 384.

56. See Lansing, *Power and Purity*.

57. Among numerous examples, 27 September 1251, *BOP*, vol. 1, 199–200; 11 March 1251, ibid., 207–8; 13 March 1252, ibid., 208; 14 March 1252, ibid., 208–9; and 31 October 1252, no. 446 (wrongly numbered no. 646), *BF*, vol. 1, 636.

58. Nicholas of Carbio, *VI*, 284.

59. 12 August 1254, *BOP*, vol. 1, 253–54. The Milanese carried through on the threat, sacking the city. See Prudlo, *Martyred Inquisitor*, 76.

60. 15 March 1252, *BOP*, vol. 1, 209–12.

61. For some of Innocent's earliest plans regarding the Regno, see his letter to the faithful in Sicily, 25 January 1251, no. 32, *MGH epp. saec. XIII*, vol. 3, 24–25. For the series of letters appointing Peter as legate to the Regno, see same date, nos. 33–38, ibid., 25–28; also, the series of letters to his Franciscan envoy, Roger de Lentino, 7 March 1251, nos. 85–88, 91, ibid., 67–89, 71–72. Other examples include the pope's letter to the Cistercian abbot Stephen de Busco and the Franciscan prior Jacob de Pernis about reconciling excommunicates in Italy still banned due to their participation in the attack on the Genoese fleet in May 1241, 26 November 1252, no. 452, *BF*, vol. 1, 642. For the bull revoking Frederick's privileges in the Regno, see 23 August 1252, no. 156, MGH epp. saec. XIII, vol. 3, 133–34.

62. This episode features in contemporary chronicle by Thomas of Split, *Historia pontificum Salonitanorum et Spalatinorum*, 597–98.

63. Nicholas of Carbio, *VI*, 282–83.

64. 5 September 1252, no. 163, *MGH epp. saec. XIII*, vol. 3, 139–40.

65. Matthew Paris, *CM*, vol. 5, 284, 300–302. Saba Malaspina (*Die Chronik*, 35, 99) claims that Manfred poisoned Conrad, encouraged by barons who indicated that they would prefer him as king.

66. Matthew Paris, *CM*, vol. 5, 346–48, 457–59. Also, Matthew Paris, *HA*, vol. 3, 126–27.

67. Marc-Bonnet, "Saint-Siège et Charles d'Anjou."

68. Nicholas of Carbio, *VI*, 283.

69. 7–12 June 1253, no. 208, *MGH epp. saec. XIII*, vol. 3, 173–81.

70. 11 July 1253, no. 219, *MGH epp. saec. XIII*, vol. 3, 189–90.

71. See Weiler, *Henry III*, 147–71; and Weiler, "Henry III and the Sicilian Business."

72. Nicholas of Carbio, *VI*, 286.

73. Nicholas of Carbio, *VI*, 285.

74. Nicholas of Carbio, *VI*, 286.

75. Matthew Paris, *CM*, vol. 5, 372–73; *Dunstable Annals*, 191; and Nicholas of Carbio, *VI*, 286.

76. Salimbene of Adam, *CA*, vol. 2, 671; and Saba Malaspina, *Die Chronik*, 35, 96.

77. 4 February 1254, no. 255, *MGH epp. saec. XIII*, vol. 3, 218. Nicholas of Carbio, *VI*, 286, describes how Conrad sent a delegation to the curia in the name of "peace and concord" but that really acted "falsely and deceptively."

78. Matthew Paris, *CM*, no. 150, vol. 6, 299–304.

79. Matthew Paris, *CM*, vol. 6, 299–304.

80. No. 255, *MGH epp. saec. XIII*, vol. 3, 218. Thomas of Savoy, among others, interceded on Conrad's behalf with the pope.

81. 9 April 1254, no. 278, *MGH epp. saec. XIII*, vol. 3, 242–45.

82. Salimbene of Adam, *Chronica*, vol. 2, 671–72; Matthew Paris, *CM*, vol. 5, 459–61.

83. *Cum dilectum filium*, 24 July 1251, no. 119, *MGH epp. saec. XIII*, vol. 3, 99–101. Saba Malaspina (*Die Chronik*, 97) dwells on Conrad's "fraternal affection" toward Manfred, while Nicholas of Jamsilla [pseud.] (*Historia de rebus gestis Friderici II*, 21–22) stresses Conrad's envy of his brother, despite Manfred's loyalty.

84. Innocent described the scene to William of Holland, 12 September 1254, no. 314, *MGH epp. saec. XIII*, vol. 3, 283–84.

85. Nicholas of Carbio, *VI*, 289; and Saba Malaspina, *Die Chronik*, 101–2.

86. 2 September 1254, no. 311, *MGH epp. saec. XIII*, vol. 3, 276–82. See also Nicholas of Carbio, *VI*, 290. Nicholas of Jamsilla [pseud.] (*Historia de rebus gestis Friderici II*, 32) complains about William Fieschi's abusive behavior of nobles in the Regno.

87. For Innocent's arrangements with Manfred, including the recognition of Conradin's claims, see 27 September 1254, nos. 318–320, *MGH epp. saec. XIII*, vol. 3, 287–90.

88. Saba Malaspina, *Die Chronik*, 104.

89. Saba Malaspina, *Die Chronik*, 105–6; and Nicholas of Jamsilla [pseud.], *Historia de rebus gestis Friderici II*, 45–55.

90. On this campaign, see Saba Malaspina, *Die Chronik*, 106; Nicholas of Jamsilla [pseud.], *Historia de rebus gestis Friderici II*, 61; Nicholas of Carbio, *VI*, 291; *Annales Placentini Gibellini*, 506; and *Annales Ianuenses*, 232.

91. Matthew Paris, *CM*, vol. 5, 430–31; and Nicholas of Carbio, *VI*, 291–92.

Postlude

1. Nicholas of Carbio, *VI*, 292; and Salimbene of Adam, *CA*, vol. 2, 634–35.

2. Matthew Paris, *CM*, vol. 5, 429–30, 470–72.

3. Charansonnet, *L'université, l'eglise et l'etate*, vol. 2, 804–11. See also Cole, d'Avray, and Riley-Smith, "Application of Theology," 234–44.

4. Charansonnet, *L'université, l'eglise et l'etate*, vol. 2, 807, 810–11.

5. Waley, *Papal State*, 164.

6. On this transformative point in the Western political tradition, see the typical sentiments offered by Skinner, *Foundations of Modern Political Thought*, vol. 1, 3–22; McClelland, *History of Western Political Thought*, 129–48; and Maiolo, *Medieval Sovereignty*.

7. See Melloni, "William of Ockham's Critique."

8. Canto X, XIII. On Dante's attitudes toward empire, see Cassell, Monarchia *Controversy*.

Epilogue

1. Hobbes, *Leviathan*, 434–35, 536–45. For the epigraph to this chapter, see ibid., 367. See also Martinichi, *Two Gods of Leviathan*, 279–310, 331–32.

2. Bellarmine, *On Temporal and Spiritual Authority*, 241. Bellarmine wrote this book in response to Barclay, *De potestate papae*. See Tutino, *Empire of Souls*.

3. Bellarmine, *On Temporal and Spiritual Authority*, 161, 181, 239–40.

4. Joseph de Maistre, *Works of Joseph de Maistre*; for the epigraph to this chapter, see ibid., 142.

5. As Armenteros, *French Idea of History*, 116, describes de Maistre's work: "For if there is one historical argument to *Du pape*, it is that the pope has made Europe.

6. Ranke, *History of Latin and Teutonic Nations*, 6; and Ranke, *History of the Popes*, vol. 1, 26–27.

7. Perkins, *Christendom and European Identity*, 20.

8. Laski, *Foundations of Sovereignty*, 1, 21.

9. Gierke, *Political Theories*, 10–11, 30–37.

10. Wulf, "Society of Nations," 224.

11. Schmitt, *Political Theology*, 15, 36. Schmitt's controversial reputation turns not just upon his "decisionism" as a critique of liberalism, but his later elaborations of the idea in the context of Nazi politics and membership in the Nazi party. For his views of the medieval empire, papacy, and Roman Catholic Church, see Schmitt, *Roman Catholicism*, 34–46; and Schmitt, *Nomos of the Earth*.

12. Dawson, *Dividing of Christendom*, 20; and Dawson, *Formation of Christendom*, 206. For similar views, see Krey, "International State." See also Perkins, *Christendom and European Identity*, 154–71.

13. Acton, "History of Freedom," 62–63.

14. Tierney, *Religion, Law*, 10. For some similar claims, see Ladner, "Aspects of Mediaeval Thought"; and Morrall, *Political Thought*, 10–11. See also Gray, "Carl Schmitt," which critiques Schmitt's "decisionism" as misunderstanding the divided nature of sovereignty in the Middle Ages, characterized by there being "two exception-bearers" that placed a source of restraint upon each other.

15. See also Tierney, "Canonists and the Medieval State"; Tierney, "Medieval Canon Law"; Muldoon, "Contribution"; and the essays in Oakley, *Natural Law*. Tierney, Muldoon, and Oakley draw on Figgis, *Studies of Political Thought*, in which he locates the origins of constitutional ideas in the conciliar movement of the fifteenth century. For a somewhat shrill critique of this position, see Nederman, *Lineages*, 29–48, where he calls Tierney, Oakley, and others "Neo-Figgistes" for their stress on continuities between medieval and modern law and political ideas.

16. Davis, *Periodization and Sovereignty*, 50. Davis aptly describes "feudalism," not Christendom, in these terms.

17. Dawson, *Religion*, 15–16, emphasis is mine; and Tierney, *Religion, Law*, 8, 12–13.

18. Casanova, "What Is a Public Religion?," 130–31. See also de Vries and Sullivan, *Political Theologies*, 1–88.

Bibliography

Manuscript Sources

London, British Library (BL)
- add. 46352
- Cotton Cleopatra E 1
- Royal 14 C VII

London, Lambeth Palace Library, no. 37
London, National Archives, 7/64/47
Padua, Biblioteca Antoniana, cod. 79
Paris, Archives Nationales, L 245, n. 84
Paris, Bibliothèque National de France (BNF)
- Lat. 4039
- Lat. 5152A
- Lat. 8989
- Lat. 8990
- Lat. nouv. acq. 2128

Rome, Archivio Segreto Vaticano (ASV)
- Reg. 14–20
- Reg. 21–23

Rome, Biblioteca Apostolica Vaticana (BAV)
- Lat. 4860
- Pal. Lat. 953
- Ottob. Lat. 2546
- Lat. Ross. 957

Printed Primary Sources

Alberic of Trois-Fontaines. *Chronicon*. *MGH SS* 23, 631–950.

Alberigo, Joseph, et al., eds. *Conciliorum oecumenicorum decreta*. Basilae: Herder, 1962.

Albert of Stade, *Annales*. *MGH SS* 16, 271–379.

Alexander Minorita. *Expositio in Apocalysim*. Edited by Alois Wachtel. MGH, Quellen zur Geistesgeschichte des Mittelalters, vol. 1. Weimar: H. Böhlaus Nachfolger, 1955.

Annales Augustani minores a. 1137–1321. *MGH SS* 10, 8–11.

Annales Erphordenses a. 1220–1254. *MGH SS* 16, 26–40.

Annales Ianuenses. *MGH SS* 18, 226–48.

Annales et notae Sancti Emmerammi. *MGH SS* 17, 567–76.

Annales Mantuani. *MGH SS* 19, 19–31.

Annales Placentini Gibellini. *MGH SS* 18, 457–581.

Annales Placentini Guelfi. *MGH SS* 18, 411–57.

Annales Sanctae Justinae Patavini. *MGH SS* 19, 148–93.

Annales Sancti Pantaleonis Coloniensis. *MGH SS* 22, 529–47.

Annales Sancti Rudberti Salisburgenses. *MGH SS* 9, 758–810.
Annales Scheftlarienses maiores. *MGH SS* 17, 335–50.
Annales Veronenses. *MGH SS* 19, 1–18.
Auvray, Lucien, ed. *Les registres de Grégoire IX, recueil des bulles de ce pape publiées ou analysées d'après les manuscrits originaux du Vatican*. 4 vols. Paris: Ernest Thorin, 1890–1955.
Barclay, William. *De potestate papae*. London, 1609.
Bartholomaeis, Vincenzo de, ed. *Poesie Provenzali storiche relative all'Italia*. Rome: Tipografia del Senato, 1931.
Bartholomew the Scribe. *Annales a. 1225–1248*. *MGH SS* 18, 156–225.
Bartolini, Franco, ed. *Codice diplomatico del Senato romano dal MCXLIV al MCCCXLVII*. Fonti per la storia d'Italia pubblicate dall' Istituto storico italiano per il Medio Evo, no. 87. Rome: Tipografia del Senato, 1948.
Bellarmine, Robert. *On Temporal and Spiritual Authority*. Edited and translated by Stefania Tutino. Indianapolis: Liberty Fund, 2012.
Berger, Élie, ed. *Les registres d'Innocent IV, publiées ou analysées d'après les manuscrits originaux du Vatican et de la Bibliothèque Nationale*. 4 vols. Paris: Ernest Thorin, 1884–1911.
Bird, Jessalynn, Edward Peters, and James M. Powell, eds. *Crusade and Christendom: Annotated Documents in Translation from Innocent III to the Fall of Acre, 1187–1291*. Philadelphia: University of Pennsylvania Press, 2013.
Boos, Heinrich, ed. *Chronicon Wormatiense*. Quellen zur Geschichte der Stadt Worms, vol. 3: Chroniken. Berlin: Weidmannsche, 1893.
Breve chronicon de rebus Siculis. *MGH SRG*, vol. 77.
Burchard of Ursburg. *Chronicon*. *MGH SS* 23, 333–83.
Burton Annals. *AM*, vol. 1, 183–500.
Carducci, G., and V. Fiorini, eds. *Rerum Italicarum scriptores*, n.s., 34 vols. Città di Castello, 1900–75.
Christian of Mainz. *Liber de calamitate ecclesiae Moguntinae*. *MGH SS* 25, 236–48.
Chronica regia Coloniensis, *MGH SRG*, vol. 18.
Chronica S. Petri Erfordensis moderna a. 1072–1335. *MGH SS* 30, 335–457.
Close Rolls for the Reign of Henry III Preserved in the Public Record Office. 14 vols. London, 1916–64.
Cole, Henry, ed. *Documents Illustrative of English History in the Thirteenth and Fourteenth Centuries*. London, 1844.
Duchesne, André. *Historiae Francorum scriptores coaetani*. 5 vols. Paris: Lutetiae Parisiorum, 1649.
Dunstable Annals. *AM*, vol. 3, 3–408.
Ernst-Lupprian, Karl. *Die Beziehungen der Päpste zu islamischen und mongolischen Herrschern im 13. Jahrhundert anhand ihres Briefwechsels*. Studi e testi, vol. 291. Vatican City: Biblioteca Apostolica Vaticana, 1981.
Estoire de Eracles. *RHC*, *Historiens occidentaux*, vol. 2.
Fabre, Paul, ed. *Le Liber censuum de l'église Romaine*. Bibliothèque des écoles française d'Athènes et de Rome. 7 vols. Paris: Thorin et fils, 1889–1905.
Fredericq, Paul, ed. *Corpus documentorum inquisitionis haereticae pravitatis Neerlandicae*. 5 vols. Ghent: J. Vuylsteke, 1889–1902.
Frenz, Thomas, and Peter Herde, eds. *Das Brief- und Memorialbuch des Albert Behaim*. MGH Briefe des späteren Mittelalters. Munich: Monumenta Germaniae Historica, 2000.
Friedberg, Aemelius, ed. *Corpus iuris canonici*. 2 vols. Graz: Akademische Druck-U. Verlagsanstalt, 1955.
García y García, Antonius, ed. *Constitutiones concilii quarti Lateranensis una cum commentariis glossatorum*. Series A: Monumenta iuris canonici, vol. 2. Vatican City: Biblioteca Apostolica Vaticana, 1981.
Gerard Maurisius. *Cronica dominorum Ecelini et Alberici fratrum de Romano (1183–1237)*. Edited by Giovanni Soranzo. *RIS*, vol. 8/4.
Gesta Treverorum Continuata. *MGH SS* 24, 368–488.
Gieben, Servus. "Robert Grosseteste at the Papal Curia, Lyons, 1250: Edition of the Documents." *Collectanea Franciscana* 41 (1971): 340–93.

Halushchyn'skyi, Theodosius, and Meletius Voinar, eds. *Acta Innocentii PP. (1243–1254). Pontificia commissio ad redigendum codicem iuris canonici orientalis, fontes, III.* 4 vols. Rome, 1962.

Hampe, Karl, ed. *Die Aktenstücke zum Frieden von S. Germano 1230, MGH epistolae selectae,* vol. 4. Berlin: Wiedmannsche Buchhandlung, 1926.

Hobbes, Thomas. *Leviathan: Or the Matter, Forme and Power of a Commonwealth Ecclesiasticall and Civil.* Edited by Michael Oakeshott. 1962. New York: Simon and Schuster, 2008.

Huillard-Bréholles, J.-L.-A., ed. *Historia diplomatica Friderici secundi Romanorum imperatoris, Jerusalem et Siciliae regis.* 6 vols. Paris, 1854–55.

Innocent IV. *Commentaria Innocentii quarti pontificis maximi super libros quinque decretalium.* Frankfurt, 1570.

Jacob de Aquis. *Chronicon imagines mundi.* Monumenta Historiae Patriae, vol. 3. Turin: Augusta Taurinorum, 1848.

Jaques de Vitry. *Lettres de Jacques de Vitry: 1160/1170–1240, évêque de Saint-Jean d'Acre.* Edited by R. B. C. Huygens. Leiden: Brill, 1960.

John of Plano Carpini. *Itinera et relationes fratrum minorum saeculi XIII et XIV.* Sinica Franciscana, vol. 1. Edited by Anastasius Vanden Wyngaert, 3–130. Quaracchi: Apud Collegium S. Bonaventurae, 1929.

Jones, W. H. R., ed. *Vetus registrum Sarisberiense, alias dictum registrum S. Osmundi episcopi.* 2 vols. London, 1883–84.

Joseph de Maistre. *The Works of Joseph de Maistre.* Translated by Jack Lively. New York MacMillan, 1965.

Kempf, Friedrich, ed. *Regestum Innocentii III papae super negotio Romani imperii.* Miscellanea. Historia Pontificae, vol. 12. Rome: Pontificia Università Gregoriana, 1947.

Lange, Christian C. A., and Carl R. Unger, eds. *Diplomatarium Norvegicum: Oldbreve til Kundskab om Norges Indre og Ydre Forholde, Sprog, Slaegter, Saeder, Lovgivning og Retterhand i Midelalderen.* 22 vols. Christiana: P. T. Mallings Forlagshandel, 1847.

Lavaud, René, ed. *Poésies complètes du troubadour Peire Cardenal (1180–1278).* Toulouse: Édouard Privat, 1957.

Levi, Guido, ed. *Registri dei cardinali Ugolino d'Ostia e Ottaviano degli Ubaldi.* Fonti per la storia d'Italia. Rome: Istitutio Storico Italiano, 1890.

Matthew Paris. *Chronica majora.* Edited by Henry Richard Luard. 7 vols. Rerum Britannicarum medii aevi scriptores. London, 1872–83.

———. *Historia Anglorum.* Edited by Frederic Madden. 3 vols. London: Longmans, Green, Reader, and Dyer, 1866–69.

Menko. *Chronica a. 1234–1273. MGH SS* 23, 523–61.

Nicholas of Jamsilla [pseud.]. *Historia de rebus gestis Friderici II. imperatoris ejusque filiorum Conradi et Manfred.* Edited by Ferdinando Ughelli. Naples: Jahannis Gravier, 1770. Translated by Louis Mendola as *Frederick, Conrad, and Manfred of Hohenstaufen: The Chronicle of Nicholas of Jamsilla, 1210–1258* (New York: Trinacria Editions, 2016).

Osney-Thomas Wykes Annals. AM, vol. 4, 3–354.

Peters, Edward, ed. *Heresy and Authority in Medieval Europe: Documents in Translation.* Philadelphia: University of Pennsylvania Press, 1980.

Powell, James, M., trans. *The Liber Augustalis or Constitutions of Melfi Promulgated by the Emperor Frederick II for the Kingdom of Sicily in 1231.* Syracuse: Syracuse University Press, 1971.

Powicke, F. M., and C. R. Cheney, eds. *Councils and Synods with Other Documents Relating to the English Church.* 2 vols. Oxford: Oxford at the Clarendon Press, 1964.

Psuedo-Joachim of Fiore. *Super Jeremiam Prophetam.* Cologne, 1516.

Reichert, B. M., ed. *Acta capitulorum generalium ordinis praedicatorum ab anno 1220 usque ad annum 1303.* Monumenta ordinis fratrum praedicatorum historica. Rome, 1898.

Richard of San Germano. *Cronica a. 1189–1243. MGH SS* 19, 321–84.

Ripoll, Thomas, ed. *Bullarium ordinis FF. Prædicatorum: sub auspiciis SS. D. N. D. Benedicti XIII, pontificis maximi, ejusdem Ordinis.* 8 vols. Rome, 1729–40.

Rodenburg, Carl. *Monumenta Germaniae Historica: epistolae saeculi XIII e regestis pontificum Romanorum selectae*. 3 vols. Berlin, 1883–87.
Roger of Wendover. *Chronica, sive Flores historiarum*. Edited by Henry O. Coxe. 4 vols. London, 1841.
Roland of Padua. *Chronica*. *MGH SS* 19, 32–147.
Rymer, Thomas, and Robert Sanderson, eds. *Foedera, conventiones, literae et cujuscunque generis act et publica inter reges Angliae et alios imperatores, reges, pontifices, principes, vel communitates*. 3rd ed. Hague: Apud Joannem Neaulme, 1845.
Saba Malaspina. *Die Chronik des Saba Malaspina*. *MGH SS*, vol. 35.
Salimbene of Adam. *Chronica*. Edited by Guiseppe Scalia. 2 vols. *Corpus Christianorum, Continuatio Mediaevalis*, 125–125A. Turnhout: Brepols, 1998.
Sambin, Paolo. *Problemi politici attraverso lettere inedite di Innocenzo IV*. Memorie classi di scienze morali e lettere, vol. 31, fasc. 3. Venice: Istituto Veneto, 1955.
Sbaralea, J. H., ed. *Bullarium Franciscanum Romanorum Pontificum constitutiones, epistolas, ac diplomata continens*. 4 vols. 1768; Santa Maria degli Angeli: Edizioni Porziuncola, 1983.
Teulet, Alexandre, et al., eds. *Layettes du trésor des chartes*. 4 vols. Paris: Henri Plon, 1863–1902.
Tewksbury Annals. *AM*, vol. 1, 43–182.
Theiner, Augustin, ed. *Vetera monumenta historica Hungariam sacram illustrantia*. 2 vols. Rome: Typis Vaticanis, 1859–60.
Thomas of Cantimpré. *Bonum universal de apibus*. *Acta Sanctorum*, vol. 28 (July 2).
Thomas of Eccleston. *De adventu fratrum minorum in Angliam*. Edited by J. S. Brewer. Rerum Britannicarum medii aevi scriptores, vol. 48. London, 1858.
Thomas of Split. *Historia pontificum Salonitanorum et Spalatinorum*. *MGH SS* 29, 569–98.
Tondelli, Leone, ed. *Il libro delle figure dell'abate Gioachino da Fiore*. 2 vols. Turin: Società editrice internazionale, 1953.
Waverley Annals. *AM*, vol. 2, 129–412.
Weiland, Ludwig. *MGH Constitutiones et acta publica imperatorum et regum*. Legum, section IV. 4 vols. Hannover, 1893–1911.
William de Puylaurens. *Chronique, 1203–1275: Chronica magistri Guillelmi de Podio Laurentii*. Translated by Jean Duvernoy. Paris: Éditions du Centre National de la Recherche Scientifique, 1976.
William of Andres. *Chronica*. *MGH SS* 24, 684–773.
Winkelmann, Edward, ed. *Acta imperii inedita seculi XIII: Urkunden und Briefe zur Geschichte des Kaiserreichs und den Königsreichs Sicilien in den Jahren 1198 bis 1273*. 2 vols. Innsbruck: Wagner'schen Universitäts-Buchhalndlung, 1880.
———. *Fratris Arnoldi Ord. Praed. de correctione ecclesiae epistola et anonymi de Innocentio IV. P. M. antichristo libellus*. Berlin: E. S. Mittler and Sons, 1865.

Secondary Literature

Abate, Giuseppe. "Lettere 'secretae' d'Innocenzo IV e altri documenti in una raccolta inedita del sec. XIII." *Miscellanea Franciscana* 55 (1955): 317–73.
Abulafia, David. *Frederick II: A Medieval Emperor*. London: Allen Lane, 1988.
———. "The Kingdom of Sicily and the Origins of the Political Crusades." In *Società, istituzioni, spiritualità: studi in onore di Cinzio Violante*, 65–77. Spoleto: Centro Italiano di studi sull'alto medioevo, 1994.
Acton, Lord John. "The History of Freedom in Christianity (1877)." In *Essays on Freedom and Power*, edited by Gertrude Himmelfarb, 58–87. Boston: Beacon Press, 1948.
Adut, Ari. *On Scandal: Moral Disturbance in Society, Politics, and Art*. Cambridge: Cambridge University Press, 2008.
Alberzoni, Maria P. "La legazioni di Ugo d'Ostia (1217–1221) e l'organizzazione della crociata." In *Legati, delegati el'impressa d'Oltremare (secoli XII–XIII)/ Papal Legates, Delegates and the Crusades (12th–13th Century)*, edited by Maria P. Alberzoni and Pascal Montaubin, 283–326. Turnhout: Brepols, 2014.

Ames, Christine Caldwell. *Righteous Persecution: Inquisition, Dominicans, and Christianity in the Middle Ages*. Philadelphia: University of Pennsylvania Press, 2009.

Anderson, Benedict. *Imagined Communities: Reflections on the Origin and Spread of Nationalism*. London: Verso, 2006. First published in 1983.

Araujo, Robert John, and John A. Lucal. "A Forerunner for International Organizations: The Holy See and the Community of Christendom: With Special Emphasis on the Medieval Papacy." *Journal of Law and Religion* 20 (2004–5): 305–50.

Armenteros, Carolina. *The French Idea of History: Joseph e Maistre and his Heirs, 1794–1854*. Ithaca, NY: Cornell University Press, 2011.

Arnold, Benjamin. "Emperor Frederick II (1194–1250) and the Political Particularism of the German Princes." *Journal of Medieval History* 26 (2000): 239–52.

Auvray, Lucien. "Le registre de Grégoire IX de la bibliothèque municipale de Pérouse." *Bibliothèque de l'École des Chartes* 70 (1909): 313–34.

Baaken, Gerhard. *Ius Imperii ad Regnum: Königreich Sizilien, Imperium Romanum und Romisches Papsttum vom Tode Kaiser Heinrichs VI. bis zu den Verichterlärungen Rudolfs von Habsburg*. Cologne: Böhlau, 1993.

———. "Die Verhandlungen von Cluny (1245) und der Kampf Innocenz' IV. gegen Friedrich II." *Deutsches Archiv für Erforschung des Mittelalters* 50 (1994): 531–79.

Bachrach, David. "The Friars Go to War: Mendicant Military Chaplains, 1216–c. 1300." *Catholic Historical Review* 90 (2004): 617–33.

———. "Making Peace and War in the 'City-State' of Worms, 1235–1273." *German History* 24 (2006): 505–25.

Bagliani, Agostino Paravicini. *Cardinali di curia e 'familiae' cardinalizie dal 1227 al 1254*. Italia Sacra: Studi e documenti di storia ecclesiastica. 2 vols. Padua: Editrice Antenore, 1972.

Barber, Malcolm. "The Crusade of the Shepherds in 1251." In *Crusaders and Heretics, 12th– 14th Centuries*, 1–23. Aldershot, UK: Ashgate, 1995.

Barraclough, Geoffrey. *The Medieval Papacy*. New York: Harcourt, Brace and World, 1968.

Barry, William. *The Papal Monarchy from St. Gregory the Great to Boniface VIII (590–1303)*. London: T. Fisher Unwin, 1902.

Battelli, Giulio. "I transunti di Lione del 1245." *Mittheilungen des Instituts für Oesterreichische Geschichtsforschung* 62 (1954): 336–64.

Beaulande, Véronique. "La force de le censure: l'excommunication dans les conflits de pouvoir au seins des villes au XIIIe siècle." *Revue historique* 646 (2008): 251–78.

Benham, Jenny. *Peacemaking in the Middle Ages: Principles and Practice*. Manchester: Manchester University Press, 2011.

Benson, Robert L. "*Plenitudo Potestatis*: Evolution of a Formula from Gregory IV to Gratian." *Studia Gratiana* 14 (1967): 192–217.

Berend, Nora. *At the Gate of Christendom: Jews, Muslims, and 'Pagans' in Medieval Hungary, c. 1000–1300*. Cambridge: Cambridge University Press, 2001.

Berger, Élie. *Saint Louis et Innocent IV: Études sur les rapports de la France et du Saint-Siège*. Paris: Thorin & Fils, 1893.

Bloomfield, Morton, and Marjorie Reeves. "The Penetration of Joachimism into Northern Europe." *Speculum* 29 (1954): 772–93.

Bock, Friedrich. "Studien zu den Registern Innocenz' IV." *Archivalische Zeitschrift* 52 (1956): 11–48.

Boureau, Alain. "The Letter-Writing Norm, a Mediaeval Invention." In *Correspondence: Models of Letter-Writing from the Middle Ages to the Nineteenth Century*, edited by Roger Chartier, Alain Boureau, and Cécile Dauphin, 24–58. Translated by Christopher Woodall. Princeton, NJ: Princeton University Press, 1997.

Brem, Ernst. *Papst Gregor IX. Bis zum Beginn seines Pontifitats: ein biographischer Versuch*. Heidelberg: Carl Winters, 1911.

Brown, Daniel A. "The Alleluia: A Thirteenth Century Peace Movement." *Archivum Franciscanum Historicum* 81 (1988): 3–16.

Brundage, James. *Medieval Canon Law and the Crusader.* Madison: University of Wisconsin Press, 1969.

Buc, Philippe. *The Dangers of Ritual: Between Early Medieval Texts and Social Scientific Theory.* Princeton: Princeton University Press, 2001.

Campbell, G. J. "Protest of St. Louis." *Traditio* 15 (1959): 405–18.

Cantini, J. A. "De autonomia judicis saecularis et de Romani Pontificis plenitudine potestatis in temporalibus secundum Innocentium IV." *Salesianum* 23 (1961): 407–80.

Carlyle, R. W., and A. J. Carlyle. *A History of Mediaeval Political Theory in the West.* 2nd ed. 6 vols. Edinburgh: W. Blackwood and Sons, 1938.

Casanova, José. "What Is a Public Religion?" In *Religion Returns to the Public Square: Faith and Policy in America,* edited by Hugh Heclo and Wilfred M. McClay, 111–39. Washington, DC: Woodrow Wilson Center Press, 2003.

Cassell, Anthony K. *The* Monarchia *Controversy: An Historical Study with Accompanying Translations of Dante Alighieri's* Monarchia, *Guido Vernani's* Refutation of the "Monarchia" Composed by Dante, *and Pope John XXII's Bull* Si fratrum. Washington, DC: Catholic University Press of America, 2004.

Cassidy-Welch, Megan. "'O Damietta': War Memory and Crusade in Thirteenth-Century Egypt." *Journal of Medieval History* 40 (2014): 346–60.

Caumanns, Volker. "Die Kreuzzugsmotivation Friedrichs II." *Crusades* 8 (2009): 131–72.

Charansonnet, Alexis. *L'université, l'eglise et l'etate dans les sermons du cardinal Eudes de Châteauroux (1190?–1273).* 2 vols. Lyons: Université Lumière Lyons 2, 2001.

Chiodi, Giovanni. "Istituzioni e attività della seconda Lega Lombarda (1226–1235)." In *Studi di storia del diritto,* vol. 1, 79–262. Milan: Giuffrè, 1996.

Chodorow, Stanley. *Christian Political Theory and Church Politics in the Mid-Twelfth Century: The Ecclesiology of Gratian's Decretum.* Berkeley: University of California Press, 1972.

Clanchy, M. T. *From Memory to Written Record: England 1066–1307.* 3rd ed. Malden: Wiley Blackwell, 2013. First published in 1979.

Clarke, Peter D. *The Interdict in the Thirteenth Century: A Question of Collective Guilt.* Oxford: Oxford University Press, 2007.

Claverie, Pierre-Vincent. "Deux lettres inédites de la première mission en orient d'André de Longjumeau (1246)." *Bibliothèque de l'école des Chartres* 158 (2000): 283–92.

———. *Honorius III et l'orient (1216–1227): étude et publication de sources inédites des archives vaticanes (ASV).* Boston: Brill, 2013.

Clementi, Dione. "Further Notes on the 'Transcripts of Lyons of 1245' (Rouleaux de Cluny)." In *Studi in onore di Riccardo Filangieri,* vol. 1, 189–97. Naples: L'Arte Tipografica, 1959.

Cole, Penny, David L. d'Avray, and Jonathan Riley-Smith. "Application of Theology to Current Affairs: Memorial Sermons on the Dead of Mansurah and on Innocent IV." In *Modern Questions about Medieval Sermons: Essays on Marriage, Death, History and Sanctity,* edited by Nicole Bériou and David L. d'Avray, 217–45. Spoleto: Centro Italiano di Studi sull'Alto Medieovo, 1994.

Constable, Giles. *Letters and Letter-Collections.* Typologie des Sources du Moyen Âge Occidental, vol. 17. Turnhout: Brepols, 1976.

Congar, Yves. "Quod omnes tangit, ab omnibus tractari et approbari debet." *Revue historique de droit français et étranger* 35 (1958): 21–59.

d'Alatri, Marino. *L'inquisizione francesana nell'Italia centrale nel secolo XIII.* Rome: Istituto Storico dei Frati Minori Cappuccini, 1954.

Davis, Kathleen. *Periodization and Sovereignty: How Ideas of Feudalism and Secularization Govern the Politics of Time.* Philadelphia: University of Pennsylvania Press, 2008.

Dawson, Christopher. *The Dividing of Christendom.* New York: Sheed and Ward, 1965.

———. *The Formation of Christendom.* New York: Sheed and Ward, 1967.

———. *Religion and the Rise of Western Culture.* New York: Sheed and Ward, 1950.

de Vries, Hent and Lawrence E. Sullivan, eds. *Political Theologies: Public Religion in a Post-Secular World.* New York: Fordham University Press, 2006.

Dehio, Ludwig. *Innocenz IV. und England: Ein Beitrag zur Kirchengeschichte des 13. Jahrhunderts*. Berlin: G. J. Göschen'sche Verlagshandlung, 1914.

Denifle, Heinrich. "Das Evangelium Aeternum und die Commission zu Anagni." *Archiv für Litteratur- und Kirchengeschichte des Mittelalters* 1 (1885): 49–142.

Diehl, Peter. "'Ad Abolendam' (X 5.7.9) and Imperial Legislation Against Heresy." *Studia Gratiana* 19 (1989): 1–11.

———. "Overcoming the Reluctance to Prosecute Heresy in Thirteenth-Century Italy." In *Christendom and Its Discontents: Exclusion, Persecution, and Rebellion, 1000–1500*, edited by Scott Waugh and Peter Diehl, 47–66. Cambridge: Cambridge University Press, 1996.

Donne, Fluvio Delle. "Il Papa e l'anticristo: poteri universali e attese escatologische all'epoca di Innocenzo IV e Federico II." *Archivio Normanno-Svevo* 4 (2014): 17–44.

Doran, John. "Rites and Wrongs: The Latin Mission to Nicaea, 1234." In *Unity and Diversity in the Church*, edited by R. N. Swanson, 131–44. Oxford: Blackwell, 1996.

Dotson, John. "The Genoese Civic Annals: Caffaro and His Continuators." In *Chronicling History: Chroniclers and Historians in Medieval and Renaissance Italy*, edited by Sharon Dale, Alison Williams Lewin, and Duane J. Osheim, 55–86. University Park: Pennsylvania State University Press, 2007.

Edbury, Peter W. *John of Ibelin and the Kingdom of Jerusalem*. Woodbridge, UK: Boydell Press, 1997.

———. "The Lyon *Eracles* and the Old French Continuations of William of Tyre." In *Montjoie: Studies in Crusade History in Honour of Hans Eberhard Mayer*, edited by Benjamin Z. Kedar, Jonathan Riley-Smith, and Rudolf Hiestand, 139–54. Aldershot, UK: Variorum, 1997.

Felten, Franz. *Papst Gregory IX*. Freiburg: Herder, 1886.

Fenster, Thomas, and Daniel Lord Smail, eds. *Fama: The Politics of Talk and Reputation in Medieval Europe*. Ithaca, NY: Cornell University Press, 2003.

Figgis, J. N. *Studies of Political Thought from Gerson to Grotius*. 2nd ed. Cambridge: Cambridge University Press, 1916.

Figuerira, Robert C. "*Legatus Apostolicae Sedis:* The Pope's *Alter Ego* According Thirteenth-Century Canon Law." *Studi Medievali* 27 (1986): 527–74.

———. "Papal Reserved Powers and the Limitations on Legatine Authority." In *Popes, Teachers, and Canon Law in the Middle Ages*, edited by James Ross Sweeney and Stanley Chodorow, 191–211. Ithaca, NY: Cornell University Press, 1989.

Freed, John B. *The Friars and German Society in the Thirteenth Century*. Cambridge: Medieval Academy of America, 1977.

Fuhrmann, Horst. "Konstantinische Schenkung und abendländisches Kaisertum." *Deutsches Archiv für Erforschung des Mittlealters* 22 (1966): 63–178.

Gatto, Ludovico. "Federico II nella cronaca di Salimbene de Adam." In *Federico II e le nuove culture: atti del XXXI convegno storico internazionale, Todi, 9–12 Ottobre, 1994*, 507–38. Spoleto: Centro Italiano di studi sull'alto medioevo, 1995.

Gierke, Otto von. *Political Theories of the Middle Age*. Translated by Frederic W. Maitland. Cambridge: At the University Press, 1951. Partial translation of *Das deutsche Genossenschaftsrechte*. 4 vols. Berlin, 1868–1913.

Given, James. *Inquisition and Medieval Society: Power, Discipline, and Resistance in Languedoc*. Ithaca: Cornell University Press, 1997.

Goering, Joseph. "The Internal Forum and the Literature of Penance and Confession." In *The History of Medieval Canon Law in the Classical Period, 1140–1234: From Gratian to the Decretals of Pope Gregory IX*, edited by Wilfried Hartmann and Kenneth Pennington, 379–428. Washington, DC: Catholic University of America Press, 2008.

Goez, Werner. *Translatio Imperii: ein Betrag zur Geschichte des Geschichtsdenkens und der politischen Theorien im Mittelalter und in der frühen Neuzeit*. Tübingen: Mohr, 1958.

Goodich, Michael. "The Politics of Canonization in the Thirteenth Century: Lay and Mendicant Saints." *Church History* 44 (1975): 294–307.

Gouguenheim, Sylvain. *Frédéric II: un empereur de legends*. Paris: Perrin, 2015.

Graefe, Friedrich. *Die Publizistik in der letzen Epoche Kaiser Friedrichs II: Ein Beitrag zur Geschichte der Jahre 1239–1250*. Heidelberg: Carl Winter's Universitätsbuchhandlung, 1909.

Gray, Phillip W. "Carl Schmitt and Medieval Christian Political Thought." *Humanitas* 20 (2007): 175–200.

Gregorovius, Ferdinand. *History of the City of Rome in the Middle Ages*. Translated by Annie Hamilton. 8 vols. London: George Bell & Sons, 1895–1906.

Grieco, Holly J. "Pastoral Care, Inquisition, and Mendicancy in the Medieval Franciscan Order." In *The Origin, Development, and Refinement of Medieval Religious Mendicancies*, edited by Donald S. Prudlo, 146–53. Leiden: Brill, 2011.

Habermas, Jürgen. *The Structural Transformation of the Public Sphere: An Inquiry into a Category of Bourgeois Society*. Translated by Thomas Burger. Cambridge, MA: MIT Press, 1989). First published as *Strukturwandel der Öffentlichkeit: Untersuchungen zu einer Kategorie der bürgerlichen Gesellschaft*. Darmstadt: Luchterhand, 1962.

Hageneder, Othmar. "Das päpstliche Recht der Fürstenabsetzung: seine kanonistiche Grundlegung (1150–1250)." *Archivum Historiae Pontificae* 1 (1963): 84–90.

Hamilton, Bernard. *The Latin Church in the Crusader States: The Secular Church*. London: Variorum Publications, 1980.

Hampe, Karl. *Ein ungedruckter Bericht über das Conclave von 1241 im römischen Septizonium*. Sitzungsberichte Heidelberger Akademie der Wissenschaften, philosophisch-historische Klasse, vol. 4. Heidelberg, 1913.

———. "Über die Flugschriften zum Lyoner Konzil von 1245." *Historisches Vierteljahrsschrift* 11 (1908): 297–313.

Harris, Matthew Edward. *The Notion of Papal Monarchy in the Thirteenth Century: The Idea of Paradigm in Church History*. Lampeter, UK: Edwin Mellen Press, 2011.

Hechelhammer, Bodo. "Zwischen Martyrermord und Todesstrafe: Die Hinrichtung des Bischofs Marcellino von Arezzo in Jahre 1248." In *Bischofsmord im Mittelalter / Murder of Bishops*, edited by Natalie Fryde and Dirk Reitz, 303–19. Göttingen: Vandenhoeck and Ruprecht, 2003.

Herde, Peter. "Literary Activities of the Imperial and Papal Chanceries during the Struggle Between Frederick II and the Papacy." In *Intellectual Life at the Court of Frederick II Hohenstaufen*, edited by William Tronzo, 227–39. Washington, DC: National Gallery of Art, 1994.

———. "Ein Pamphlet der päpstlichen Kurie gegen Kaiser Friedrich II. von 1245/46 ('Eger cui lenia')." *Deutsches Archiv für Erforschung des Mittlealters* 67 (1967): 468–538.

Hiestand, Rudolf. "Friedrich II. und der Kreuzzug." In *Friedrich II.: Tagung des Deutschen Historischen Instituts in Rom im Gedenkjahr 1994*, edited by Arnold Esch and Norbert Kamp, 128–49. Tübingen: Max Niermeyer, 1996.

Hilpert, Hans-Eberhard. *Kaiser- und Papstbriefe in den Chronica Majora des Matthaeus Paris*. Veröffentlichungen Des Deutschen Historischen Instituts London / Publications of the German Historical Institute London, vol. 9. Stuttgart: Klett-Cotta, 1981.

Hobbins, Daniel. *Authorship and Publicity Before Print: Jean Gerson and the Transformation of Late Medieval Learning*. Philadelphia: University of Pennsylvania Press, 2009.

Höfler, Constantin. *Albert von Beham und Regesten Pabst Innocenz IV*. Bibliotek Des literarischen Vereins in Stuttgart, vol. 16. Stuttgart: Literarischer Verein, 1847.

Housley, Norman. *The Italian Crusades*. Oxford: Clarendon Press, 1982.

———. "Politics and Heresy in Italy: Anti-Heretical Crusades, Orders and Confraternities, 1200–1500." *Journal of Ecclesiastical History* 33 (1982): 193–208.

Huillard-Bréholles, J.L.A. "Examen des chartes de l'église Romaine continues dans les rouleaux dits rouleaux de Cluny." *Notices et extraits des manuscrits de la Bibliothèques imperial et autres bibliothèques de France* 21, no. 2 (1865): 267–363.

Hyams, Paul. *Rancor and Reconciliation in Medieval England*. Ithaca, NY: Cornell University Press, 2003.

Jackson, Peter. "The Crusade Against the Mongols (1241)." *Journal of Ecclesiastical History* 42 (1991): 1–18.

Jones, Philip. *The Italian City-State: From Commune to Signoria*. Oxford: Clarendon Press, 1997.

Jordan, William Chester. *Louis IX and the Challenge of the Crusade: A Study in Rulership*. Princeton, NJ: Princeton University Press, 1979.

Jostmann, Christian. *Sibilla Erithea Babilonica: Papsttum und Prophetie im 13. Jahrhundert*. MGH Schriften, vol. 54. Hannover: Hahnsche Buchhandlung, 2006.

Kantorowicz, Ernst. *Frederick the Second, 1194–1250*. Translated by E. O. Lorimer. New York: Richard R. Smith, 1931. First published as *Kaiser Friedrich der Zweite*. Berlin: Georg Bondi, 1927.

———. *Kaiser Friedrich der Zweite: Ergänzungsband*. Berlin: Georg Bondi, 1931.

Kempf, Friedrich. "La deposizione di Federico II alla luce della dottrina canonistica." *Archivio della Società Romana di Storia Patria* 21 (1968): 1–16.

Kennan, Elizabeth T. "Innocent III, Gregory IX, and the Political Crusades: A Study in the Disintegration of Papal Power." In *Reform and Authority in the Medieval and Reformation Church*, edited by Guy Fitch Lytle, 15–35. Washington, DC: Catholic University of America Press, 1981.

Kintzinger, Martin, and Bernd Schneidmüller. "Politische Öffentlichkeit im Spätmittelalter: Eine Einführung." In *Politische Öffentlichkeit im Spätmittelalter*, edited by Martin Kintzinger and Bernd Schneidmüller, 7–20. Ostfildern: Jan Thorbecke, 2008.

Krey, August C. "The International State of the Middle Ages: Some Reasons for Its Failure." *American Historical Review* 28 (1922): 1–12.

Kuttner, Stephan. "Die Konstitutionen des ersten allgemeinen Konzils von Lyon." *Studia et Documenta Historiae et Iuris* 6 (1940): 70–131.

Laarhoven, Jan van. " 'Christianitas' et réforme grégorienne." *Studi Gregoriani* 6 (1959–61): 1–98.

Ladner, Gerhart. "Aspects of Mediaeval Thought on Church and State." *Review of Politics* 9 (1947): 403–22.

———. "The Concepts of 'Ecclesia' and 'Christianitas' and Their Relation to the Idea of Papal 'Plenitudo Potestatis' from Gregory VII to Boniface VIII." *Miscellanea Historiae Pontificiae* 17 (1954): 49–77.

Lansing, Carol. *Power and Purity: Cathar Heresy in Medieval Italy*. Oxford: Oxford University Press, 1998.

Laski, Harold J. *The Foundations of Sovereignty and Other Essays*. 1921. Freeport, NY: Books for Libraries, 1968.

Le Bras, Gabriel. "Innocent IV Romaniste: Examen de l'Apparatus." *Studia Gratiana* (1967): 305–26.

Legassie, Shayne Aaron. *The Medieval Invention of Travel*. Chicago: University of Chicago Press, 2017.

Le Goff, Jacques. *Saint Louis*. Translated by Gareth Evan Gollard. 1996. Notre Dame: University of Notre Dame Press, 2009.

Lerner, Robert. "Frederick II, Alive, Aloft and Allayed, in Franciscan-Joachite Eschatology. In *The Uses and Abuses of Eschatology in the Middle Ages*, edited by Werner Verveke, Daniel Verhelst, and Andries Welkenhuysen, 359–84. Leuven: Leuven University Press, 1988.

Lewin, Alison Williams. "Salimbene de Adam and the Franciscan Chronicle." In *Chronicling History: Chroniclers and Historians in Medieval and Renaissance Italy*, edited by Sharon Dale, Alison Williams Lewin, and Duane J. Osheim, 87–112. University Park: Pennsylvania State University Press, 2007.

Leyser, Karl J. "The Polemics of the Papal Revolution." In *Trends in Medieval Politics Thought*, edited Beryl Smalley, 42–64. Oxford: Basil Blackwell, 1965.

Lomax, John Phillip. "A Canonistic Reconsideration of the Crusade of Frederick II." In *Proceedings of the Eighth International Congress of Medieval Canon Law*, edited by Stanley Chodorow, 207–26. Vatican City: Biblioteca Apostolica Vaticana, 1992.

———. "Frederick II, His Saracens, and the Papacy. In *Medieval Christian Perceptions of Islam: A Book of Essays*, edited by John Victor Tolan, 175–97. New York: Garland, 1996.

———. "*Ingratus* or *Indignus:* Canonistic Argument in the Conflict Between Pope Gregory IX and Emperor Frederick II." PhD diss., University of Kansas, 1987.

———. "The *Negotium Terrae Sanctae* in Papal-Imperial Discourse (1226–1244)." *Proceedings of the Fourteenth International Congress of Medieval Canon Law, Toronto, 5–11 August 2012*, edited by

Joseph Goering, Stephan Dusil, and Andreas Their, 915–48. Monumenta Iuris Canonici, Series C: Subsidia, vol. 15. Vatican City: Biblioteca Apostolica Vaticana, 2016.

Longère, Jean. "Le concile oecuménique Lyon I (1945): Quelques aspects canoniques et pastoraux des décrets 1–22." *Revue d'Histoire de l'Église de France* 84 (1998): 337–48.

Loud, G. A. "The Case of the Missing Martyrs: Frederick II's War with the Church 1239–1250." In *Martyrs and Martyrologies*, edited by Diana Wood, 141–52. Oxford: Blackwell, 1993.

———. "The Papal 'Crusade' Against Frederick II in 1228–1230." In *La papauté et les croisades: actes du VIIe congrès de la Society for the Study of the Crusades and the Latin East*, edited by Michel Balard, 91–103. Farnham, UK: Ashgate, 2011.

Lower, Michael. *The Baron's Crusade: A Call to Arms and Its Consequences*. Philadelphia: University of Pennsylvania Press, 2005.

Lunt, William E. *Financial Relations of the Papacy with England to 1327*. 2 vols. Cambridge, MA: Medieval Academy of America, 1939.

———. *Papal Revenues in the Middle Ages*. 2 vols. New York: Columbia University Press, 1935.

———. "The Sources for the First Council of Lyons, 1245." *English Historical Review* 33 (1918): 72–78.

Maccarrone, Michele. "*Ubi est papa, ibi est Roma*." In *Aus Kirche und Reich: Studien zu Theologie, Politik und Recht im Mittelalter*, edited by Hurbert Mordek, 371–82. Sigmaringen: Jan Thorbecke, 1983.

———. *Vicarius Christi: storia del titolo papale*. Rome: Facultas Theologica Pontificii Athenaei Lateranensis, 1952.

Mah, Harold. "Phantasies of the Public Sphere: Rethinking the Habermas of Historians." *Journal of Modern History* 72 (2000): 153–82.

Maier, Christoph T. *Preaching the Crusades: Mendicant Friars and the Cross in the Thirteenth Century*. Cambridge: Cambridge University Press, 1994.

Maiolo, Francesco. *Medieval Sovereignty: Marsilius of Padua and Bartolus of Saxoferrato*. Delft: Eburon, 2007.

Maleczek, Werner. "La propaganda antiimperiale nell'Italia Federiciana: l'attività dei legati papali." In *Federico II e la città Italiane*, edited by Pierre Toubert and Agostino Paravicini Bagliani, 290–303. Palermo: Sallerio, 1994.

Malegam, Jehangir. *The Sleep of Behemoth: Disputing Peace and Violence in Medieval Europe, 1000–1200*. Ithaca, NY: Cornell University Press, 2013.

Mann, Horace K. *Honorius III to Celestine IV., 1216–1241*. The Lives of the Popes in the Middle Ages, vol. 13. London: Kegan Paul, Trench, Trubner, 1925.

———. *Innocent IV., the Magnificent, 1243–1254*. The Lives of the Popes in the Middle Ages, vol. 13. London: Kegan Paul, Trench, Trubner, 1928.

Manselli, Raoul. "Ezzelino da Romano nella politica Italiana del sec. XIII." In *Studi Ezzeliniani, Istituo storico Italiano per il medio evo: studi storici*, 35–79. Rome: Nella sede dell'isituto, 1963.

Marazzato, Primo Ottilio. "L'appello di Federico II contro la setenza del concilio di Lione." In *Istituto di diritto pubblico*, vol. 4. Trieste, 1955.

Marc-Bonnet, Henry. "Le saint-siège et Charles d'Anjou sous Innocent IV et Alexandre IV." *Revue Historique* 200 (1948): 38–65.

Marcone, Arnaldo. "Gli affreschi Constantiniani nella chiesa Romana dei Quattro Coronati (XIII seculo)." *Rivista Storica Italiana* 118 (2006): 912–32.

Martin, Susan. "Biblical Authority in the Writing of Pope Innocent IV (1243–1254)." In *The Church and the Book*, edited by R. N. Swanson, 98–195. Woodbridge, U K.: Boydell Press, 2004.

Martinichi, A. P. *The Two Gods of Leviathan: Thomas Hobbes on Religion and Politics*. Cambridge: Cambridge University Press, 1992.

Marx, Jakob. *Die Vita Gregorii IX. quellenkritisch Untersucht*. Berlin: Speyer and Peters, 1889.

Massimo, Oldomi. "Pier della Vigna e Federico." In *Federico II e le nuove culture: atti del XXXI convegno storico internazionale, Todi, 9–12 Ottobre, 1994*, 347–62. Spoleto: Centro italiano di studi sull'alto medioevo, 1995.

Mastnak, Tomaz. *Crusading Peace: Christendom, the Muslim World, and Western Political Order*. Berkeley: University of California Press, 2002.

Mayer, Hans Eberhard. *The Crusades*. Translated by John Gillingham. 2nd ed. Oxford: Oxford University Press, 1988. First published in 1965.

McClelland, J. S. A. *A History of Western Political Thought*. London: Routledge, 1996.

McGinn, Bernard. "Apocalyptic Traditions and Spiritual Identity in Thirteenth-Century Religious Life." In *The Roots of the Modern Christian Tradition*, edited by E. Rozanne Elder, 1–26. Kalamazoo, MI: Cistercian Publications, 1984.

———. *The Calabrian Abbot: Joachim of Fiore in the History of Western Thought*. New York: Macmillan, 1985.

Melloni, Alberto. "Ecclesiologia ed institutioni: Un aspetto della concezione della cristianità." In *Proceedings of the Eighth International Congress of Medieval Canon Law*, edited by Stanley Chodorow, 285–307. Vatican City: Biblioteca Apostolica Vaticana, 1992.

———. *Innocenzo IV: La concezione e l'esperienza della cristianità come regimen unius personae*. Genoa: Marietti, 1990.

———. "William of Ockham's Critique of Innocent IV." *Franciscan Studies* 46 (1986): 161–204.

Melve, Leidulf. "Assembly Politics and the 'Rules-of-the-Game' (ca. 650–1150)." *Viator* 41 (2010): 69–90.

———. " 'Even the Very Laymen Are Chatting About It': The Politicization of Public Opinion, 800–1200." *Viator* 44 (2013): 25–48.

———. *Inventing the Public Sphere: The Public Debate During the Investiture Contest (c.1030–1122)*. Leiden: Brill, 2007.

Menache, Sophia. *The Vox Dei: Communication in the Middle Ages*. Oxford: Oxford University Press, 1990.

Merlo, Grado Giovanni. "Federico II, gli eretici, i frati." In *Federico II e le nuove culture: atti del XXXI convegno storico internazionale, Todi, 9–12 Ottobre, 1994*, 45–67. Spoleto: Centro italiano di studi sull'alto medioevo, 1995.

Mierau, Heike Johanna. "Exkommunikation und Macht der Öffentlichkeit: Gerüchte im Kampf zwischen Friedrich II und der Kurie." In *Propaganda, Kommunikation under Öffentlichkeit (11.–16. Jahrhundert)*, edited by Karel Hruza, 47–80. Vienna: Verlag der österrichischen Akademie der Wissenschaften, 2002.

Miethke, Jürgen. "Die Konzilien als Forum der öffentlichen Meinung im 15. Jahrhundert." *Deutsches Archiv für Erforschung des Mittelalters* 37 (1981): 736–73.

Miller, Maureen C. *The Bishop's Palace: Architecture and Authority in Medieval Italy*. Ithaca, NY: Cornell University Press, 2000.

Mirbt, Carl. *Die Publizistik im Zeitalter Gregors VII*. Leipzig: J. C. Hinrich, 1894.

Montaubin, Pascal. "Innocent II and Capetian France." In *Pope Innocent II (1130–43): The World vs the City*, edited by John Doran and Damian J. Smith, 172–80. London: Routledge, 2016.

Moore, R. I. *The War on Heresy*. Cambridge, MA: Belknap Press of Harvard University Press, 2012.

Moorman, John. *A History of the Franciscan Order from Its Origins to the Year 1517*. Chicago: Franciscan Herald Press, 1988. First published in 1968.

Moos, Peter von. "Das Öffentliche und das Private im Mittelalter: für einen kontrollierten Anachronismus." In *Das Öffentliche und Private in der Vormoderne*, edited by Gert Melville and Peter von Moos, 3–83. Cologne: Böhlau Verlag, 1998.

———. *"Öffentlich" und "privat" im Mittelalter: Zu einem Problem historischer Begriffsbildung*. Heidelberg: Universitätsverlag Winter, 2004.

Morrall, John. *Political Thought in Medieval Times*. London: Hutchinson University Library, 1971. First published in 1958.

Morris, Colin. *Medieval Media: Mass Communication in the Making of Europe*. Southampton: University of Southampton, 1972.

———. *The Papal Monarchy: The Western Church from 1050–1250*. Oxford: Clarendon Press, 1989.

Mostert, Marco, ed. *A Bibliography of Works on Medieval Communication*. Turnhout: Brepols, 2012.

———, ed. *New Approaches to Medieval Communication*. Turnhout: Brepols, 1999.

Mostert, Marco, and P. S. Barnwell, eds. *Medieval Legal Process: Physical, Spoken, and Written Performance.* Turnhout: Brepols, 2011.

Moynihan, Robert. "The Development of the 'Pseudo-Joachim' Commentary 'Super Hieremiam': New Manuscript Evidence." *Mélanges de l'école française de Rome* 98 (1986): 109–42.

———. "Joachim of Fiore and the Early Franciscans: A Study of the Commentary 'Super Hieremiam.,'" 2 vols. PhD diss., Yale University, 1988.

Muldoon, James. "The Contribution of the Medieval Canon Lawyers to the Formation of International Law." *Traditio* 28 (1972): 483–97.

Nederman, Cary J. *Lineages of European Political Thought: Explorations Along the Medieval/Modern Divide from John of Salisbury to Hegel.* Washington, DC: Catholic University of America Press, 2009.

Novikoff, Alex J. *The Medieval Culture of Disputation: Pedagogy, Practice, and Performance.* Philadelphia: University of Pennsylvania Press, 2013.

Oakley, Francis. "Celestial Hierarchies Revisited: Walter Ullmann's Vision of Medieval Politics." *Past and Present* 60 (1973): 3–48.

———. *The Mortgage of the Past: Reshaping the Ancient Political Inheritance, The Emergence of Western Political Thought in the Latin Middle Ages.* New Haven, CT: Yale University Press, 2012.

———. *Natural Law, Conciliarism, and Consent in the Later Middle Ages.* London: Variorum. 1984.

Orallo, Santiago Panizo. *Persona jurídica y ficción: estudio de la obra de Sinibaldo de Fischi (Inocencio IV).* Pamplona: Ediciones Universidad de Navarra, 1975.

Pacaut, Marcel. "L'autorité pontificale selon Innocent IV." *Le moyen âge* 66 (1960): 85–199.

Pagnotti, Francesco. "Niccolò da Calvi e la sua *Vita d'Innocenzo IV* con una breve introduzione sulla istoriografia pontificia nei seculo XIII e XIV." *Archivio della società Romana di storia patria* 21 (1898): 5–120.

Painter, Sidney. "The Crusade of Theobald of Champagne and Richard of Cornwall." In *A History of the Crusades: The Later Crusades, 1189–1311,* edited by Robert Lee Wolff and Harry W. Hazard, vol. 2, 474–77. Madison: University of Wisconsin Press, 1969.

Pardue, Brad. *Printing, Power, and Piety: Appeals to the Public During the Early Years of the English Reformation.* Leiden: Brill, 2012.

Partner, Peter. *The Lands of St. Peter: The Papal State in the Middle Ages and the Early Renaissance.* Berkeley: University of California Press, 1972.

Patschovsky, Alexander. "The Holy Emperor Henry 'the First' as One of the Dragon's Heads of Apocalypse: On the Image of the Holy Roman Empire Under German Rule in the Tradition of Joachim of Fiore." *Viator* 29 (1998): 291–322.

Pegg, Mark. *A Most Holy War: The Albigensian Crusade and the Battle for Christendom.* Oxford: Oxford University Press, 2008.

Pennington, Kenneth. "Gregory IX, Emperor Frederick II, and the Constitutions of Melfi." In *Popes, Teachers, and Canon Law in the Middle Ages,* edited by James Ross Sweeney and Stanley Chodorow, 53–61. Ithaca, NY: Cornell University Press, 1989.

———. "Pope Innocent III's Views on Church and State: A Gloss to *Per venerabilem.*" In *Law, Church, and Society: Essays in Honour of Stephan Kuttner,* edited by Kenneth Pennington and Robert Sommerville, 1–25. Philadelphia: University of Pennsylvania Press, 1977.

———. *Popes and Bishops: The Papal Monarchy in the Twelfth and Thirteenth Centuries.* Philadelphia: University of Pennsylvania Press, 1984.

Perkins, Mary Anne. *Christendom and European Identity: The Legacy of a Grand Narrative Since 1789.* Berlin: Walter de Gruyter, 2000.

Perry, Guy. *John of Brienne: King of Jerusalem, Emperor of Constantinople, c. 1175–1237.* Cambridge: Cambridge University Press, 2013.

Peters, Edward. *Inquisition.* Berkeley: University of California Press, 1989.

———. "Rex Inutilis: Sancho II of Portugal and Thirteenth-Century Deposition Theory." *Studia Gratiana* 14 (1967): 253–305.

Piergiovanni, Vito. "Sinibaldo dei Fieschi decretalista." *Studia Gratiana* 14 (1967): 126–54.

Pixton, Paul B. *The German Episcopacy and the Implementation of the Decrees of the Fourth Lateran Council, 1216–1245: Watchmen on the Tower*. Leiden: E. J. Brill, 1995.
Potestà, Gian Luca. *Il Tempo dell'Apocalisse: Vita di Gioacchino da Fiore*. Rome: Laterza, 2004.
Powell, James M. *Anatomy of a Crusade 1213–1221*. Philadelphia: University of Pennsylvania Press, 1986.
———. "Church and Crusade: Frederick II and Louis IX." *Catholic Historical Review* 93 (2007): 251–64.
———. "Frederick II and the Church: A Revisionist View." *Catholic Historical Review* 48 (1963): 487–97.
———. "The Papacy and the Early Franciscans." *Franciscan Studies* 36 (1976): 248–62.
———. "Patriarch Gerold and Frederick II: The Matthew Paris Letter." *Journal of Medieval History* 25 (1999): 19–26.
Prudlo, Donald. *The Martyred Inquisitor: The Life and Cult of Peter of Verona*. Aldershot, U K: Ashgate, 2008.
Purcell, Maureen. *Papal Crusading Policy: The Chief Instruments of Papal Crusading Policy and Crusade to the Holy Land from the Final Loss of Jerusalem to the Fall of Acre*. Leiden: E. J. Brill, 1975.
Raccagni, Gianluca. "The Crusade Against Frederick II: A Neglected Piece of Evidence." *Journal of Ecclesiastical History* 67 (2016): 721–40.
———. *The Lombard League, 1167–1225*. Oxford: Oxford University Press, 2010.
Rader, Olaf B. *Friedrich II. Der Sizilianer auf dem Kaiserthron*. Munich: C. H. Beck, 2010.
Ranke, Leopold von. *History of Latin and Teutonic Nations from 1494 to 1514*. Translated by Philip A. Ashworth. London: George Bell and Sons, 1887. First published in 1824.
———. *The History of the Popes During the Last Four Centuries*. Translated by G. R. Dennis. 3 vols. London: George Bell and Sons, 1908. First published 1834–36.
Reeves, Marjorie. *The Influence of Prophecy in the Later Middle Ages*. Notre Dame, 1993. First published in 1969.
Rennie, Kriston. *The Foundations of Papal Legation*. Houndmills, UK: Palgrave MacMillan, 2013.
Richard, Jean. "L'attitude du pape Grégoire IX envers les souverains musulmans." In *La Correspondance entre souverains, princes et cités-états: Approches croisées entre l'Orient musulman, l'Occident latin et Byzance (XIIIe–début XVIe s.)*, edited by Denise Aigle, 101–5. Turnhout: Brepols, 2013.
———. *La papauté et les missions d'Orient au moyen âge*. Collection de l'école française de Rome, vol. 33. Rome: École française de Rome, 1977.
———. *Saint Louis: Crusader King of France*. Translated by Jean Birrell. Cambridge: Cambridge University Press, 1992. First published in 1983.
Robinson, I. S. *Authority and Resistance in the Investiture Contest*. Manchester: Holmes & Meier, 1978.
———. *The Papacy 1073–1198: Continuity and Innovation*. Cambridge: Cambridge University Press, 1990.
Rodenberg, Carl. "Die Friedensverhandlungen zwischen Friedrich II. und Innocenz IV. 1243–1244." In *Festgabe für Gerold Meyer von Knonau*, 165–204. Zurich: Berichthaus, 1913.
———. *Innocenz IV und das königreich Sicilien 1245–1254*. Halle: M. Niemeyer, 1892.
———. "Die Verhandlugen zum Frieden San Germano 1229–1230." *Neues Archiv der Gesellschaft für ältere deutsche Geschichtskunde* 18 (1893): 178–205.
Ruehl, Martin A. "'In This Time Without Emperors': The Politics of Ernst Kantorowicz's *Kaiser Friedrich der Zweite* Reconsidered." *Journal of the Warburg and Courtauld Institutes* 63 (2000): 187–242.
Runciman, Steven. "The Crusader States, 1243–1291." In *A History of the Crusades: The Later Crusades, 1189–1311*, edited by Robert Lee Wolff and Harry W. Hazard, vol. 2, 557–98. Madison: University of Wisconsin Press, 1969.
———. *The Sicilian Vespers: A History of the Mediterranean World in the Later Thirteenth Century*. Cambridge: At the University Press, 1958.
Rupp, Jean. *L'idée de chrétienté dans la pensée pontificale des origins à Innocent III*. Paris: Presses Modernes, 1939.

Sawyer, Jeffrey K. *Printed Poison: Pamphlet Propaganda, Faction Politics, and the Public Sphere in Early Seventeenth-Century France*. Berkeley: University of California Press, 1990.

Sayers, Jane E. *Papal Government and England During the Pontificate of Honorius III (1216–1227)*. Cambridge: Cambridge University Press, 1984.

———. *Papal Judges Delegate in the Province of Canterbury 1198–1254: A Study in Ecclesiastical Jurisdiction and Administration*. Oxford: Oxford University Press, 1971.

Schaller, Hans Martin. "Die Antwort Gregors IX. auf Petrus de Vinea I, 1 'Collegerunt pontifices.' " *Deutsches Archiv für Erforschung des Mittelalters* 11 (1954/55): 140–65.

———. "Endzeit-Erwartung und Antichrist-Vorstellungen in der Politik des 13. Jahrhunderts." In *Festschrift für Hermann Heimpel zum 70. Geburtstag*, 924–47. Göttingen: Vandenhoeck and Ruprecht, 1972.

———. *Kaiser Friedrich II: Verwandler der Welt*. Gottingen: Musterschmidt, 1964.

———. "Das letzte Rundschreiben Gregors IX. gegen Friedrich II." In *Festschrift Percy Ernst Schramm zu seinem siebzigsten Geburtstag von Schülern und Freunden*, edited by Peter Classen and Peter Scheibert, vol. 1, 309–21. Wiesbaden: Franz Steiner, 1964.

———. *Politische Propaganda Kaiser Friedrichs II. und seiner Gegner*. Munich: S. Stahlmann, 1965.

———. "Zur Entstehung der sogenannten Briefsammlung des Petrus de Vinea." *Deutsches Archiv für Erforschung des Mittelalters* 12 (1956): 114–59.

Schmitt, Carl. *The Nomos of the Earth in the International Law of the* Jus Publicum Euopaeum. Translated by G. L. Ulmen. New York: Telos Press, 2003. First published in 1950.

———. *On Dictatorship: From the Origin of the Modern Concept of Sovereignty to Proletarian Class Struggle*. Translated by Michael Hoelzl and Graham Ward. Cambridge: Polity, 2014.

———. *Political Theology: Four Chapters on the Concept of Sovereignty*. Translated by George Schwab. Cambridge, MA: MIT Press, 1985. First published in 1922.

———. *Roman Catholicism and Political Form*. Translated by G. L. Ulmen. Westport, CT: Greenwood Press, 1996. First published in 1923.

Schmolinsky, Sabine. *Der Apokalypsenkommentar des Alexander Minorita: zur frühen Rezeption Joachims von Fiore in Deutschland*. MGH, Studien und Texte 3. Hannover: Hahnsche Buchhandlung, 1991.

———. "Prophezeite Geschichte und früher Joachitismus in Deutschland: zur Apokalypsendeutung des Alexander Minorita." In *Ende und Vollendung: eschatologische Perspektiven im Mittelalter*, edited by Jan Aertsen and Martin Pickavé, 523–44. Berlin: Walter de Gruyter, 2002.

Schmutz, Richard. "Medieval Papal Representatives: Legates, Nuncios, and Judges-Delegate." *Studia Gratiana* 15 (1972): 442–63.

Setton, Kenneth M. *The Papacy and the Levant (1204–1571): The Thirteenth and Fourteenth Centuries*. Vol. 1. Philadelphia: University of Pennsylvania Press, 1976.

Shepard, Laurie. *Courting Power: Persuasion and Politics in the Early Thirteenth Century*. New York: Garland, 1999.

Siberry, Elizabeth. *Criticism of Crusading 1095–1274*. Oxford: Clarendon Press, 1985.

Sibilia, Salvatore. *Gregorio IX*. Milan: Casa Editrice Ceshina, 1961.

Skinner, Quentin. *The Foundations of Modern Political Thought*. 2 vols. Cambridge: Cambridge University Press, 1978.

Smail, Daniel Lord. *The Consumption of Justice: Emotions, Publicity, and Legal Culture in Marseille, 1264–1423*. Ithaca, NY: Cornell University Press, 2003.

Smith, A. L. *Church and State in the Middle Ages: The Ford Lectures Delivered at Oxford in 1905*. Oxford, 1913.

Smith, Thomas W. "Between Two Kings: Pope Honorius III and the Seizure of the Kingdom of Jerusalem by Frederick II in 1225." *Journal of Medieval History* 41 (2015): 41–59.

———. *Crusade and Curia: Pope Honorius III and the Recovery of the Holy Land 1216–1227*. Turnhout: Brepols, 2017.

———. "The Role of Honorius III in the Fifth Crusade." In *The Fifth Crusade in Context: The Crusading Movement in the Early Thirteenth Century*, edited by E. J. Mylod et al., 15–26. Crusades-Subsidia, vol. 9. London: Routledge, 2017.

Sohn, Andreas. "Bilder als Zeichen der Herrschaft: Die Silvesterkappelle in SS. Quattro Coronati (Rom)." *Archivum Historiae Pontificae* 35 (1997): 7–48.

Southern, Richard. *Robert Grosseteste: The Growth of an English Mind in Medieval Europe*. Oxford: Clarendon Press, 1986.

Spence, Richard. "Gregory IX's Attempted Expeditions to the Latin Empire of Constantinople: The Crusades for the Union of the Latin and Greek Churches." *Journal of Medieval History* 5 (1979): 163–76.

———. "The Impact of Historical Events on the Compilation of the *Litterae curiales* from Pope Gregory IX's Twelfth Year." *Archivum Historiae Pontificiae* 18 (1980): 383–93.

Stickler, Alfons M. "Concerning the Political Theories of the Medieval Canonists." *Traditio* 7 (1949–51): 450–63.

Stock, Brian. *The Implications of Literacy: Written Language and Models of Interpretation in the Eleventh and Twelfth Centuries*. Princeton, NJ: Princeton University Press, 1983.

Strayer, Joseph R. "Political Crusades of the Thirteenth Century." In *A History of the Crusades: The Later Crusades, 1189–1311*, edited by Robert Lee Wolff and Harry W. Hazard, vol. 2, 343–75. Madison: University of Wisconsin Press, 1969.

Stürner, Wolfgang. *Friedrich II*. 2 vols. Darmstadt: Wissenschaftliche Buchgesellschaft, 2000.

Sullivan, Karen. *The Inner Lives of Medieval Inquisitors*. Chicago: University of Chicago Press, 2011.

Symes, Carol. *A Common Stage: Theater and Public Life in Medieval Arras*. Ithaca, NY: Cornell University Press, 2007.

———. "Out in the Open, in Arras: Sightlines, Soundscapes, and the Shaping of a Medieval Public Sphere." In *Cities, Texts, and Social Networks, 400–1500: Experiences and Perceptions of Medieval Urban Spaces*, edited by Caroline Goodson, Anne E. Lester, and Carol Symes, 279–302. Farnham: Ashgate, 2010.

Szabari, Antónia. *Less Rightly Said: Scandals and Readers in Sixteenth-Century France*. Stanford: Stanford University Press, 2010.

Szittya, Penn. *The Antifraternal Tradition in Medieval Literature*. Princeton, NJ: Princeton University Press, 1986.

Takayama, Hiroshi. "Frederick II's Crusade: An Example of Christian-Muslim Diplomacy." *Mediterranean Historical Review* 25 (2010): 169–85.

Tangl, Michael. "Die soganannte *Brevis nota* über das Lyoner Council von 1245." *Mittheilungen des Instituts für osterreichische Geschichtsforschung* 12 (1881): 247–53.

Taylor, Charles. *Modern Social Imaginaries*. Durham, NC: Duke University Press, 2004.

Thompson, Augustine. *Cities of God: The Religion of the Italian Communes 1125–1325*. University Park: Pennsylvania State University Press, 2005.

———. *Revival Preachers and Politics in Thirteenth-Century Italy: The Great Devotion of 1233*. Oxford: Clarendon Press, 1992.

Thouzellier, Christine. "La légation en Lombardie du Cardinal Hugolin (1221): en épisode de la cinquième croisade." *Revue d'histoire ecclésiastique* 45 (1950): 508–42.

Throop, Palmer A. *Criticism of the Crusade: A Study of Public Opinion and Crusade Propaganda*. Amsterdam: N. v. Swets & Zeitlinger, 1940.

Thumser, Matthias. "Antistaufische Propaganda in einer Prager Handschrift: Der Brief *Grande piaculum* des Kardinals Rainer von Viterbo (1248)." *Mediaevalia Historica Bohemica* 12 (2009): 7–41.

———. "Kardinal Rainer von Viterbo (d. 1250) und seine Propaganda gegen Friedrich II." In *Die Kardinäle des Mittelalters und der frühen Renaissance*, edited by Jürgen Dendorfer and Ralf Lützelschwab, 187–99. Florence: Edizioni del Galluzzo, 2013.

———. "Kuriale Briefkultur: Konturen eines vernaxchlässigten Forschungsgebeites." In *Kuriale Briefkultur im späteren Mittelalter: Gestaltung-Überlieferung-Rezeption*, edited by Tanja Broser, Andreas Fischer, and Matthias Thumser, 9–34. Weimar: Böhlau, 2015.

———. "Perfekte Harmonie. Kardinal Stefano Conti und der Freskenzyklus bei SS. Quattro Coronati im Rom." *Zeitschrift für Kirchengeschichte* 123 (2012): 145–72.

Tierney, Brian. "The Canonists and the Medieval State." *Review of Politics* 15 (1953): 378–88.

———. "The Continuity of Papal Political Theory in the Thirteenth Century: Some Methodological Considerations." *Mediaeval Studies* 27 (1965): 227–45.

———. *The Crisis of Church and State, 1050–1300: With Selected Documents*. Engelwood Cliffs, NJ: Prentice-Hall, 1964.

———. *Foundations of the Conciliar Theory: The Contributions of the Medieval Canonists from Gratian to the Great Schism*. Leiden: Brill, 1998. Rev. ed. 1955.

———. "Medieval Canon Law and Western Constitutionalism." *Catholic Historical Review* 52 (1966): 1–17.

———. *Religion, Law, and the Growth of Constitutional Thought 1150–1650*. Cambridge: Cambridge University Press, 1982.

———. "Some Recent Works on the Political Theories of the Medieval Canonists." *Traditio* 10 (1954): 594–625.

Tillmann, Helene. "Datierungsfragen zur Geschichte des Kampfe zwischen Innocenz III. und Kaiser Otto IV." *Historisches Jahrbuch* 84 (1964): 34–85.

Töpfer, Bernhard. *Das kommende Reich des Friedens: zur Entwicklung chiliasticher Zukunftshoffnungen im Mittelalter*. Berlin: Akademie Verlag, 1964.

Tutino, Stefania. *Empire of Souls: Robert Bellarmine and the Christian Commonwealth*. Oxford: Oxford University Press, 2010.

Tyerman, Christopher. *God's War: A New History of the Crusades*. Cambridge, MA: Belknap Press of Harvard University Press, 2006.

———. *How to Plan a Crusade: Reason and Religious War in the High Middle Ages*. London: Allen Lane, 2015.

Ullmann, Walter. "Frederick II's Opponent, Innocent IV, as Melchisedek." In *Atti del convegno internazionale di studi Federiciani: VII centenario della morte di Federico II imperatore e re di Sicilia (10–18 Dicembre 1950)*, 53–81. Palermo: Stabilimento d'Arti Grafische A. Renna, 1952.

———. *The Growth of Papal Government in the Middle Ages: A Study in the Ideological Relation of Clerical to Lay Power*. London: Methuen, 1965. 2nd ed. 1955.

———. *Medieval Papalism: The Political Theories of the Medieval Canonists*. London: Methuen, 1949.

———. *Principles of Government and Politics in the Middle Ages*. New York: Barnes and Noble Inc., 1961.

———. "Some Reflections on the Opposition of Frederick II to the Papacy." *Archivio Storico Pugliese* 13 (1962): 16–39.

Van Cleve, Thomas C. "The Crusade of Frederick II." In *A History of the Crusades: The Later Crusades, 1189–1311*, edited by Robert Lee Wolff and Harry W. Hazard, vol. 2, 429–62. Madison: University of Wisconsin Press, 1969.

———. *The Emperor Frederick II of Hohenstaufen, Immutator Mundi*. Oxford: Oxford at the Clarendon Press, 1972.

Vauchez, André. "Grégoire IX et la politique de la sainteté." In *Gregorio IX e gli ordini mendicanti: atti del XXXVIII convegno internazionale*, 351–77. Spoleto: Centro Italiano di studi sull'alto medioevo, 2011.

Vaughan, Richard. *Matthew Paris*. Cambridge: At the University Press, 1958.

Verga, Guido. "Gregorio de Monte Longo, legato apostolico in Lombardia (1238–1251)." *Archivio storico Lombardo* 93–94 (1966–67): 173–82.

Vincent, Nicholas. *Peter des Roches: An Alien in English Politics, 1205–1238*. Cambridge: Cambridge University Press, 1996.

Voci, Anna Maria. "Federico II imperatore e i medicanti: privilegi papali e propaganda anti-imperiale." *Critica Storica* 22 (1985): 3–28.

Vodola, Elisabeth. *Excommunication in the Middle Ages*. Berkeley: University of California Press, 1986.

Waley, Daniel Philip. *The Italian City Republics*. 3rd ed. London: Tauris Academic Studies, 1996.

———. *The Papal State in the Thirteenth Century*. London: MacMillan, 1961.

Warner, Michael. *Publics and Counterpublics*. New York: Zone Books, 2002.

Watt, J. A. "Medieval Deposition Theory: A Neglected Canonist *Consultatio* from the First Council of Lyons." In *Studies in Church History*, edited by G. J. Cuming, vol. 2, 197–204. London: Nelson, 1965.

———. "Spiritual and Temporal Powers." In *The Cambridge History of Medieval Political Thought c. 350–c. 1450*, edited by J. H. Burns, 367–423. Cambridge: Cambridge University Press, 1988.

———. "The Theory of Papal Monarchy in the Thirteenth Century." *Traditio* 20 (1964): 179–317.

Webb, Diana M. "Cities of God: The Italian Communes at War." In *Studies in Church History*, edited by W. J. Sheils, vol. 20, 111–27. Oxford: Ecclesiastical History Society, 1983.

Weber, Hans. *Der Kampf zwischen Papst Innocenz IV. und Kaiser Friedrich IV. bis zur Flucht der Papstes nach Lyon*. Berlin: E. Ebering, 1900.

Weiler, Björn. "Gregory IX, Frederick II, and the Liberation of the Holy Land." In *The Holy Land, Holy Lands, and Christian History: Studies in Church History*, edited by R. N. Swanson, vol. 36, 192–206. Woodbridge, UK: Boydell Press, 2000.

———. *Henry III of England and the Staufen Empire, 1216–1272*. Woodbridge, UK: Boydell Press, 2006.

———. "Henry III and the Sicilian Business: A Reinterpretation." *Historical Research* 74 (2001): 127–50.

———. "Matthew Paris on the Writing of History." *Journal of Medieval History* 35 (2009): 254–78.

Wenck, Karl. "Das erste Konklave der Papstgeschichte, Rom August bis Oktober 1241." *Quellen und Forschungen aus italienischen Archiven und Bibliotheken* 18 (1926): 101–70.

Werner, Matthias, ed. *Heinrich Raspe—Landgraf von Thüringen und römischer König: Fursten, König und Reich in spätstaufischer Zeit*. Frankfurt: Peter Lang, 2003.

Werzstein, Thomas. "The Deposition of Frederick II (1245)—A Public Lesson in Procedural Law." In *Proceedings of the Fourteenth International Congress of Medieval Canon Law: Toronto, 5–11 August 2012*, 949–64. Vatican City: Biblioteca Apostolica Vaticana, 2016.

West, D. C. "The Education of Fra Salimbene of Parma: The Joachite Influence." In *Prophecy and Millenarianism: Essays in Honour of Marjorie Reeves*, edited by Ann Williams, 191–26. Harlow, UK: Longman, 1980.

Westenholz, Elizabeth von. *Kardinal Rainer von Viterbo*. Heidelberg: Carl Winter, 1912.

Whalen, Brett Edward. "Corresponding with Infidels: Rome, the Almohads, and the Christians of Thirteenth-Century Morocco." *Journal of Medieval and Early Modern Studies* 41 (2011): 487–513.

———. *Dominion of God: Christendom and Apocalypse in the Middle Ages*. Cambridge, MA: Harvard University Press, 2009.

———. "Joachim the Theorist of History and Society." In *A Companion to Joachim of Fiore*, edited by Matthias Riedl, 88–108. Leiden: Brill, 2017.

Williamson, Dorothy M. "Some Aspects of the Legation of Cardinal Otto in England, 1237–41." *English Historical Review* 64 (1949): 76–97.

Wulf, Maurice de. "The Society of Nations in the Thirteenth Century." *International Journal of Ethics* 29 (1919): 210–29.

Zaret, David. *Origins of Democratic Culture: Printing, Petitions, and the Public Sphere in Early-Modern England*. Princeton, NJ: Princeton University Press, 2000.

Zimmermann, Heinrich. *Die päpstliche Legation in der ersten hälfte des 13. Jahrhunderts von Regierungsantritt Innocenz' III. bis zum Tode Gregors IX. (1198–1241)*. Paderborn: Ferdinand Schöningh, 1913.

Zutschi, Patrick. "Innocent III and the Reform of the Papal Chancery." In *Innocenzo III, urbs et orbis: atti di congresso internazionale Roma, 9–15 September 1998*, edited by Andreas Sommerlechner, 84–101. Rome: Presso la società alla Biblioteca Vallicelliana, 2003.

———. "The Personal Role of the Pope in the Production of Papal Letters in the Thirteenth and Fourteenth Centuries." In *Vom Nutzen des Schreibens: Soziales Gedächtnis, Herrschaft und Besitz im Mittelalter*, edited by Walter Pohl and Paul Herold, 225–36. Vienna: Verlag der Österreichischen Akademie der Wissenschaften, 2002.

———. "The Roman Curia and Papal Jurisdiction in the Twelfth and Thirteenth Centuries." In *Der Ordnung der Kommunikation und die Kommunikation der Ordungen, Band 2, Zentralität: Papsttum und Orden im Europa des 12. und 13. Jahrhunderts*, edited by Cristina Andenna, Klaus Herbers, and Gert Melville, 213–27. Stuttgart: Franz Steiner Verlag, 2013.

Index

Note: Page numbers in italic type indicate illustrations.

Acknowledgments

When I started my research for this book several years ago, I initially planned to write a straightforward biography of Innocent IV, an important but in many ways understudied pope. I was especially interested in his missionary outreach to the Mongols and the Islamic world. As my work progressed, I came to realize that Innocent's contentious relationship with Frederick II represented the defining element of his papacy. To understand Innocent's attitude toward the "Wonder of the World," as Frederick is sometimes called, I found myself inevitably looking back at the papacy of his predecessor, Gregory IX, who had his own problematic interactions with the Hohenstaufen ruler. My book on one pope had become a book on two of them. As I dug into the sources for the time span of their papacies, I became especially intrigued by the various iterations of the "public" that appeared during the crisis between the papacy and empire, linked not just to abstract ideas about sovereignty but also to the forms of communication that made the question of the "two powers" so vital for contemporaries. In this way, I eventually produced a very different kind of historical study than I originally envisioned.

Given all of those twists and turns, I was extremely fortunate to benefit from the generous support and patience of various institutions, colleagues, and friends throughout the entire process. During the early stages of my research, I had the good fortune to be one of the inaugural 2013 Kingdon fellows at the Institute for Research in the Humanities in Madison, Wisconsin. At the IHR, I would like to thank Susan Friedman, Gregory Milton, Justine Andrews, Ayelet Ben-Yishai, Anne Duncan, Ben LaBreche, Joseph Marchal, Benedict Robinson, Molly Zahn, and Jordan Zweck. My thanks also to the Institute for Arts and Humanities at the University of North Carolina, Chapel Hill, which provided a semester of research leave associated with my Chapman Teaching Award. The College of Arts and Sciences at UNC-CH provided an additional semester of research and study leave. Additional thanks are owed to the American Philosophical Society; to the Vatican Film Library, in Saint Louis, Missouri; to the Biblioteca Antonia, in Milan; to the British Library; and to the Bodleian Library, at the University of Oxford.

At different stages in this book's development, I also had the chance to present my work in progress at various seminars, benefiting from the feedback of the participants. These included the Medieval Intellectual History Seminar at the Newberry Library, in Chicago, in December 2013 (with special thanks to Robert Lerner and Dyan Elliott); the Triangle Medieval Studies Seminar at the National Humanities Center, Research Triangle Park, NC, in September 2015 (with a nod to Jehangir Malegam and Neslihan Senocak); and the Stanford University Medieval Studies Seminar in October 2015 (with gratitude to Paula Findlen, Fiona Griffiths, and Maureen Miller). My additional thanks go to Bjorn Weiler, Jay Rubenstein, Carol Symes, Ed Peters, Philippe Buc, William Jordan, John Philip Lomax, Robert Swanson and T. F. X. Noble. At the University of Pennsylvania Press, I would like to express my appreciation to Ruth Mazo Karras, Jerome Singerman, Hannah Blake, and Lily Palladino. Needless to say, the shortcomings that remain are entirely my responsibility.

Finally, my heartfelt gratitude goes to colleagues and friends in Durham and Chapel Hill, North Carolina, who offered support, encouragement, and, when needed, commiseration about the challenges of historical research and writing. These included Emily Burrill, Ben Waterhouse, John Martin, Kathleen DuVal, Christian Lentz, Adrian Lentz-Smith, Marcus Bull, Wayne Lee, Melissa Bullard, Fitz Brundage, and Lloyd Kramer. In its final stages of revision, this book benefited immensely from the editorial prowess of Mark Hornburg, a member of the history department at Chapel Hill. The Durham Lakewood YMCA helped to keep me healthy and compos mentis while I lived the life of the mind. As always, I would like to express my gratitude toward my family, including my mother Lynn, Paul, Bradley, Diana, Bob, and Robert. I continue to benefit from my childhood interest in history that, in different ways, my mother and my father, Thomas, encouraged. I am dedicating this book to my nephew, Jack, and niece, Amelia, whose intellectual futures are still taking shape. Above all, I cannot thank enough my wife, Malissa, my companion for the last twenty-five years and the best writing coach a person could ask for. I look forward to the next twenty-five years with her, and beyond.